5a1

THE
POTTERIES

Keele Hall, the historic centre of Keele University, the host institution of the 1993 meeting of the British Association for the Advancement of Science.

THE
POTTERIES

Continuity and Change in a
Staffordshire Conurbation

EDITED BY A. D. M. PHILLIPS

ALAN SUTTON

First published in the United Kingdom in 1993 by
Alan Sutton Publishing Limited
Phoenix Mill · Far Thrupp · Stroud · Gloucestershire

First published in the United States of America in 1993 by
Alan Sutton Publishing Inc · 83 Washington Street · Dover · NH 03820

British Library Cataloguing in Publication Data

Phillips, A D M
Potteries
I. Title
942.463

ISBN 0–7509–0223–X

Library of Congress Cataloging in Publication Data applied for

Typeset in 10/12pt Times.
Typesetting and origination by
Alan Sutton Publishing Limited.
Printed in Great Britain by
Butler & Tanner Ltd, Frome and London.

Contents

List of Figures

List of Plates

List of Tables

Preface

The occasion for the publication of this collection of essays is the visit of the British Association for the Advancement of Science to Keele University in 1993. As this is the first time that the British Association has visited the Potteries, the custom of the host institution to provide an introduction to the region is particularly appropriate. However, the volume is intended to be more than a guide: the visit of the British Association has presented the opportunity to produce a new and far-ranging overview of the conurbation, examining its development and challenges, its character and originality.

The Potteries forms one of the most remarkable and yet little known conurbations in the United Kingdom. A product of the industrial revolution and comprising the six pottery towns of Tunstall, Burslem, Hanley, Stoke, Fenton, and Longton, together with the adjacent market centre of Newcastle-under-Lyme, it is the only conurbation to be named after its dominant manufacturing activity. Moreover, the emergence of the conurbation, by the formal fusing of these independent towns at the beginning of the twentieth century, represents a distinctive and singular process in recent British urban history. The development of the pottery industry among a cluster of small, but separate communities, so strikingly recorded in the novels of Arnold Bennett, bequeathed a unique industrial-urban landscape, summed up by J B Priestly in his *English journey* of 1933 as grim, ugly, smoke-filled, a clutter of towns that gave the impression of uniformity and littleness, relieved only by a 'fantastic collection of narrow-necked jars or bottles peeping up above the house tops on every side, looking as if giant biblical characters, after a search for oil and wine, had popped them there, among the dwarf streets'.

Today that image of the Potteries has largely disappeared. Technological change has removed the need for the most distinctive hallmark of the landscape, the bottle oven: the 900 or so of 1945 have dwindled to 34, in the main skulking unused in forgotten sidestreets. The present-day landscape of the Potteries yields little or no evidence of its eponymous industry. The traditional image has been further eroded through the impact of government legislation, local authority initiatives (even to the extent, with the naming in 1975 of Stoke-on-Trent City Council's new office building Unity House, of attempting to supersede loyalties to local towns), environmental regeneration and economic diversification. While problems from the past still persist in the present conurbation – the existence of seven, separate towns, the lack of unitary authority, the scale of pre-1914 housing – these are offset by the challenges and opportunities presented by a population of around half a million and a role as a leading regional centre in the West Midlands.

In portraying the past and present development of the Potteries, the essays in this volume have been organized around three themes. The first group places the conurbation in its broader regional setting in terms of its geology and physical resources, its physical environment and early settlement. The making of the industrial-urban complex proper between 1660 and 1945 forms the theme of the second group, tracing the emergence of the dominant pottery industry and the subsidiary but vital coal and iron industries; the spread of the conurbation and the difficulties of its administration, culminating in federation in 1910; and the creation of a regional identity. The essays that make up the final section have concentrated on the major aspects of the economic well-being and the quality of life of the contemporary conurbation. In particular, they are orientated to assessments of the structure and performance of the region's economy, and the changing nature and pattern of industrial activity; the effectiveness of planning strategies and the regeneration of derelict land; the distinctive social structure and health profile of the conurbation; and finally education policies and cultural traditions in the Potteries.

The volume has provided a welcome opportunity to bring together the established interests of researchers from a variety of backgrounds. The Potteries represents a research focus not only for many staff at Keele University but also for colleagues at other institutions and bodies in the region – Staffordshire University, North Staffordshire Health Authority, Staffordshire County Council – and beyond. The planning of the volume began in late 1991, and since then advice and help have come from many quarters. In particular, the suggestions and encouragement of Professor Brian Fender, Vice-Chancellor of Keele University, Sue Bramley, Local Organizer for the British Association meeting, and the advisory Editorial Board have been much appreciated. Special thanks are due to the Librarian in charge of Special Collections, Keele University, for making available the delights of the Warrillow Collection of photographs. The maps and diagrams have all been prepared by Andrew Lawrence of the Geography Department, Keele University, with his customary skill and care.

In listing the failings in Edwin Clayhanger's education in the schools of Oldcastle (Newcastle), Arnold Bennett drew specific attention to his ignorance of the local region. He knew nothing of the geology of the Potteries, though the whole district's 'livelihood depended on the scientific use of geological knowledge', of its topography – 'he could not have found the Trent in a day's march' – and of the forces that transformed 'the Five Towns [into] the great seat of manufacture'. If nothing else, it is hoped that this collection of essays would have provided Clayhanger with a sound base to remedy his lack of understanding of the Potteries.

A D M Phillips

PART ONE

The Regional Setting

1. The Landscape

EDWARD DERBYSHIRE

The north Staffordshire landscape is one of broad horizons. This is largely because it has evolved by the differential erosion of a number of different rock types and structures forming part of three landscape provinces: the south-western flanks of the Derbyshire Dome of the southern Pennines lie to the east; the margins of the Cheshire–Shropshire Basin make up its north-western edge; and the undulating periphery of the Midlands Plateau extends to the south. The region straddles the 200 m contour, and so embraces parts of both 'upland' and 'lowland' Britain. Open to the full force of polar maritime air from across the low surface of the Cheshire Plain, the hilly lands of north Staffordshire provide a rich range of natural habitats from the river flats and lowland mires of the Cheshire margins, close to sea-level, to the high heather moorlands and thin, acidic soils of north-central England's low, sub-alpine mountains. This is an impressive variety in a region only 25–30 km across. Such diversity is readily overlooked in the face of the human modification of the landscape which accompanied the course of its industrial history. The region's resources of coal, iron and clay made it an early contributor to the world's first industrial revolution. Although its developed expertise in iron-working and its pre-eminence in potting ensured survival (despite the early need to import superior iron ores and fine china clays), the decline of coal in late twentieth-century Britain is again placing strains on the economy of this region. The drastic landscape modification which accompanied the vigorous nineteenth-century economic activity has been smoothed over as iron, and now coal, decline. The result is a smoother, but locally spurious, landscape (Pl 1.1).

This chapter discusses the geological basis of the north Staffordshire landscape and looks in particular at the thin but important 'top dressing' of erosional forms and sedimentary deposits left behind by the dramatic surface processes of the Quaternary era with its alternations of ice sheets, warm periods, dry arctic cold, dust storms, and the action of violent meltwaters.

THE BEDROCK LANDSCAPE

The conurbation of Stoke-on-Trent and the towns and villages of its hinterland are built across a diverse landscape of ridges and hills making up part of the main watershed of England. The divide between the headwaters of the Trent (flowing to the North Sea) and the minor affluents of the Mersey system (flowing to the Irish Sea) consists of the ridge country around Kidsgrove and Biddulph at a little over 200 m above sea-level. The watershed between two of the master-streams of England, the Trent and the Severn, includes the Maer Hills, just 8 km west of Trentham (Fig 1.1).

The general form of both the landscape and the river network clearly reflects the regional geological structure. The broadly triangular platform of the Potteries coalfield occurs as a sharp salient of the Pennines which extends in a line of outcrops of Upper Carboniferous age from Goldenhill, Audley and Barlaston south-westwards through Market Drayton to and beyond Shrewsbury (Fig 2.1). To the east lie the six towns of the Potteries, aligned north-north-west to south-south-east along the strike of the Productive Coal Measure rocks. Further east, the gentle

PLATE 1.1 Etruria Vale in the Potteries coalfield, looking east from Basford, with Hanley on the right: top, 1940; bottom, 1993 (Warrillow Collection, Keele University Library and E Derbyshire).

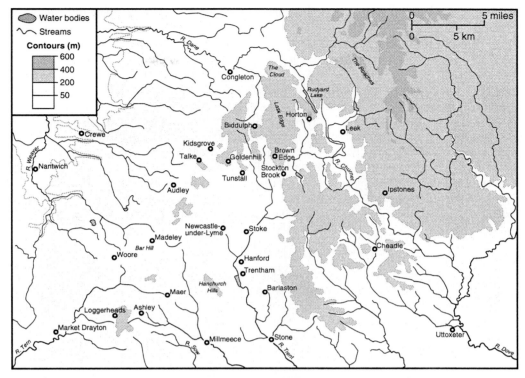

FIGURE 1.1 River network and drainage divides in north Staffordshire and adjacent areas.

coalfield ridges give way to the bolder and sharper lines of the scarps and backslopes (cuestas) developed on the Namurian interbedded sandstones and shales, the coarser sandstones including the 'Millstone Grits'. These 'edges', including Congleton Edge, the Cloud (343 m), and Brown Edge, give rise to a relative relief of over 100 m and essentially define the north-west, and part of the north-east, rim of the Potteries syncline. From here, the syncline plunges southwards to the much gentler country south of Stone which, on rocks of Triassic age, makes up the northern edge of the Midlands Plateau. These younger and characteristically red rocks, which include pebble beds, sandstones and mudstones, surround the coalfield on all sides other than the north-east. Outcrops reach over 200 m above sea-level around Ashley and Maer, about 15 km south-west of Stoke, but the landscape to the north and west, along the eastern margins of the Cheshire Plain, is mantled by varying thicknesses of glacial deposits and is a gentle terrain less than 100 m above the sea. The geological diversity of the region is thus reflected in the major landform units as exemplified by the relative relief (Fig 1.2).

The key to an understanding of the history of the landscape prior to the extreme events of the Quaternary (the last two and a half million years) has been regarded by a number of authors as lying in a topographical sequence of surfaces of low relief including small plateau remnants, flat-topped hills and ridges, and a succession of river terraces. The highest of these surfaces is found around the northern rim of the coalfield at altitudes of over 300 m, below which is a surface at about 225 m above sea-level typified by the area around Ashley but also distributed across the ridges of the coalfield to the east. A third, undulating surface has also been recognized at an altitude of between 195 and 160 m, the highest and apparently compound westernmost element of which has been called the Keele surface. Hill summits in the range 125–150 m are frequent in the undulating hill country along minor interfluves associated with the river Sow and Millmeece drainage, and an extensive surface at about 100 m altitude has been described for the interfluves west of Stafford. The Trent and its tributaries flow in rather broad and gently sloping valleys within this set of surfaces, floodplain and remnants of alluvial terraces being up to 1–2 km wide south of the coalfield. The traditional view has been that the higher the landscape remnant, the older it is likely to be, although there is little definitive evidence for the age of the remnants of higher level surfaces in north Staffordshire. Sediments found on such surfaces, even when they can be reliably dated, provide only a minimum age for the erosion surface itself which may be orders of magnitude older than any associated deposits. Nevertheless, this succession or 'staircase' of surfaces is certainly striking when seen from vantage points such as Foxholes (near Talke), the Hanchurch Hills and, in the south, the castle mound at Stafford, and it provides a useful basis for descriptions of landscape elements.

THE QUATERNARY ICE AGES: THE LANDSCAPE LEGACY

Much of the detail in the landscape of north Staffordshire and the adjacent areas is the product of the last two and a half million years or so (the Quaternary era), during which time surface processes included extreme events such as the advance of ice sheets across the region (the glacial evidence) and perennial deep freezing of the ground in conditions cold enough but too dry to generate ice sheets and glaciers (the periglacial evidence).

Glacial erosion and deposition in the landscape
Although the ridges of the Potteries coalfield bear only a thin and patchy drape of the distinctive deposits (known as 'till') derived from direct deposition from glacier ice, recognition that the low, sinuous ridge between Whitchurch, Woore and Bar Hill near Madeley is a moraine deposited at the front of an ice sheet which covered the Cheshire Plain goes back almost a century. Over 60 years ago, studies of meltwater gorges and glacial deposits in the southern Pennines to the east of the coalfield demonstrated beyond reasonable doubt that, in one or more stages of the Quaternary, the northern ice sheets had overridden the Potteries region. The first major synthesis of the evidence of multiple glaciation of the west midlands is that by L J Wills, published over 55 years ago. According to this work, study of the glacial deposits indicates that the Potteries coalfield was affected by continental-scale ice sheets on three separate occasions in the last half a million years. The first and second glaciations for which there is evidence (the deposits of which Wills termed the 'Older Drift series') completely inundated the region, being characterized by far-travelled rock particles ('erratics') from the Pennines and the Irish Sea Basin. The third and youngest of the glaciations, with its 'Newer Drift series' of deposits dominated by rock particles from the Irish Sea Basin, transgressed the coalfield but terminated close by, along a north-south line running from the tor mass known as the Roaches, just east of Leek, to Ipstones, recurving to the west of Cheadle and extending a lobe of ice as far east as the Churnet-Dove confluence near Uttoxeter. Wills was struck by the freshness of the moraine topography north of Wolverhampton compared to that further south, and he recognized evidence for a later ice sheet advance as far as Ellesmere and Whitchurch.

Although known to occur sporadically above 800 m above sea-level, the drift deposits of the coalfield and the south-west Pennines (Fig 2.9) provide little basis for a description of more than the last ice sheet glaciation of Britain. By comparison, the drift deposits of the nearby

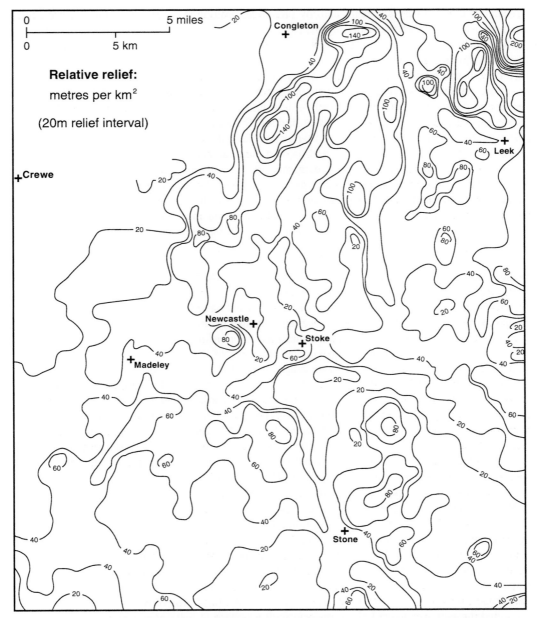

FIGURE 1.2 Relative relief map of the Potteries coalfield and environs. Relative relief is the altitudinal difference between tops and bottoms of slopes per unit area (here m per km²).

Cheshire Plain are very abundant and, by inference, provide information on the environmental changes which affected the wider region.

The north-western flanks of the south-west Pennines and the Potteries coalfield, as well as that part of the west-south-west trending ridge of Upper Coal Measures east of Market Drayton, are cut by steep-sided, open-ended valleys now either dry or with very small ('underfit') streams. These valleys range in dimensions from the Madeley-Whitmore Gap, which is 1 km wide and 6 km long, to channels only a few tens of metres wide running obliquely to the contours or cutting across minor bedrock divides. Reaching as high as 400 m above the sea on the Pennine flanks to the east of the Potteries coalfield, the channels record at least one episode when an ice sheet diverted drainage and its own meltwaters along routes which, in many cases, form little or no part of the modern stream network. This glacial drainage system was diverse in pattern, the melting ice sheet frequently generating water discharges many orders of magnitude greater than those typical of the streams which occupy the valleys today. The hydrological system included glacial lakes of variable dimensions and duration, rock channels cut by the overflowing lakes and by streams controlled by the ice margin, and channels cut by subglacial meltwaters.

The most striking series of meltwater channels can be seen cut into the Trent-Weaver watershed between Woore, in the west, and Congleton. Although opinion has varied over the years as to the primary process responsible for these and similar channels (notably river capture versus glacial meltwater erosion), all agree the channels have been modified by meltwaters. The precise relationship to the ice sheet, however, may still be argued. For example, if it is assumed that all the channels between Kidsgrove and Lask Edge resulted from the overspill of a glacial lake, their distribution broadly approximates the form of the ice front at that stage of glacier retreat. If, on the other hand, the channels are interpreted as of subglacial origin, the inferences on ice thickness, ice distribution and the location of the former ice front may be quite different. The general trend of most channels in this area is southward, indicating the overall hydrological gradient during ice wastage: however, the evident fact that the floors of several channels, including some of the larger ones such as the Rudyard-Churnet valley, rise to their highest point some tens of metres along their courses has led to the view that these erosional forms are the product of subglacial meltwater streams which can flow uphill because of the great water pressures generated beneath thick glaciers. This shift in opinion has been reinforced by the general paucity of information on extensive lacustrine deposits in the depressions within these hill lands once thought to have been the sites of lakes. It must be admitted that, in view of the strong likelihood that the region was inundated by ice sheets during two or three distinct glaciations, such meltwater channels were almost certainly used more than once, so that any role played by proglacial lake drainage remains cryptic. On the western slopes of the coalfield, however, the relationship between channels and former lakes is rather more clear. This may be regarded as the north-eastern margin of a large and complex ice-dammed lake series which developed on the north and west side of the Trent-Mersey-Severn watershed, and which included the very extensive Lake Lapworth with a surface at just under 100 m above sea-level. Lake waters stood at an altitude of c 128 m on the north side of the interfluve into which the Madeley channel is cut. As the ice sheet retreated across the Cheshire Plain, it left several lower channels which breach the Bar Hill–Woore–Whitchurch moraine.

A number of anomalous river alignments and acute tributary junctions have been explained as a result of derangement of the drainage, largely because of multiple glaciation. The broad gap at Stockton Brook has been interpreted as the upper reaches of the Horton Brook when it was a left bank tributary of a former north-flowing Churnet river. Further west, around

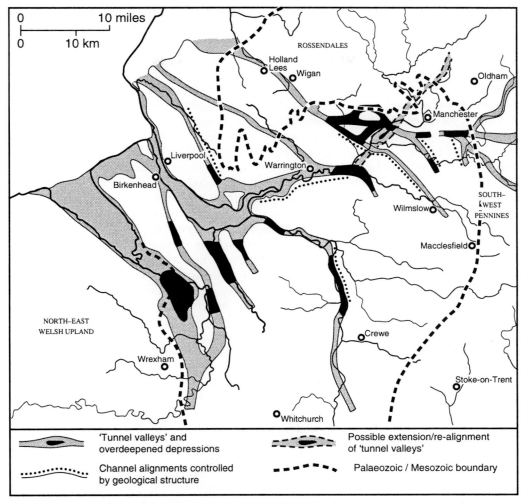

FIGURE 1.3 The general shape of the bedrock surface below the glacial deposits of the northern part of the Cheshire Plain (*Source*: R H Johnson, 'The imprint of glaciation on the west Pennine uplands', in R H Johnson, ed, *The geomorphology of north-west England*, Manchester, 1985, 252).

Madeley, the river Lea diverts sharply northwards from an easterly course some 3 km east of Woore at a point where the Woore moraine terminates and the Whitmore gap lies open to the south. Deposition of the Woore moraine also effectively reversed the flow direction of the river Tern to an anomalously westerly course, as well as diverting meltwaters into the Sow drainage. The Trent itself also shows some anomalous characteristics. Instead of following the broad valley along the line of the Trent and Mersey Canal between Stoke and Barlaston, it lurches westwards to join the Lyme Brook at Hanford before returning to the main valley floor about 2 km south of Trentham. Glacial deposition, in the form of a morainic mass at Sideway, has been proposed in explanation, but the long history of land disturbance hereabouts may mean that this hypothesis will never be adequately tested.

The sedimentary cover left behind by the Quaternary glaciations varies from a thin and discontinuous drape on the ridges of the south-west Pennines and the coalfield to complex mantles over 40 m thick both to the north and west (Cheshire Plain) and the south. Near Nantwich, for example, organic silty clays underlie an interbedded succession of sands and bouldery clays totalling 43 m in thickness. In the Sow valley, halfway between Stafford and Seighford, the surface alluvium is underlain by peats and silts which rest upon at least 45 m of glacial meltwater gravels. Accumulation of such thick sequences of deposits in this watershed region has modified the drainage pattern to varying degrees. The bedrock surface below the drift cover of parts of Cheshire, for example, reveals a valley system quite different from that at the present. The pattern is a composite one, reflecting the effects of pre-glacial river systems, glacial erosion, and the concentrated erosion by major subglacial rivers to form 'tunnel valleys' (Fig 1.3). It thus appears that the Mersey-Trent interfluve has been shifted some distance to the north-west as a direct result of thick glacial and proglacial deposition on the Cheshire Plain.

The glacial deposits of the western margins of this region provide the stratotype for the Last Glacial Stage in Britain, the stage name 'Devensian' being derived from the 'Devenses', an ancient British tribe which lived hereabouts. The Devensian ice sheet, in reaching the Potteries coalfield, was close to the limit of its advance: there is little visible evidence here of glacial erosion, the subglacial tills and erratic boulders of the extreme limit beyond most of the recognizable moraines are discontinuous and generally thin, and the complex glacial retreat which eventually occurred left a thick drape of deposits across the Cheshire Plain. The general explanation of the diverse and complexly interbedded glacier-derived deposits in this small region involves widespread stagnation of an ice sheet rich in englacial debris. As it downwasted, till was released and became concentrated on the stagnant ice masses, between

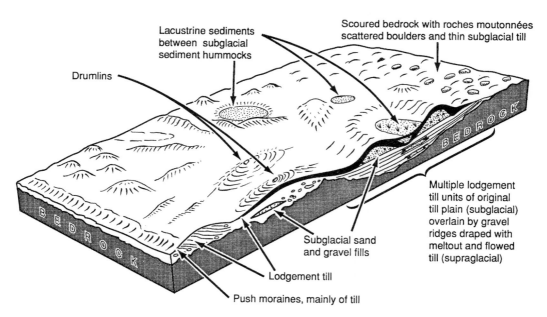

FIGURE 1.4 Schematic diagram showing the complexity of the supraglacial sediment association to be found in parts of east Cheshire.

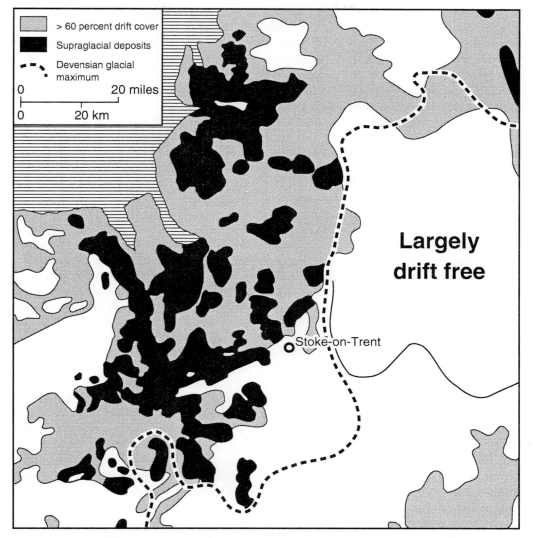

FIGURE 1.5 Dominance of the supraglacial sediment association along the western side of the Potteries region.

which there was abundant deposition of both the fine sediments typical of proglacial lakes and outwash (glaciofluvial) sands and gravels (the latter making up a variety of forms, including kames – gravel hillocks and terraces, and eskers – sinuous gravel trains marking the former sites of englacial or subglacial streams). With the final melting out of the buried cores of ice, a very hummocky terrain was produced consisting mainly of supraglacial debris (Figs 1.4 and 5).

Ice in the ground: the periglacial landscape changes
The evidence of former severe modification of the landscape of north Staffordshire and the eastern edge of the Cheshire Plain by periglacial (literally, 'near-glacial') processes is

widespread: processes which, in today's world, are typical of those parts of the sub-polar and polar regions not covered by glaciers. The contrast with the present day, in which freeze-thaw action is limited to relatively brief disturbance of a very thin surface layer, is striking.

Isolated bedrock stacks or 'tors' have been interpreted as the result of frost action, bedding planes and rock joints being wedged apart by the growth of lensoid ice bodies, and the main mass of the exposed 'corestones' breaking down by the process of granular disaggregation, the essential energy for which comes from the growth of ice crystals as frost penetrates into the rock. The 'gritstones' (arkosic sandstones) of the Namurian of the Pennines, including the Roaches syncline on the north-eastern edge of the Potteries region, have weathered into a well-known series of tors (Pl 1.2). Many of the valley side slopes below such tors include a broad apron or fan of granular debris which is vegetated and stable under the present climate, suggesting that during the period when the tors were actively being stripped, there were few obstacles to substantial slope debris transport and accumulation.

Some of the many 'dry valleys' and small valleys with underfit streams to be found on the Triassic sandstones and conglomerates have been regarded as glacial meltwater channels, while others may be old valley heads created by normal stream-and-slope processes (Fig 1.6). Many, however, have been modified by periglacial processes. In permafrost conditions, the sandstones would have been much less permeable than they are today, so that they would have been much more subject to enhanced stream erosion as well as frost action. A significant number of these features are short valleys with steep headwalls, and some can best be described as bowl-shaped. These have been regarded as the result of snowpatch erosion ('nivation hollows'). Although none has been dated, sandstone debris at least 2 m thick is known from one or two, suggesting that such periglacial modelling of the landscape occurred relatively recently, perhaps towards the end of the last glaciation.

The most widespread evidence of severe periglacial climates during the Quaternary, however, is provided by the many diverse deposits to be found in the region. The general term 'head' has been used for decades to distinguish this complex of slope deposits from the equally heterogeneous products of glacial deposition, with which it has frequently been confused. The term is loosely defined so as to include a wide range of materials translocated on slopes by periglacial mass movements, but incorporates the slow, cyclic downslope creep of seasonally-thawed soil known as solifluction. Head drapes many slopes on the higher Pennine margins in the north-east of the region, and appears to be more abundant outside the Devensian ice limits in north Staffordshire.

Failures of more-or-less coherent masses of slope deposits are common, especially in the north and east, and include, for example, bedding-plane slip, subsidence, rotational sliding and mudslides. The mudslides are of particular interest, both because of what they tell us about environmental conditions at the time of their activation and because their unsuspected presence within some hillsides has been troublesome and expensive. A particular case concerned the construction, begun in 1958, of a motorway section near Walton's Wood 2.5 km north-east of Madeley. By 1961, the roadline had moved at least 1.5 m downhill, so the toe of the feature was loaded with slag and deep piles were driven into the failing mass. However, it continued to move, cracks soon appearing on the newly constructed road embankment. Despite the insertion of additional piles of sheet steel, the embankment was moving at a rate of 4 cm per month by 1962, and deep cracks, some 60 cm wide, ran down the centre of the roadline. It was only then that detailed investigation showed that this innocent-looking hillside had been cut by a steep-sided glacial meltwater channel at the end of the last glaciation. It had then been filled with 15 m of fine lake clays, sands and peats over which a head deposit, some 10 m thick, had

PLATE 1.2 One of the masses making up Ramshaw Rocks, developed in Namurian arkosic sandstones of the Roaches syncline, with Rudyard Lake in the middle distance (E Derbyshire).

accumulated. This head proved to be full of rather gently-inclined shear (failure) surfaces along which the clay was found to have much lower residual strength values than in the intact (undisturbed) clay making up most of the deposit. To make matters worse, it rested in part on impermeable mudstone bedrock, so that a local 'perched' water table could develop. It soon became clear that, with gradients as low as 7°, the basal failure surface in the head, although stable if undisturbed under the present climate, was the principal failure plane of a periglacial mudslide. The likely environmental conditions required for such a movement include deep freezing of the upper layers of the ground with consequent trapping of the liquid water below it and above the impermeable mudstone, so that excess pore water pressures were able to develop in the head. Such conditions have been recognized on present-day slopes with active mudslides in sub-polar periglacial regions such as Spitsbergen. Clearly, in the case of Walton's Wood, the meltwater erosion phase of the last glaciation was followed by severe periglacial conditions. By cutting and loading this old failed mass, the motorway construction changed the gradient and drainage conditions, so that an ancient but stable periglacial mudslide was reactivated.

Because pore size and space vary in natural sediments, slow but deep freezing of moist terrain results in an irregular distribution of ice in the ground. Such segregated ground ice may occur as veins, wedges, sheets, lenses and irregularly shaped concretionary masses. Given that some expansion occurs as water turns to ice and also because high soil atmosphere pressures are generated in the finest soil pores because of preferential growth of ice nuclei in the larger pores, the development of segregated ice tends to leave a permanent mark on the structure and texture of sediments. Perhaps the most striking feature of this type is the fossil frost wedge. Initial

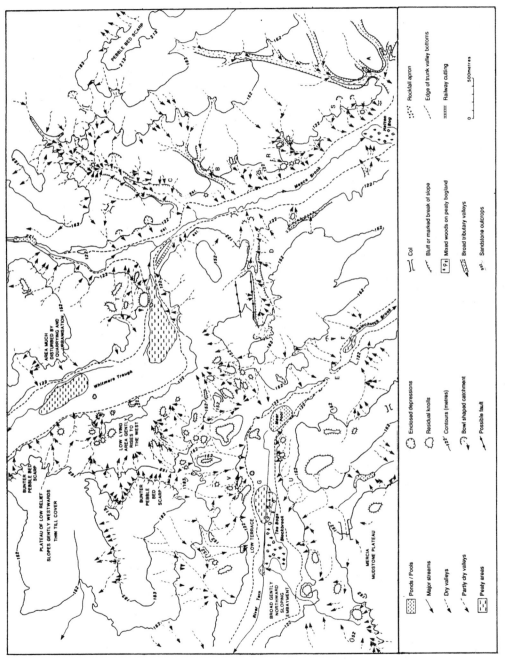

FIGURE 1.6 'Dry valleys' and valleys with underfit streams between the Maer–Ashley area and the Hanchurch Hills (*Source:* A Knowles, 'The Quaternary history of north Staffordshire', in Johnson, *The geomorphology of north-west England*, 235).

failure of a deeply-frozen and hence brittle soil induces contraction and consequent near-vertical cracking of the ground, giving rise to a polygonal crack system covering the ground surface. Wedges several metres deep and crack systems made up of polygons up to 30 m in diameter are best seen at present in extreme periglacial environments such as northern Greenland, Siberia, and Antarctica. In extremely dry periglacial regions, such as the 'dry valleys' of the Antarctic, such cracks may fill with sand each time they enlarge. In areas where some meltwater is generated in summer, however, very thin veins of dirty ice may progressively fill the wedge. With a change of climate, these wedges either preserve their sand filling or, as the ice wedge melts away, they become filled with debris from the upper soil layers. Freezing of the moist upper layers of a land surface may cause general and widespread ground heaving which, in turn, disrupts the primary (original) sedimentary structures. The resulting disturbances are known as involutions. Frost wedges and involutions together provide clear evidence of past periods of periglacial climate.

Signs that severe periglacial conditions with perennially frozen ground (or 'permafrost') prevailed in Staffordshire and Cheshire are quite widespread. Frost wedges have been described in detail from a quarry at Chelford, about 22 km north of Newcastle-under-Lyme: their presence in two distinct sand units beneath the till of the last ice advance, as well as in the upper surface of that till, indicates that permafrost conditions prevailed in this region on at least three occasions in the past 80,000 years. Wedges and involutions are also known from Baldwin's Gate, Loggerheads, and Madeley. Some of these sites have also yielded more than one horizon of wind-facetted stones (or 'ventifacts'), confirming the repeated occurrence of severe but non-glacial conditions here.

Other ground evidence indicating harsh periglacial conditions is provided by the presence of wind-blown sands and silts. Blown sands of Quaternary age have not been described from the north Staffordshire region, but some occur in the Quaternary sediment successions of the Cheshire Plain. Much more widespread, although frequently difficult to demonstrate without the use of laboratory analysis of the soils, is periglacial wind-blown silt, or loess. Although usually thin and weathered, and very often reworked into other sediments, loessic deposits have been shown to be extensive on limestone outcrops including the Carboniferous Limestone which bounds the Potteries coalfield on its eastern side. Loess contrasts strongly with such underlying bedrock, especially in its mineralogy and its distinctively high silt fraction (over 50 per cent by weight). The mineral composition of the loessic fraction in the soils is remarkably uniform over extensive areas and is very similar to that found in the Devensian tills. This has been used to argue that the loess originated on the proglacial plains outside the ice sheet margins of the last glaciation.

The thinness and patchy nature of the loess is a reminder of the importance in the evolution of any landscape of the frequently slow but continuous processes of weathering and erosion. There is no doubt that the original thin mantles of wind-blown silt have been drastically reduced by slope processes and incorporation of this mechanically-weak material into other deposits, notably the river alluvium making up the terraces and floodplains of the present. All the loess deposits in the south-west Pennines are decalcified and weathered throughout. With mean annual rainfall amounts ranging from around 700 mm in the lower lands to west and south, to about 1200 mm on the highest ground to the east, the region is dominated by the family of leached soils known as podzols. On the Cheshire side, podzolized brown acid soils developed on the hummocky drift, but are replaced by humus-iron podzols on the steeper margins of the peat-filled late-glacial lake hollows. The podzols and acid brown soils of the Carboniferous rocks of the coalfield are locally denuded to dwarf podzols on the steeper slopes of the arkosic sandstones of the 'edges' while, with passage on to the Carboniferous Limestone of the south-west Pennines, brown calcareous soils and brown rendzinas are dominant, with thin rendzinas and brown podzolics on the steeper valley sides. On the coalfield itself, of course, much of this primary soil population has been reworked and reconstituted by intensive settlement, construction and industrial development over the past two centuries. This is recognized in the legends of most current soil maps which refer to the soils of urban and industrial areas as 'unsurveyed'.

AN AMENDED LANDSCAPE

Despite the relatively late appearance of human populations in the Potteries coalfield region, the spread of agriculture, the growth of dense industrial populations, and the concentration of routeways for coaches, canals, railways, roads and motorways along the Trent, Churnet, Lyme Brook and Whitmore channels over the past two to three hundred years had created, by the middle of the twentieth century, a land surface which was in many details artificial. Although a good deal of this activity has declined or disappeared, extractive industry continues to supply clay for the brickyards and tileries, and sand and gravel for the construction industries. Thus, new landforms continue to appear in the form both of holes in the ground and piles of waste. Some of these artifacts are now being deliberately preserved, so that a new kind of landform association, grassed over and planted with trees and bushes, is emerging. A primary motive for such major undertakings was to cover with imported materials, including soil, many huge accumulations of industrial debris such as colliery spoil, iron slag, and chemical waste, some of which contain toxic components. Increasingly, however, social imperatives have stimulated work leading to the creation of new city parks for the use of an urban population with increasing amounts of time on its hands. The newest landscape elements in the Potteries region, therefore, are parks and lakes bulldozed from areas of formerly extensive industrial waste. As the latest examples of rapid and severe landscape change, the scale of such work is impressive. It is worth noting, in conclusion, that the industrial waste making up Central Forest Park (between Burslem and Hanley) is thicker than any known glacial or periglacial deposits within the coalfield, its slopes are steeper, and its artificial 'downs' higher than most of the hummocky moraine which it so much resembles.

BIBLIOGRAPHY

K R Early and A W Skempton, 'Investigations of the landslide at Walton's Wood, Staffordshire', *Quart Jnl Eng Geol*, 5, 1972, 19–41.

A M D Gemmell and P K George, 'The glaciation of the west midlands: a review of recent research', *N Staffs Jnl Fld Stud*, 12, 1972, 1–20.

R H Johnson, 'The imprint of glaciation on the west Pennine uplands', in R H Johnson, ed, *The geomorphology of north-west England*, Manchester, 1985, 237–62.

A Knowles, 'The Quaternary history of north Staffordshire', in Johnson, *The geomorphology of north-west England*, 222–36.

L J Wills, 'The Pleistocene history of the west midlands', *Rep Brit Assoc*, 1937, 71–94.

P Worsley, 'Pleistocene history of the Cheshire-Shropshire Plain', in Johnson, *The geomorphology of north-west England*, 201–21.

E M Yates and F Moseley, 'A contribution to the glacial geomorphology of the Cheshire Plain', *Trans Inst Brit Geogr*, 42, 1967, 107–25.

2. Geology

B M BESLY

The Potteries conurbation is built on the approximately triangular outcrop of Coal Measures that forms the north Staffordshire coalfield. This area of rounded hills of moderate relief (maximum elevation 355 m OD) forms a south-western appendage of the higher land underlain by older Carboniferous rocks in the southern termination of the Pennine chain. To the west and the south, generally lower ground of gentler topography is underlain by Triassic rocks, locally blanketed by thick Quaternary sediments. The geology of the region around Stoke-on-Trent is, therefore, representative of that of much of the north midlands, and of the contrast between 'lowland' England, underlain by soft, Mesozoic rocks, and 'upland' northern England, formed largely of Carboniferous rocks.

The solid geology outcrop of north Staffordshire and south Cheshire is illustrated in Figure 2.1. The stratigraphic succession is summarized in Figures 2.3–5 and 8. In this brief summary, published data are in places supplemented with the results of recent unpublished work, and the past and present availability of natural resources is discussed.

GEOLOGICAL HISTORY

The geological sequence of the district falls into four main units, separated by unconformities representing major phases of earth movement and erosion. These units are, in chronological order: Precambrian and Lower Palaeozoic, the geological basement of the area, comprising rocks that were deformed in the mid-Devonian Caledonian mountain building events; Upper Palaeozoic (Devonian and Carboniferous), mainly sedimentary rocks, disrupted by folding and faulting in the late Carboniferous Variscan mountain building event; Latest Palaeozoic and Mesozoic (Permian to Jurassic), sedimentary rocks, disrupted by faulting, folding and igneous intrusion during Tertiary earth movements; and Quaternary, a veneer of clays, sands and gravels deposited as a result of glaciations during the last 300,000 years.

Precambrian and Lower Palaeozoic basement

The thick sequences of Carboniferous and Triassic rocks mean that basement rocks are neither exposed nor penetrated in boreholes. Evidence for the nature of the basement is derived from geophysical interpretation and from boreholes around the edges of the district, and its nature remains speculative. Boreholes near Market Drayton suggest that the area lying to the east of the major Wem/Red Rock Fault system (Fig 2.1) is underlain by Precambrian metamorphic rocks, and Cambrian and Silurian sedimentary rocks. To the west the basement is formed of Ordovician sedimentary rocks. This contrast has been employed to argue that the Wem/Red Rock Fault system marks the continuation of the bounding faults of the Lower Palaeozoic Welsh basin. This fault system is one of the most important geological features in the district, having been demonstrably active from Carboniferous to Tertiary times, and forming the boundary of the Mesozoic Cheshire Basin. It is significant that it corresponds to the extension of an important Precambrian and/or Lower Palaeozoic lineament. Most of the other major faults displacing late Palaeozoic and Mesozoic rocks have probably also been formed by the reactivation of older fault lines in the basement.

Devonian and Carboniferous

The Lower Palaeozoic rocks of central England underwent regional folding and erosion in mid-Devonian times, after which a new regime of subsidence and sedimentation was initiated. Deposition of Devonian and Carboniferous sediments took place in three phases, reflecting an evolving pattern of subsidence (Fig 2.2). Firstly, between the late Devonian and early/mid-Namurian rapidly subsiding rift basins (graben) developed, showing a strong contrast to the adjoining shelf areas which underwent little subsidence or were emergent (Fig 2.2A). To the south of the district, much of the central midlands was uplifted and emergent. Secondly, between mid-Namurian and early Westphalian times the contrast between the areas of high and low subsidence became less pronounced: more uniform thicknesses of sediment were deposited, and deposition encroached southwards over the formerly emergent central midlands (Fig 2.2B). Finally, during the late Westphalian and Stephanian, more irregular patterns of subsidence evolved in response to the onset of the late Carboniferous Variscan mountain building events (Fig 2.2 C and D).

The disposition of the high areas and graben is fairly well known at outcrop in north-east Staffordshire, but little known beneath the Triassic cover further south, where reconstructions rely on a few boreholes. The earlier phases of infill of the late Devonian and early Carboniferous graben are covered by thick later Carboniferous deposits. Devonian rocks do not outcrop, and are only known from boreholes. They consist of red sandstones and mudstones of Old Red Sandstone type, and are interpreted to have been deposited by subaerial river systems.

Lower Carboniferous sediments (Fig 2.3) are dominated by limestones, which accumulated in clear tropical seas. The deposits reflect stages in the progressive drowning of the late Devonian rift basin topography by rising sea-level. Early Lower Carboniferous (Tournaisian) deposits consist of shallow-water limestones, with textures that indicate the former presence of the evaporite mineral anhydrite. With rising water-level and continuing subsidence during the Dinantian, emergent areas became flooded. Massively-bedded white and pale grey limestones were deposited, containing fossils of shallow water organisms and small reefs. At the same time, the rift basins were occupied by deeper, mainly stagnant water. Limestones were deposited by catastrophic subaqueous density flows of carbonate material derived from the shallow shelf areas. In contrast to the massive, pale limestones of the shallow water areas, these deep water limestones are thinner bedded, and have a dark grey colour reflecting the accumulation of fine grained organic matter in the stagnant conditions.

Locally, clastic sediments were contributed by uplifted areas undergoing erosion, notably around Astbury, to the north-west of the Potteries coalfield, where a thin sequence of coal-bearing deltaic sediments is present in the latest Dinantian (Brigantian stage). To the south-west of this a significant volcanic centre developed in the later part of the Lower Carboniferous in the western part of what is now the Potteries coalfield. The volcano, represented by the occurrence of more than 830 m of basaltic ash and breccia in the Apedale-2 borehole, sourced ash beds, which can be identified over much of the north of the district.

This fairly stable pattern of palaeogeography and depositional environments underwent a major disruption in the latest Lower Carboniferous and early Namurian. This occurred in two phases. In the Brigantian (latest Lower Carboniferous) a phase of tectonic compression caused a local inversion of the subsidence pattern of graben and shelf areas. This resulted in the development of a local angular unconformity between the latest Lower Carboniferous rocks and

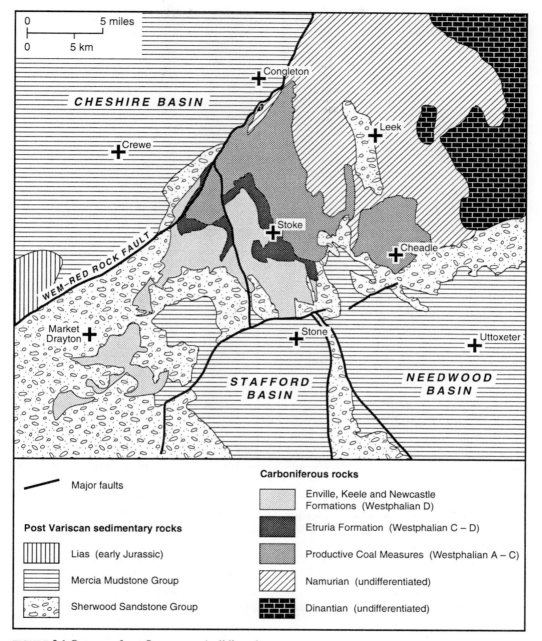

FIGURE 2.1 Outcrop of pre-Quaternary, 'solid' geology.

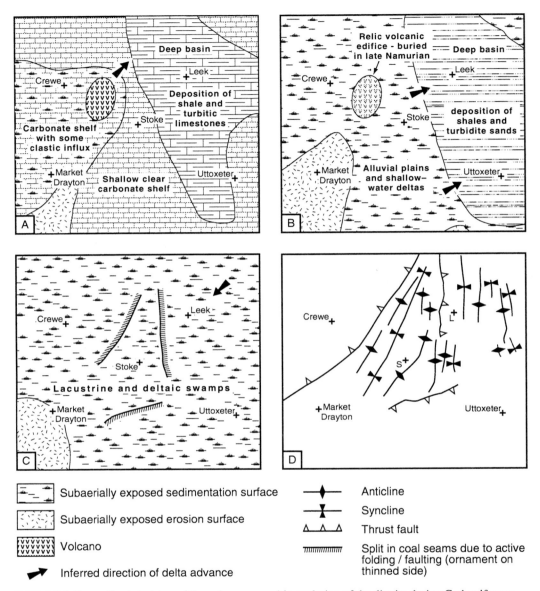

FIGURE 2.2 Generalized sketches of the palaeogeographic evolution of the district during Carboniferous time: A) Dinantian; B) Namurian; C) early Westphalian; and D) pattern of major folding in Variscan orogeny. Map areas as in Fig 2.1.

the succeeding Namurian strata, and led to the introduction of mud and sand which formed intercalations in the limestones; hence the latest part of the basinal graben deposits consist of calcareous shale. A more far-reaching change occurred at the beginning of the Namurian. A flood of sandy and muddy sediment was introduced into Staffordshire, which led to the cessation of limestone formation. At about the same time, the pattern of differential subsidence between graben and shelf areas was replaced by a more uniform pattern of subsidence. The

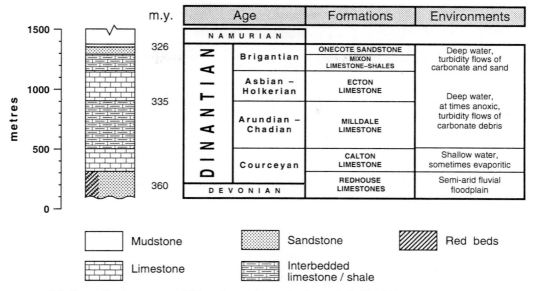

FIGURE 2.3 Generalized sequence of Dinantian rocks present in north Staffordshire.

whole of the north midlands, with the exception of marginal parts of the depositional basin in south Staffordshire, became covered by deep, predominantly fresh, water, in which the former areas of shallow water limestones formed submerged topographic highs.

The Namurian sediments (Figs 2.2B and 4) record the progressive infilling of this fairly uniformly subsiding basin by extensive delta systems. Small deltas were sourced by rivers flowing from a rejuvenated source in the south midlands, and much larger, ultimately dominant deltas spread southwards, fed by rivers sourced from uplifted areas lying to the north and north-west of Scotland. The deposits can be differentiated by the composition of the sandstones: those from the south are quartz-rich and lack significant feldspar; those from the north are much coarser, and contain abundant feldspar. The latter form the Millstone Grits of northern England.

The sequence of Namurian sediments is similar throughout northern England, consisting of three main phases: a sequence of shale-dominated basinal sediments predating the advance of the major delta systems; a thick sequence of interbedded sandstone and shales marking the infilling of the deep water body by the advance of a major delta; and a succession of thinner sequences of shales and sandstones, capped by root beds and coal seams, marking the growth and abandonment of smaller delta systems in shallower water. The second phase, containing the first major beds of sandstone, usually comprises a basal sequence of turbidites, formed by sediment density flows down the delta front, a siltstone sequence marking the advance of the delta slope, and a sandstone-dominated sequence formed by the fills of the distributary channels of the delta top. The early, shale-dominated phase is restricted to areas that formed deep basins at the end of the Lower Carboniferous, where it and the succeeding turbidites blanket and infill the pronounced topography of the Lower Carboniferous carbonate platforms.

By late-Namurian time, the combination of more uniform subsidence and the infilling of relict topography had created a wide area of shallow water, into which small deltas repeatedly

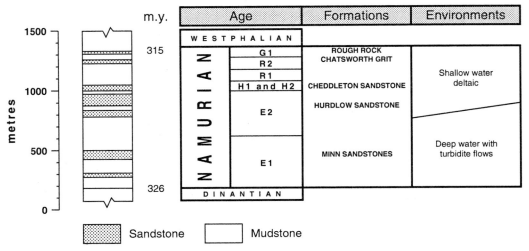

FIGURE 2.4 Generalized sequence of Namurian rocks present in north Staffordshire.

advanced, leading to periods of emergence and plant colonization. These conditions heralded those of the early to mid-Westphalian, where plant growth on abandoned subaerial delta surfaces became dominant, and led to the formation of thick peat deposits, now preserved as coal seams (Figs 2.2C and 5). The principal phases of coal formation occurred in late Westphalian A to early Westphalian B, and in late Westphalian C times. Between these periods, the delta plain was more subject to marine flooding and fewer coals formed.

Although sedimentation during the early Westphalian superficially resembles that of the late Namurian, subtle changes in subsidence pattern from Westphalian A onwards mark the beginning of the deformation of the basin fill. This culminated, during the latest Carboniferous, in the cessation of deposition, and in major folding, faulting, uplift and erosion. The earliest signs of these events were changes in the loci of subsidence. Until late Namurian time, the thickest sequences had been deposited to the east of a major structure – the Lask Edge Fault – defining the western side of the north Staffordshire 'Gulf'. From Westphalian A time the pattern reversed, a thinner sequence accumulating to the east of this line and the centre of deposition moving into the main coalfield area around Stoke-on-Trent. This reversal is interpreted to mark the onset of regional compression, which initially had the effect of reversing the relative subsidence pattern associated with deep-seated major faults. Further evidence for these events is found in the pattern of splitting of coal seams. In the early Westphalian B, seams in the Hams, Ragman, Rough 7 ft and Yard group amalgamated to form thick composite seams over the crests of what later became the major anticlinal fold structures of the coalfield (Fig 2.2C). This amalgamation marks a phase of differential subsidence caused by the initiation of these folds. The onset of compression was due to the beginning of major deformations in the Variscan mountain belt in the region now occupied by the English Channel and south-west England.

Towards the end of the Westphalian, the increasing intensity of deformation led to marked geographical and environmental changes. Between mid-Westphalian B and late Westphalian C major folding and uplift occurred in the south midlands, giving rise, in Shropshire and south Staffordshire, to an angular unconformity within the sequence. The products of this uplift and

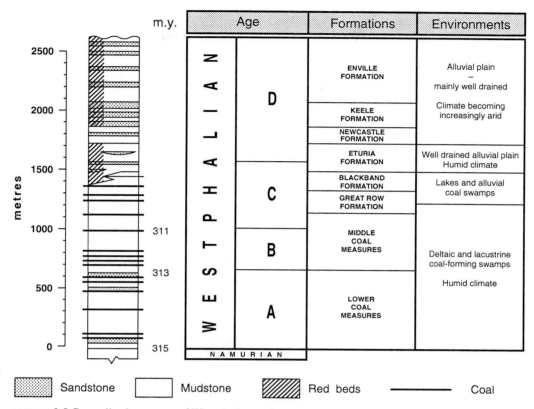

FIGURE 2.5 Generalized sequence of Westphalian rocks present in north Staffordshire.

erosion form a distinctive set of fluviatile red-bed deposits, known collectively as the Etruria Formation, whose depositional area spread northwards, culminating in late Westphalian C. By this time, the formation of coal-bearing sediments was restricted to a small area of rapid subsidence around Stoke-on-Trent, where a series of lakes developed, which were infilled by small deltas and river systems. The unusual chemistry in these lakes allowed the formation of bedded ironstones, freshwater limestones and oil shales – rock types that are generally unusual in British Coal Measures. By the end of Westphalian C time this lacustrine area was also invaded by red-bed forming fluviatile environments.

During the final phase of Carboniferous sedimentation (Westphalian D–Cantabrian), the district formed part of a large foreland basin – a rapidly subsiding downwarp formed by loading of the crust to the north of the Variscan mountain belt. Dominantly red fluvial sediments accumulated to form the Newcastle, Keele and Enville Formations. The sediments were derived from major mountain uplifts to the south of the midlands. Soon after their deposition, major Variscan deformations spread northwards through the midlands. Deformation occurred in two phases (Fig 2.2D), with the formation of large-scale north-south and north-east–south-west oriented folds, and subsequently large normal faults, generally trending north-south and north-west–south-east. The pattern of deformation was controlled by the pre-existing faults (Fig 2.6). The accompanying uplift and erosion locally removed up to 4 km of the Carboniferous sequence before deposition resumed during the Permo-Triassic.

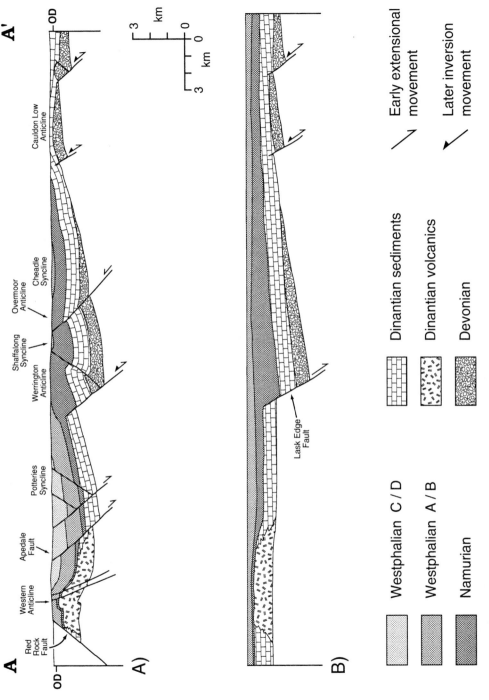

FIGURE 2.6 True-scale, structural cross-section through north Staffordshire: A) present situation; and B) situation at end of Westphalian B. Note the control on the size and position of Variscan fold structures exercised by the Dinantian Apedale volcanic pile and the Lask Edge Fault.

Latest Palaeozoic and Mesozoic

The patterns of sediment deposition and palaeogeographic evolution of the north midlands during these periods were entirely different to those that had prevailed before the Variscan deformation. Devonian and Carboniferous basin formation and infilling had been dominated by extension, and later compression, that had acted in generally north-south directions. After the Variscan Orogeny, tensional stress developed, acting in a dominantly east-west direction. The result was the formation of elongate north-south rift basins, bounded by mainly north-south trending faults. Three such basins were formed around Stoke-on-Trent (Fig 2.1): the Stafford Basin to the south; the Needwood Basin to the south-east; and the Cheshire Basin to the west. The faults bounding these basins were in part formed by re-activation of pre-existing fault lines, probably along Precambrian trends.

Permian and Triassic sedimentation (Figs 2.7 and 8) took place under arid non-marine conditions, depositional environments including aeolian dune fields, gravelly and sandy rivers, and intertidal zones, lagoons and salt lakes. Three broad phases can be recognized.

Permian (Fig 2.7A). Following the initial extensional faulting, curve-crested ridge dunes driven by an easterly trade wind occupied the centres of the basins. These deposited sands which now form the Bridgnorth Sandstone Formation (Stafford Basin) and the Kinnerton Sandstone Formation (Cheshire Basin).

Early – mid-Triassic (Scythian – Anisian; Fig 2.7B). Regional river systems became established, carrying sediment northwards from the Variscan mountains in southern England. These rivers deposited the thick sequences of gravels and sandstones of the Sherwood Sandstone Group. Intermittent aeolian dune fields were formed by wind reworking of the dried out river plains. These led to intercalations of dune bedded sandstones in the fluvial deposits. At this time, deposition spread from the axes of the rift basins to the adjoining areas. Thus Carboniferous rocks are unconformably overlain by Kidderminster/Chester Pebble Beds over a wide area. Upfolds and uplifts formed during the Variscan deformation remained as areas of positive relief. In the Leek area pebbly Triassic sediments occupy a fossil valley at least 250 m deep cut through one such uplift.

Later Triassic (Anisian – Norian; Fig 2.7C). Lessening relief in the sediment source areas led to a diminution in the amount of pebbles and sand delivered to the basins. Sedimentation became dominated by the accumulation of dolomitic and gypsum-bearing mudstones in saline lakes, occasionally affected by marine flooding events. The resulting sequence forms the Mercia Mudstone Group. Two periods of enhanced marine influx led to the development of the thick rock salt (halite) beds of the Northwich and Wilkesley/Stafford Halite Formations.

The characteristic desert environments of the Triassic came to an end in the latest Triassic, when a widespread transgression of the sea ushered in the long Jurassic and Cretaceous period of dominantly marine sedimentation. In the north midlands post-Triassic sediments are restricted to a small area around Prees in Shropshire, where a sequence of *c* 600 m of early Jurassic marine shales and mudstones is present. As this is the thickest sequence of this age in the UK onshore area, it is reasonable to suppose that subsidence continued in the north midlands during the later Jurassic and Cretaceous, but that these sediments have been removed by pre-Quaternary erosion. Support for this comes from the study of the degree of coalification in the coals in the underlying Carboniferous rocks. The pattern of coal rank development shows that these coals experienced their maximum burial after the folding and faulting of the Variscan deformation. The deepest burial is inferred during the Cretaceous. Since then more than 2 km of post-Triassic sediment has been eroded from the Cheshire and Stafford Basins.

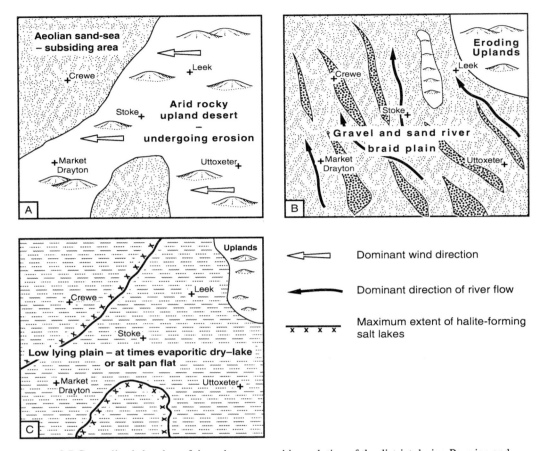

FIGURE 2.7 Generalized sketches of the palaeogeographic evolution of the district during Permian and Triassic time: A) late Permian; B) early Triassic; and C) late Triassic. Map areas as in Fig 2.1.

Tertiary

Although no Tertiary sedimentary rocks are preserved, a few lines of evidence relate to the geological evolution of the district during this period. The Permo-Jurassic rocks in the Cheshire Basin are folded into a gentle syncline, dissected by faults. The folding could have occurred at any time between the early Jurassic and the Quaternary, but regional patterns of deformation and uplift, for instance in the east midlands and southern North Sea, suggest that it is most likely to have occurred during the latest Cretaceous or early Tertiary. Some constraint is provided by the presence of two groups of Eocene dykes – the nepheline olivine dolerite dykes of the Butterton/Swynnerton/Yarnfield dykes of north Staffordshire, and the tholeiitic dolerite Grinshill dykes of Shropshire. These postdate the folding, and reflect a period of north-east–south-west regional tension. Recent work suggests that each dyke swarm is composed of several magma suites, and that the dykes are related to the Mull-Arran, and Northern Ireland centres respectively. Mineralization (Cu-Pb-Zn-Co-Ba) of the Triassic sandstones of the Cheshire Basin postdates dyke emplacement.

The Tertiary was largely a time of uplift and denudation. During these processes there was

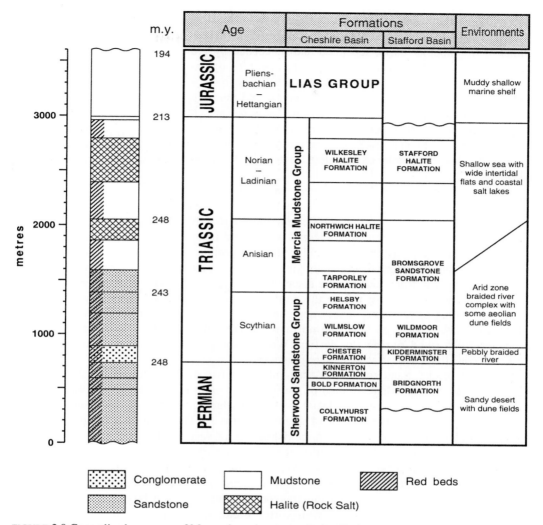

m.y.	Age		Formations		Environments
			Cheshire Basin	Stafford Basin	
194	JURASSIC	Pliens-bachian – Hettangian	LIAS GROUP		Muddy shallow marine shelf
213	TRIASSIC	Norian – Ladinian	Mercia Mudstone Group — WILKESLEY HALITE FORMATION	STAFFORD HALITE FORMATION	Shallow sea with wide intertidal flats and coastal salt lakes
248		Anisian	NORTHWICH HALITE FORMATION		
			TARPORLEY FORMATION	BROMSGROVE SANDSTONE FORMATION	Arid zone braided river complex with some aeolian dune fields
243		Scythian	Sherwood Sandstone Group — HELSBY FORMATION		
			WILMSLOW FORMATION	WILDMOOR FORMATION	
			CHESTER FORMATION	KIDDERMINSTER FORMATION	Pebbly braided river
248			KINNERTON FORMATION		
	PERMIAN		BOLD FORMATION	BRIDGNORTH FORMATION	Sandy desert with dune fields
			COLLYHURST FORMATION		

Conglomerate ☐ Mudstone ☐ Red beds

Sandstone ☐ Halite (Rock Salt)

FIGURE 2.8 Generalized sequence of Mesozoic rocks present in the district.

significant renewed movement on some of the faults, implied by the vertical offset of rank levels in the Westphalian coals between seams in the exposed coalfields and their correlatives beneath the Triassic basin fills. By Pliocene time, a regional peneplain had formed, which now forms an eastward tilted platform at a level 450–550 m OD. Further uplift and denudation have dissected this surface, which is still recognizable in central Wales and the Pennines, where resistant rocks now form uplands.

Quaternary
The most recent events contributing to the stratigraphic sequence were the glaciations of the last 300,000 years. These were largely responsible for moulding the present landscape of the area, and have left thick deposits of gravel, sand and clay over much of the lower ground (Fig 2.9). In

the mid-nineteenth century, a tradition developed in which glacial deposits were divided into two: the so-called Older and Newer Drifts. This division was based on the occurrence of two units of till (boulder clay), separated and succeeded by gravels, sands and clays deposited during interglacial periods. Recently, it has been recognized that the stratigraphy is more complex, and represents the deposits of at least three main glaciations, each characterized by interaction of ice sheets from several sources, and involving several glacial advances. The deposits are related only to the Anglian to Devensian glacial episodes. Although evidence in East Anglia implies that there were earlier, pre-Pastonian or Beestonian, glaciations in Wales and the midlands, no deposits can yet be attributed to these episodes. In all but the easternmost part of the district deposits of the latest Devensian glaciation mantle or modify earlier glacial deposits.

The Quaternary sediments fall into three main groups.

Till. Till is a poorly sorted, unstratified mixture of rock fragments in a matrix of clay and sand-size material. It represents material eroded and incorporated into glacier ice, that has been deposited directly from ice melting. Its composition and texture vary, and are largely dependent on the nature of the underlying bedrock. Apart from locally derived fragments, 'erratics' derived from considerable distances allow recognition of the direction of origin of different ice sheets. Thus, tills to the north, west and south of the district were generally formed during Devensian advances, and contain a suite of erratics that includes volcanic and granite pebbles derived from the north-west. Tills to the east of Stoke-on-Trent were generally formed during the earlier, Wolstonian glaciation, and include significant Cretaceous flints indicating an eastern provenance.

Sand and gravel. Sand and gravel accumulated in two distinct settings in relationship to glaciers. In the immediate vicinity of the fronts and sides of the glaciers, outwash streams reworked material dumped by glacial melting, producing mounds of sandy sediment, and locally more extensive ridges of sand and gravel. The former were produced by sedimentary infilling of hollows on the degrading ice surface, the latter as moraines at the ice front. A major moraine relating to the Devensian glaciation forms a series of arcuate ridges stretching westwards from Alsager and Madeley, towards Whitchurch and Wrexham. The second major setting of sand deposition was located in front of the ice sheet. Meltwater streams and wind transported and reworked large volumes of sandy sediment, depositing sheets of well-sorted clean sand. Sands of this type form the economically important Congleton Sand.

Lacustrine and organic deposits. In the latest stages of retreat, lakes were formed by the decay of melting masses of ice, or by the damming of valley systems by the retreating ice front. Initial fill of these lakes consisted of clay, but with climatic amelioration they became the sites of many small accumulations of peat. Large peat-filled depressions around Alsager and Betley may owe their origin to subsidence brought about by solution of underlying Triassic rock salt.

Quaternary deposits show widely varying thicknesses. On high ground in the east of Stoke-on-Trent, only thin veneers of till are present. Thicknesses increase on the lower ground to the west, reaching more than 40 m around Congleton, mainly formed of the Congleton Sand. Locally the Quaternary sediments infill deeply incised channels, one example, at Ettiley Heath north of Crewe, containing more than 100 m of sand, clay and till.

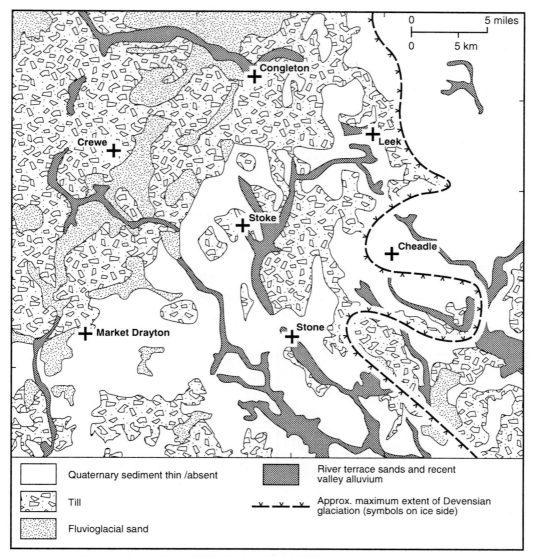

FIGURE 2.9 Outcrop of Quaternary sediments. Map area as in Fig 2.1.

ECONOMIC GEOLOGY

Ceramic raw materials

The pottery industry of the region was based on the occurrence of clays suitable for manufacturing coarse earthenware in the upper part of the Productive Coal Measures. By the early nineteenth century most indigenous clays had been displaced by imported ball clays. Plastic clays in the weathered zone of the Etruria Formation have also been used for making red-bodied pottery (Fig 2.10A).

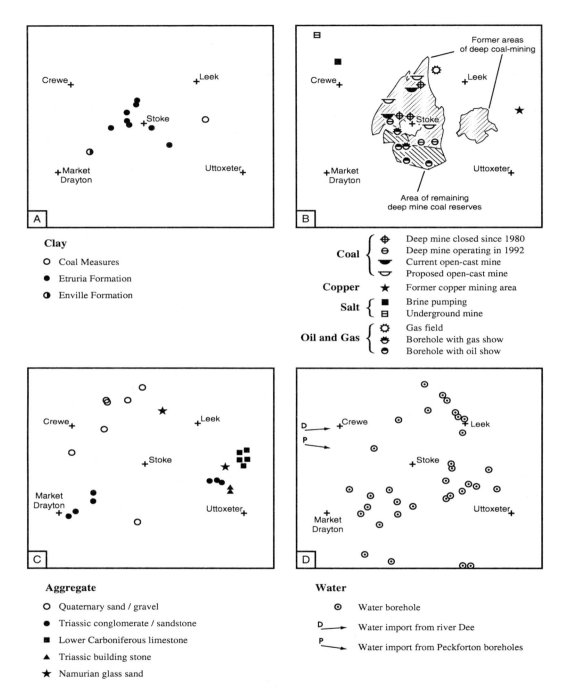

Clay

O Coal Measures
● Etruria Formation
◐ Enville Formation

Coal
⊕ Deep mine closed since 1980
⊖ Deep mine operating in 1992
◒ Current open-cast mine
◡ Proposed open-cast mine

Copper ★ Former copper mining area

Salt
■ Brine pumping
⊟ Underground mine

Oil and Gas
✿ Gas field
❀ Borehole with gas show
● Borehole with oil show

Aggregate

O Quaternary sand / gravel
● Triassic conglomerate / sandstone
■ Lower Carboniferous limestone
▲ Triassic building stone
★ Namurian glass sand

Water

⊙ Water borehole
D→ Water import from river Dee
P→ Water import from Peckforton boreholes

FIGURE 2.10 Locations of extractive industries: A) clay; B) coal, oil and gas, metals, salt; C) sand, gravel, limestone; and D) water.

Clays in the Productive Coal Measures and the Etruria Formation have also formed the basis for an extensive brick and tile industry. Shales in the Westphalian B and C Coal Measures have been worked on a small scale for making common bricks, but the industry has been based mainly on the fireclays in the upper Westphalian C, and the red clays of the Etruria Formation. The former were widely worked around Hanley, Burslem and Tunstall for manufacturing stock bricks and high quality buff-coloured facing bricks. Although substantial volumes of clay remain, extraction has ceased and fireclays are now imported.

The brick and tile industry based on the Etruria Formation is still very active. These clays are dominated by the mineral kaolinite, and have exceptionally high contents of ferric oxide. These features allow the manufacture of products of consistently high quality and strength. The traditional 'Staffordshire Blue' engineering bricks are no longer produced, having been rendered largely obsolete by the increased use of reinforced concrete. Instead, the industry concentrates on producing high-quality facing bricks and roofing tiles, the high iron content of the clays allowing the production of a wide range of satisfying colours. Red clays are also worked, on a very small scale, in the Enville Formation at Willoughbridge Wells.

Much of the outcrop of the Etruria Formation has been developed, and is no longer available for new clay pits. Remaining areas lie largely in the upper portion of the Formation, which contains clays of inferior quality. Continued availability of Etruria Formation clays for brick and tile making will depend on maximum use being made of the now limited reserves of high-grade clay in the lower and middle parts of the Formation; and on improvements in techniques of extraction and processing of the poorer clays in its upper part. The former may require the granting of planning protection to these reserves. One aspect of the latter lies in the possibility of making increased use of the clays from the Enville Formation, which impart beneficial properties when blended with poor quality clays from the Etruria and other Formations.

Clays from the Mercia Mudstone Group and the Quaternary have also locally been worked for brickmaking, but are not currently important.

Coal

The north Staffordshire coalfield contains one of the thickest sequences of coal-bearing strata in Britain: 1600 m of measures containing more than 30 seams over 2 m thick. Coal-mining developed in tandem with the other industries, production reaching a plateau of 6–7 million tonnes per year by the late nineteenth century, a figure maintained until recently. For most of the history of mining, the coal produced was mainly consumed locally. In the early part of the twentieth century, some coal from the western part of the coalfield was exported for making gas in neighbouring cities. From 1945 onwards coal has increasingly been exported for electricity generation outside the district, currently at Fiddlers Ferry (Warrington), Rugeley and Ironbridge (Fig 2.10B).

The character of the seams depends on their initial composition and on their rank, the latter being largely a function of depth of burial during the Mesozoic.

Composition. The principal coal seams occur in three stratigraphic units marked by distinctly different coal compositions (Fig 2.11): Upper Westphalian A – lower Westphalian B, characterized by extensive, thick seams having low ash and sulphur contents; Upper Westphalian B – lower Westphalian C, containing rather few coals of mineable thickness – the two major seams having abundant clay partings and high sulphur contents; and Upper Westphalian C, containing abundant thick seams, and thinner seams that have been extensively worked as a by-product of ironstone mining. The upper Westphalian C coals

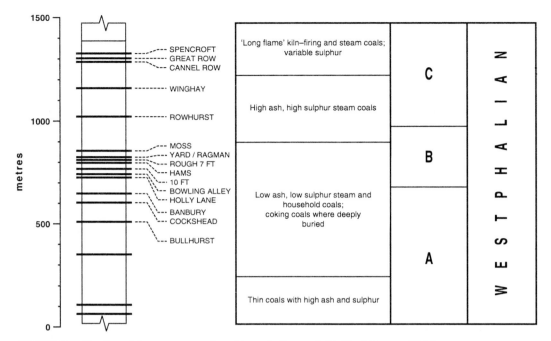

FIGURE 2.11 Stratigraphic occurrence of coal types in the north Staffordshire coalfield.

generally have abundant associated cannel coal. Apart from stratigraphical variation in character, there is a general increase in chlorine content with burial depth which is independent of stratigraphical horizon.

Rank. At outcrop most seams are high-volatile bituminous coals, suited for general steam-raising and industrial use. The more deeply buried seams, towards the centre of the Potteries Syncline, are strongly caking, high-volatile bituminous coals suitable for gas making, coking and household use.

Variations in coal type have led to an evolving pattern of coal utilization. Until the middle of this century mining activity was concentrated in the coals of the upper Westphalian A–low Westphalian B, and of the upper Westphalian C. The former, with their coking properties and low sulphur content, were employed in the iron industry, and for gas making and household use. The latter commanded a ready market as 'long flame' coals, particularly well suited to kiln firing in the pottery and brick industries.

With the decline, from about 1950, in household and industrial use, the principal market for coal became the electricity industry. At the same time, increasing mechanization restricted workable seams to those that were thick and geologically undisturbed. These were mainly in the south, where the seams have lower dips, but are more deeply buried. This led to increased exploitation of the thick, low quality, high sulphur coal in the Rowhurst and Winghay seams. In the last five years, the increasing need for low-sulphur coal, to reduce acid emissions, has led to renewed interest in the coals in the lower Westphalian B.

Between the 1957 and 1992 the combination of increasing productivity and a declining market for coal has led to a remorseless contraction in the number of deep mines. Large reserves of potentially mineable coal remain to the south and south-west of the north Staffordshire conurbation. This coal is generally deeply buried below Late Carboniferous red beds and Triassic rocks, and access to it may be prohibitively expensive, once the existing mines close.

The major development in coal-mining since 1950 has been the development of large-scale open-cast mining. This started as a means of rapid extraction during the Second World War, but with increasingly powerful excavating plant, open-cast mines have expanded, reaching depths of 120 m. Because it lies in the weathering zone, open-cast coal has lower levels of sulphur and chlorine, and is used for blending with deep-mined coal to reduce the levels of these pollutants in fuel for power stations. Open-cast mining has also permitted the extensive reclamation of land made derelict by former industrial activity.

Oil and gas

Oil seeps, generated from organic-rich shales interbedded within the Coal Measures, have been extensively recorded in coal-mines. Methane is still being generated naturally in large quantities in the more deeply buried coal seams. To date ten exploratory wells have been drilled. Although some are reputed to have contained shows of oil and gas, none has proved a commercial discovery, largely for want of sufficiently permeable reservoir rocks (Fig 2.10B).

A small gasfield has been discovered deep beneath Lask Edge. Although the discovery well flowed gas at potentially economic rates, the field is too small for development at current gas prices. The gas was probably generated from organic-rich shales in Dinantian or early Namurian rocks. The reservoir rock is formed by the late Dinantian Onecote Sandstone, the problem of low permeability being reduced by intense fracturing in the highly deformed Lask Edge Anticline.

Because of the lack of reservoir rocks, further potential for conventionally trapped hydrocarbon accumulations seems low. It may, however, be possible to produce natural gas directly from gas-rich coals, by drilling networks of boreholes into the seams and liberating the absorbed gas by fracturing the coal under high pressure. The technique has yet to be successfully implemented.

Iron ore

Iron working existed on a small scale in north Staffordshire from medieval times. The ores, from the Productive Coal Measures, were of both 'clayband' and 'blackband' type. The former consist of nodular concretions of iron carbonate (siderite) disseminated through mud- and siltstones associated with the coal seams. The latter were richer ores, occurring as stratified deposits overlying the coals in the highest part of the Productive Measures. The latter ores contain significant quantities of disseminated organic matter, rendering them partly self-calcining. The industry expanded greatly during the mid to late nineteenth century when it was found that the low phosphorus content of the blackband ores rendered them suitable for steel making. Underground mining of blackband ore, often in conjunction with coal, continued until about 1940. Considerable reserves remain, but it is unlikely that further working will take place.

Other metals

In the east of the district lead, zinc and copper ores were worked from vein deposits in Lower Carboniferous limestones around Mixon, Ecton and the Weaver Hills. All workings had ceased by 1890. The principal mine was that of the dukes of Devonshire at Ecton, which between 1760 and 1820 produced more than 50 per cent of the total UK copper output. The ores were smelted in the Cheadle area, where copper manufacturing is still carried out at Froghall. Unsuccessful trials for copper have also been made in the Triassic sandstones in the south-east and south-west of the district (Fig 2.10B). In all cases the vein deposits are interpreted to have formed from formation waters that had migrated out of adjacent deeply buried sedimentary basin fills. The main mineralization, of Carboniferous rocks, occurred during the Permian. Reduced rates of fluid flow and mineralization continued into Tertiary times.

Salt
Rock salt and brine have been extensively produced from the Triassic halite deposits in the Cheshire and Stafford Basins, probably from Roman times (Fig 2.10B). The main centre now lies around Winsford and Middlewich, to the north-west of the district. Brine production was carried out around Alsager until the 1920s, and continues at Warmingham, west of Sandbach. Early works relied on pumping 'wild brine', formed by natural solution of the rock salt by groundwater at the contact with the overlying Quaternary sediments. Current extraction involves controlled solution within the rock salt by injection of water through boreholes. This technique has much reduced the associated subsidence problems. The only underground rock salt mine in the UK is situated at Winsford. The salt produced is entirely used for winter treatment of roads.

Limestone
The Lower Carboniferous Milldale and Kevin Limestones are worked in five quarries near Cauldon Low, in the east of the district. In the late nineteenth century the limestone was used as a fluxing agent in the blast furnaces of north and south Staffordshire, and was exported to the chemical industries around Northwich. Although the limestone is of high chemical purity, all but one of the quarries currently produce aggregate. Limestone from one quarry at Cauldon Low is blended with the adjoining Namurian shales to produce cement (Fig 2.10C).

Sand, gravel, sandstone and refractories
Sand and gravel are quarried for aggregate and specialized uses from three main horizons (Fig 2.10C).

Namurian. These sandstones were formerly quarried extensively for building stone. High purity sandstones have been worked for the manufacture of refractory furnace bricks from the mid-Namurian Minn Beds and the late Namurian 'ganisters' near Mow Cop. The uppermost Namurian Rough Rock continues to be quarried for glass sand east of Biddulph and at Moneystone near Cheadle.

Triassic. All but the conglomerates of the Sherwood Sandstone Group have been worked locally for building stone. In most cases the stone has been of indifferent quality, but in the south-east, around Cheadle and Hollington, good quality yellow-grey freestone was widely worked before 1900. Quarrying continues on a small scale. Major reserves of sand and gravel are present in the Kidderminster Conglomerate Member. These are extensively worked around the southern periphery of the Stoke-on-Trent conurbation, at Croxden and Draycott Cross near Cheadle, and at Willoughbridge and Hales Almington, south-west of Newcastle-under-Lyme.

Quaternary. Substantial reserves of fluvioglacial sand exist in the Quaternary, particularly around Congleton, and in the moraines running westwards from Madeley. In the former area, extensive pits extract sand for construction, glass making, and for use as foundry sand. Elsewhere sand and gravel are used for aggregate.

Water supply

Water supply to the district is provided by the Severn Trent and North West Water Companies. Their boundary follows the watershed between the Trent and Weaver catchments, and runs in an irregular line between Market Drayton and Congleton. In the Severn Trent area, supply is almost exclusively from underground sources, the single major reservoir at Tittesworth supplying only some 15 per cent of demand. Underground extraction is from the Sherwood Sandstone aquifer, which has extremely good porosity and permeability. For historical reasons, a significant proportion of the supply to the Potteries is drawn from wells near Peckforton, west of Nantwich, in the Dee catchment of North West Water. Groundwater from the Sherwood Sandstones is also extensively abstracted in the North West Water area. Such supplies are supplemented by water from the river Dee and from Lake Vyrnwy. In both areas springs and boreholes into Namurian sandstones provide small-scale private supplies in the northern and eastern uplands (Fig 2.10D).

Geothermal energy

Recent research has demonstrated that the groundwater in deeply buried underground aquifers may be at a sufficiently high temperature to be usable as a low grade source of heat for horticultural purposes and district heating. A potentially exploitable source of hot water has been discovered in the Sherwood Sandstone aquifer, where it is deeply buried below Crewe and Nantwich. This resource has yet to be exploited.

BIBLIOGRAPHY

General reviews

J Blunden, *The mineral resources of Britain*, 1975.

P McL D Duff and A J Smith, eds, *Geology of England and Wales*, Geological Society, London, 1992.

B A Hains and A Horton, *British regional geology: central England*, Institute of Geological Sciences, London, 3rd ed, 1969.

Local studies

British Geological Survey Memoirs

N I Aitkenhead, J I Chisholm and I P Stevenson, 'The geology of the country around Buxton, Leek and Bakewell', *Mem Br Geol Surv*, sheet 111, 1985.

J I Chisholm, T J Charsley and N I Aitkenhead, 'The geology of the country around Ashbourne and Cheadle', *Mem Br Geol Surv*, sheet 124, 1988.

W B Evans, A A Wilson, B J Taylor and D Price, 'The geology of the country around Macclesfield, Congleton, Crewe and Middlewich', *Mem Geol Surv Gt Brit*, sheet 110, 1968.

J G Rees and A A Wilson, 'The geology of the country around Stoke-on-Trent', *Mem Br Geol Surv*, sheet 123, in preparation.

T H Whitehead, E E L Dixon, R W Pocock, T Robertson and T C Cantrill, 'The geology of the country between Stafford and Market Drayton', *Mem Geol Surv Engl & Wales*, sheet 139, 1927.

General geology and stratigraphy

B M Besly, 'Palaeogeographic implications of late Westphalian to early Permian red-beds, central England', in B M Besly and G Kelling, eds, *Sedimentation in a synorogenic basin complex: the Upper Carboniferous of north-west Europe*, Glasgow, 1988, 200–21.

J D Collinson, 'Controls in Namurian sedimentation in the Central Province basins of northern England', in Besly and Kelling, *Sedimentation . . . of north-west Europe*, 85–101.

P D Guion and C R Fielding, 'Westphalian A and B sedimentation in the Pennine Basin, UK', in Besly and Kelling, *Sedimentation . . . of north-west Europe*, 153–99.

A Knowles, 'The Quaternary history of north Staffordshire', in R H Johnson, ed, *The geomorphology of north-west England*, Manchester, 1985, 222–36.

D B Thompson, *The Permo-Triassic sediments of the Cheshire and adjacent Basins*, Poroperm-Geochem Ltd, Chester, 1985.

L J Wills, 'A palaeogeological map of the Lower Palaeozoic floor below the cover of Upper Devonian, Carboniferous and later formations', *Mem Geol Soc London*, 7, 1978.

P Worsley, 'Pleistocene history of the Cheshire-Shropshire Plain', in Johnson, *The geomorphology of north-west England*, 201–21.

Economic geology

D McC Bridge and D S Kneebone, 'The limestone and dolomite resources of the country north and west of Ashbourne, Derbyshire', *Miner Assess Rep Inst Geol Sci*, 129, 1983.

F W Cope, 'The north Staffordshire coalfields', in A E Trueman, ed, *The coalfields of Great Britain*, 1954, 219–43.

I N Gale, C J Evans, R B Evans, I F Smith, M T Houghton and W G Burgess, 'The Permo-Triassic aquifers of the Cheshire and west Lancashire Basins', *Invest Geotherm Potent UK: Br Geol Surv*, 1984, 1–46.

A B Malkin, *The conglomerate resources of the Sherwood Sandstone Formation between Stoke-on-Trent and Stone, Staffordshire*, Wardell and Partners, Newcastle-under-Lyme, 1984.

D Piper, 'The conglomerate resources of the Sherwood Sandstone Group of the country east of Stoke-on-Trent, Staffordshire', *Miner Assess Rep Inst Geol Sci*, 91, 1982.

3. Environmental History and Early Human Occupancy

F M CHAMBERS AND DAVID WILSON

This chapter is concerned both with the general vegetational history of the Potteries region, and with archaeological, palaeoenvironmental and other evidence for the presence, settlement and impact of humans in the region from the end of the Pleistocene and start of the Holocene, some 10,000 radiocarbon years ago,[1] to the end of the Roman occupation in AD 410. It covers, therefore, some 85 per cent of the Holocene epoch, and thereby encompasses the Mesolithic, Neolithic, Bronze Age, Iron Age and Roman periods. However, the dating of landscape changes and of human settlement in prehistory are mere approximations, derived via one or a range of techniques that are themselves not immediately compatible either with each other or with the sidereal calendar.

Several methods of citing dates are used here. Dates cited as BC or AD are calendar dates; dates or age ranges given as BP are in conventional (that is, uncalibrated) radiocarbon years (and beyond 2000 BP may be expected to underestimate the calendar age by a significant and possibly increasing amount); whereas those cited as Cal BC or Cal AD are radiocarbon ages that have been calibrated to calendar years using the Belfast-Seattle international tree-ring calibration curve.[2] In addition, where neither calendar nor radiometric dates are available, an age approximation is given by reference to one of the cultural periods – Neolithic, Bronze Age – based on typology of artefacts or monuments (Table 3.1).

In this review, the Potteries region is given a fairly wide brief, with reference made to specific sites in the Welsh borders to the west, to areas of the Peak District to the east and north-east, and to parts of Cheshire to the north.

VEGETATIONAL AND ENVIRONMENTAL HISTORY

Studies of Holocene vegetational history rely upon a suite of 'palaeoecological' techniques, which have been developed and refined over the years. These techniques have mainly been employed at specific sites to reconstruct pictures of past ecosystems through time, and thereby to construct a narrative of the changing environments of the site and its region.[3] Since the 1960s, the principal palaeoecological techniques employed have been pollen analysis – the identification, counting and interpretation of microscopic pollen grains and fern spores found in sediments – and radiocarbon dating, the dating of the organic components of sediments by measurement of the radioactive decay of an isotope of carbon – carbon-14.

Information on prehistoric vegetation and landscape change can thus be derived from analysis and dating of sediments containing abundant pollen and other plant micro- and macrofossils. Though pollen and plant remains can be found at archaeological sites, they are usually better preserved in the deposits of lakes and mires. The sediments of such lakes or mires need to be largely undisturbed and to have accumulated over a suitable time period. It is not possible, for example, to use Westport Lake, south of Tunstall, to chronicle the postglacial

Table 3.1

Relationships between geological epochs and cultural stages in England, and the approximate ages of their boundaries both in uncalibrated radiocarbon years and in calibrated or calendar years.

Geological Epoch	Cultural Stage	Radiocarbon Age (uncalibrated years before present)	Calibrated age (cal) BC or Calendar Years AD
H O L O C E N E	Roman	*c* 1950 BP	AD 43 to *c* AD 407
	Iron Age	*c* 2500 BP until *c* 1950 BP	765/673/667/613/608 cal BC to AD 43
	Bronze Age	*c* 4000 BP until *c* 2500 BP	2564/2541/2499 to 765/673/667/613/608 cal BC
	Neolithic	*c* 6000 BP until *c* 4000 BP	4993/4925/4903 to 2564/2541/2499 cal BC
	Mesolithic	*c* 10,000 BP until *c* 6000 BP	until 4993/4925/4903 cal BC
LATE PLEISTO-CENE	Upper Palaeolithic	until *c* 10,000 BP	

environments of the Potteries as it was only recently created as part of a twentieth-century programme of derelict land clearance. Indeed, such has been the industrial and post-industrial impact of human settlement and activity on the landscape of the Potteries that there are few, if any, sites suitable for long-term palaeoenvironmental studies within the conurbation. Certainly, none has been found that can produce anything like the full postglacial (Holocene) pollen diagrams of Crose Mere or Whixall Moss in Shropshire.[4] Nevertheless, there are suitable mire (bog) and mere (lake) sites on the western and north-western fringes of the Potteries region, particularly in south Cheshire, on the Staffordshire-Cheshire border, and most notably in Shropshire. Several of these sites have sediment records that span much or all of the Holocene, but few have been examined in any detail.

One site that has recently been investigated and found to produce a vegetational history covering the period of time from the end of the Pleistocene through to the latter part of the Holocene is White Moss, near Alsager, a 50-ha mire abutting the route of the M6 motorway. Deposits covering the historical period at this site have been lost through hand peat-cutting earlier this century, but a record from *c* 12,000 BP until say 3000 BP was found in lake muds and overlying peats. Much of the site has recently been destroyed by mechanized peat removal and by extraction of underlying Pleistocene sands. What initially attracted archaeologists and palaeoecologists to the site were the exhumed remains of substantial sub-fossil pine stumps, which at first sight seemed to represent a buried prehistoric forest (Pl 3.1). Detailed study by J Lageard showed that the pine stumps in fact represented the undecayed remains of several populations of pine trees that established themselves on the drying surface of a large peat bog in the period 4500–4000 BP. Pollen analysis and radiocarbon dating produced a general vegetational history of the site,[5] shown in summary form in Figure 3.1. This pollen diagram is the closest and most detailed record yet of vegetational change adjacent to the Potteries conurbation. Other nearby sites with published records are Wybunbury Moss, south of Crewe, and the King's Pool, Stafford.[6] There are several others further to the west and north in Shropshire and in Cheshire.

PLATE 3.1 Remains of exhumed pine stumps at White Moss, Alsager, south Cheshire   (J Lageard).

The Pleistocene legacy

Preceding the Holocene was the Pleistocene – an epoch of alternating cold (latterly, glacial) and temperate (interglacial) stages. The last cold stage – the Devensian – is held to have lasted some 100,000 years, but it was not all cold, as it included some warmer episodes (interstadials). The last of these – the Windermere interstadial – postdated the major Devensian ice advance that peaked perhaps 19,000 radiocarbon years or 22,500 calendar years ago.[7] The Windermere interstadial is apparently recorded (though imprecisely and inaccurately dated) in the deposits of a former lake at White Moss and shows evidence of local birch (both tree birches and the dwarf birch – *Betula nana*). These birch populations appear to have succumbed in a return to cold conditions at the close of the Pleistocene when an open, treeless environment obtained during a late-glacial stadial known as the Younger *Dryas*. This was a 500-year period of intense cold that brought a readvance of glaciers in the Scottish Highlands (the Loch Lomond readvance) and at high altitude in south Wales (in the Brecon Beacons), but saw periglacial activity elsewhere in Britain. Though conditions would have been hospitable during the Windermere interstadial, with summer temperatures almost as high as those of today, there is relatively scant evidence of human habitation in the Potteries region in the Late-Devensian (see below).

The early- and mid-Holocene environments

The start of the Holocene appears to have been a time of rapid climatic amelioration from the preceding short-lived cold snap that marks the end of the Pleistocene in the northern hemisphere. The Younger *Dryas* ended abruptly, so that by the early Holocene, summer

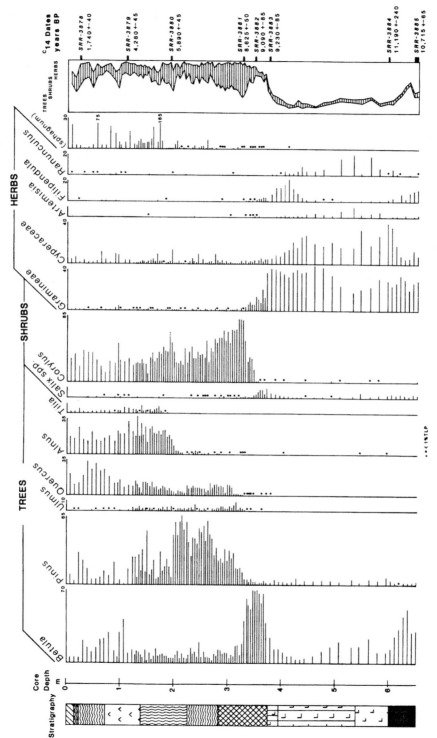

FIGURE 3.1 Summary pollen diagram from White Moss, near Alsager, Cheshire, showing pollen taxa changing with depth. The taxa are (left to right) birch, pine, elm, oak, alder, lime, willow, hazel, grasses, sedges, and other herbs. Records of *Sphagnum* spores (excluded from the pollen count) are also shown. Radiocarbon dates are uncalibrated, in conventional radiocarbon years BP (Data courtesy of J Lageard).

temperatures in the Potteries region had risen significantly, but still permitted the continuation of snow-bed plant communities in some localities, as evidenced by records of *Salix herbacea* (arctic willow). The early Holocene environment was thus very different from that of today and has been characterized as having '. . . very cold winters, relatively cool summers, a marked seasonal temperature range and frequent development of summer water deficit'.[8]

The record of vegetational change shown in Figure 3.1 is a product both of natural vegetational change – influenced by climate, soil, herbivores and the plants themselves – and of human activity, expressed either directly by the burning and clearing of woodland and later by the sowing of crops, or indirectly by the browsing and grazing activities of favoured hunted (quarry) species and later by domestic livestock. Pollen analysts use various pollen and spore taxa as 'anthropogenic indicators'.[9] Human activities – both direct and indirect – can be inferred from the records of these taxa in pollen diagrams, but the pollen evidence is seldom conclusive, and in the early Holocene the records of so-called anthropogenic indicators are at best ambiguous, and often contentious.

In the early Holocene, human subsistence was by hunting and gathering; these Mesolithic hunter-gatherers were previously thought to have had very little impact upon the landscape, and instead to have been so dominated by their environment that their activities were confined to coast and lakeshore, with seasonal forays inland to hunt deer and wild boar. Increasing finds of Mesolithic artefacts (largely, flints), some associated with charcoal records, and the production of more detailed pollen diagrams from the early Holocene in Britain, have led to views of Mesolithic human impact changing significantly: the propensity and ability of Mesolithic peoples to effect vegetational change have thus been reassessed,[10] with so-called 'anthropogenic' interpretations of vegetational change often taking precedence over interpretations invoking 'natural' change. Thus, charcoal records in sediments of Mesolithic age are now often interpreted as indicating human-induced firing of the landscape, perhaps to drive game or to improve the browse of the principal quarry, the red deer. However, it has recently been recognized that there was a maximum of summer radiation in the northern hemisphere in the early Holocene. With a more continental climatic regime and possible greater incidence of electrical storms and lightning strikes,[11] the early-Holocene woodland, which contained easily combustible species such as Scots pine, may have experienced widespread natural fires. It is equally possible then that humans could have moved into clearings created by natural fires, rather than humans themselves being responsible for creating the clearings.

At White Moss, there are records of charcoal from early-Holocene sediments, but their significance in terms of human activities is not known. In the Potteries region there are very few Mesolithic finds: Mesolithic settlement sites from the Potteries conurbation are unknown, and so the scale and impact of any human activity in the region in the early Holocene are very difficult to assess. Any hunter-gatherers of this period in the region would probably have been heavily dependent on red deer, on local plant resources, and particularly on a seasonal harvest of hazel nuts.

In general, vegetational history in the Potteries region during the early and mid-Holocene mirrors that elsewhere in lowland Staffordshire and south Cheshire, but with some local differences. The pollen record in Figure 3.1 shows that initial birch and pine-hazel woodland was succeeded by elm-oak-hazel woods, with the later establishment of alder, lime and ash by 6000 BP. Pine was then confined to the fringes of mires, rather like at Wybunbury Moss today, until its final demise at White Moss *c* 4000 BP. Indeed, the pollen record from White Moss probably over-emphasizes the role of pine in the region – away from the mire it was probably very rare by the mid-Holocene.

The impression, and as yet it is little more than that, is that human influence upon the Potteries region was relatively slight until the Neolithic. Even in the Neolithic (see below) there is not a great deal of pollen evidence for marked human impact upon vegetation, although to the east, in the Peak District, there are both archaeological sites and pollen records that testify to a significant impact of Neolithic peoples on the landscape.[12] However, the major prehistoric human impacts on woodland in the region seem to have been rather later, in the Bronze Age and subsequent cultural periods. Nearby, on the sands of south Cheshire, from the analysis of pollen beneath Bronze Age tumuli, and beneath cairns and stone circles on the Gritstone moors of the Peak District, comes abundant evidence for considerable vegetational change during the Bronze Age. Woodland clearance, arable crops and pastoral activity all left their mark on the prehistoric landscape. In south Cheshire, woodland gave way to fields, whereas in the Peak District open woodland seems to have degenerated to upland heath after episodes of human disturbance and possible cultivation (Fig 3.2).

It is possibly as late as the Early Bronze Age then, that the major influence upon the landscape of the Potteries region changes from that of natural agency to that of its people, whereas in uplands to the north-east – in the southern Pennines – human activity has been invoked as a major influence upon the landscape from the Mesolithic onwards.[13] Indeed, as close as Buxton – an upland settlement just outside the Peak District National Park – there are records of local human activity in both the Mesolithic and Neolithic, together with some of the earliest dated crop records in England, including remains of wheat and flax from house structures covering the period 5025±125 BP to 4680±70 BP.[14] The variability in the timing of first human impact suggests that palynological studies at more sites need to be undertaken before a full assessment can be made of human impact upon the prehistoric woodlands of the Potteries region, *sensu stricto*.

The late-Holocene environment

For Britain, generally, Jones has described a general trend '. . . between the Middle Bronze Age and the Early Iron Age, towards an increase in the range of cereals and legume crops . . .' such

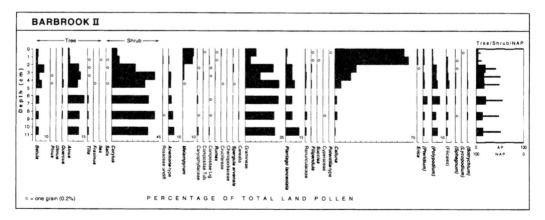

FIGURE 3.2 Pollen diagram from a vertical profile of soil buried under the enclosing bank of a prehistoric stone circle at Barbrook II, Derbyshire Peak District. AP/NAP (arboreal pollen/non-arboreal pollen) ratios are shown, based on a total land pollen (TLP) sum. Taxa in parentheses were excluded from the pollen sum.

that '. . . from the Middle Bronze Age, we begin to see large tracts of the landscape divided up and enclosed', with '. . . existing ecosystems . . . replaced by agricultural ecosystems'.[15] Although there are data that point to significant climatic shifts in Britain in the late-Holocene, it might be expected that the changing vegetational environments of the Potteries region during this period would largely have reflected an increasing impact of human activity. Pollen studies carried out on sediments at a site to the south of the region – at the King's Pool, Stafford – bear this out. There, the first significant human impact upon forest was estimated at *c* 4170 BP, in the (late) Neolithic; but more major impacts were noted in the Bronze Age, and particularly at the beginning of the Iron Age, *c* 2700–2500 BP, when a period of major forest clearance at Stafford was accompanied by agriculture.

By Roman times, the regional landscape would have been substantially disforested, with perhaps a predominantly agricultural landscape, although there is evidence from the King's Pool for an increase in the cultivation of cereals and of *Cannabis* (hemp, for fibre and rope) near or just after the end of the Roman period. The peak in the King's Pool cereal pollen curve was dated at 1370±70 BP (calibrated by the authors to Cal AD 650), whilst the first peak in the *Cannabis* pollen curve was somewhat later, implying that the major cultivation of hemp in the region began in Anglo-Saxon times. The authors infer that a high level of agricultural activity continued '. . . from the Roman period at least until the end of the Saxon period',[16] and they point to Roman settlements in the region and to a Saxon origin for Stafford itself.

ARCHAEOLOGICAL EVIDENCE

Having reviewed the general changes in environment and vegetation, the archaeological evidence for human presence and settlement in the region will be discussed in more detail. As the activities of man from the Industrial Revolution onwards have ensured the loss of sites for palaeoenvironmental studies so have they destroyed, or at the very best masked, virtually all early archaeological sites in the Stoke-on-Trent area. Consequently, apart from the occasional chance-find spot, it is the surrounding area that has to be examined for archaeological evidence, for prehistory at least.

The earliest period from which material remains is the later Palaeolithic (*c* 15,000–10,000 BP), and this is very limited in terms of both artefacts and sites; in fact, it is only in some of the numerous caves and fissures of the Limestone Peak that evidence is forthcoming, such as at Elder Bush Cave, near Wetton, where a number of flint points and blades were found together with a scatter of split bones, mainly reindeer, and fragments of charcoal. This limited amount of debris suggests that the cave was occupied, presumably by hunters, for only a relatively brief period. Ossums Cave, Grindon, produced some possibly Cresswellian blades, and at Thor's Cave and Thor's Fissure, both at Wetton, late Palaeolithic finds have been made.

The next prehistoric phase, the Mesolithic, spans the period from the end of glaciation to the Neolithic, roughly from 10,000 to 6000 BP, although there is clearly no sharp dividing line between the late Palaeolithic and the early Mesolithic, or the late Mesolithic and the early Neolithic. One major event of the Mesolithic was a rise in temperature which brought about a melting of the glacial ice, a consequent rise in sea-level and the separation of Britain from the rest of Europe. In addition, the postglacial soils were maturing, and woodland, of predominantly birch and pine, was developing and supporting an animal population including deer, both roe and red, and pig. Probably as a consequence of the woodland habitation of his animal prey, Mesolithic man developed new types of tools, notably microliths, which were used as points for arrows in the hunt.

Some 30 sites or find-spots within the general area can be dated to the Mesolithic, although the total number of artefacts is very small indeed. A perforated macehead of the later Mesolithic was found at Northwood Farm, Clayton, and similar artefacts have been found at Waterhouses, Blithfield, Leekfrith, Rowley Bank in Stafford, and two at Cold Norton in Chebsey, whilst at Coton Hill, Stafford, a 'chipping floor' produced later Mesolithic flint artefacts, similar in date to those found at Branston, Aldridge and Cannock Wood.

As was the case in the Palaeolithic, caves and fissures were also occupied during the Mesolithic in the Peak area of north Staffordshire. Particularly interesting in this context is the Wetton Mill Rock Shelter[17] where the collection of flint and chert microliths recovered during excavation suggests both early and late Mesolithic sporadic occupation of the shelter, which probably provided summer cover for deer hunters. It is a pity that the radiocarbon date for this site (8847± 210 BP) cannot be directly related to any of the artefacts, as this would provide conclusive evidence of early Mesolithic occupation, which is sadly lacking generally, the evidence at the moment being purely typological. Another possible hunting camp site is at Colwich, where a cave produced an assemblage of Mesolithic flint and a hearth.

The evidence for these two early phases of prehistory in the area is limited both in terms of material remains and of topographical location, but on turning to the Neolithic (c 6000–4000 BP), that is to a period when the hunter-gathering life of the Mesolithic has gradually given way to more settled farmsteads with domesticated animals and crops and the introduction of pottery and large field monuments, then the evidence, in terms of chance finds anyway, becomes more plentiful and widespread, although habitation sites remain elusive. The most common of the Neolithic chance finds are the polished stone axe-heads which, apart from some instances of ceremonial use, must have been the basic implement for woodland clearance, a process which began in the late Mesolithic but which accelerated in Britain in the Neolithic with the need for more permanent settlement and agricultural land.

Thousands of intact and broken polished axe-heads have been found throughout the country, and within the north Staffordshire area they are too numerous to mention individually, spanning as they do the area from Fawfieldhead in the north-east to Stoke-on-Trent in the west. An almost equal number have been found on lower-lying land and on the upland areas of the north-east, although in the middle and upper Trent basin generally over half of the known stone axes were found in the highland zone and almost exclusively on the Carboniferous Limestone as opposed to the Millstone Grit,[18] where on grade 4 agricultural land, at least, the soil would probably have been richer and deeper than today. Petrological analysis of a number of polished stone axes from north Staffordshire has shown that they derive mainly from stone from the Lake District (Great Langdale and the Coniston area) and from north Wales (Graig Llwyd in Gwynedd). Rare examples also come from Dyfed, north Wales and from near Camborne, Cornwall.

As these polished axe-heads are evidence for woodland clearance and consequent settled farming, so the occasional finds of leaf-shaped arrowheads (as, for example, at Weston, Leek, and in Seven Ways Cave, Grindon, in this last case with a disarticulated skeleton) and oblique-type transverse arrowheads (as, for example, at Alsager and Smethwick, in south Cheshire) clearly indicate that, farmers though they were, the people of the Neolithic were happy to supplement their diet by hunting, and a variety of animal bones has been found in sites in Britain, including ox, red deer, wild boar and brown bear.

In the north Staffordshire area the range of major monuments to be found in the south of England is lacking, particularly those associated with burial. The most obvious is the Bridestones, lying above Congleton on the boundary between Cheshire and Staffordshire. These are the rather sad remains of a gallery grave with a gallery c 5.5 m long surviving, and divided into two by what is left of a porthole stone. In addition, a large stone lies across the entrance and there are three standing stones (replaced) of the crescent-shaped forecourt. At one time there were also two smaller lateral chambers c 50 m from the existing chamber, and the whole was covered with a cairn probably some 110 m long and c 12 m wide. Unfortunately, all these features seem to have been destroyed in the eighteenth century to provide material for road metalling, although much of it looks to have gone to making the 'grotto' in the adjacent farm garden. It has been suggested that the Bridestones is the earliest of the Peak District long cairns,[19] but the excavations earlier this century added little to knowledge of the site, and no real dating evidence has since been forthcoming and nothing is known of any burials. It would seem that the monument and its immediate environment would greatly repay further examination. Other possible remains of a chambered tomb are at Mucclestone, which is in a lowland position unlike the Bridestones. All that now exist are two standing stones, one with a porthole c 50 m in diameter.

Three further sites, this time in the north-east of the county, may represent Neolithic burial mounds. The first of these is Grub Low, Waterhouses, excavated by Samuel Carrington in 1849, where the only dating evidence was the presence of two leaf-shaped arrowheads associated with an inhumation and a cremation. Similar evidence comes from Long Low, Wetton, where two round barrows connected by a bank c 200 m long were again excavated by Carrington. The northernmost barrow, perhaps the earlier of the two, contained a massive stone cist with limestone-slab paving, containing the remains of thirteen crouched skeletons with two leaf-shaped arrowheads; it may be that the cist is a late version of the earlier gallery graves.[20] The third site, at Low Farm, Fawfieldhead, has been excavated much more recently and has the benefit of a radiocarbon date. The burial mound was composed of turf, with no evidence of stonework, and covered a single cremation. The date of 4220 ± 180 BP was derived from large pieces of charcoal from within the mound rather than the burial itself, which had no charcoal, but if this evidence can be accepted, then it puts the burial well into the Neolithic. A rim sherd of late Neolithic Grooved Ware was found beneath the mound, and as this type of pottery is not normally found in burial contexts but often in domestic contexts, it may indicate a settlement nearby.[21]

Although the burial sites noted above are the only ones of which there is knowledge, mainly because, with the exception of the last, they contain a substantial stone element that has survived, it is possible that further similar structures once existed in other parts of the area, but with timber or turf-stacks taking the place of stone, consequently decomposing and later being reduced by ploughing. Such sites could only be revealed by aerial photography as have others in the county, notably in the area of Barton-under-Needwood where a large group of Neolithic-Early Bronze Age monuments have been shown to exist near the Tame-Trent confluence, including causewayed enclosures, a possible cursus and a henge.

The transition from the Neolithic to the Early Bronze Age, as with all transitions from one prehistoric phase to another, was a gradual one, and mainly evidenced in the north Staffordshire area, as elsewhere, by a change in burial practice with round barrows superseding the earlier communal tombs. Round barrows nationally represent the most common archaeological monument, and over three hundred are known in Staffordshire, being particularly apparent on the highlands of the north-east of the county where many were opened in the first half of the nineteenth century by Thomas Bateman or his proxy-digger Samuel Carrington.

The distribution of round barrows shown in Figure 3.3, however, is more likely to represent the distribution of survival rather than the *actual* original distribution of the monuments. Soils

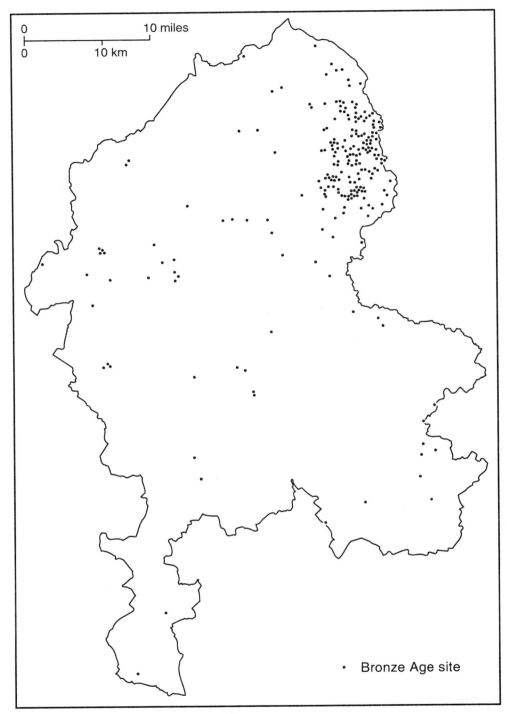

FIGURE 3.3 Bronze Age round barrows in Staffordshire (*Source*: Staffordshire County Sites and Monuments Record).

on the limestone and Millstone Grit of the north-eastern uplands have been far less subject to ploughing than the clay lowlands. Indeed, aerial photography is increasingly revealing ploughed-out barrows, such as those at Norbury, Rocester and Barton-under-Needwood. In addition, chance finds of pottery might well indicate now-vanished barrows, such as the beakers found at Normacot sandpit and Rocester both during quarrying, and the collared urns found at the same Normacot sandpit and at Trentham. Beakers tend to be earlier and associated with inhumations, and collared urns later and containing cremations. Although these barrows fall within what is traditionally called the 'Early Bronze Age' only a small proportion of them has actually produced metalwork among their grave goods, usually bronze daggers with primary inhumation burials such as at Thorncliff Low and Musden Low, Waterhouses, Lidlow, Warslow, and at Grindon, although a tanged dagger was found with a cremation at Blore. At King's Low, Tixall, which is still under excavation, a bronze bracelet was found, but not in a closed context and it is likely to be a secondary feature. This lowland mound was constructed of turf, which has decomposed to sand in a similar way to those of lowland south-east Cheshire, which again have not usually produced bronzework, although at one recently excavated barrow near Jodrell Bank the bone pommel of a dagger was found with a cremation in a collared urn, the metal part of the artefact never having been buried, presumably because of the scarcity of this material. After about 3500 BP the raising of burial mounds dies out, although they continue to have secondary cremation burials inserted into them. In some parts of Britain, particularly the south, flat cremation cemeteries supersede barrows, but in the north Staffordshire area there is little evidence of post-barrow burials.

The polished axe-heads noted when discussing the Neolithic undoubtedly continue to be used in the Early Bronze Age, so that it is difficult to see their distribution as specifically indicative of Neolithic settlement or Early Bronze Age. However, another commonly found artefact, the axe-hammer, seems more likely to relate to the latter, and was probably used for tillage, and hence for cultivation rather than woodland clearance. In Staffordshire these axe-hammers tend to be found in lowland rather than highland areas, perhaps indicative of a greater tendency towards land cultivation in the lowlands as opposed to stock rearing on the highland areas. Petrological analysis has shown that virtually all of them derive from one of two sources, either from the Shropshire-Powys border or from Cumbria, and interestingly stone from these sources is not used for polished axe-heads.

The later phases of the Bronze Age, from c 3500 to 2500 BP, are represented in and around north Staffordshire only by chance finds of metal ware. The most common are bronze palstaves, especially associated with the middle Bronze Age, which have been found at, for example, Norbury, near Chartley Hall, Stone, Keele, Uttoxeter, Biddulph and Marchington. Like the Early Bronze Age axe-hammers, but unlike the polished axes, palstaves appear to be more common in the lowland than the highland region, and if they are to be considered as land clearance implements then it may be that they are associated with the regenerated woodland in the lowland areas which often followed periods of agriculture. Also probably from the middle Bronze Age is the hoard of metalwork found at Norbury which appears to have comprised palstaves and fragments of rapiers and swords, although there are some doubts about the actual contents. Other middle Bronze Age artefacts from the area include a bronze spearhead from Eccleshall, dirks from Butterton and Whitmore, and a superb gold armlet from Stanton.

The latest phase of the Bronze Age is even more sparsely represented by chance finds which include a gold bracelet, again from Stanton, a spearhead from Whitgreave, socketed axes from Trentham Park, Stoke and Waterhouses, and a sword from Alton Towers. Unfortunately, the limited information concerning the later phases of the Bronze Age makes it difficult to discuss

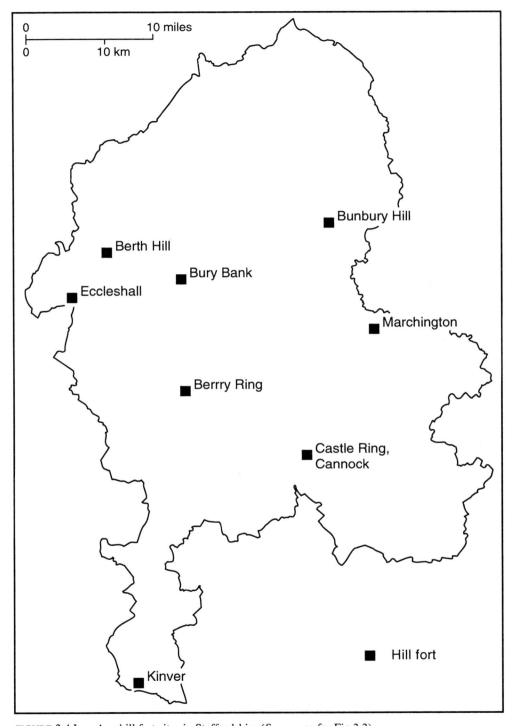

FIGURE 3.4 Iron Age hill fort sites in Staffordshire (*Source*: as for Fig 3.3).

them in any detail, but it does seem possible that, as appears to be the case in the middle Bronze Age, there is a greater level of population in the lowland than in the highland areas, although even this is a dangerous assumption, based as it is on little other than chance finds of bronzework. What is lacking in the area, as well as in others, are recognizable settlement sites which would enable more positive statements about population densities and distribution to be made.

The pre-Roman Iron Age (c 2500 BP–AD 50) in north Staffordshire is basically represented by a number of hill forts, but these have been subjected to little or no serious investigation except for recent surveys by the Royal Commission on Historical Monuments, whose results are not yet published. Consequently it is difficult to speak of these hill forts with any degree of authority.

Bury Bank, just outside Stone, is a hill fort of c 1.5 ha enclosed by a bank and ditch with an internal entrance on its western side. It has traditionally been believed that the site had been re-used or refortified to enclose a Saxon palace, but the Royal Commission's survey suggests that this is unlikely. Bunbury Hill camp at Alton Towers was much destroyed in the building of the Towers and in the laying out of the gardens. Limited excavation in 1963 revealed a rampart faced with a massive drystone wall close enough to the edge of the steep hillside to preclude the need for a ditch. Other sites within the area include Berry Ring at Bradbury, a univallate fort; Berth Hill at Maer, an irregular enclosure of some 4 ha bounded by a single bank and ditch; and two possible promontory forts at Marchington and Eccleshall. The distribution of hill forts in Staffordshire is shown on Figure 3.4.

In other parts of the country evidence has been found from excavation that hill forts were not, as it was often thought, merely refuges in times of trouble but rather permanently occupied centres, with facilities for grain storage and milling, and the herding of animals and the processing of animal products. In addition, each hill fort had its own territory. There is also plentiful evidence for some hill forts being extended or elaborated over a period of time whilst others were abandoned. Sadly, because of the limited work done on the Staffordshire forts, these are aspects that are little known, but which call for serious study.

The chance finds from the Iron Age are so few in number that they add nothing to the overall picture of the period in the area. The most striking of these is the second-century large gold torc from Hanbury, found not a great distance from a probably Iron Age D-shaped enclosure at Tatenhill. The remaining finds are an iron spearhead from Stone, a knife from Knutton, a spindlewhorl from Eccleshall and a bronze terret ring inlaid with red enamel from Baswich.

There is considerable evidence for Romano-British settlement and activity in north Staffordshire, as the county distribution (Fig 3.5) shows. As yet there has been no published synthesis of all of this material and unfortunately space here precludes all but brief comments concerning some of the major sites and finds.

Excavations in 1969–71[22] located the south-east defences and the two corresponding corners of the Roman fort at Chesterton, Newcastle. The rampart was some 8 m wide, with a ditch, cut into bedrock, 1.5 m wide and 2 m deep. Behind the rampart was a baking oven. Pottery evidence suggests a date late in the first century for the construction of the fort, and the narrow date range of the Samian ware indicates a very short period of occupation. It is interesting that no pottery of the mid-late first-century Trent Vale type was found at Chesterton, although the fort and the kiln were only a few miles apart. The Trent Vale kiln was abandoned still with pottery in it, after being gutted by fire.

A few hundred yards from the Chesterton fort is the civilian settlement at Holditch. Restricted excavation in the late 1950s[23] exposed the site over an area of c 400 m by 250 m,

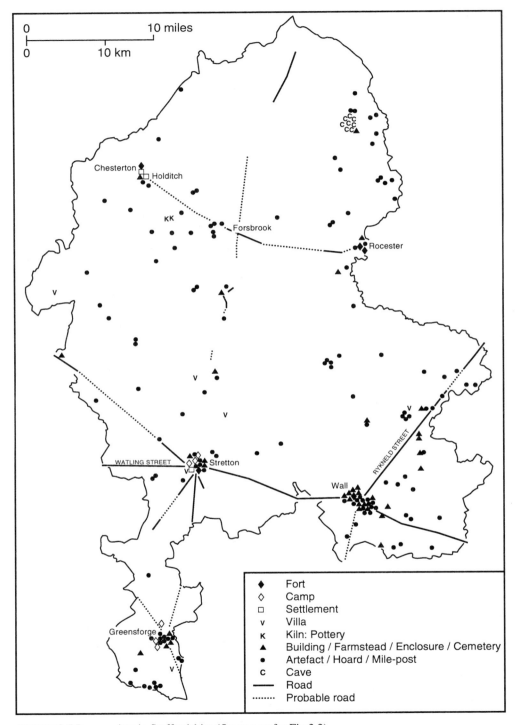

FIGURE 3.5 Roman sites in Staffordshire (*Source*: as for Fig 3.3).

although it clearly extended beyond this. The pottery evidence indicated an occupation date range from c AD 80 to the third century, and once again the Trent Vale kiln seems to have had little influence, only half a dozen sherds from there being found at Holditch. A road running eastwards from the Chesterton-Holditch complex links it to the fort and later the small Roman town of Rocester. Here the fort appears to have had a three-phase occupation, being finally abandoned in the second half of the second century, and the town wall was erected no earlier than AD 200.

The site of the villa at Hales was considered by its excavator to have been in more or less continuous occupation from the late Bronze Age to the middle of the fourth century AD. The villa's bath-house dates from the early second century, with some re-jigging in the later second and third century. Coin dating from the latest well on the site indicates that it was destroyed in the second half of the fourth century, a date borne out by the pottery evidence from a working floor.[24]

In addition to these sites, numerous finds of Roman coins have been made in the north Staffordshire area, at such places as Eccleshall, Stone, Stoke, Bradley and Keele, and hoards have been found at, for example, Sandon, Leek, Newcastle, and especially at Longton where there were 2461 third-century coins. One particularly interesting possibility for future research is suggested by Figure 3.5. It will be seen that the heavy concentrations of Roman sites in the south of the county, at Wall, Stretton and Greensforge, all occur at conjunctions of major Roman roads. A similar conjunction occurs on the stretch of road running through the parishes of Forsbrook, Draycot-in-the-Moors and Checkley, and it may well be that detailed study in this area would yield important results. The evidence, then, from north Staffordshire and its environs is one of considerable Romano-British activity, perhaps more than is generally realized outside the county. This activity spans virtually the whole Roman period, from the mid-first century forts indicative of Roman advance and consolidation, to the last activities of a villa in the latter part of the fourth century.

REFERENCES

1. That is, 10,000 BP, where BP means 'before present', with 'present' standardized as AD 1950.
2. F M Chambers, ed, *Climate change and human impact on the landscape*, 1993, xix–xx and appendix.
3. B E Berglund, ed, *Handbook of Holocene palaeoecology and palaeohydrology,* Chichester, 1986; H H and H J B Birks, P E Kaland and D Moe, eds, *The cultural landscape – past, present and future*, Cambridge, 1988.
4. P W Beales, 'The Late Devensian and Flandrian vegetational history of Crose Mere, Shropshire', *New Phytologist*, 85, 1980, 113–61; J Turner, 'The anthropogenic factor in vegetational history, 1: Tregaron and Whixall Mosses', *New Phytologist*, 63, 1964, 73–89.
5. J G A Lageard, 'Vegetational history and palaeoforest reconstruction at White Moss, south Cheshire, UK', unpublished PhD thesis, Keele University, 1992; F M Chambers, J G A Lageard and P A Thomas, 'Pollen and tree-ring studies at White Moss, Alsager', *Cheshire Past*, 1, 1992, 4–5.
6. B H Green and M C Pearson, 'The ecology of Wybunbury Moss, Cheshire. II, post-glacial history and the formation of the Cheshire mere and mire landscape', *J Ecol*, 65, 1977, 793–814; D D Bartley and A V Morgan, 'The palynological record of the King's Pool, Stafford', *New Phytologist*, 116, 1990, 177–94.
7. W S Broeker, 'Discovery of a large offset in the radiocarbon time scale', *Eos*, 73, 1992, 32.
8. B Huntley, 'Rapid early-Holocene migration and high abundance of hazel (*Corylus avellana* L.): alternative hypotheses', in Chambers, *Climate change*, 212.
9. K-E Behre, *Anthropogenic indicators in pollen diagrams*, Rotterdam, 1986.

10. I G Simmons, 'Vegetation change during the Mesolithic in the British Isles: some amplifications', in Chambers, *Climate change*, 109–18.
11. J E Kutzbach and P J Guetter, 'The influence of changing orbital parameters and surface boundary conditions on climate simulations for the past 18,000 years', *Jnl Atmospheric Science*, 43, 1986, 1726–59; Huntley, 'Rapid early-Holocene migration', 205–15
12. S P Hicks, 'The impact of man on the East Moors of Derbyshire from Mesolithic times', *Archaeol Jnl*, 129, 1972, 3–21; J Barnatt, *The henges, stone circles, and ringcairns of the Peak District*, Sheffield Archaeological Monographs 1, Sheffield University, 1990; R Hodges and K Smith, eds, *Recent developments in the archaeology of the Peak District*, Sheffield University, 1991.
13. R M Jacobi, J H Tallis and P A Mellars, 'The southern Pennine Mesolithic and the ecological record', *Jnl Archaeological Science*, 3, 1976, 307–20.
14. P E J Wiltshire and K J Edwards, 'Mesolithic, early Neolithic and later prehistoric impacts on vegetation at a riverine site in Derbyshire, England', in Chambers, *Climate change*, 157–68.
15. M Jones, 'The arable field: a botanical battleground', in M Jones, ed, *Archaeology and the flora of the British Isles*, Oxford, 1988, 89.
16. Bartley and Morgan, 'The palynological record of the King's Pool', 193.
17. J H Kelly, *The excavation of Wetton Mill rock shelter, Manifold valley, Staffordshire*, City of Stoke-on-Trent Museum Archaeological Society Report 9, 1976.
18. P M Vine, *The Neolithic and Bronze Age cultures of the middle and upper Trent basin*, Oxford, 1982.
19. T G Manby, 'Chambered tombs of Derbyshire', *Derbys Archaeol Jnl*, 78, 1958, 38.
20. Ibid, 39.
21. D Wilson and F Cleverdon, 'Excavations of two round barrows at Low Farm and Low Bent, Fairfieldhead, Longnor', *Trans S Staffs Archaeol Hist Soc*, 27, 1987, 1–26.
22. F H Goodyear, 'The Roman fort at Chesterton', *N Staffs Jnl Fld Stud*, 10, 1970, 103–5, and 16, 1976, 1–15.
23. J M T Charlton, 'Excavations at the Roman site at Holditch', *N Staffs Jnl Fld Stud*, 1, 1961, 26–50.
24. F H Goodyear, 'The Roman villa at Hales, Staffordshire', *N Staffs Jnl Fld Stud*, 14, 1974, 1–20.

4. Early Medieval Settlement in North Staffordshire

R STUDD

The earliest historians of this county were impressed by the rugged quality of the landscape of north Staffordshire and with good reason. 'One of the barrenest countries I know' was how Sampson Erdeswick described the valley of the Churnet between Rocester and Dieulacres. A century later Robert Plot complained of the roads in these northern parts 'where between the three shires heads, and Longnor, the Hills and Boggs are such that a Horse can scarce pass between the two places'. 'A third part at least, if not half this County', he wrote, 'must be confest when all's done, to be barren heathy, and gorsy grounds, and woodland.'[1] It was a way of saying that even in the later seventeenth century the region was not conducive to easy settlement, was relatively underproductive agriculturally and presented problems of political organization. It is indeed true that the topography of north Staffordshire has played a large part in determining the progress and nature of its political and ecclesiastical settlement and its economic development from the earliest period of the Middle Ages.

Very little land in the county north of a line drawn through Burton-on-Trent and Stafford lies below the 150 m contour; beyond Leek much is situated above the 250 m contour and has therefore been of small use to man and beast. The valley land formed out of the courses of the rivers Blithe and Dove was confined over the greater part of their lengths, opening out into relatively fertile floodplains only below Blithebridge and Okeover, respectively. Almost all land in the north-eastern quarter lies on the thin soils. In the north-western quarter, the rivers Sow and Trent cut fertile swathes suitable for cattle rearing, and for a little arable, through an upland landscape of heath and woodland[2] (Figs 1.1 and 2.1). Land in this sector remained available for colonization and exploitation until relatively late in the medieval period, but it was always a tough prospect to clear the woodland and render productive the heavy clays which predominate.

None was ever likely to make a fortune from the agricultural productivity of this area either as lord or tenant. Lords frequently resorted to leasing as a solution to the challenge of securing a profit from such land and so handed over the task of exploitation to others. Diversification into urban and quasi-industrial activities offered an alternative prospect for some. After AD 1000 several religious houses were set up and endowed for the salvation of their founders' souls with tracts of some of the most unyielding land in the area. All were modest foundations, arriving relatively late in the north Staffordshire landscape and consequently impoverished for the whole of their existence. Only two houses in the whole county, Burton and Dieulacres, had a sufficient annual income to exempt them from the terms of the first Dissolution Act of 1536. Such was the continuing response to the difficult nature of the terrain of north Staffordshire in the Middle Ages.

This chapter is concerned primarily with the two northern hundreds of Staffordshire, Totmonslow, in the north-east, and Pirehill in the north-western sector. It will pursue these themes further by looking first at the political and ecclesiastical settlement which occurred in the Anglo-Saxon period and then, and only briefly, looking forward to developments after the arrival of the Normans in the area after the Conquest.

In the Anglo-Saxon period this part of England lay first within the kingdom, then the ealdormanry and later, the earldom, of Mercia; but, when, precisely, the Anglo-Saxons arrived in the area remains largely a matter of conjecture. A later Mercian tradition had it that the tribes which formed the nucleus of the Mercian kingdom were led to Britain by a man called Icel, now known to have been active at the beginning of the sixth century. This suggests that among the Anglo-Saxons, the Mercians can be identified with the later arrivals from the continent, and that fact has been used to explain why, passing along the Trent river system, they came eventually to settle in midland England. Excavation at the Anglo-Saxon settlement of Catholme, near Barton-under-Needwood, provides evidence for the continuous settlement of that site from the middle of the sixth century and gives some credence to the hypothesis.[3] But beyond this kind of chance archaeological find, the precise locations and manner of their settlement in the area cannot now be known.

Indeed, how far a Mercian 'kingdom' was organized politically in the sixth century, it is impossible to tell. Political stability was not a feature of the period as tribes grouped and re-grouped and kingdoms appeared and disappeared. Two more leaders in Mercia are known from the last decade of the century but in circumstances which do not conclusively demonstrate that they were ever recognized as kings with sway over a defined territory. Recently, a case has been argued for the secure establishment and comparative antiquity of a Mercian dynasty by the end of the sixth century, but even its author admits that this 'can only be an exercise in controlled conjecture'.[4] By the seventh century, however, a rather more settled pattern emerged and certainly by the end of it, Tamworth was recognizable as the principal centre of a tribal group called the Tomsaetan who had established an hegemony in the region stretching northwards to Derby and the Peak, southwards into the territory of the Stoppingas of the Forest of Arden and westwards towards the ridge that later became Cannock Chase, as well as along the entire length of the upper Trent valley.[5]

This was the nucleus of the kingdom of King Cearl, 'a successful pagan', and as such, ignored by Bede. Under his authority, which lasted until his overthrow at, or in association with, the battle of Chester (616), it has been suggested that Mercia expanded into an 'overkingship', which extended to the frontiers of Deira in the north and stretched from Lindsey in the east to the Wrekin.[6] That seems highly likely. But King Aethelfrith of Northumbria, the victor at Chester, was himself defeated shortly afterwards by the forces of King Radwald of East Anglia and was succeeded on his throne by the Deiran Christian, Edwin, the consort of King Cearl's daughter. Mercia emerged from this series of political crises as a client kingdom of Northumbria under the rule of a king who was certainly a Northumbrian appointee, and possibly of Northumbrian stock or, more probably, someone sprung from a collateral branch of King Cearl's family.

Was the nominee, Eobba, Penda's brother, or were the brothers named as co-kings? Who ruled in Mercia between 616 and 632 is now not certainly known. It is evident that Penda ruled in his own right in Mercia only after 632/3; it is possible that he had succeeded by 626 or even earlier. Under his rule Mercian independence was re-asserted.[7] The seventh-century kings of Mercia were politically enormously successful, first Penda (?626/632–655) and later, Wulfhere (658–675). Together with the two mighty kings of the eighth century, Aethelbald (716–757) and Offa (757–796), they created and then re-created the Mercian hegemony that lasted until the acquisition of the Mercian throne, at the beginning of the ninth century, by a collateral branch of the royal house whose political centre was no longer at Tamworth but in London.

Certainly, within a very short time of the battle of Chester itself, Mercian overlordship was extended north-westwards into the areas of Hales and Lyme in north Shropshire, Cheshire and north-western Staffordshire, although the precise details of how and when this was accomplished are not known. It has been quite reasonably suggested that this move towards the Dee was associated with a seventh-century refortification of the Iron Age hill fort at Bury Bank at Darlaston that has come to be attributed to Penda's son, King Wulfhere (Fig 3.4). The twelfth-century chronicler, Hugh Candidus, suggests as much. He was a monk of Peterborough who was commissioned to write a history of his house from its foundation by Wulfhere until his own day. He was therefore in a position to gain access to earlier writings and to transmit any oral tradition of a link between Peterborough and Darlaston and Stone, the last being the site of a hermitage founded by the seventh-century Mercian king close by the hill fort. That the Peterborough chronicler should comment at all is evidence of his quality as an historian since, by the chronicler's day, there were no particular reasons why any emphasis should be given to this early political and religious connection.[8]

Two twelfth-century charters recorded in the Stone cartulary, nevertheless lend support to the thesis.[9] Both record deeds of gift by daughters of Ingulph de Gresley before the lands to which they refer were acquired by the Augustinian priory at Stone. Both refer to Bury Bank as 'Wulfhere's camp' (*Wulfecestre*); neither speak of it as Darlaston, 'Deorlaf's estate', a name which the settlement/manor in which it was situated is unlikely to have gained before *c* 750 or after *c* 950, and so called from the royal thegn who acquired its lordship. The second of the charters records both the connection with Wulfhere and the name by which the place was known in the twelfth century, *le Buri*, a description applied in the later Anglo-Saxon period to pre-Viking defensive strongholds.[10] Unfortunately no trace of seventh-century work has turned up in recent archaeological investigation of Staffordshire's hill forts,[11] but the evidence presented here certainly points to the political settlement of the area as having happened by the end of the third quarter of the seventh century and this would be consistent with what is revealed of the extent of the Mercian hegemony in this century by the document known as the Tribal Hidage.[12]

Unfortunately, Mercia lacks both charter evidence before the tenth century and its own chronicle and that is unhelpful in attempting to uncover the tortuous political events of these centuries and the progress in detail of the Mercian colonization. *Mercia* means 'a march'; its people were marcher folk in the sense that at some point they lived along the frontiers of the Anglo-Saxon settlement with the British. Stenton sought to identify this boundary physically with that line of hills that begins in north Warwickshire in Arden, runs northwards along Cannock Chase to the west of the Trent valley, and eventually becomes the central Cheshire ridge. There is some evidence in place names to support that view. To the east there is a well-known cluster of names with clear pagan association, similar to others Gelling has noted as occurring along the borders of the early Anglo-Saxon kingdoms.[13] Wednesbury is 'Woden's fort', Wednesfield, 'Woden's open land', Weoley, 'a heathen temple' and Weeford, 'the ford at the heathen temple'. All are names of the pre-Christian era in Mercia which dates them in origin certainly to before the last quarter of the seventh century and most likely to before 650; they also suggest that because of their survival into the post-Christian period these were either already so firmly fixed as place names that the change of state religion made no difference to them, or indeed surviving pockets of paganism. Geographically, all lie on or to the east of Stenton's line while to its west lay the lands acquired as part of the seventh-century westward expansion of the kingdom. Striking as the group is, none is located in the north of Staffordshire.

Almost all the place names in this area contain relatively late elements, as Gelling's work demonstrates. Brocton, Broughton, Darlaston, Longton, Moreton, and Wooton share the habitative *tūn* element which is now to be dated to the two centuries between *c* 750 and *c* 950. Badenhall, Bucknall, Endon, Moddershall, and Tittensor, like Darlaston noted above, represent a group of settlement names including the personal name of a thegn exercising authority in the location during approximately the same period. Gelling's analysis of the common topographical elements in north Staffordshire place names suggests that many of these too date from the mid-to-late rather than the early Anglo-Saxon period. *Leah*, for instance, meaning a clearing in woodland, is one of the commonest of place name elements in the area today. In the vicinity of Stoke-on-Trent and Newcastle-under-Lyme, it is present, amongst others, in Ashley, Bromley, Linley, Keele, Stanley and Wetley–clearings among ash trees, broom, lime trees (or ? flax), for cows, on stony ground and on wet land respectively, and, in characteristic later Anglo-Saxon form, coupled with thegnly names, as in Audley, Baddeley, Betley, Balterley, Barthomley and Onneley. Hanley and Heighley also contain the late, more usually northern, formation *heah*, meaning 'high ground', which once again indicates later settlement, while, with the possible exception of Madeley, all are names of secondary settlements.[14]

Gelling also points to a number of individual place names in the vicinity which clearly demonstrate its later settlement. First there is Leek, if, as seems possible, the place name is derived from an Old Norse word for a stream and it is to be regarded as a new Norse settlement, as Gelling argues, rather than a renamed pre-existing settlement. Chebsey, which contains the element indicating a position on an island site above water-meadows or marsh, is also to be dated to the early eighth century. The contention seems to be correct for the date complements quite precisely what can be inferred of the early organization of the church in the area, after the conversion of the Mercians, with the creation of the field church/preaching station which remains so obvious a feature of the landscape of the settlement to this day. A similar eighth-century date is convincingly attributed to the origins of Broughton, *Hereborgestone* in the Domesday survey ('the army's *burh*'), which was clearly the site of one of the Mercian king's defended military posts probably established after the political expansion of the kingdom into the district of Hales.[15]

The place-name evidence, therefore, confirms what can be inferred from the political development of the area, indicating that the upland character of north Staffordshire, with its extensive tracts of woodland, was unattractive to the earliest settlers, and that it began to be cleared only during the period, in the eighth century, of Mercian greatness and of relative political stability associated with the reigns of Aethelbald and Offa. As high kings, these two dominated the southern English in this century but, for all that, they were unable to secure the succession of their direct line and, by the beginning of the next century, a collateral branch of the family based on London rather than on the Lichfield-Tamworth-Repton triangle had taken over the reins of the kingdom.

The story of Mercia thereafter is one of internecine fighting as first one and then the other branch of the family tried to assert authority while her client kings regained their independence. Of the four kings who succeeded Cenwulf (796–821), two were deposed – one of them twice – and two were murdered by their vassals. Few of her ninth-century monarchs succeeded in gaining more than a temporary hold on the kingdom as real authority in England passed into the hands of her principal English opponents, the kings of Wessex. Mercia was first conquered by the West Saxons in 829 and, although the Mercians were able to reassert their independence in the following year, the kingdom was effectively broken backed by its experience of internal squabbling and external warfare. Worse still, the Vikings arrived in Britain in these same years and achieved their first major political success when, in 851, they drove the Mercian king,

Beorhtwulf, out of London and into exile. In 855 the Vikings sailed up the Trent, and for the first time crossed Staffordshire and reached Wroxeter. Each year they returned somewhere in England and, twelve years later, in 867, they wintered in Mercia for the first time and so drove the Mercian king to seek the assistance of the old enemy, Wessex. By 873, in spite of King Alfred's accession to the West Saxon throne two years previously, the Vikings were able to establish a headquarters at Repton, to expel the Mercian king, to establish a puppet ruler in his place and systematically to dismember the Mercian kingdom.

What remained of Mercia in the 880s, after Alfred and Guthrum's Peace had created the division between the Danelaw and the West Saxon parts of England, became dependent upon the kingdom of Wessex, and fortunately so. For, it was King Alfred, whose queen was of Mercian stock, who consequently selected the able Aethelred, probably another descendant of the Mercian dynasty, as his ealdorman and, in 889, married him to his exceptionally competent daughter, Aethelflaed. Territorially, Mercia was limited to a western strip stretching southwards from the Mersey through modern Cheshire and Staffordshire, and on southwards through the west midland counties into Gloucestershire.[16] With a common code of law operating in Mercia and Wessex the two kingdoms are virtually indistinguishable politically from this date, but the political link which was established in this period served Mercian interests, as well as West Saxon, particularly well.

A second major Viking onslaught began in 892 and this time the northmen turned their attention more directly to the western rump of the former Mercian kingdom. The Trent valley settlement at Catholme was destroyed irrevocably at this time. It has been argued that the attacks that followed were part of a political plan to annex the entire area to the Danelaw. Three times in as many years between 893 and 895 Danish armies crossed the region and three times they were overcome by a combined army of Mercians and West Saxons, at Buttington by Welshpool in the summer of 893, at Chester towards the end of the same year and at Bridgnorth in 895. When, finally, in 907 the Norse settlers of the Wirral and the Lancashire seaboard were beaten in a battle at Chester by Aethelflaed, Lady of the Mercians, and a further Viking army was defeated in 910 by Edward the Elder at Tettenhall, the West Saxon political hold on Mercia was secured and further consolidated by the creation of Alfredian style *burhs* at Chester (907), Bridgnorth (912), Tamworth (913), Stafford (913), Eddisbury (914), Warwick (914), Chirbury (915), Runcorn (915), Derby (917), and at a number of other not definitely identified locations elsewhere.[17]

The Viking impact in this region was, therefore, very slight. There was little opportunity for Viking colonization outside the Wirral peninsula and so it is not surprising that there are no examples of place names with the commonest Scandinavian forms in the hundreds of Pirehill and Totmonslow, nor for that matter in the county as a whole. Celtic and British place-name elements, in fact, survive in reasonable number emphasizing the Viking failure in the area. Two places having the Danish element *hulme*, signifying water, occur, one in each hundred. But both are found close to the larger groupings of the element in east Cheshire and beyond the Trent. In any case, it is not certain that the element is not from Old Norse, *holmr*, and so of considerably greater antiquity than the ninth century.[18] The place name Normacot, in Stoke-on-Trent, which hints at Norse settlement, was undoubtedly named by antipathetic Mercians rather than by the Norse farmers of the place. Archaeology seems to confirm this view. The only piece of clearly identifiable Scandinavian work in the county is the Rolleston cross, the wheel-head type usually associated with the Norse settled districts of Cheshire, which may have been introduced from western Cheshire or, more likely, brought over the river Dove from Danish Derbyshire. The rivers Trent and Tame and, to the south, Watling Street certainly formed an effective political and social boundary between the two areas of England defined in the reign of King Alfred.

The administrative and political settlement of the region therefore followed West Saxon lines. Victory over the Danes was completed by the kings, Edward the Elder and Athelstan between 920 and 937, who could from then on justify their claim to rule *de facto* as kings of the whole English people. The West Saxon practice of dividing the kingdom into shires and of sub-dividing shires into smaller administrative units called hundreds was now extended throughout the absorbed territory of Mercia. Shires, 'shares' of the kingdom handed over to lesser members of the royal dynasty to administer as ealdormen, on the West Saxon model, were created with centres at the episcopal see of Worcester, at Shrewsbury, and at the *burhs* of Warwick, Chester and Stafford. There is some debate as to whether Edward the Elder or Athelstan was responsible since the earliest written evidence for any of them, for Cheshire, dates only from 980. All were extremely artificial creations, as alien to their inhabitants, in that they showed little consideration for topography and cut across tribal divisions, as the redrawn county map of 1974. The newly created 'Stafford-shire' was a particularly unsatisfactory amalgamation of the Tomsaetan of the lowland Trent and Tame valleys, the Pencersaetan, whose territory lay to the west of the central ridge, those of the Wreocansaetan whose lands stretched into the district of Hales, and part of the Pecsaetan who occupied Lyme and the uplands of the Peak District.[19] That the Mercians rebelled against West-Saxon rule – in 918, when it was necessary for Edward the Elder to march on Tamworth and again in 924, when the same king found it necessary to campaign in the Dee valley at the very moment that these political arrangements were being made – may hint at the existence of a deliberate policy of undermining the opportunity for reasserting Mercian independence. Were the rebellions caused by these very proposals? The new boundary between Warwickshire and Staffordshire was drawn through the main streets of Tamworth, the former chief town of Mercia, while Stafford, the administrative centre of the new shire, although a Roman road station in origin and still the site of an important minster church, is not known to have been of political significance under the Mercian dynasty.

The five hundreds, each, in theory, a grouping of one hundred hides, were also essentially administrative in concept and so, technically, equally unresponsive to the pre-existing social organization in the area. That there were only five compared with thirty-four in Norfolk, fifteen in Shropshire, twelve in Worcestershire and twelve in pre-Conquest Cheshire, can be viewed as yet further evidence of the relative poverty of the county, but it also points to the essentially artificial administrative nature of such divisions. Hundreds inevitably varied considerably in size in order to reflect potential tax-bearing, and military and legal capacity, so that in Staffordshire the smaller hundreds of Offlow, Cuttlestone and Seisdon were found in the lowland and more fertile south and south-west between the Tame and the Severn. The two sprawling northern hundreds, Totmonslow and Pirehill, took in almost all the highest land. Each took its name from the meeting place of the hundred court, at a prominent hill site in the case of Pirehill, and from a probable burial tumulus which later became the site of a small settlement in the case of Totmonslow. Offlow was named from a tumulus in the parish of Hints, Cuttlestone from a probable memorial lith situated near Penkridge and Seisdon from a settlement in the parish of Trysull. The strangeness of this is that, even in the period in which they were formed, these were not the principal political, religious, or economic centres in them, but seem to coincide with the location of the traditional meeting places of the Mercian tribal groups which settled in the districts they covered. The hundreds in Staffordshire may in the end, therefore, be tribally based with, for instance, Offlow for the Tomsaetan, Cuttlestone for the Pencersaetan, and Totmonslow for those of the Pecsaetan who found themselves included in the shire, and so be of much greater antiquity than the tenth century. There is no doubt that this was an enduring administrative organization that outlasted the Middle Ages but that it may well be no more than the reimposition of an existing order made as the price of West-Saxon conquest.

If the political settlement of Mercia was first effected in the seventh and eighth centuries, was destroyed in the ninth, and was remodelled as part of the kingdom of the whole of England in the tenth century, the early ecclesiastical settlement of the region was equally enduring. Christianity was adopted by the Mercians in the 650s. Lichfield, already the site of a Celtic monastic establishment became the see for the kingdom after the appointment of Theodore of Tarsus as archbishop at Canterbury and, when in 669 King Wulfhere asked for a bishop, St Chad was named. He must surely have been a man of considerable charisma for, although he lived only until 672, his grave became the site of a popular, local, Mercian pilgrimage which endured for the remainder of the Middle Ages. The possession of his bones was responsible both for the success of Lichfield as a bishopric in the Anglo-Saxon period, its continuation across the Conquest, and the development and growth in the twelfth century of a newly planned town close by the cathedral complex. Even before the end of the seventh century, the church had acquired a unitary organization throughout Mercia and Lindsey far ahead of the political organization of the state, and it provided an example and model for the latter. Under the aegis of the church, and within a very short period of time, an influential school was established at Lichfield, designed to produce literate priests for the diocese, and clerks and advisors for the kingdom. By the eighth century the school was known for its fine manuscript production.[20]

The early organization of the Mercian church is usually attributed to King Wulfhere and his younger brother and successor, Ethelred (674–704), and it is certain that the estates which the cathedral still held at the time of the Domesday survey were, in the main, acquired in these earliest years of Mercian Christianity as the kingdom of Mercia expanded westwards and northwards over the Cannock ridge and into the districts of Hales and Lyme. A major group of these was situated close to Lichfield in Offlow hundred in the south-east and in Cuttlestone hundred in the mid-west of Staffordshire, but the single manor of Ellastone, in the Dove valley, was in Totmonslow hundred, while a major holding centred on Eccleshall together with the manors of Adbaston, Coley, Drointon, Moreton and Seighford, in the hundred of Pirehill, formed a distinct group of estates in the north-west of the county. Along with other properties at Wybunbury in the Cheshire hundred of Nantwich, and in the Dee valley towards Chester, the cathedral acquired its principal and wealthiest territorial holdings in a swathe of land linking the see to Chester during the last third of the seventh century, if not in the time of the bishopric of St Chad himself, in the manner of thank offerings to a helpful Christian god for a conquest successfully accomplished.[21] Some confirmation of this view is afforded by the inclusion of Eccleshall, the site of a pre-Mercian, Celtic church, which was, it appears, already situated at the centre of a vast and complex ancient estate. Eccleshall remained the most extensive manor in the county in the Middle Ages, and by about 1200, its castle had become a favoured place of residence for the bishop of the diocese.[22] Even today its church contains a small Anglo-Saxon relief, built into a wall and probably from a cross shaft, which appears to represent Bede's description of Chad's method of carrying out his pastoral work on foot, in the manner of the Apostles, rather than on horseback, in the Roman way, as decreed at the Synod of Whitby and as required of him by his archbishop, Theodore, linking the church to the founding bishop and saint of the diocese.

In the Anglo-Saxon period, a cathedral had general supervisory responsibilities for the see, was required to maintain spiritual standards and needed to provide a literate priesthood to serve the diocese and kingdom in which it was located. This necessitated the acquisition of landed wealth. However, besides endowing the headminster at Lichfield, Wulfhere is also said to have founded other *monasteria*, minster churches, throughout his kingdom with various roles in the localities in which they were situated. We cannot now be sure where these were sited and such evidence that exists is inevitably circumstantial. Nevertheless, reasonable arguments based upon oral tradition and later documentation have put forward suggestions for his foundation of houses at Stone and Burton-upon-Trent which were most likely double-houses of nuns and canons in the usual early Anglo-Saxon form, and for a nunnery, which had become a house for men by the 870s, at Hanbury on the summit of the Needwood escarpment (Fig 4.1).

The term 'minster' is ambiguous for, as Deansley demonstrated more than half a century ago, it was used to apply without differentiation both to communities of clerks and to monastic groups.[23] Minsters are perhaps most easily to be identified as baptisteries – for baptism, the point of entry to the church, was jealously guarded as yet – and as mission churches serving as mother churches of a district with a staff of priests who could be despatched as required to attend to the spirtual needs of a local flock, and, when feasible, to set up dependent chapels. There were no parishes of the kind that would be recognizable to us; these came to be defined in this area only from the tenth century and over several centuries, sometimes growing out of these dependent chapels or from private manorial churches in a process which is far from clear anywhere in England. Each minster, however, had jurisdiction over an area represented later in the Middle Ages and in the post-Reformation period by several parishes. It has recently been argued convincingly that the efficacy of the minster system in Anglo-Saxon England retarded parish development.[24] That certainly seems to be illustrated by what happened in north Staffordshire.

A famous letter written by Bede to the bishop of York in 734, in which he argued for an extension of their number in order to provide wider access to their services, reveals the existence of a system of mother churches already in operation in Northumbria. By also indicating that these minsters had been set up in royal vills and former tribal centres Bede implies the close linkage between the political arm and the church throughout the English kingdoms, including Mercia, in the eighth century. Bede has nothing to say of Wulfhere, because he was a Mercian, but by bringing together what the Northumbrian monk has to say on this subject with what we know is claimed in oral tradition, and is revealed by Peterborough evidence, to have been the Mercian king's contribution to the organization of the church in his kingdom, it becomes reasonable to argue a very early date for the foundation of most of the major churches of the Mercian region. In these terms, the churches at Lichfield, Tamworth and Repton were clearly defined as minsters, but where else in the diocese, and, in particular, where in north Staffordshire could such institutions be found; what was the pre-parochial organization of the church in the area?

Minsters were frequently collegiate, staffed by colleges of priests in varying numbers. The Domesday survey of 1086 provides clear indications of some of the most important. Lichfield, with its very large staff of twenty canons before the see was moved in 1075, on Archbishop Lanfranc's instructions, to Chester, was situated in Offlow hundred and was merely the grandest among them. But Domesday also surveyed the major colleges at Wolverhampton (Seisdon), Tettenhall (Seisdon), Penkridge (Cuttlestone), Gnosall (Cuttlestone) and Stafford (Pirehill) within the county and at Derby, Chester and Shrewsbury in the wider diocese.[25] For none of these is there written testimony before the tenth century, but such documentary evidence as there is, for Penkridge, Wolverhampton and Chester in particular, points to their foundation in the earliest years after the conversion of the Mercians. St Mary's at Stafford, St Peter's, Wolverhampton, St Michael's, Penkridge and, one suspects, St Edith's at Tamworth also served as hundredal churches. In the post-Conquest period all the colleges surveyed in Domesday were recognized as royal free chapels with a status unique in Europe as ecclesiastical peculiars in which the crown acted in its own right as dean and from which the local diocesan's authority was entirely excluded.

FIGURE 4.1 Pre-Conquest ecclesiastical settlement in north Staffordshire.

Yet of these, only St Mary's, Stafford, in the farthest south of its hundred, was in Pirehill while no hundredal minster is recorded for Totmonslow, and no claim was ever advanced in support of this status by any other church in either of the two northern hundreds – evidence of the uncompleted task of the Domesday commissioners in the north of the county as well as further proof of the relative poverty and underdeveloped nature of the region. Nevertheless, Domesday is known to understate the evidence for the number, wealth and status of churches; only 30 priests are recorded in the whole county, and only one and half a church in Totmonslow hundred. That statistic, however, seems to confirm the thesis that the more modest of churches, even small minsters, are unlikely to be recorded in the survey of those parts of the county dominated by superior minsters.[26]

In 1086 St Mary's, Stafford, had a complement of thirteen canons. Penkridge and Gnosall had nine and Tettenhall had five. No figure is given for Wolverhampton which maintained up to seven in the twelfth century. Norbury, just on the Cuttlestone side of the boundary with Pirehill hundred, is the only church in Staffordshire, other than the colleges, with more than a single recorded priest.[27] Elsewhere this might be sufficient evidence for its mother church status before the Conquest but, because it is unusual in the county, it is difficult to draw firm conclusions from this fact alone, while the existence here of a single pair of clerks points to a relatively modest establishment. Other evidence must therefore be sought for the existence of the lesser minster churches of the region.

Dedications of churches have been used to point to early principal churches. A dedication to St Peter, for instance, is generally considered to be a significant pointer towards a foundation of considerable antiquity by the Conquest. In Totmonslow and Pirehill this could establish the status of the churches at Alstonefield, Alton, Caverswall, Ellastone, Maer and Stoke. For some there is no other supportive evidence. The formation of later parishes adjacent to Alton, Ellastone and Maer, and the appropriation of lands by post-Conquest monastic foundations in the same area has further complicated the story. For others, like Stoke, the evidence is unequivocal. Besides its indicative dedication, Stoke still has the shaft of a Mercian cross standing in its churchyard and, throughout the Middle Ages, was the central church of a very large parish with six dependent chapels at Bagnall, Bucknall, Burslem, Newcastle, Norton-in-the-Moors and Whitmore (Fig 9.1). The evidence for Alstonefield – indicative dedication, dependent chapelries and a whole group of Mercian and other cross shafts – is very similar.

Churches dedicated in the post-Conquest period to Anglo-Saxon saints can also, often, but not always, provide an indication of their early status. Dedications did sometimes change as fashions in saints changed. Hanbury, the early 'nunnery', is still, and probably always was, dedicated to St Werburgh, the Mercian daughter of King Wulfhere (d c 700); it was from here that, in 874, her relics were translated to Chester. The extent of its medieval parish hints at the survival of a very sizeable monastic estate in Needwood with Hanbury at its centre. There were dependent chapels at Marchington and, after the Norman Conquest, at Newborough, while the configuration of the adjacent parish of Tutbury suggests that it too was created out of Hanbury when the Norman lord, Henry de Ferrers, built his new castle and laid out a new town there sometime between 1071 and 1086. We can surely recognize here the relic of a once substantial pre-Viking *monasterium*.

Two dedications in Staffordshire to St Edith (arguably, but unlikely, two different saints bearing the same name, one an aunt, the other a grand-daughter of Alfred the Great) at Tamworth and Church Eaton nevertheless warrant caution. They are unlikely to date from before the West-Saxon seizure of Tamworth and its district by Edward the Elder in 918 and, because of their West-Saxon association, would suggest that the Mercian dedication of the church at Tamworth was suppressed. Church Eaton, in any case, seems to have acquired its dedication after the Norman Conquest and so provides no evidence for the siting of an earlier principal church.[28] The two dedications to Edward the Confessor, at Leek and Cheddleton, were clearly also later – thirteenth-century acquisitions owing much to the foundation of Dieulacres abbey by Ranulph, earl of Chester, and the developing cult of the Confessor during the reign of Henry III.

With St Bertolin, almost certainly a Mercian contemporary of Werburgh, we seem to be on surer ground. The church at Ilam contains his shrine and was clearly the focus at least of a local cult which would have brought people in some numbers to the remoter parts of the Dove and Manifold valleys in this period. It had a least one dependent chapel, at Sheen, a detached jurisdiction south of Longnor, while confirmation that this was a church of standing before the Conquest is provided archaeologically by the Anglo-Saxon fragments remaining in the present church building and by the several cross shafts, of different types, which still stand either in the churchyard or close by. Evidence for the status of two other churches dedicated to the saint is less clear-cut. The early Anglo-Saxon church, whose footings can be viewed outside the west end of St Mary's at Stafford, was also dedicated to Bertolin and stood in a relationship to the minster church which suggests dependency, while at Barthomley, whose later parish was bisected by the boundary between Cheshire and Staffordshire, the existence of several dependent chapels, as well as the early dedication itself, seems to confirm its importance in the organization of the church in Mercia.[29] Dedications to Chad are uncommon, occurring on the estates of the bishopric and, except for Wybunbury in Cheshire, are not particularly identified with early minsters. There are only three certain medieval dedications to St Chad in Staffordshire, at Pattingham, Seighford and Stafford. None appears to have been of more than local or manorial church status but the last two were located in Pirehill hundred.

In spite of the keen observation of H M Taylor, Staffordshire is not particularly rich in Anglo-Saxon archaeological remains, and some that he confidently dated to the period have been reassigned.[30] It is likely that until the eleventh century, or even later, most churches in the area were insubstantial structures of timber, which was always available in plenty in the county during the medieval period. Betley, and perhaps Whitmore, though later medieval structures, are probably surviving examples of this type. The exceptions were the principal minsters. To this day Gnosall and, less so, St Mary's, Stafford, retain elements in their plan which indicate their Anglo-Saxon origin.[31] In a number of settlements, perhaps a majority, in the two northern hundreds, however, the provision of a church building is unlikely to have happened in the pre-Conquest period. A timber or stone cross is likely to have stood, sometimes in an enclosed area of land, at a convenient meeting place for worship within the township which was frequently favoured as the site for burial of the dead. Eventually this often became the site of the parish church. Field churches of this type date from the earliest days of the Christian mission and were encouraged by Archbishop Theodore in the later seventh century.

In north Staffordshire it seems reasonable to interpret the presence of a notable surviving group of cross shafts as evidence for the early local organization of the church. Although most can be ascribed to the tenth or eleventh centuries and may even, in some instances, date from after the Conquest, they should perhaps be seen as stone replacements for earlier wooden crosses of the kind claimed to have been discovered by archaeologists in the footings of St Bertolin, Stafford. Several are also clearly associated with minster churches, as, for instance, at St Peter's, Wolverhampton, where the single eighth-century cross is the finest of all in the county. As at Stoke, which also has a single cross shaft, other evidence points to its having been the major church in its area. The presence of several crosses, usually more than simply a single pair, in one location, as at Alstonefield, Checkley, Eccleshall, Ilam, Leek, and most famously at Sandbach (Cheshire), is also strong evidence, as has been argued above, for the location of pre-Conquest mother churches. The presence and siting of the single cross at Chebsey and of cross shafts at Heaton and Swythamley in north Staffordshire, and at Rainow, Disley and Wincle in Cheshire – all of them of characteristic late-Mercian form – appear to indicate something of the pre-parochial organization of the church in the region. All, except Chebsey which became a parish in its own right in the post-Conquest period but may have been dependent on Eccleshall before it, were located in townships themselves attached to dependent chapelries of a much larger *parochia*, suggesting that they are merely the survivors of a pre-Conquest system of local spiritual provision. Parishes were not a feature of the pre-Conquest ecclesiastical settlement in this region. They were slow to appear in the area even after Lanfranc's injunctions intended to secure the appointment of a resident priest with cure of souls in each locality. There is evidence to suggest that although a new emphasis was placed upon the pastoral role of the priesthood in the later eleventh century, the impact of such change was not felt in these upland hundreds of Staffordshire for some time and that parishes went on being formed in the area for all of the Middle Ages.

The Domesday survey of 1086 confirms the impression of a conservatively backward, underpopulated, and economically underdeveloped shire. The two northern hundreds in particular were especially unappealing to the new Norman masters of England. With small acreages of pasture, decreasing in extent the higher up the Trent, Blithe and Dove valleys that settlements were located, and with the amount of the woodland cover increasing before giving way in the far north to moorland, the Normans viewed as unattractive everything beyond the lower Trent and Tame valleys in the south of the county. Manorial values were generally of miserable proportions in the north and seemed to offer little prospect of immediate gain. Much in the two northern hundreds was dismissed by the commissioners as 'waste', unassigned and unassignable, or untaxable or not worth the pains of taxing. Manorial structures also lagged behind counties to the south with several composite manors, such as Eccleshall, which were survivors from an early Anglo-Saxon private estate system and had only a rudimentary manorial organization. There was also a lack of urban settlements in the county with only Tamworth and Stafford, according to the survey, recognizable as such. But Domesday is a poor record of the towns of later eleventh-century England and what looks suspiciously like an incipient borough at Newcastle may be subsumed within the entry for the manor of Trentham.[32] Nevertheless, in spite of the size of the shire, the commissioners seem to have spent relatively little time on their task, and produced the second shortest account of all the counties surveyed in 1086.

It is not, therefore, particularly surprising that the Normans who came to colonize Staffordshire after the confiscation of the Earl Edwin of Mercia's lands following his rebellion (1069–71) were never particularly numerous. Besides the king himself, only nine new Norman landholders arrived between 1071 and 1086. It is true that, as well as Earl Roger of Shrewsbury, they included Robert de Stafford, Henry de Ferrers and William fitzAnsculf who were to found major dynasties based on their holdings in the county, but the holders of the greatest estates as tenants-in-chief of the crown remained the seven ecclesiastical tenants, four of whom had occupied their lands since the seventh or early eighth century. It should also be noted that seventeen English thegns, a higher concentration than elsewhere, were recorded as still holding directly from the crown in the county, indicating the incomplete nature of the Norman colonization of Staffordshire at this date. Because land was still available to the crown to grant out new tenancies at the beginning of the twelfth century at the expense of the English thegns, several Frenchmen, who came to England in the wake of Henry I's successful coup, received rewards of grants in the county including two, the Audleys, lords of Audley and Heighley, and the Verduns, lords of Alton, whose families were to leave a considerable mark on its future history and on the development of the two northern hundreds in particular. But this was always difficult terrain and, in a sense, it could be argued that the Normans never fully completed the colonization of the northern parts of the county. 'Alstonfield (no man affecting to seat himself in that cold, wild country) was divided into many parts', wrote Erdeswick, pointing out the consequential fragmented state of lordship after the Conquest.[33]

It should, of course, never be forgotten that the Normans came to England, and so to

Staffordshire, as conquerors. They wished to make money and to exploit their new territories to the advantage of their estates in Normandy. Besides the obvious defensive and offensive purposes, the construction of a castle provided an opportunity to achieve this end, and castles appeared throughout the county up to the twelfth century. In the north of Staffordshire, the castle-building programme represented the first systematic effort to develop the economic possibilities of the area, and castles were erected at Alton, Audley, Biddulph, Chartley, Newcastle, Stafford, Tyrley, Tutbury and Castle Church by tenants-in-chief and their under-tenants.[34]

Castles were centres of consumption; they attracted tradesmen and others seeking service to their gates, and in short order new permanent settlements began to be founded. In one of the best known entries in the whole of the Domesday survey, Henry de Ferrers' newly planted town at Tutbury is described: 'In the borough round the castle are 42 men living only from their trade, and they render with the market £4 10*s*'. The grid plan that that new town foundation represents is visible only on the ground. The Domesday entry explicitly confirms what can be seen in the landscape – a newly planted town close to the castle where townsmen, deriving all their income from commerce and not at all from agriculture, trade in the new market to the profit of the local lord. Such concentrated, urban-based economic activity was entirely new to the region. What Domesday fails to tell is that even closer to the castle, Henry de Ferrers and his wife founded a Benedictine priory, a cell of the Norman house at St Pierre-sur-Dives which by the early twelfth century had also acquired a parochial role at the centre of a new parish.[35] Here was a second centre of consumption served by the Tutbury market and a further reason why the town, the castle, the convent and the Ferrers family prospered. The political stability that the Conquest imposed on England also created a climate in which trade could flourish, while the sharp rise in the population between *c* 1000 and *c* 1300 provided the additional consumers so necessary for prosperity.

The example of Henry de Ferrers' success at Tutbury encapsulates Norman attitudes to their new acquisitions and demonstrates the process whereby they took advantage of them. As a consequence many new markets were set up by many different lords in the county in the next two centuries, most as speculative ventures in an attempt to diversify their income. In Pirehill hundred, the bishop of Lichfield set up a market at Eccleshall, the earl of Chester created one at Chartley and Henry de Audley another, doomed to fail, at Betley. In Totmonslow hundred the earl of Chester established a market at Leek, the monks of Burton abbey set up others at Burton and Abbots Bromley, and the Ferrers family, now earls of Derby, at Uttoxeter. The most successful market centres were sometimes established as boroughs, usually by royal charter, so that even in north Staffordshire besides Stafford, the shire town, and Newcastle, which was by the mid-twelfth century already a substantial urban settlement, Abbots Bromley, Alton, Betley, Colton, Eccleshall, Leek, Stone and Uttoxeter acquired that distinction at some time before the early fourteenth century.[36] Profits were often spent on conspicuous display and in a search for personal salvation; it was at this time that the new manorial lords created more permanent arrangements for worship by building new parish churches in timber and stone to serve the spiritual needs of the local community as can still occasionally be determined archaeologically, as at Caverswall. The territories which had been the pastoral responsibilities of the pre-Conquest minsters were broken up to form new parishes. No written evidence of this process survives, which can only be inferred, but it probably provides the explanation for the complicated pattern of small parishes which emerged in the vicinity of Alton in Totmonslow hundred and Maer in Pirehill.[37] It was certainly at this time that the broad lines of the parish map of Staffordshire that outlasted the Reformation were drawn up.

The Normans had, in part, justified their conquest, as an attempt to restore the Anglo-Saxon church to the rightful way of continental Christendom. In reforming the regular church, it was inevitable, therefore, that they should follow the example of the Conqueror himself who founded a new abbey on the site of his victory over King Harold. Henry de Ferrers followed the king-duke very closely with his foundation of the Benedictine priory at Tutbury, but by the twelfth century the new religious orders were considered more fashionable, demanded less by way of endowments and were regarded as spirtually more efficacious than the Benedictines. Consequently, apart from a weakly nunnery at Blithbury, no other house of the Benedictine subscription was founded in the north of the county. The new houses were for Augustinian canons, founded in the course of the twelfth century by successful Norman settlers at Calwich (c 1125), Ranton (c 1150), Rocester (c 1145), Stafford (c 1174), Stone (c 1140) and Trentham (c 1150), and for the Cistercians, at Croxden (1179), Dieulacres (1214) and Hulton (1219).[38] The Knights Templars were given lands to clear in order to found a preceptory at Keele between 1155 and 1163 and had succeeded in doing so before c 1250.[39]

All the religious orders played their part in clearing the woodland and making the land yield as much as could be got from it given the relatively limited technology of the period. Sheep rearing to produce a wool cash crop dominated the agriculture of the northern hundreds in these years; all the religious houses of the area had flocks in grazing on the moorlands and elsewhere. Dieulacres, Croxden and Burton owed much of their relative prosperity to the success of their wool clip. Cattle were successfully reared on the grasslands of the Blithe and central Trent valleys as, for example, by the bishop at his large manor of Haywood in Pirehill hundred. Horse breeding was to become a profitable feature of the earldom/duchy of Lancaster estates centred on Needwood Forest and Tutbury by the fourteenth century. Assarting, the process of bringing new land under the plough, is a noticeable consequence of the rise in the population first observable in the northern parts of the county in Needwood and the Trent valley in the twelfth century, but occurred everywhere in the area by the thirteenth.[40]

Yet the character of the northern hundreds of Staffordshire was little changed by the arrival of the Normans. It remained an area of sparse settlement and small communities. There was little scope here for increasing the size of demesnes and manorial values generally. Ekeing out an existence for lords and tenants alike in these more inhospitable and socially conservative parts of the county was never an easy business in the Middle Ages, 'the north being divided into moorland and woodland', according to Erdeswick.[41] The Normans certainly arrived in England at a propitious moment, and by capitalizing on the dramatic population increase of the three centuries after 1000 were able to exploit their achievement fully. But even in the seventeenth century, as Erdeswick and Plot bear witness, exploiting and taming this part of the county still presented almost as many problems to its landholders as it did to the Anglo-Saxons who first came to the area exactly one thousand years before.

REFERENCES

1. S Erdeswick, *A survey of Staffordshire* (T Harwood, ed), 1820, 364; R Plot, *The natural history of Staffordshire*, Oxford, 1686, 110.
2. M W Greenslade and D G Stuart, *A history of Staffordshire*, Chichester, 2nd ed, 1984, 12–14; D M Palliser, *The Staffordshire landscape*, 1976, 30–5.
3. W Davies, 'Annals and the origin of Mercia', in A Dornier, ed, *Mercian studies*, Leicester, 1977, 23; G Losco-Bradley, 'Catholme', *Current Archaeology*, 59, 1976, 358–69.
4. N J Higham, 'King Cearl, the battle of Chester and the origins of the Mercian "Overkingship"', *Midl*

Hist, 17, 1992, 10–12.

5.   F M Stenton, *Anglo-Saxon England*, Oxford, 3rd ed, 1971, 40; C Hart, 'The kingdom of Mercia', in Dornier, *Mercian studies*, 53–4. Evidence from a grave discovered at Barlaston provides archaeological support for this statement: A J H Gunstone, 'An archaeological gazetteer of Staffordshire, part 1: chance finds and sites, excluding barrows and their contents', *N Staffs Jnl Fld Stud*, 4, 1964, 15.

6.   Higham, 'King Cearl', 1–5, 8–10 and map.

7.   Davies, 'Annals and the origin of Mercia', 20–2, 27; Hart, 'The kingdom of Mercia', 53–5.

8.   W T Mellows, ed, *The chronicle of Hugh Candidus, a monk of Peterborough*, Oxford, 1949, 152–3.

9.   G Wrottesley, ed, 'The Stone cartulary', *Collections for a History of Staffordshire*, 5(1), 1885, 9–10.

10. M Gelling, 'Some thoughts on Staffordshire place names', *N Staffs Jnl Fld Stud*, 21, 1981–85, 4, 17–19; Stenton, *Anglo-Saxon England*, 292.

11. P Everson and M Jecock of the Keele Office of the Royal Commission on Historical Monuments of England and Wales provided this information.

12. This survives only in a tenth-century copy and has been subject to considerable redating and re-interpretation, most recently by Higham, 'King Cearl', 1–15. It is claimed here that the document can be dated to 625, as the work of Paulinus at the court of King Edwin of Northumbria, and that, while based upon a Mercian tribute list of early seventh- or late sixth-century date, it is a Deiran recension in the form in which it has been transmitted. Stenton, *Anglo-Saxon England*, 43, 295–7, 300–1, accepts its Mercian origin and asserts that it belongs to a date between the accession of Wulfhere and the end of Offa's reign.

13. M Gelling, *Signposts to the past: place names and the history of England*, 1978, 158–61, and 'Staffordshire place names', 2–3, 14.

14. Gelling, *Signposts to the past,* 126–9, and 'Staffordshire place names', 2–3; E Ekwall, *The concise Oxford dictionary of English place names*, Oxford, 3rd ed, 1951, 218–19.

15. Gelling, 'Staffordshire place names', 5–6, 17–18.

16. D Hill, *An atlas of Anglo-Saxon England*, Oxford, 1981, 46–7, map 70.

17. F T Wainwright, 'Aethelflaed, Lady of the Mercians', in H P R Finberg, ed, *Scandinavian England*, Chichester, 1975, 305–24.

18. F T Wainwright, 'North-west Mercia', in Finberg, *Scandinavian England*, 122.

19. Hart, 'The kingdom of Mercia', 43–54.

20. R Studd, 'Pre-Conquest Lichfield', *Trans S Staffs Archaeol Hist Soc*, 22, 1980–81, 24–30; British Museum, *The making of England*, Exhibition Catalogue, 1992.

21. The usual formula in response to the Domesday commissioners' question 'who held the land in the reign of Edward the Confessor?' is 'St Chad held it' (*Sanctus Cedde tenuit*), implying that the territory formed part of the original endowment of the church of Lichfield and was made in the saint's own day: C F Slade, 'Introduction and translation of the Staffordshire Domesday', in *Victoria County History of Staffordshire (VCH Staffs)*, 1958, iv, 41–3; P H Sawyer and A T Thacker, 'The Cheshire Domesday', in *Victoria County History of Cheshire*, 1987, i, 343–5.

22. P and M Spufford, *Eccleshall: the story of a Staffordshire market town and its dependent villages*, Keele University, 1964, 5–11, 36–7.

23. M Deansley, 'Early English and Gallic minsters', *Trans Royal Hist Soc*, 4th series, 23, 1941, 25ff.

24. J Blair, 'Local churches in Domesday Book and before', in J C Holt, ed, *Domesday studies*, 1987, 267–71.

25. D Styles, 'The early history of the king's chapels in Staffordshire', *Birmingham Archaeol Jnl*, 60, 1936, 56ff; J H Denton, *English royal free chapels, 1100–1300: a constitutional study*, Manchester, 1970, 1–90.

26. J Blair, 'Secular minster churches in Domesday Book', in P H Sawyer, ed, *Domesday Book: a reassessment*, 1985, 112, and 'Local churches in Domesday Book', 275; Slade, 'Staffordshire Domesday', 24.

27. Blair, 'Secular minster churches', 105–14.

28. J E Buckler, *Church Eaton: a short history and guide*, privately published, 1978; J Gould, 'Saint Edith of Polesworth and Tamworth', *Trans S Staffs Archaeol Hist Soc*, 27, 1987 for 1985–86, 35–8.

29. D Sylvester and G Nulty, eds, *The historical atlas of Cheshire*, Chester, 1958, 36–7.

30. M O H Carver, 'A twelfth-century tympanum fragment at Caverswall, Staffordshire', *N Staffs Jnl Fld Stud*, 20, 1980, 1–8.

31. Blair, 'Secular minster churches', 121–2.

32. R Studd, 'Medieval Newcastle-under-Lyme: a hidden Domesday borough?' *Staffs Stud*, 3, 1990–91, 1–21.

33. Erdeswick, *Staffordshire*, 353.

34. L M Cantor, 'The medieval castles of Staffordshire', *N Staffs Jnl Fld Stud*, 6, 1966, 38–46; D M Palliser, 'Staffordshire castles: a provisional list', *Staffs Archaeol*, 1, 1972, 5–8.

35. A Saltman, 'The priory of Tutbury', in *V C H Staffs*, 1970, iii, 331.

36. D M Palliser and A C Pinnock, 'The markets of medieval Staffordshire', *N Staffs Jnl Fld Stud*, 11, 1971, 50–63; D M Palliser, 'The boroughs of medieval Staffordshire', *N Staffs Jnl Fld Stud*, 12, 1972, 63–73.

37. Compare Norman treatment of the county's royal free chapels, which were alienated apparently out of ignorance of their unique status: Denton, *English royal free chapels*, 41–2, 69–71.

38. M W Greenslade *et al*, 'Religious houses', in *V C H Staffs*, iii, 135–273.

39. R Studd, 'A Templar colony in north Staffordshire: Keele before the Sneyds', in C J Harrison, ed, *Essays in the history of Keele*, Keele University, 1986, 5–21.

40. J Birrell, 'Medieval agriculture', in *V C H Staffs*, 1979, vi, 1–48.

41. Erdeswick, *Staffordshire*, 3.

PART TWO

The Development of the Potteries

5. The Beginnings of Industrialization: Pottery Manufacture, 1660–1760

LORNA WEATHERILL

... the potters were never confined to any Mode or fashion for the making of their earthen ware but each potter did from tyme to tyme vary and alter the same ...[1]

This chapter deals with the early period in the industrialization of north Staffordshire and concentrates on the major industry in the area, pottery manufacture.[2] Industrialization has not been a simple linear process; so many aspects of commercial and technical change need to be explored to show how the industry and the locality developed. This chapter is arranged in five sections in order to show the scope of the early developments: it starts by outlining chronological change; technical change is then considered as a background to the development of new sectors; the assets and organization of the potteries are examined; the markets for the output and how it was sold are considered in detail; and the impact of industrial change on the locality forms a conclusion.

GROWTH OF THE POTTERY INDUSTRY, 1660–1760

This first section lays out a framework of chronological change for the rest of the discussion by presenting some estimates of growth and change from 1660 to 1760. There were no contemporary measurements of the size of the industry and so there are considerable limitations in making estimates because the source material is diverse and the figures rest on a large number of assumptions.[3] Figures 5.1 and 2 display the capacity of the industry in terms of the number of people estimated as employed in it. The first shows the estimated growth of the industry in north Staffordshire in comparison with that in London and elsewhere. Expansion was characteristic of the whole century from 1660 to 1760, and changes in north Staffordshire were not at the expense of other areas, for the industry in London (especially before 1750) and many places in the north and midlands expanded at the same time. Expansion in the late seventeenth century in north Staffordshire was based on increases in the number of coarse earthenware potteries. Surviving pieces bear witness to the wide range of styles made for domestic use, as well as large dairy wares and butter pots. In the eighteenth century, production became more diversified than previously, and stoneware was established in the last decade of the seventeenth century, with expansion and diversification in the early decades of the eighteenth century. The development of fine earthenware was slow until the 1750s, when a period of rapid growth began which continued into the nineteenth century.

Some of the dynamics of change are illustrated in Figure 5.2, which shows the estimated size

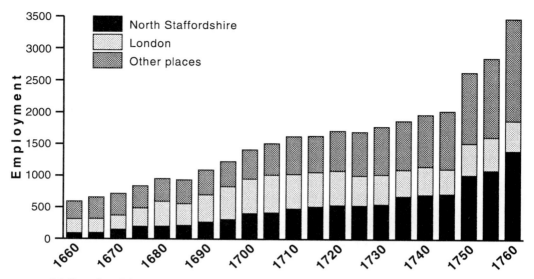

FIGURE 5.1 Capacity of the pottery industry in north Staffordshire, 1660–1760, expressed in terms of the number of people working in pottery production (*Source*: L Weatherill, 'The growth of the pottery industry in England, 1660–1815', unpublished Ph D thesis, London University, 1981, appendix 1).

of three sectors in the whole of England. Expansion everywhere in the later seventeenth century was based on traditional types of products, sold in broadly traditional, expanding home markets. Expansion in the early eighteenth century was due to the new kinds of pottery, notably stoneware, which was made in north Staffordshire, London and elsewhere. There was a time of sustained growth from the 1740s, based on finer stoneware and fine earthenware; production of these was not confined to north Staffordshire but these sectors were more concentrated in the area than previous production. These new products were sold mainly in the home market through a developing network of dealers. Just before 1760 the fine earthenware sector emerged in north Staffordshire and grew so rapidly thereafter that it accounted for four-fifths of the whole industry in England by 1780. The foundations for that growth are to be found in the period of early industrialization that is the subject of this chapter.

There are other measures of the growth of industry in the area, the best of which are recorded in Figures 5.3 and 4, which display the tonnages of cratesware, flint and fine clay carried on the Weaver Navigation after 1733. These figures clearly support the pattern shown in Figure 5.1, with continuous growth before 1760 and a tendency for greater expansion in the 1750s. Figure 5.3 supports the point that growth was based on new products, using new raw materials. Increasing output and changing product range were associated with larger potteries, with greater investment in working capital and with an expanding market, but before the commercial aspects are examined in detail, the technical changes essential to expansion are described.

TECHNICAL CHANGE

Technical change in the period before 1760 in north Staffordshire was characterized by gradual and continuous transformation of basic processes and raw materials.[4] The growth of the industry did rely on technical change, although in the late seventeenth century growth was also

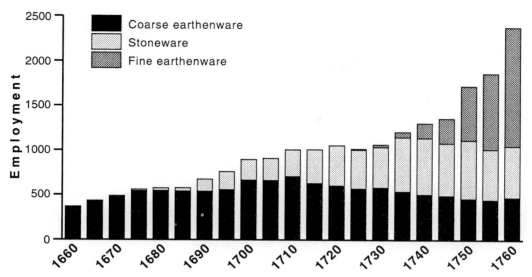

FIGURE 5.2 Capacity of the coarse earthenware, fine earthenware, and stoneware sectors in England, 1660–1760, expressed in terms of the number of people working in pottery production in each sector (*Source*: as for Fig 5.1. A very small amount of china was produced in the area in the 1750s but this has been excluded; the china sector was largely concentrated in London until later in the eighteenth century. Delftware was never made in the area).

due to the addition of new productive capacity using essentially the same techniques as before. The association between changes in capacity and technical development was a subtle one, for the result of technical change arising from what was already known was a series of new products. Each technical change in itself was small but taken together they resulted in stoneware, fine earthenware and china production. These developed in north Staffordshire as a result of improvements over a long period to the earthenwares made there in the seventeenth century. The impact at a national level is indicated in Figure 5.2, which illustrates the gradual diversification of the industry as a whole. For example, early stoneware may have been influenced by developments in London but later developments seem to have originated from this area. Thus, none of the tools associated with new wares has been found in the probate inventories of potters in other parts of the country. It is difficult to distinguish the scientific from the pragmatic in this industry; potteries developed their own formulae as a result of trial, error and handed-down wisdom. There are few examples of 'inventions', but developments were based on a growing body of practical knowledge about materials, processes and kilns.

Pottery was made (as it still is) in a series of stages in which materials were acquired, prepared, made into vessels, fired and decorated. That there were numerous processes was important, for modifications were necessary at several stages if a new kind of ware were to be made. The hotter ovens of stoneware firing, for example, necessitated different raw materials and restricted decorations to colours not destroyed by high temperatures.

It is well known that the earthenware industry depended on the clay resources of the coalfield area and there is fortunately a detailed description by Dr Plot of the clays used in the late 1670s.[5] New materials were gradually introduced, and changes in raw material supplies were essential to the new sectors and represented considerable commercial change, for ball clay, flint

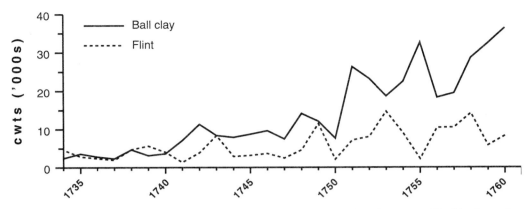

FIGURE 5.3 Flint and ball clay carried upstream on the river Weaver, 1733–60 (*Source*: Cheshire Record Office, Weaver Navigation, tonnage accounts. This is only one of three water-borne routes into the area and does not represent the total amount of ball clay and flint available).

and other materials were 'imported' into the area from places remote from north Staffordshire. White ball clay was known in London in the late seventeenth century and appears in documents in north Staffordshire by 1710. Until the 1750s it was used for decoration in relatively small amounts. Its importance was in enabling the bodies of some stoneware and fine earthenware to be made white. The bodies for fine earthenware and stoneware were similar by the 1760s with each pottery having its own formulae being established in the 1740s and 1750s. The extent of the imports of ball clay into north Staffordshire can be seen from Figure 5.3, which shows the amounts brought upstream on the river Weaver from 1733 to 1760. Flint was certainly in use in north Staffordshire before 1720 for it is referred to several times in documents around 1720. It was obtained from a variety of places along the south coast. However, it was difficult to prepare before flint milling under water, a process patented in 1732. Supply may have been erratic, the annual figures shown in Figure 5.3 certainly varying more than those for clay.

Clay preparation was an entirely manual process and mechanized methods (apart from flint milling) were not developed until later in the eighteenth century. It was washed and beaten to get the correct consistency; skill was needed at this stage to avoid disaster later; careful preparation was essential to make finer bodies, involving manual labour and attention over mixing and filtering. By the 1760s heated tanks were used for drying slip but improved control through indoors slip kilns was sought earlier for there are references by the 1720s in north Staffordshire to kilns for 'boiling' clay.

The vessels themselves were shaped from balls of prepared clay on a potter's wheel. Gradual modifications included regular turning on a lathe to make the surface smoother; potters' lathes were well known by the 1720s. There was more specialization and the thrower came to have assistants to 'tread the wheel', to ball the clay, and to remove boards of completed pots. Wheels improved, for they have a higher valuation in inventories after 1720. Large moulds for shaping wares or plaster of Paris have not been found in documents before 1760, but small amounts of ware were moulded into various shapes to make novelties or such things as spouts for teapots.

Firing was a crucial stage as much could go wrong at this point, and understanding of the process was essential. In making coarse earthenware the pots were fired only once, so glazing was done before any firing had taken place. In the seventeenth century ovens in north

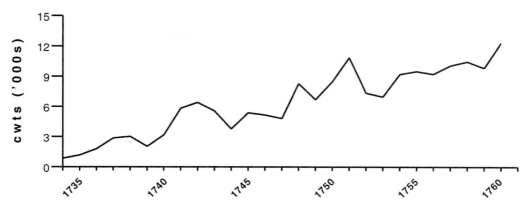

FIGURE 5.4 Cratesware carried downstream on the river Weaver, 1733–60 (*Source*: as for Fig 5.3. This is only one of three water-borne routes from the area and does not measure total production).

Staffordshire were circular and were quite small, up to 7 ft internal diameter, built of brick, tile and stone. Potters built their own ovens without following a clear plan, so improvements could be made spasmodically. Because stoneware and earthenware ovens were similar, the new sector could build on understanding gained in the older one, although stoneware required a hotter kiln, at 1100°C rather than 800°C. More care over the management of firing was necessary for stoneware and so 'hovels' were built to give greater control over draughts and temperature. The earliest documented example was in 1719–21 when a stoneware pottery was required to have the 'case' of the kiln 'nine yards in height'. From the late seventeenth century, saggars were used in the stoneware sector to protect fine wares although the earliest descriptions are to be found in the 1760s. A later development (from the 1740s) was that earthenware was fired twice, once called 'biscuit', the second 'glost'. This practice gave more control over the glaze and the decoration, and was essential in the production of fine earthenware.

Decoration had commercial importance because higher prices could be obtained for decorated wares. Coarse earthenware was not often decorated and decoration on stoneware was limited in scope. The possibility of painting on pottery was known in the main markets in London where painted delftware had been available from the seventeenth century and chinaware was painted. There was some blue painting on white stoneware and a little overglaze painting in the 1760s; attempts at decoration were made from the 1730s by using coloured clays to make mottled and tortoiseshell wares.

The significance of numerous technical changes can be seen in tracing the origins of stoneware and fine earthenware production. As far as the origin of stoneware production in north Staffordshire is concerned it seems that there were two lines of development, one associated with the London stoneware potter, John Dwight, the other the independent development of stoneware out of earthenware production in the late seventeenth century. There seems to have been a little interaction between the London and north Staffordshire potters. Fine earthenware derived from careful preparation of clays, the production of pale coloured bodies and double firing. It was the product of gradual technical change in the 1740s and 1750s, and was closely associated with stoneware. There is a powerful tradition in the literature that Wedgwood invented creamware and writers express surprise that he did not patent it. Whilst he made high quality products in the 1760s, these were based on many and numerous technical changes made by many unidentified potters over a long period of early industrialization, and even the high-class creamware itself was not an 'invention'.

In north Staffordshire the production of fine earthenware, stoneware and china was associated because the skills needed to make the new wares were also needed for china. The soft paste porcelain made in the mid-eighteenth century was fired at about 1000°C, similar to stoneware temperatures. The glazes and clays were also comparable. By the 1740s there was an incentive to produce china, and the two most successful concerns were in London, at Bow and Chelsea, both dating from about 1747. They were preceded by a number of earlier attempts in north Staffordshire, probably influenced by the London merchants, Weatherby and Crowther.

The expansion of the growth sectors in the 1740s and 1750s relied on technical change, although it was not due to any single 'invention'. Expansion also required suitably-financed potteries and an effective demand for new goods; it is to these commercial aspects that we now turn.

FINANCING EXPANSION

The industry was made up of a large number of relatively small producers and no single firm was ever dominant in north Staffordshire, although there were large-scale producers in London. There were clear differences between the semi-rural producers of the seventeenth century and the larger, more complex units of the 1760s. This section focuses on the commercial environment of early industrialization, and presents some scattered data on individual producers to show what capital was needed and what costs were incurred. Of particular note is that working capital was needed in order to allow credit to wholesale merchants in the distributive trades, and that the investment in fixed capital was relatively modest.[6] This, and the differences between potteries in different sectors, illustrate that notable commercial change occurred during early industrialization.

Table 5.1

Capital employed in a typical large coarseware pottery in the late seventeenth century

Items of capital		Amount (£)
Buildings:	workhouses	40
	oven	20
	other buildings	20
Tools and utensils		4
Stocks of materials		2
Stocks of ware		4
Debts due		10
Cash		?
Total		100

Source: The evidence comes largely from probate inventories and the values for the buildings were estimated from contemporary insurances: Weatherill, 'Growth of the pottery industry', 140.

Table 5.1 shows estimates of the capital employed in coarseware potteries in the seventeenth century. It draws on scattered data from probate inventories and other sources. Buildings are included in the fixed capital because it is unrealistic to leave them out as a workshop and an oven, which represented considerable investment, were essential. Working capital was probably more significant than the modest value suggested here because the value of stocks could vary. Yet even so, stocks of materials and ware were more valuable than the tools and utensils, and in some cases they were much larger than those shown in the table. For example, Thomas Daniel of Burslem (he probably made butter pots) had clay and materials valued at £14 in 1669. The same Thomas Daniel also had £14 in money and £15 owing to him. Credit may have been given to some customers, and so some allowance is needed for the debts due in the course of business. The table also shows that even the early potteries were not the kind of enterprise where raw materials were 'worked up' in living rooms but required some sort of workroom and an oven. There were wide variations in the amounts of farming undertaken by individual potters. In north Staffordshire potters normally had a few cows or pigs, and horses were common; in some cases there was no farming at all, as is shown in Table 5.2.

Table 5.2

Farming and pottery production in north Staffordshire, 1660–1760: evidence from probate inventories

| Location | Number of inventories indicating | | | |
	farming and pottery	limited farming	no farming	total
Burslem	3	6	3	12
Elsewhere in north Staffordshire	4	9	0	13
Total	7	15	3	25

Source: Weatherill, 'Growth of the pottery industry', appendix 2.

The capital needed by early stoneware potteries outside London is demonstrated in Table 5.3. They were notably larger than those in the coarse earthenware sector, which is interesting as the two were often closely associated. Some were even larger than suggested in the table: Joshua Astbury, for example, left tools and assets to the value of £132 in 1722, far more than any other contemporary pottery in north Staffordshire. In general, the higher valuations for tools, buildings and other fixed items are reflections of technical and commercial change. It is, however, the difference in working capital between the old and new sector that is most notable. Larger, more valuable stocks of materials are indicative of the need to acquire raw materials from a wider range of sources and to maintain supplies of appropriate mixtures of different clays and sand. Larger stocks of finished wares were also held in these potteries. There was also a need to cover the value of wares sent to dealers on credit, with a result that larger sums are listed as debts due. Credit of this kind is indicative that stoneware producers were already entering into a complex distribution network. Such was the importance of capital that some potters needed the support of a partnership in order to trade effectively, although there were also sole proprietors.

Stoneware potteries became larger as they made finer wares in the middle of the century. A good example of a pottery in the stoneware sector at this time is that of Peter Bagnall (Table 5.4), with other inventories, although not as detailed, revealing similar assets in the 1740s and 1750s. For example, the largest sum due in an inventory was to William Taylor (1736) at £300, with £332 for stock in hand; John Meir (1729) had £160 due and £60 in stock; and John Boulton (1737) £140 due and £30 in stock. Table 5.4 lists the values of Bagnall's fixed and working capital. It shows that the value of fixed capital was dominated by the buildings; tools

Table 5.3

Capital needed for an early stoneware pottery outside London in the early eighteenth century

Items of capital	Amount (£)
Buildings: workhouses	60
oven	30
drying rooms	10
others	30
Tools and utensils	20
Stocks of materials	15
Stocks of ware	50
Credit: debts due	25
Cash	25
Total	265

Source: Weatherill, 'Growth of the pottery industry', 150.

were all manual; and working capital comprised the stocks of made wares in the various warehouses and rooms in the house, together with the money owing to him. The debtors were dealers to whom sales had been made on credit, and therefore represent a considerable investment in the distribution of the finished articles. Twice as much was invested in this part of the business as was invested in fixed assets and buildings. The cash was needed for immediate expenditure, especially for wages normally paid weekly.

Table 5.4

Assets of a large stoneware pottery: Peter Bagnall, 1761

Items of capital	Amount (£)
Buildings	280
Tools and utensils	19
Stocks of materials	13
Stocks of wares	99
Debts due: good	393
doubtful	203
Cash	20
Total	1027

Sources: Lichfield Joint Record Office, Probate inventory of Peter Bagnall, April 1761. This is a very detailed inventory which suggests that he made wheel-thrown stoneware. The valuation of his property was made possible using figures from another document, the insurance of William Banks of Stoke on Trent, 1763, Guildhall Ms 11936, vol 150, no 204458. Banks made stoneware and the site became the Spode factory after 1776.

The commercial requirements for the production of fine earthenware are well documented by the business of John Baddeley, whose assets in 1761 are listed in Table 5.5. This concern illustrates that fine earthenware needed more buildings, for there were more processes, but that the value of equipment was no more than the stoneware potteries and relatively little other investment in fixed capital was demanded. However, large amounts of working capital were essential and Baddeley's book debts were normally about £3000 in the early 1760s. Baddeley's business was amongst the larger ones at this time but he was not unique: for example, Enoch Booth of Tunstall insured his buildings for £400 in 1756 and William Banks for £500 in 1763.

Table 5.5

Assets of a large fine earthenware pottery: John Baddeley, 1761

Items of capital	Amount (£)
Buildings	700
Equipment	38
Stock of material	6
Stock of ware: in pottery	21
in warehouse	48
Book debts	1200
Cash	?
Total	2013

Sources: Staffordshire Record Office, Inventory of the assets of John Baddeley of Shelton, 22 July 1761, D1788, 14(2). The values are likely to have been lower than usual because he was in some financial problem in 1761. The inventory does not value the buildings and estimates were made on the basis of valuations for insurance of William Banks (Table 5.4). The 'first cost' of the buildings was entered at £732 in accounts (D1788 v99) and the book debts were also recorded in the account books (D1788, v102).

Analysis of the costs of production and profitability requires detailed business records. These are not available before the 1770s, and in their place retrospective estimates have been calculated of the weekly costs of making earthenware and stoneware in the early eighteenth century (Tables 5.6 and 7). Both estimates show that labour accounted for the largest proportion of the costs, with raw materials and fuel next in importance. Labour cost has always been important in pottery manufacture and figures from the later eighteenth century suggest that it would form about 40 to 45 per cent of total costs. In the later eighteenth century materials varied from about 30 to 45 per cent depending on the quality of the ware made and the amount of fuel used. The cost of equipment and buildings was relatively low, at about 5 per cent, largely because other costs were incurred, such as packing and carriage. The absolute costs of making stoneware in the early to mid-eighteenth century were greater than those for making coarse earthenware, due to higher costs of firing and of raw materials. However, as stoneware could command better prices, it is likely that the resulting profit was larger, the more so if producers were also able to make any of the novelty wares that sold for enhanced prices. (Coarseware mugs were priced 1s to 2s 6d a dozen, flintware mugs 9s to 12s a dozen, and stoneware mugs 2s a dozen in late seventeenth-century lists.)

By the middle of the eighteenth century profits would seem to have fallen for stoneware, which may have been due to a market which favoured the new fine earthenware. Prices are notoriously hard to trace, but it seems that stoneware mugs sold at 2s a dozen with earthenware ones at 4s a dozen. Earthenware could also have value added through decoration, whereas stoneware was more difficult to decorate. In the 1750s and 1760s some stoneware firms moved to produce earthenware. There were no significant obstacles to this, the only change being a new oven, for the raw materials and skills were similar. An example is Thomas Wheildon. He

Table 5.6

Estimated weekly costs of production in a coarseware pottery in the early eighteenth century

Production items	Value (s)	Percentage of total
Clay	4	4.5
Glaze	14	15.7
Coal	14	15.7
Labour	46	51.7
Rent	2	2.3
Utensils and oven	4	4.5
Packing and sales expenses	1	1.1
Profit	4	4.5
Total	89	100

Source: Based on retrospective estimates undertaken by Josiah Wedgwood in 1776, printed in E Meteyard, *The life of Josiah Wedgwood*, 1865, i, 190.

began making stoneware at Fenton Low around 1740 but by 1750 he had leased his pottery to another potter (Edward Warburton, who continued to make stoneware into the 1760s). He moved to Fenton Vivian and excavation of the site suggests that he made earthenware with coloured glazes; his notebook has jottings about tortoiseshell and cream colour in 1749 and 1750.

MARKETS AND MARKETING

Who bought pottery and how was it sold to buyers? The answers are that it was sold to the 'middling' ranks in society and that it was sold increasingly through shops in the eighteenth century. Expansion was closely associated with demand from the middling ranks in society, whose incomes and lifestyles enabled them to own a growing range of goods in the pre-industrial period. Consumption by the poorest in society was not significant in the eighteenth century. Exports were not as important as the home market to the growth of the industry in

Table 5.7

Estimated weekly costs of production in a stoneware pottery in the early eighteenth century

Production items	Value (s)	Percentage of total
Clay	8	6.6
Glaze	7	5.8
Coal	30	24.8
Labour	52	43.0
Rent	4	3.3
Utensils and oven	10	8.3
Packing and sales expenses	4	3.3
Profit	6	4.9
Total	121	100

Source: As for Table 5.6

north Staffordshire before 1760, although some goods were exported. A network of shops and dealers developed from the early eighteenth century in order to distribute imported china from London to the provinces; this network was developed and extended later for selling stoneware and earthenware so that by 1760 there was a well-established network of wholesale dealers throughout Britain ready to buy new types of pottery.[7]

Tracing the demand for pottery necessitates documentation that refers to the people who owned it, or wanted to own it. There were many thousands of households throughout England and Scotland which have left few documents referring to the purchase or ownership of household goods. Probate inventories do give some indication of ownership, although coarse earthenware was probably not fully listed in many cases; finer wares and china were more likely to be noticed. Table 5.8 reveals that ownership of earthenware did increase so that it was listed in the goods of more than half of middling households by the 1720s. Plate 5.1 illustrates that the heavy pottery was not used as tableware, but for storage and serving; this mealtime scene also shows that pewter was more important as tableware, and continued to be so well beyond the middle of the eighteenth century. Even so there was a large potential demand for quite plain and functional pottery. There were, in addition, new uses for pottery with the increased use of tea from the end of the seventeenth century. At least a quarter of all middling households were already in the market for tea wares by the 1720s, as demonstrated by the evidence from inventories. Plate 5.2 portrays a well-off family drinking tea from imported china cups and illustrates the different context of the demand for the new, finer wares of all kinds. The new uses for earthenware and stoneware, and the influence of china, represented a large potential market if potteries could substitute their own wares for those imported from the Far East; once this was done they could also take advantage of the growing demand for decoration in the home in general and produce decorative plates and other utensils for eating. Changes to mealtimes and the demand for decorated dinner wares date from the 1750s, so the main stimulus to the industry from the demand side came from the use of the new drinks alongside other decorated items. Thus, there was a potential demand for the goods produced by the industry in north Staffordshire if they fulfilled the purchasers' requirements and could be sold in a convenient manner.

Table 5.8

Ownership of earthenware, china and utensils for hot drinks in a sample of middle-ranking households, 1675–1725

Date	No of inventories	Earthenware	China	Utensils for hot drinks
			percentage of total	
1675	520	27	0	0
1685	520	27	1	0
1695	497	34	2	1
1705	520	36	4	2
1715	455	47	8	7
1725	390	57	9	15

Source: The figures are derived from a sample of inventories in eight parts of England taken in the middle year of each decade. Probate inventories are unusual after about 1730 in most areas of the country, so they do not cover the expansion of the mid-eighteenth century: L Weatherill, *Consumer behaviour and material culture in Britain, 1660–1760*, 1988, tables 2.1 and 2.

PLATE 5.1 Grace before a meal, J Van Aken, *c* 1720 (Ashmolean Museum, Oxford). The picture provides a good impression of the uses of pottery in seventeenth-century households. There are heavy vessels on the cupboard and a few earthenware plates on the shelf. The table setting is simple and the vessels used are of pewter: pottery tablewares were not common until the end of the eighteenth century.

There was already a distribution network serving the industry in the seventeenth century and there was a subtle change from traditional sales in the seventeenth century to new methods in the eighteenth century. Direct sale to the consumer at potteries was limited, even in the seventeenth century, for potteries in north Staffordshire were distant from the main centres of population and consumption. Wares from north Staffordshire undoubtedly were sold outside the area through markets, fairs and itinerant tradesmen. Seventeenth-century Staffordshire earthenware has been found widely distributed in the midlands and northern England. Dr Plot (of the 1670s) reported sale '. . . is chiefly to the poor *Crate-men* who carry them at their *backs* all over the country . . .' However, the growth of the industry was not based on small-scale dealing of this kind, and it was the development of a network of middlemen dealing on a larger scale that provided the commercial environment for early industrialization. By the mid-eighteenth century it is possible to trace a complex network of wholesale and retail dealers centred largely, but not exclusively, on London. This network had several origins, such as the need to distribute chinaware imported in large amounts through London from the late

PLATE 5.2 Family at tea, R Collins, 1732 (Victoria and Albert Museum, London). The tea wares here were more lavish than those in most houses of middle rank, and few had such extensive collections of silver. The cups and saucers are typical of those imported from China, which inspired the development of new forms of pottery in the mid-eighteenth century.

seventeenth century. Shops that specialized in glass and earthenware date from the late seventeenth century. In 1691 the Glass-sellers Company claimed (with some exaggeration) that glass and earthenware was '. . . sold by shopkeepers in all Cittys, Townes and Corporate Market Townes and boroughs and allmost all villages in England . . .' There are a few probate inventories of shopkeepers.

By the mid-eighteenth century a wealth of references to individual dealers from producers' ledgers, advertisements, directories and other sources points to an extensive network. The references can be accumulated as evidence about the networks available to producers by the middle of the eighteenth century for distribution. The trade was focused on London: for example, after 1758 between a quarter and a half of John Wedgwood's sales were to London dealers. London was both a large concentration of consumers and an entrepôt for re-distribution of goods made in the provinces. Wholesale and retail techniques were probably pioneered by London chinamen: for example, their shops had a reputation as fashionable lounges, although they were not involved in earthenware and stoneware trades. There was a group of merchants who dealt in stoneware and earthenware from many different producers. For example, William Strapham of Thames Street received large amounts from John Wedgwood and John Baddeley in the 1750s. Just as no one producer dominated production, no one dealer dominated the distribution trades. There was also a large network of dealers in the provinces, although their businesses were on a smaller scale than the London ones, and many grocers and general dealers sold earthenware. There were numerous places with more than five dealers (Bristol, Newcastle, Liverpool, Hull, Manchester, Cambridge, Norwich and Bath) and a further 84 places with between one and four dealers, including the main urban centres. There were 482 dealers and purchasers recorded in miscellaneous sources before 1780. So there existed a well-developed network of sales outlets through which wares from north Staffordshire (and elsewhere) could be sold directly to the retail customer. Shops could display new items and markets could be established, especially in the larger towns, where these could be seen and desired.

From the point of view of producers, selling to dealers was clearly recognized by the time of the earliest surviving sales' ledgers dating from the 1750s. These give the impression of a well-established trade; the dealers wrote their orders with detailed comment about requirements, and manufacturers do not seem to have sent unsolicited orders. Potteries may have maintained contacts in person: for example, there is internal evidence in the sales' ledger of John Wedgwood that someone, possibly his brother, undertook infrequent journeys to collect money due and take new orders. The larger dealers probably visited north Staffordshire as early as 1760, although the best documented instances date from advertisements in the 1770s.

EARLY DEVELOPMENTS AND THE GROWTH OF THE CONURBATION

That the growth of the pottery trade and other industries in north Staffordshire had an impact on the area can be taken for granted, but what sort of impact?[8] Firstly, other industries associated with pottery were established. Flint milling dates from the 1720s, and by 1730 the entire production was in the hands of mills. They were frequently owned or leased to potters who did not work them themselves but employed a miller. John Baddeley, for example, had interests in several mills: in 1760 his total output was 25,318 pecks (each peck of 2 gall) of ground flint, of which he bought only 600 pecks for his own use. The mills were powered by water and were thus located along the streams of the coalfield area, some of them several miles from the producers. There was also an increase in the need for carriers to transport coal, flint, raw materials and various wares both within the area and to the head of navigation along the main water routes out of the midlands. The demand was met by the use of pack-horses belonging to carriers, farmers and the potters themselves, and the road improvements that allowed carts and waggons to be used occurred only after 1760. Specialist carriers in the area date from the 1690s and there are seven of their probate inventories before 1740. Probate inventories of farmers and other individuals in the district indicate that horse ownership was common. For example, William Coxton of Sneyd Green (1671/2) had three pack-saddles and three horses; he was a small moorland farmer. Over half the ground flint from Baddeley's mills was carried by two carriers.

Secondly, the early eighteenth century saw an increase in the variety of service occupations which provided for a population reliant on cash wages for part of their household income. These included trades like kettleman and leatherworker, butchers and bakers, general shops and tailors. The organization of a formal market in Burslem was arranged in 1760 when a body of trustees leased land on which to have a public building. On the other hand, agriculture became less important in the eighteenth century, as would be expected. In Burslem, for example, there were fewer animals on holdings, even in outlying hamlets.

Thirdly, population in the whole of the north Staffordshire area grew. For example, in Burslem there was a marked expansion in population from around 600 in the main settlement before 1675 to over 2000 by 1760, with the greatest increase in the twenty years from 1740, when the figure was about 1400. It seems likely that this growth was indigenous and not a result of net inward migration. Birth rates in Burslem and other manufacturing hamlets were high: in Burslem 40 per 1000, in Hanley 46 per 1000, and in Shelton, 42 per 1000. This pattern was common at this time in areas where industry was growing and was probably due to younger age at marriage and consequently more children per family.

REFERENCES

1. Public Record Office, C/6/404/24, Hammersley's deposition in a Chancery case about making stoneware.
2. This chapter is based on research carried out for Lorna Weatherill, *The pottery trade and north Staffordshire, 1660–1760*, Manchester, 1971; 'The growth of the pottery industry in England, 1660–1815', unpublished PhD thesis, London University, 1981 (a facsimile of which was published by Garland Publishing, New York, 1986); and *Consumer behaviour and material culture in Britain, 1660–1760*, 1988.
3. The sources include probate papers, directories, investigations of kiln sites, work done by collectors on various sites and wares, and estate papers: Lorna Weatherill, 'The growth of the pottery industry in England, 1660–1815: some new evidence and estimates', *Post-Medieval Archaeology*, 17, 1983, 15–46, and 'Growth of the pottery industry', appendix 1.
4. Weatherill, 'Growth of the pottery industry', chaps 2 and 8, and appendix 2 for probate inventories used, and *Pottery trade*, chaps 2 and 3.
5. R Plot, *The natural history of Staffordshire*, Oxford, 1686: he visited in the late 1670s.
6. No business records survive for any pottery before the 1740s so that statements have to be based on detail from scattered records, although some of these (such as inventories and insurance records) give good information: Lorna Weatherill, 'Capital and credit in the pottery industry before 1770', *Business History*, 26, 1982, 243–58.
7. Tracing shopkeepers and wholesalers relies on scattered evidence from sources like sales' ledgers, probate inventories, early directories and advertisements: Lorna Weatherill, 'The business of middleman in the English pottery trade before 1780', *Business History*, 28, 1986, 51–76, and 'Marketing English pottery in Scotland: a study in the inland trade', *Scottish Economic and Social History*, 2, 1982, 18–43.
8. Material for this section is taken from Weatherill, *Pottery trade*, chaps 8 and 9.

6. The Beginnings of Industrialization: Coal, Iron and Related Concerns

PETER LEAD

Although pottery manufacture was destined to dominate the economy, consciousness and image of the region, it was but one of a number of emerging industries in north Staffordshire in the seventeenth and eighteenth centuries. Similarly based on and benefitting from local natural resources, coal-mining and iron production were the chief rivals to pottery amongst these growing industrial enterprises. Both came to contribute significantly to the employment structure and settlement pattern, and to the industrial landscape and legacy of the conurbation. The purpose of this chapter is to outline the early development of these major components of the Potteries' economy.

COAL-MINING

During the last half of the seventeenth century there occurred a modest but sustained growth in the north Staffordshire coal industry. It appears that the stimulus for this was the relative high price of wood (dictated by the iron industry), which in turn drove saltmakers to start looking for an alternative fuel. Roger Wilbraham of Nantwich relates how salt was made in lead pans using wood as the sole fuel, until in 1632 'some fancifull persons, thought it would be more for their profit to boyle their salt in Iron Pannes . . . pretending [that] wood grew scarce.'[1] Such a move would also have helped the north Staffordshire iron industry, especially the forges at Keele and Knutton that specialized in pan forging.

During the Commonwealth there were several prospectors looking for coal in the Apedale-Talke-Kidsgrove areas, which all sit close to the border with Cheshire. They ranged from the small-scale prospector like the Mr Poole who looked without success in 'a little piece of land [that he owned] at Talke', to the regicide Major-General Thomas Harrison who clearly sponsored more extensive explorations in the Apedale valley which led to productive mines before 1660. These workings were in the same area in which Dr Plot inspected drift or 'footerill' mines around 1677.[2] In this period, the pottery industry must also have been influenced in its choice of fuel by the high cost of wood and blessed its close proximity to the Coal Measures. Coal also found a ready market with the nailors and other skilled metalworkers concentrated around Newcastle and Audley. Richard Parrott provides plentiful evidence of a thriving metalworking industry about Audley and various small-scale coal concerns. A more significant demand was that from the chafery and slitting forges of the local iron industry where coal was in use before 1693–4 at less than half the cost of charcoal. Coal production could be highly profitable as in the case of Thomas Poole (possibly a nailor of Talke) who drew '£800 clear profit' from his mine in 1674–5.[3]

There is much evidence to suggest that coal production during this time was largely seasonal and even then very much at the mercy of the weather. Bell pits were very prone to flooding as were any adit mines that were driven against the natural flow of the water. The removal of water using buckets or primitive pumps was expensive in terms of the labour employed, so it is not surprising to discover that the preferred method of drainage involved driving an adit (or sough) at a lower level than the workings. These sometimes served a surprisingly large area such as that driven in 1719 by order of Lord Parker from a point near Burslem church into his own adjacent workings. Another major drainage adit served the Fenton-Longton area by 1775 and various leases give evidence of others. Primitive pumps were also used and again Plot provides a description of one type, although he does not describe the water-engines that were quite widely used because of neglige running costs. Brindley erected such an engine in 1759 near Cheadle and the Cockshead colliery relied on another for the first fifteen years of its working life.[4]

The role of Sparrow and Parrott in the promotion of the Newcomen steam-engine is discussed below, but it is very probable that they inspired James Brindley to take an interest in early steam-engines. Brindley built the first local steam-engine to pump out Thomas Broade's mines at Fenton in 1756 and through perseverance got it to work satisfactorily, although it subsequently suffered because it was not properly maintained. Interestingly, it was the only one of his 'credited inventions' for which Brindley obtained a patent and this further indicates the financial backing provided by Broade, before the more lucrative canal business turned Brindley's mind from any further developments.[5]

Until about 1775, coal was normally conveyed either in pannier loads on pack-horses or in waggons where road conditions were more favourable. At first glance this would appear to be an enormous disadvantage, but it needs to be remembered that five out of the six pottery centres lie on the outcrop of the Upper Coal Measures and in most instances a supply of coal was never more than half-a-mile away. Stoke was the only one which did not enjoy this advantage, but it was close to the mines around Fenton in which many Stoke-based potters had shares. Even the opening of the Trent and Mersey Canal in 1777 did not encourage a large-scale migration of works to its banks. Stoke was the only one of the six centres that the canal ran through, although later branch canals and tramroads brought the others closer to the main system. Some potteries were established on the canal at Longport and Etruria and this enabled them to draw on the Harecastle mines. It now seems curious that the plan produced in 1758 (for what became the Trent and Mersey Canal) envisaged a canal from Longbridge (later Longport) towards the river Trent and the sea, but it did not embrace the idea of a northern link towards Liverpool. Then it was proposed to extend the canal into the southern end of the Harecastle Hill so that a partnership which comprised the Gilbert brothers, Hugh Henshall, Robert Williamson and John Brindley (younger brother to James) could work the various rich coal seams after the fashion pioneered at Worsley. As late as 1765 there were still heated discussions over the northern extension of this scheme, although by then it had been agreed that the line be projected towards Liverpool. When the Harecastle tunnel was complete coal was worked within the hill from lateral canals which drained the workings, helped to fill the canal and allowed the smooth outward movement of the coal.[6]

No satisfactory figures exist for total coal production in north Staffordshire before the 1850s, but it is clear from the number of pits sunk and from the known demands of the pottery industry that coal output was rising significantly between 1750 and 1840. In 1836, some 55,000 tons of coal and slack left the Potteries by canal, which can be equated with the annual output of two to three medium-sized local collieries. It is also known that some 67,500 tons of earthenware and china left the area in this same year. S H Beaver calculated that for every ton of clay goods produced between nine and twelve tons of coal needed to be burnt, so it could be suggested that the pottery industry alone accounted for between 607,500 and 810,000 tons of coal in that year. This takes no account of brick and tile production, lime-burning, use by steam-engines, domestic consumption or the demands of the iron industry after 1785; so it would not be unreasonable to suggest that total production was approaching 1 million tons by 1836.[7]

Significantly, the areas where mining was taking place did not alter a great deal within the passage of time, but the depths from which coal was being won increased at an amazing rate. When Jars, a French engineer, visited the Newcastle area in 1765 he saw a large number of mines, the deepest being 120 ft and the norm between 50 and 60 ft. This represented the working limit imposed by the limitations of water-engines and other less sophisticated pumping devices. The first Newcomen-style engines appeared at Dilhorne and Pooldole (Meir Heath) before 1786, the second of these engines being valued at £1300. Boulton and Watt later supplied engines for winding at Apedale and Cockshead collieries, plus pumping engines for Fenton Park and Cockshead. In all eleven engines are known to have been erected at collieries in the period 1790–9, with a further fifteen between 1800 and 1811. Depths of 300 ft were exceeded by 1810 due to the more widespread use of steam-engines. Thomas Smith writing in 1836 recorded workings at 2145 ft at Apedale, 975 ft at Kidsgrove, and 1038 ft at Longton, each figure representing a record for that section of the coalfield.[8]

Some of the earliest large-scale workings of coal were organized on behalf of the major local landowners like the Leveson-Gowers, Parkers, Sneyds, and Gresleys. They appear to have generally preferred to lease out the mines to operators perhaps taking a sixth of the sale price of the coal as rent. These operators varied from bands of three or four men working a single small pit to 'coalmasters'. This title covered a range of individuals, from the specialist with widespread interests over a number of counties like John Gilbert to Samuel Taylor who was a farmer and ran the Foxholes colliery, near Talke. Some coalmasters were no more than financiers with a controlling interest like John Sparrow, the Newcastle solicitor who was principal shareholder in the Cockshead colliery with at least two pottery manufacturers among his partners. By 1836 this particular colliery was being operated by a company of six Longton potters who were interested in making 'themselves independent of the fluctuating prices which have prevailed for some years past'. Other potters took an interest in pits which were literally on the factory doorstep. Sneyd colliery in Burslem supplied the Hole House Potworks with 'excellent coal [delivered by railroad] . . . at a rate but little exceeding that at the pits'.[9]

IRON

The seventeenth century was a period of great expansion in the north Staffordshire iron industry, although the less viable works had closed due to diminishing supplies of the cordwood needed to produce charcoal. Pig-iron production at both the Meir Heath and Lawton furnaces was extremely high and well above the national average for a furnace which stood at 310 tons per annum. Indeed, during an exceptional campaign in 1693–4, Meir Heath produced a staggering 1098 tons. By 1717, the national average stood at 340 tons per annum and this was exceeded by the three local furnaces. Madeley produced 400 tons, Lawton 600 tons and Meir Heath 600 tons, which collectively accounted for some 6.4 per cent of total national production.[10] This is a significant indicator of an important local industry which, if considered with all the linked trades, may well have been of greater value to the local community than the pottery industry in 1700.

The local iron industry did not specialize simply in pig-iron production for the furnaces also supplied local finery forges. Forges were generally located at some distance from furnaces due to the basic need for a reliable water-power site, although in some instances the availability of coal was also a factor. An indication of the capacity of these forges can be obtained from the production figures for Consall forge, which dealt with about 282 tons of pig iron during 1693–4 when Meir Heath furnace achieved its record production figure. Production was down to 150 tons of bar-iron in 1737 during the great depression in the industry, but rose again to 300 tons in 1750 due to the closure of other local forges. The forges at Abbots Bromley and Chartley each produced some 200 tons of bar-iron annually during this period, a figure that can be taken as representative for most local forges.[11]

The success of the local iron industry at this time can be attributed to the co-operative way in which the different units were operated. Sixteenth-century furnaces and forges had been erected in the area on a purely speculative basis encouraged by landowners keen to develop their estates but not to participate actively in the developments. The earl of Shrewsbury built a forge at Oakamoor for lease prior to 1572; but it was left to a more entrepreneurial tenant, Sir Francis Willoughby, to build a blast furnace there to complement the existing forge. The Shrewsbury estate received rent for the works, plus income from the sale of ironstone and cordwood. The potential income was very significant, especially when compared with the rents derived from subsistence farming, and this was a lesson not lost on the Leveson family of Trentham Hall. By 1580, their 'Trentham ironworks' (later called the Meir Heath furnace) were being leased to John Olcoatt of Talke, who also bought his ironstone and cordwood from the estate. The Sneyd family had a similar arrangement with John Smith to operate a furnace and forge on Knutton Heath.[12] In such ventures setting up or development costs lay with the tenant, who would where possible bring in family or neighbours as partners.

During the late seventeenth century more far-reaching and complex partnerships began to evolve, centred around Philip Foley and Obadiah Lane of Longton. In 1688–9, Meir Heath furnace, attached to Consall and Oakamoor forges and slitting mills, was operated by John Wheeler. These were linked to Chartley forge by 1692 and comprised the 'Moorland works'. In the same year, they were combined with the Bromley and Cannock forges, plus Rugeley slitting mill, to form the 'Staffordshire works', bringing William Cotton and partners into a wider partnership. To this was added in 1707–8 the so-called 'Cheshire works', controlled by Thomas and Edward Hall with their partner Daniel Cotton, to create a combine which stretched across Staffordshire and Cheshire and was capitalized at £13,500. This massive concern smelted local and Cumberland ores in their furnaces to make pig-iron, which was then sent to their forges to be refined into bar-iron. Most of this bar-iron was in turn sent to the slitting mills to produce rods, although at Street plating forge it was converted into salt pan plates, pans and saw-iron.[13]

Philip Riden has put forward a convincing case for the steady increase in the average output of British charcoal furnaces during the eighteenth century, but the north Staffordshire industry does not seem to have shared in this general growth.[14] Two new and independent furnaces came into production in the first two decades of the century. The Leek furnace was in the hands of William Fallowfield by 1727, when he took out a patent for 'melting down iron ore . . . and drawing the same into bar iron' using prepared peat instead of charcoal. The other furnace at Teanford (near Cheadle) was operating at the same time. Both furnaces fell victim to the depression of 1737–8, brought on by cheap imports of foreign pig-iron from Spain, Russia, Sweden and the American colonies where fuel was plentiful and inexpensive. English ironmasters were tied to their existing works, due to the inertia effect of their investment and the national shortage of timber. Faced with such unfavourable market conditions, many local ironmasters left-off operating their works, especially after 1737–8, when the full force of foreign competition was felt. Lawton furnace closed and never worked again, so in 1744 Thomas Adams (a close relative of the pottery family) agreed to 'take, farme & Rent ye old ffurnace at Lawton & convert it into a fflint mill'. Adams already operated coal-mines locally and this investment represented a keen awareness of the emerging raw materials needs of the pottery industry. As regards hopes for a revival in the iron industry it represented the loss of an important water-power site and this happened elsewhere, most notably at Consall forge.[15] Meir Heath and Madeley furnaces were able to survive longer by an increased involvement in the production of cast-iron.

By 1780 the iron industry in north Staffordshire had declined to near extinction and, as the water-power sites had been largely redeveloped for other uses, a new technology was needed as the basis for any renaissance of the industry. This came when the steam-engine was adapted to provide the blast for iron furnaces about 1766, and for many years it has been thought that the Partridge Nest ironworks (near Chesterton) represents an early local example of this new technology. Recent research has shown that these works were not erected until 1790, when the landowner, Sir Nigel Bowyer Gresley appears to have granted a lease to Thomas Kinnersley, a Newcastle banker, and his partner. Some six years earlier, Gresley had leased a site further down the Apedale valley (on the banks of his estate canal) to the Parker brothers, ironmasters of Tipton, to whom should be accorded the credit for reviving the local iron industry. As Gresley owned most of the local mines in Apedale, he also drew revenue from coal and ironstone production, in much the same way as the countess of Shrewsbury had done nearly two hundred years earlier. The developments on the adjacent estate did not go unobserved by the Sneyd family, and their estate agent put together a partnership which launched the Silverdale Iron Company in 1792. The close proximity of this new generation of works was not accidental as each stood close to outcropping coking coals and clayband ironstone.[16]

By 1839 the output of the seven furnaces then operating in north Staffordshire reached 18,200 tons and a major expansion was being planned to meet a new market. Thomas Kinnersley (son of the Newcastle banker) erected four furnaces at Kidsgrove and Earl Granville (a descendant of the Levesons of Trentham) erected three blast furnaces at Etruria. A local writer observed in 1842 that it was 'the recent demand for iron for railways, &c., [that] has given increased importance to the trade in the district'.[17] The North Staffordshire Railway Company's system was planned with connections to the works at Etruria, Silverdale and Apedale, thus linking them directly to markets in the north and midlands. This also enabled the wrought-iron industry to be established alongside the furnaces such as was done at Etruria in 1852.

ENGINEERING

North Staffordshire has never been noted for a large and thriving engineering industry, but it is now clear that the other main local industries did trigger developments in machine development and construction. There is clear evidence to show that Madeley furnace was involved in high quality casting by 1680, which almost certainly involved the casting of pipes and other components for man, horse and water-powered pumps for local collieries throughout the coalfield. This was also linked to a developing expertise among some local smiths or 'engineers' in the earliest sense of that term.

This group of smiths played a vital role in the manufacture and erection of Newcomen engines in north Wales, the Black Country and Tyneside in the period 1716–30. They were closely linked to Street forge, where the first iron boiler for a steam-engine was fabricated in 1716 as part of an order for a steam-engine for a mine at Whitehaven. This was built under licence from Thomas Newcomen by Stonier Parrott of Bignall Hill, at a time when even the Coalbrookdale Company had not yet begun its long involvement with the production of steam-engines. Writing in 1744, Desaguliers refers to 'the manner of joining together and riveting the Iron Plates of Mr. Parrott's Invention, which lasts much longer and costs five times less than the Copper-Boilers'. A description of this first boiler indicates that it had all the features of a prototype but overcame an early flaw in the Newcomen engine.[18]

Thomas Benson, described as 'engineer' of Newcastle-under-Lyme, has been noted for contributing the first piece of large machinery used in the pottery industry. He proposed that flint be ground in a wet state, so as to protect the operatives from the serious effects of silicosis. For his first patented mill in 1726, he proposed a type of edge runner mill, followed by grinding with two large iron balls each weighing 60 lb. The balls and the large iron vessel in which they ran were cast at Meir Heath furnace, but 'the abrasion of the iron among the flints . . . [was] . . . found injurious to the ware made with it'. Benson's solution to this problem was simple but effective: he replaced the iron vessel and balls with a stone pan and balls. This is of interest as it shows that practical men of the group frequently termed 'mill-wrights' addressed specific technological challenges with far reaching consequences for local industry.[19]

William Sherratt I who called himself a 'mill-wright' was in many ways as 'ingenious' as the well known James Brindley. One example of his work was the water-engine erected at Keele Hall in 1771 to pump water for the domestic system. He is also credited with finishing and bringing into operation Spode's engine (c 1776), which had been started by Joseph Hateley, who had himself patented a 'fire engine with boiler' in 1768. This marks Sherratt's first involvement with steam-engines, and later his son moved to Lancashire where he joined with James Bateman to form the partnership of Bateman and Sherratt. They are best known as the defendants in a legal action brought by the less than saintly Boulton and Watt, but their engines played a vital role in the development of the Lancashire cotton industry.[20]

Richard Trevithick spent some time in the Potteries area in 1804. One of his engines had been erected locally early in 1803, which justifies the view that north Staffordshire was one of the areas where the Trevithick engine was pioneered. Further engines were erected by William Heath, a local engineer with wide ranging interests and close connections with William Sherratt and Trevithick. Heath had a foundry in Hanley which in 1811 was producing a range of parts for steam-engines and mills, plus specialist machinery like 'Potters' printing presses'.[21] There were others like the Stone-based firm of Rangeley and Dixon, a partnership made up of an inventive engineer and a manufacturer of shoes who provided most of the capital. They produced patent 'roller pumps' after 1818, which could be powered by horses, water or steam. Not surprisingly, the partnership also manufactured small steam-engines which were complementary to their pumps. The premises that they occupied had previously been the home of the inventive genius, Robert Bill, whose first patent was for a washing machine and who at the end of his life was doing pioneering work with iron masts for ships.[22]

The interests of the educated landed class and the manufacturers of north Staffordshire were far reaching and often surprisingly varied. The committee of the Trent and Mersey Canal Company was talking about bridges of iron in 1768 and had a model built to demonstrate their potential. The same group of people were discussing the use of inclined planes in 1773, so it is hardly surprising to trace links between Thomas Gilbert and William Symington about the possibilities of steam haulage on canals.[23] In such an environment it seems less unlikely that Edward Massey from Newcastle should come up with a string of inventions including instruments for taking soundings at sea, chronometers, and 'apparatus for measuring the speed of vessels through water'. Even the Fourdrinier family, noted for their paper-making and -cutting machines, turned their attention to the problems of the coal industry. Mr Edward Newman Fourdrinier of Cheddleton paper-mill produced the first safety cage for use in winding which was installed at Sneyd Green colliery in February 1848.[24]

In the study of the industrial development of the Potteries, research interest has tended to focus on the enterprise and fortunes of pottery manufacture. Whilst understandable, this emphasis has served to eclipse the role, importance and scale of change in other local industries, and the influence of their associated entrepreneurs both inside and beyond north Staffordshire. The scope for research in these other industries of the Potteries is large, with the hope of eventually producing a more balanced perspective of the development of the north Staffordshire economy.

REFERENCES

1. J Hall, *A history of Nantwich*, Nantwich, 1883, 203.
2. R L Galloway, *Annals of coal mining and coal trade*, 1898, i, 193; J Ward, *The borough of Stoke-upon-Trent*, 1843, appendix lxvii; R Plot, *The natural history of Staffordshire*, Oxford 1686, 129–31.
3. S A H Burne, ed, 'Parrott's Audley survey, 1733' *Collections for a History of Staffordshire (SHC)*, 1944 vol, 1947, 1–74; B L C Johnson, 'The iron industry of Cheshire and Staffordshire: 1688–1712', *Trans N Staffs Field Club*, 88, 1953–4, 50–1; Galloway, *Annals of coal*, i, 193.
4. Ward, *Stoke*, 209; A D M Phillips, ed, 'A map of the county of Stafford by William Yates, 1775, *SHC*, 4th series, 12, 1984; Plot, *Staffordshire*, 148–9; P Lead, *Agents of revolution*, Keele, 1990, 58–9; Lady K E Farrar, ed, *Letters of Josiah Wedgwood*, Didsbury, 1973, ii, 435.
5. Ward, *Stoke*, 165–6.
6. Lead, *Agents*, 69–73.
7. Ward, *Stoke*, 389; *Staffordshire Advertiser*, 2 August 1828; S H Beaver and B J Turton, *The Potteries*, Sheffield, 1979, 33.
8. Galloway, *Annals of coal*, i, 334; P Lead and J R Robey, 'Steam power in north Staffordshire, 1750–1850', *Jnl Staffs Industrial Arch Soc*, 9, 1980, 16–17; J H Jackson, 'Notes on early mining in Staffordshire and Worcestershire', *Trans Institution Mining Engineers*, 27, 1903–4, 105; T Smith, *The miner's guide*, 1836, 92.
9. Lead, *Agents*, 113–37; W White, *Directory of Staffordshire*, Sheffield, 1851, 430–1; J Thomas, *The rise of the Staffordshire Potteries*, Bath, 1971, 72–3; Staffordshire Record Office (SRO), D239/M/3725; *Staffordshire Advertiser*, 2 August 1828 and 10 February 1816.
10. P Lead, 'The north Staffordshire iron industry, 1600–1800', *Jnl Hist Metallurgy Soc*, 11, 1977, 5–7.
11. Johnson, 'The iron industry', 49–52.
12. H A Chester, *The iron valley*, Cheadle, 1979, 29–34; SRO, D593/1/3/12; M W Greenslade, 'Longton: industries', in *Victoria County History of Staffordshire (VCH Staffs)*, 1963, viii, 244; P Lead, 'John Smith of Newcastle', *Staffordshire Magazine*, December 1972, 27.
13. Johnson, 'The iron industry', 33.
14. P Riden, 'The output of the British iron industry before 1870', *Econ Hist Rev*, second series, 30, 1977, 447–9.
15. Patent Office, Orpington, Patent no 490 (1727); *Gentleman's Magazine*, April 1731, 166–7; Lead, 'North Staffordshire iron', 7; P W L Adams, *A history of the Adams family of north Staffordshire*, 1914, 202–8; Stoke-on-Trent City Museum, John Wedgwood Papers, uncatalogued; SRO, D239/M/1217.
16. Lead, 'North Staffordshire iron', 10; B Hardman, 'The early history of the Silverdale Ironworks', *Jnl Staffs Industrial Arch Soc*, 3, 1972, 1–20; Beaver and Turton, *Potteries, 35.
17. A Birch, 'Iron and steel from 1750', in *VCH Staffs*, 1967, ii, 130; Ward, *Stoke*, 128.

18. M B Rowlands, 'Stonier Parrott and the Newcomen engine', *Trans Newcomen Society*, 41, 1968–9, 57; J S Allen, 'The 1715 and other Newcomen engines at Whitehaven', *Trans Newcomen Society*, 45, 1972–3, 251.
19. S Shaw, *History of the Staffordshire Potteries*, Hanley, 1829, 145.
20. Keele University, Sneyd Mss, S 1667; Lead and Robey, 'Steam power', 12; A E Musson and E Robinson, *Science and technology in the Industrial Revolution*, Manchester, 1969, 407–11.
21. P Lead and H S Torrens, 'The introduction of the Trevithick steam engine to north Staffordshire', *Jnl Trevithick Soc*, 8, 1981, 26–30.
22. *Staffordshire Advertiser*, 18 April and 26 December 1818; *Gentleman's Magazine*, November 1827, 466–8.
23. Lead, *Agents*, 40–1.
24. Information from Mr A A Treherne; Patent Office, Patent no 11,557 (1847); Galloway, *Annals of coal*, ii, 335.

7. The Development of Industrial Specialization

J H Y BRIGGS

Later urban development masks the upland farming heritage of north Staffordshire, but for most of its history agriculture has been the main occupation of the inhabitants of the area. The story of how farmers of north Staffordshire first began to make butter pots for use at Uttoxeter market has often been told. Whilst, however, in the seventeenth century it was normal for pottery manufacture to be combined with farming, that had ceased to be the case by the beginning of the eighteenth century.[1] Thus, while the towns of north Staffordshire continued and continue to service their surrounding hinterlands, providing for them an ever expanding population for which to produce, it was increasingly that which lay below the soil that was of greater importance for their developing economy. The two essential ingredients were clay and coal; their exploitation explains the prevailing shape of economic development in the area as is demonstrated by occupational statistics.

OCCUPATIONAL FOCUS

Occupational statistics are not reliably available until the 1840s but the censuses of the period 1841–61 clearly indicate the weight of the mature pottery industry within the economic enterprise of the area, and fully justify the region being designated 'the Potteries'. In this it is unique, for no other region of Britain today is titled by its industry, whereas in north Staffordshire the designations Stoke and the Potteries are virtually interchangeable.

In 1841 43.3 per cent of men and women in employment aged over 20 (the category that offers easiest comparisons with later figures) in Burslem and Wolstanton were working in the pottery industry and those enterprises which closely serviced its interests. The figure for the old parish of Stoke-upon-Trent was 38.2 per cent. The next most significant industry was mining with 10.5 and 6.1 per cent respectively. Much of this output was, moreover, devoted to the firing of the kilns of the pottery industry. In 1851, when more than 70 per cent of the 34,341 potters of England and Wales were employed in Staffordshire, the 4917 adult potters in Wolstanton and 8452 in Stoke-upon-Trent Poor Law Unions represented 33.4 and 40.2 per cent respectively of the workforce, with miners rising to 13.0 and 8.0 per cent. In 1861 the figures were 30.1 per cent for Wolstanton and 37.6 per cent for Stoke, with miners at 12.3 and 9.6 per cent.

Robert Baker, factory inspector, was concerned with investigating the pottery industry prior to the extension of the Factory Acts to discipline its productive energies in the early 1860s. His arithmetic is at times careless and his categories are approximate and doubtless include potters who lived outside the pottery towns themselves. His abstractions from the 1861 census are for all potters, including some aged 5–9 (434 males and 159 females), not as Baker himself believed all aged 5. Indeed, the pottery industry was conspicuous for the very large numbers of adolescents employed (in the age band 10–15, 2758 males and 1847 females); that is, prior to the extension of the Factory Acts to the potteries in 1864, 18.9 per cent of the workforce was aged under 15. Indeed, of pottery workers nationally aged under 20, almost 78 per cent were employed in the Potteries, though Baker was able to produce figures to show that the number of young employees was already falling, for children aged under 13 had been 5198 in 1861, but by 1864 had fallen by nearly a quarter to 3913. Whilst belatedly children were excluded from the pot-banks, no longer hidden by the deviousness of sub-contracting, the concentration of the pottery industry on north Staffordshire remained and developed.

HEAVY INDUSTRIES

Coal

The industries of north Staffordshire, for the most part direct products of the geology of the area, have thus from the earliest times linked together extractive and manufacturing processes. The inter-relationship of the two is to be seen in the take-over of technology pioneered in extraction at a later stage by manufacturing, the most notable example of which is the deployment of the steam-engine, initially developed to pump underground workings dry, then used to maintain the flow of water for water mills, and only thirdly directly applied to manufacture.

Extensive as had been the exploitation of the Coal Measures of north Staffordshire prior to the Industrial Revolution, the second half of the eighteenth century witnessed take-off to new levels of exploitation in each of these areas. Coke now outgrew charcoal as a fuel source in the production of iron, and this together with the expansion of the clay industries of the area, made heavy demands on the collier's skills and energies, for in the manufacture of pottery the ratio of coal to clay is of the order of twelve tons of coal to each ton of pottery fired. Moreover, the disadvantage of the region's lack of navigable rivers was now rectified by the cutting of canals that made Staffordshire 'the pivot of England's waterway system'.[2] Thus to the expanding urban economies of the midlands and north-west were added other users further afield.

Though not as fast to grow as south Staffordshire, development in the north of the county was considerable once the completion of the Trent and Mersey Canal in 1777 had brought the region fully into the orbit of the economic life of the nation. Population in north Staffordshire doubled between 1801 and 1841 during which period the growing utilization of the region's coal is attested by the increasing depth at which coal-getting took place. By the 1840s this was down to 2000 ft at Apedale, and this before the large-scale expansion of the iron industry in the area. As yet the output of the coalfield was to be measured in hundreds of thousands of tons, but by 1859 it was up to 2 million tons and five years later 3 million, much of the increase generated by the take-off of the local iron industry.

Mining in north Staffordshire was both difficult and perilous because of the steep-pitched and faulted nature of the coal seams, the threat of inundation from older now disused workings nearer the surface, and the large amount of gas found in many seams. All these hazards were made worse by the widespread deployment of the butty system which diffused responsibility underground and distanced senior management from day-to-day practice. The butty system was a form of sub-contracting whereby a collier with some entrepreneurial ambitions leased a pit or a coalface, and worked it to the best of his ability directly employing his own workforce so to do; his principal concern was, of course, maximum output and minimum cost in a world where profit margins were often narrow. In the late 1860s it became clear that proprietors could not evade their safety responsibilities by the use of buttymen, and an Act of 1872 required the employment of a qualified and certificated manager at every colliery, though aspects of the butty system still operated in north Staffordshire well into the twentieth century.

As the demand to extract at ever deeper levels increased so the hazards multiplied with the heightened difficulty of ventilation and winding. In the larger mines, coal-getting practice improved partly as a response to mining disaster, partly as a response to the educational encouragement of the local inspector of mines, Thomas Wynne, who sought to woo his district into better practice in the period 1852–88, and partly in terms of improving technology: winding, ventilation and haulage techniques were all improved. As early as 1880, W Y Craig in his presidential address to the North Staffordshire Institute of Mining and Mechanical Engineers argued that 'cost will not be lessened until hand labour is superseded by machinery in cutting'.[3] By 1909, the Florence Coal and Iron Company was securing nine-tenths of its output by mechanical cutting (Pl 7.1). Modest-scale mining, however, still continued even into post-nationalization years in small footrails or drift mines, which exploited those areas of shallow extraction adjacent to the outcropping of the Coal Measures.[4]

The hazards of the working collier's life – both economic and physical – lay behind the great strikes that are part of the history of the industry and of the unionization of labour. In both 1825 and 1844 north Staffordshire miners engaged in offensive strikes to better their conditions, but the prolonged strike of 1842–3 which flowed into the Plug Plot/chartist riots was the action of men made desperate by a depression of trade, which was also the cause of the 22-week long strike of 1883. The repeal of the Combination Acts in 1825 saw the beginnings of trade-union

PLATE 7.1 Florence pit, Longton, 1912 (Warrillow Collection, Keele University Library).

activity in the north Staffordshire pits but these were ephemeral and short-lived. The Miners' Association of Great Britain in 1844 secured 15,000 members within the county, but it too ran into difficulties in the 1850s, so that in 1869 a new beginning had to be made with the establishment of the North Staffordshire Miners' Federation, which early allied itself to a similar federation amongst the Lancashire miners. In the mid-1880s a new form of association was developed with the founding of the Midland Counties Federation which was largely based on Staffordshire, which in its turn became part of the Miners' Federation of Great Britain, but a large number of Staffordshire miners showed themselves reluctant to join.

By 1870 it was judged that 'Productive power in the [coal] industry had largely passed from the coalmaster as such to the ironmaster and still more to the ironmaking company'.[5] This meant that the vitality of the coalfield was directly dependent upon the health of the iron trade, accelerating as it found new and growing markets, but was equally vulnerable to the world depressions that the demand for iron faced from time to time. By the end of the nineteenth century, however, north Staffordshire was learning to release itself from this over-dependence upon a single usage and to seek a diversity of markets further afield, achieving a peak of production for the period before the First World War of a little short of 7 million tons per annum in 1907.

Iron and steel

The development of the north Staffordshire iron industry involved both aristocratic and gentry initiatives from Earl Granville (Pl 7.2), the Heathcotes and the Sneyds, together with initiatives from the new bourgeoisie through the labours of the Kinnersley, Heath, Williamson and Stanier

PLATE 7.2 Earl Granville's Shelton furnaces and collieries, *c* 1850 (Beaver Collection, Geography Department, Keele University).

families, all concerned to benefit from the new iron age ushered in by the growth of the railways. Parallel to the master potters, the ironmaster very often owned his own collieries, and in some cases the same shaft served both the extraction of ironstone and of coal, so that the two industries were in many cases indisseverably integrated. Robert Heath of Tunstall and Biddulph, who in 1880 was described as 'the largest private ironmaster in Great Britain', owned or leased at least a quarter of the whole north Staffordshire coalfield. By 1912, employing some 6000 hands, he was judged 'the largest producer of bar iron in the world', but by 1928 this mighty industrial empire, having failed in its attempts to produce mild steel at Norton, had collapsed and the receivers were called in.[6] The other forges and furnaces fared little better: Knutton forge closed in 1901 and Apedale in 1930. North Staffordshire ore was not at first amenable to the Bessemer process of steel production, but in 1888 Earl Granville's Shelton Iron, Steel and Coal Company began the manufacture of steel by the alternative Siemens-Martin open-hearth process.

CRAFT INDUSTRIES

The pottery industry was initially but one of the many craft industries of the area. These included a significant clock-making industry in Newcastle-under-Lyme where there had also developed strong interests in hatting linking it to the international fur trade, for beaver furs were then an essential ingredient for the hatter's trade. Brewing and sugar-refining further added to the town's economy, as did paper manufacture, especially as needed by the pottery industry.

Both silk and cotton were manufactured in the region from the end of the eighteenth century but north Staffordshire was not destined to rival the stronger adjacent counties of Lancashire, Cheshire and Derbyshire. The neighbouring town of Leek, however, was not alone in continuing to be essentially a textile town with an emphasis on the manufacture of narrow-weave silks, silk threads and on dyeing and colour-printing. Throughout the nineteenth century this was only partially a factory-based industry with the characteristic weavers' garrets supplementing more centralized manufacture.

Sir Thomas Wardle (1830–1909), friend of William Morris, Leek manufacturer, and for many years the leading world authority on silk manufacture, was the prime mover in establishing the Silk Association of Great Britain, over which he presided from its foundation in 1887 until his death in 1909. His wife was the founder in 1874 of the Leek School of Embroidery, which applied the highest possible design standards to the production of silk embroideries. At a more brutal level fustian-cutting continued in the area until within living memory. All these enterprises came to depend upon steam power fuelled by Potteries' coal.

THE POTTERY INDUSTRY

An older historiography, following Samuel Smiles, made Josiah Wedgwood, and his establishment of the Etruria factory in 1769, almost exclusively the agent of modernization in the pottery industry. More recent scholarship challenges that judgment as both too late and too early: too late in that from the beginning of the eighteenth century there were significant breakthroughs in both the technology of the industry and its ability to exploit both national and international markets; too early in that what Wedgwood achieved in 1769 was factory-manufacture but not mechanized production. Although much of the preparation of raw materials, such as flint-grinding, was mechanized early, with steam filter-presses following by the mid-nineteenth century, the mechanization of the process of flat and hollow-ware formation in Staffordshire only effectively came a hundred years or more after the founding of the Etruria factory.

The Flaxman monument to Wedgwood to be found in the chancel of St Peter's Church, Stoke, focuses the legend concerning the great entrepreneur, of whom it boasts 'He converted a rude and inconsiderable manufacture into an elegant art and an important part of national commerce.' But this does less than justice to his predecessors. At the end of the seventeenth century, the Elers brothers at Bradwell Wood produced expertly-turned vessels in unglazed redware which were particularly finely cast and turned, and then decorated with remarkably crisp sprigging in the style of contemporary silver articles.

Apprenticeship indentures, probate inventories, stock records, tonnage and port books, together with archaeological evidence, all indicate that at least by the time of Thomas Wedgwood, Josiah's uncle, a fairly sophisticated industry was in existence. The notion of crude and casual peasant production fits ill with the 28 sizes of porringer and the 25 varieties of teapot manufactured by the Big House Wedgwoods a generation before the opening of the Etruria factory.[7] Wedgwood was, however, important, in applying comprehensive logistical thought to the pottery trade: the Etruria factory was rationally set out on the banks of the Trent and Mersey Canal and the principle of the division of labour was remorselessly applied to the potters' art to improve the quality of the ware. The old general labourer increasingly gave way to a series of specialists, now deliberately trained to fulfil one task and one task only, but to execute it to perfection. A rigorous and determined factory discipline was to be the secret to the reliable production of an improved product: Wedgwood set himself the paradoxical task of both seeking 'to make artists of mere men', and 'to make such machines of men as cannot err'.[8]

A pioneer in the genesis of modern management,[9] he wedded together the insights of cost accountancy to market analysis. This was why commissions from the crowned heads and aristocracies of Europe were so important, for such patronage, effectively exploited through exhibitions and the like, opened up the markets of the whole continent and beyond; hence the importance of the commissions that were secured from Queen Charlotte at home – the patronage that gave authority for the rechristening of creamware as 'Queensware' in 1765 – and Catherine the Great abroad. The extent of overseas sales is clearly seen in the depression with associated bankruptcies that occurred in north Staffordshire as a result of the French wars at the end of the eighteenth and the beginning of the nineteenth centuries.

At the same time Wedgwood was adept at exploiting the North American market by encouraging it to purchase goods which had ceased to be fashionable in western Europe, and in London even opened a 'Seconds Shop' to good effect. Moreover, Wedgwood was working at that period when the popularization of hot beverages vastly increased the demand for economical ceramic wares. Prices were partly determined by what the market would bear, partly by Wedgwood's own close analysis of material and labour costs which provided a base line below which he could not sell profitably, but for the most part his profit margins were high.

Masons, who came to dominate the ironstone business, promoted their sales by the technique of auction sales which not only conveniently excluded the role of the retailer, but gave a seeming appearance of the stock coming from several sources, whereas in fact it was all factory supplied. Exposure in *The Times* in May 1828 brough this questionable procedure to an end.[10]

Wedgwood, himself, was content to work in earthenware, especially Queensware, his black basalt, and his jasper unglazed stonewares which displayed matt decoration with a superlative crispness of definition. Others sought by experiment with hard and soft-paste porcelains to imitate the imported wares from the Far East. Indeed, a manufacturer like Miles Mason

PLATE 7.3 Church Street, Stoke-upon-Trent, 1819, showing two of the manufactories of William Adams and Sons (Beaver Collection, Geography Department, Keele University).

(1752–1822) is first encountered as a London 'chinaman', that is to say an importer of china, before establishing himself as an earthenware and porcelain manufacturer in Fenton. Experiments in the manufacture of porcelain, that is to say a ceramic product with a translucent body as against the opaqueness of earthenware, had been made from the middle of the eighteenth century and before, both in Newcastle-under-Lyme and at Longton Hall,[11] though neither venture seems to have proved a commercial proposition. Josiah Spode, however, set the distinctiveness of British manufacture with his invention of bone china, the hybrid porcelain that came to dominate fine china production in Britain.

Innovative ingenuity tended to move from firm to firm, many of which continued to operate within the confines of the extended family, though sometimes with a sleeping financial partner. However, with Josiah II's involvement in political affairs, and the gentrification of other Wedgwood offspring, after the death of the first Josiah, Wedgwoods tended to over-rely upon the achievements of the first period. Indeed, it was not until Emile Lessore, one of a considerable group of designer-artists attracted to Staffordshire from the continent, began to design for Wedgwoods in the early 1860s that the firm began again to take a lead in the artistic development of the pottery industry, belatedly turning to the manufacture of bone china in the last quarter of the century (after a brief unsuccessful exploration of the medium earlier).

Meanwhile, standards of excellence in fine-china manufacture had been set by others: Spode-Copelands, Mintons, Davenports and the Ridgway brothers. Whilst useful ware was made in parallel in china or earthenware, and what now would be advertised as 'oven-to-table' ironstone, the effectiveness of ceramic statuary was much enhanced by the introduction of parian by Copelands about 1845, which was used to produce figures which offered an accurate marble-like finish very different from the earthenware flatbacks that were produced in abundance, a much more primitive form of folk art.

A little later Leon Arnoux, art director at Mintons, introduced a wide range of highly-coloured glazes used to produce decorative wares commonly called 'majolica'. From the 1860s fashion moved on to favour the 'art pottery', first produced by the Doulton Company in their London studio and later taken up by Minton, William Moorcroft and other Staffordshire manufacturers who at the turn of the century turned to *art nouveau* designs with considerable relish, especially by deploying tube-lined slip decoration to define the characteristic *art nouveau* shapes which were then in-filled with coloured glazes. At the same time *flambé* red and lustre decorations became popular.

There is a Whiggish form of history of the pottery industry that concentrates on the long-lived high-quality manufacturers of that prestigious tableware that has become the staple of collectors' interests: Wedgwood and Spode, Minton and Davenport, Masons and Doultons. Even at this level the list of firms need expanding to include the Woods and the Adams of the north of the city, the Turners of Lane End, the Alcocks of Cobridge, the Daniels of Stoke, the Ridgways and their successors, Brown-Westhead, Moore and Co, of Cauldon Place, whilst Aynsley, Shelley, Wild and Wildeman all produced quality ware at the southern end of the city (Pls 7.3 and 4). But this concentration ignores the vast number of partnerships, many of them highly unstable, that produced the day-to-day pottery used by the ordinary people of Britain in vast quantities, often under rather less desirable industrial conditions, and sometimes shamelessly plagiarizing the designs of the industry's leading companies. For all such considerations, such firms made up a very large part of the total economic enterprise of the area. There were good profits to be made in this more modest trade as was demonstrated by the two Meakin partnerships (Alfred, and J and G), Grindleys, and Johnson who specialized in cheap earthenware known as granite ware much of which was exported to North America so that these firms were called 'The Big American Four'.[12]

Decoration by transfer print had been undertaken since the mid-eighteenth century; initially the potters used either bats of glue or gelatine on glazed ware but more frequently printed

PLATE 7.4 East front of the manufactory of Enoch Wood and Sons, Burslem (J Ward, *The borough of Stoke-upon-Trent*, 1843).

papers to transfer the image underglaze. Something like the older bat-printing technique, with its advantages in speed, has in the second half of the twentieth century returned into use. By the 1840s the technology of multi-coloured printing was also available but it was not immediately successful, and awaited the successful development of a backing paper to strengthen the tissue. At the same time it remained common practice to infill outline prints by hand well on into the twentieth-century.

From the time of the Elers, ceramic ware had been cast in moulds as well as being thown upon the wheel, and clearly asymmetrical designs and complicated shapes required such a technique. Flat and hollow ware of various shapes as well as smaller articles such as decorated sprigs were also hand-pressed into moulds, whilst cup handles were extruded using a primitive machine for this purpose. From the 1870s semi-automatic hand-operated mechanical jiggers and jolleys which formed flatware or shallow dishes to the shape of a rotating mould became widespread. In addition in 1885 William Boulton exhibited a cup-making machine at the Paris Exhibition capable of producing sixteen cups a minute though this was not immediately used in the Potteries.

The other major area ripe for major technological improvement was that of firing in which Josiah Wedgwood with his pyro-technic experiments had invested considerable energy. Until the twentieth century all potters' kilns, with their characteristic shape giving a special rhythm to the townscape of the pottery towns, had been of the intermittent variety. Debates were held as to the relative merits of down-draught and up-draught technologies but all were coal-fired and all had to be packed, fired, allowed to cool and unloaded, a process both dirty and uneconomic

PLATE 7.5 Firing the kiln, *c* 1910 (Warrillow Collection, Keele University Library).

(Pl 7.5). In the twentieth century two great changes have occurred; first, the move to the continuously fired tunnel kiln through which the ware passed on trucks on a metal railway without the need to diminish the temperature in the oven; and secondly the application of other fuel sources than coal, giving both greater efficiency and greater control. The first Dessler gas-fired tunnel kiln to be deployed in Stoke was that installed at Barratt's tile works in 1912. The benefit was not only to the manufacturer, for it was the development of the tunnel kiln which provided the technological foundation for radical improvement of the hitherto horrendous pollution of the atmosphere caused by the industry.

Firms like Twyfords, but also Doultons, served the interests of a more healthy society from the 1850s onwards by the manufacture of sanitary ware in glazed earthenware. A communicating and power-hungry society also brought business to the pottery industry in the form of porcelain insulators and fittings manufactured in bulk from the last third of the nineteenth century onwards; earlier various fittings had been made for a newly-mechanized textile industry. Other firms found profits in producing such articles as artists palettes, door furniture, and chemical porcelain. The pottery industry itself consumed much of the product of the fire-clay industry in saggers and kiln-linings, but the hearths of the homes of England also provided an expanding market for this more specialized division of the industry. More trivially, even a firm of the stature of Mintons found it profitable to devote part of its resources to the production of ceramic buttons, the technique for which became most important in the way it was deployed to revolutionize tile manufacture.

Other clay industries developed local resources in the manufacture of bricks, especially the Staffordshire blue bricks used for paving and for viaduct construction because of the strength and durability secured by the high temperatures at which they were fired. Similarly tileries were of considerable importance and produced tiles of all different types from clay roof tiles, of which Downing and Co became the largest manufacturers in the country, to floor quarries and glazed wall tiles. Of particular interest were Minton's encaustic tiles produced to the designs of A W N Pugin, which by mechanical means reproduced tiles to medieval designs using the plastic clay pressing technique invented by Samuel Wright in 1830. Used to ornament the new Palace of Westminster when it was rebuilt in 1851, Minton's tiles came to be used for prestige buildings all over the world. As early as 1840 Richard Prosser developed a dry-press technology for making tiles, which, developed in the twentieth century, made for efficiencies in firing since large quantities of water had no longer to be removed in the drying and firing processes.

Wedgwood was intent on creating a new kind of labour force for his industry: 'to make such machines of men as cannot err'. Coupled with that high demand went the offer of the best that paternalistic entrepreneurial management could offer: improved housing, education for both themselves and their children, some form of health-care so important to an industry where silica dust in the atmosphere competed with the lead content of glazes in their noxious impact upon workers' mortality. But it was still paternalism. Whilst some were happy to accept its improvements, others challenged it with class protest, perhaps less thoughtfully by continuing the traditions of St Mondays and the various pottery wakes that always seemed to threaten the employers' profits, or more intelligently in the formation of trade unions.

The first potters' union emerged in 1824 campaigning against abuses such as payment in truck, reductions in piece-work prices, payment limited to 'good from oven' ware as against the working potters' demands for a more just 'good from hand', but its organization does not seem to have been adequate to the task. The union was resurrected in 1830, adding the problems of Martinmas hirings (which committed an employee to an employer for a year, even though no

PLATE 7.6 Pottery packers, *c* 1910 (Warrillow Collection, Keele University Library).

work was provided) to their list of grievances. The manufacturers seemed to have over-reacted and polarization of interests followed leading into the great strike and lock-out of 1836–7 which focused on the two issues of 'annual hirings' and 'good from oven'. But again the union was not strong enough for the united strength of the employers supported by the officers of the law.

In the early 1840s the dominant influence was that of chartism leading to the violence of the Plug Plot riots of 1842 with the ensuing sentences of so many rioters, including 54 potters and miners sentenced to transportation. In 1843 trade unionism re-emerged with the establishment of the United Branches of Operative Potters organized by William Evans. Fears of mechanization in the pot-making process within the industry led to the launching of Evans' pet emigration scheme to establish a new world of working-class freedom in Pottersville in Wisconsin, where the emigrants would not compete with their brethren by establishing rival potteries, but rather attempt to create a market by setting themselves to work as agriculturalists.[13] This was no more successful than the earlier union activity, but unions did survive in the separate pottery trades and in the 1850s learnt to prosecute their interests through arbitration procedures.

In the 1870s the labour force had to confront a general depression of trade, the gradual withdrawal of children from the industry after the extension of the Factory Acts to the potteries in 1864, and the increasing use of mechanical jiggers and jollies then occurring. At the same time, the pottery unions, not amalgamated until 1906, had to contend with the high percentage of women employed in the industry – some 50 per cent of the total workforce at the end of the century – who did not generally become a unionized workforce until the First World War.

Moreover, if unions faced a formidable task in the large factories, their difficulties in the small pot-banks, which came and went throughout the century with little coherence or stability, was far greater.

The pottery industry does not stand alone. Its dependence on local fuel stocks has properly been emphasized and in the nineteenth century many a master potter owned his own colliery so that there developed an integrated linear relationship between pit and pot-bank. The industry also provoked a wide array of dependent manufactures: the early crate manufacturers, sagger-makers, manufacturers of kiln furniture, the flint grinders who early set up their mills on the fast-flowing streams of north Staffordshire, the proprietors of bone mills, and the skilled kiln builders whose skills dominated the Stoke-on-Trent skyline for two centuries (Pl 7.6). Pottery decoration required the skills of colour-making, with its critical mineral demands, the generation of the specialized transfer papers so crucial to pottery decoration, and borax production which made the Coghill family wealthy and the manufacture of pottery less hazardous as the use of borax helped to secure the phasing out of the more dangerous lead glazes. Beyond all this, increasingly important were the pottery engineers and manufacturers of pottery equipment like William Boulton, whom Arnold Bennett called that 'lone and wonderful genius', and later the Wengers who had come to the Potteries from their native Switzerland, as the industry, albeit slowly, became more mechanized.

As early as 1775 Wedgwood had sought to persuade his fellow potters to work together in a primitive research association, though he himself was active in both the Lunar Society and more locally in the Potteries Philosophical Society. If the pottery industry at its best requires an amalgamation of the skills of both the scientist and the artist, then Wedgwood's desire for a school of design for the industry also needs to be noted. In fact this first found institutional shape in the Potteries School of Design established in 1847. With the establishment of the Wedgwood Institute (1863–9) the opportunity to promote both skills came into being. At the beginning of this century a Council for the Extension of Higher Education in north Staffordshire was established and a site near to Stoke station provided, on which colleges of Science and Technology, Ceramics and Arts were established which subsequently came together in the North Staffordshire Polytechnic which in 1992 became Staffordshire University.

In 1900 the forerunner of the British Ceramic Society came into being with its meetings and *Transactions* promoting and promulgating research. The refractory side of the industry formalized its research commitment in the founding of the British Refractories Research Association in 1920, with the industry-wide British Pottery Research Association following in 1937. The two bodies amalgamated in 1948 as the British Ceramic Research Association, institutionalizing the research function which had been present in the industry since the seventeenth century in the curiosity of the early potters and their usage of a separate kiln for the firing of experimental wares.

REFERENCES

1. Lorna Weatherill, *The pottery trade and north Staffordshire, 1660–1760*, Manchester, 1971, 71.
2. A J Taylor, 'Coal', in *Victoria County History of Staffordshire*, 1967, ii, 74.
3. Ibid, 90.
4. J I Jones, 'Licensed coal-mining in north Staffordshire', *N Staffs Jnl Fld Stud*, 9, 1969, 74–91.
5. Taylor, 'Coal', 81.
6. D J Jeremy, ed, *The dictionary of business biography*, 1985, iii, 142–8; W E Merritt, 'The north Staffordshire coal and iron district', *Colliery Guardian*, 19 March 1880.

7. Weatherill, *Pottery trade*, xviii; A Mountford, 'Thomas Wedgwood and Jonah Malkin, potters of Burslem', unpublished MA thesis, Keele University, 1972.
8. N McKendrick, 'Josiah Wedgwood and factory discipline', *Hist Jnl*, 4, 1961, 34 and 46.
9. S Pollard, *The genesis of modern management*, 1965, *passim*.
10. R G Haggar, *The Masons of Lane Delph and the origins of Mason's patent ironstone*, 1952.
11. P J Bemrose, 'Newcastle-under-Lyme: its contribution to the growth of the north Staffordshire pottery industry', unpublished MA thesis, Keele University, 1972; B Watney, *Longton Hall porcelain*, 1957.
12. J C Wedgwood, *Staffordshire pottery and its history*, nd, 194–5.
13. F Thistlethwaite, 'The Atlantic migration of the pottery industry', *Econ Hist Rev*, second series, 11, 1958, 264–78; H Owen, *The Staffordshire potter*, 1901; G Foreman, 'The settlement of English potters in Wisconsin', *Wisconsin Magazine of History*, 21, 1937–8, 375–96, and 'English settlers in Illinois', *Jnl Illinois State Hist Soc*, 34, 1941, 303–33.

8. The Growth of the Conurbation

A D M PHILLIPS

While the pace of economic activity quickened in eighteenth-century north Staffordshire, its impact on the pattern of settlement was limited. At the beginning of the final quarter of that century, William Yates' map, the first decisive step in the accurate recording of topographical detail in the county, revealed the market town of Newcastle-under-Lyme to be the major, if small, settlement concentration in the area (Pl 11.1). Just over a century later, the Ordnance Survey on its third edition 1 inch to the mile sheets identified a dramatic change in settlement. There had occurred a marked expansion in the built-up area, partly around the existing nucleus of Newcastle, but more significantly in the string of centres to its east, the pottery towns from north to south of Tunstall, Burslem, Hanley, Stoke-on-Trent, Fenton and Longton. Characterized by extensive areas of continuous development to the point of near total physical linkage, these six centres with Newcastle at the end of the nineteenth century dominated the settlement pattern of north Staffordshire and provided clearly the basis of a Potteries conurbation.[1] Comparison of these two surveys serves to emphasize the scale of expansion of the built area of the Potteries in the nineteenth century and the distinctive form of its growth through the gradual fusing not only of seven separate, although spatially close, centres but also of towns both ancient and newly-created by industrialization (Fig 8.1). This chapter, through an analysis of demographic change, housing provision and spatial development, seeks to detail the manner and process of this transformation in settlement pattern.

However, tracing the spread of Newcastle and the emerging pottery towns during the nineteenth century presents difficulties both in definition and in data. In 1800 the seven centres lay within three large, ancient parishes – Stoke-upon-Trent, Wolstanton and Trentham (Fig 9.1) – that ranged over some 37,190 acres. This area was largely agricultural land and remained so throughout the period. With the exception of Newcastle, a long-established borough, distinguishing rural from incipient urban locations in the census records for those parishes proves both problematic and arbitrary. In an attempt to reduce the rural component particularly in the early part of the century, the present study has concentrated not on the three ancient parishes but on a smaller area, that delineated on Thomas Hargreaves' map of the Staffordshire Potteries and Newcastle published in 1832 at the scale of 6.6 inches to the mile. Based on a detailed trigonometrical survey, this the first comprehensive large-scale cartographic representation of the urban and industrial development of the region was admired and appreciated by contemporaries.[2] The area depicted on the map amounts to 21,870 acres, and includes in Wolstanton parish the townships of Tunstall and of Wolstanton; in Burslem parish the township of Burslem with Sneyd and Rushton Grange, and the lordship of Abbey Hulton; the borough of Newcastle-under-Lyme; in Stoke-upon-Trent parish the townships of Penkhull and Boothen, of Hanley and Shelton, of Longton and Lane End, of Fenton Vivian and Fenton Culvert, of Botteslow, of part of Bucknall, and of Clayton and Seabridge; and finally the six

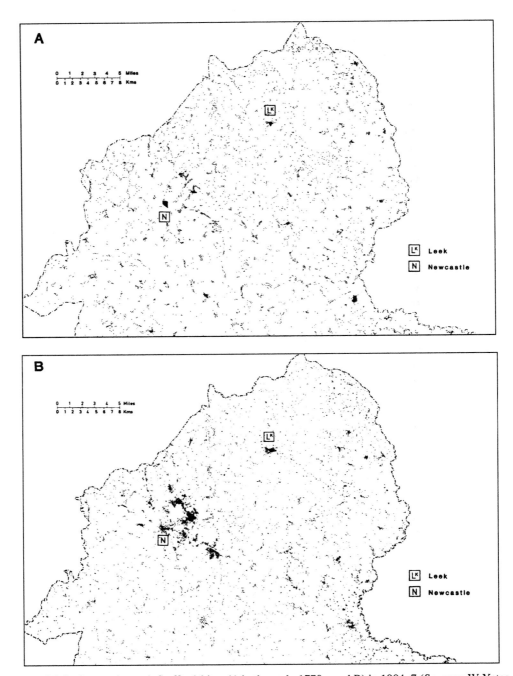

FIGURE 8.1 Settlement in north Staffordshire: A) in the early 1770s; and B) in 1904–7 (*Sources*: W Yates, *A map of the county of Stafford*, 1775; Ordnance Survey, *Third edition 1 inch to the mile large sheets*, nos 45, 52–4, 61–3, 71–2, Southampton, 1904–7).

townships of Trentham parish (Fig 8.3). With the exception of Longton and Lane End, the combined area of which was extended by some thousand acres in the 1880s largely at the expense of Blurton township in Trentham, the extent of these townships was but little modified at the end of the century: Tunstall township was transformed into Tunstall Urban District, that of Burslem with Sneyd and Rushton Grange into Burslem Municipal Borough, those of Hanley and Shelton into Hanley County Borough, those of Penkhull with Boothen into Stoke-on-Trent Municipal Borough, those of the two Fentons into Fenton Urban District, those of Longton and Lane End into Longton Municipal Borough, with Newcastle remaining as a municipal borough. Hargreaves' pioneering map, therefore, encompasses the major arena in which urban development in the conurbation took place in the nineteenth century, and at its detailed scale permits direct comparison with the later 6 and 25 inch series of the Ordnance Survey.

POPULATION CHANGE

Within this designated area, total population expanded rapidly from 30,053 in 1801 to 244,315 in 1901, a rate of increase – 813 per cent – that was twice that for England and Wales and of the same order as overall urban growth in the country (Fig 8.2). If, instead of being dispersed over a number of locations, this population had been focused on a single centre, the Potteries at the end of the nineteenth century would have ranked as one of the top ten conurbations of the country. Although growth was continuous in the area over the century, it was far from even. Thus, increase was more marked in the earlier part of the century, with the average decadal rate of growth of 23 per cent being exceeded or equalled in the first five decades. Between 1851 and 1881, the growth rate was relatively uniform, at just below the decadal average, while over the last twenty years of the century it declined, being no more than 13 per cent in the period 1891–1901.

The components of population increase in the area fluctuated over the century in response to changing economic and social conditions. Weatherill has emphasized the dominance of natural increase over net in-migration to account for expansion in the late eighteenth century, buoyant and rising birth rates stemming from reduction in the age of marriage in an environment of early industrialization more than offsetting the high but stable death rates associated with advancing urbanization. In the first part of the nineteenth century, while natural increase maintained its importance, the developing economic base of the area attracted growing numbers of migrants to its pottery, coal and iron industries. Because of the limited nature of the censuses before 1841 and of the declining relevance of parish register data prior to civil registration in 1837 in a region increasingly succumbing to nonconformity, the scale of inward migration in overall population growth is difficult to determine. The census footnotes provide some indication of the process: the rapid increase of population in Stoke-upon-Trent parish in the decade 1821–31 was 'attributed to the immigration of families from the agricultural districts who find ready employment'. Statistical evidence of the movement on the wane is to be found in Lawton's analysis of population change by registration district from 1841 to 1901 (Table 8.1). The registration districts of Stoke-upon-Trent and Wolstanton correspond closely to the area under consideration, the former comprising Stoke parish, the latter Burslem and Wolstanton parishes. And, in the decade 1841–51, 46 per cent of the absolute growth in those two registration districts resulted from net in-migration of population.[3]

Whilst net in-migration contributed significantly to the overall expansion of population in the Potteries in the first half of the nineteenth century, the field from which migrants were lured – even allowing for the predominance of short-range drift in such movements – was relatively

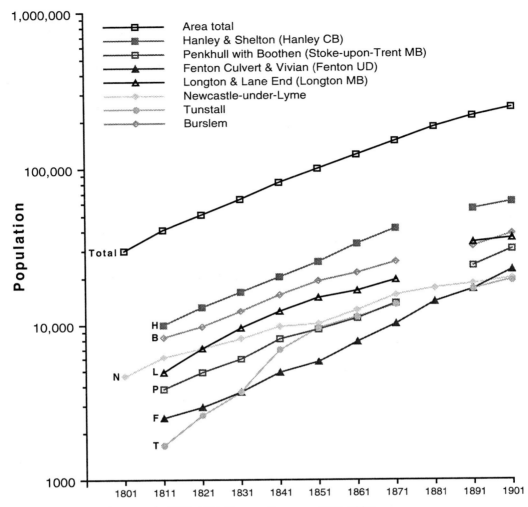

FIGURE 8.2 Population growth, 1801–1901 (*Source*: Censuses, 1801–1901).

limited, and largely confined to Staffordshire itself. Although the total population of the area exceeded 100,000 in 1851, its dispersion among a number of centres lessened the force of attraction. Thus, in 1841 and 1851, in Stoke and Wolstanton registration districts 88 and 82 per cent respectively of the population were born within Staffordshire, proportions higher than for the county as a whole. Studies of the centres of Burslem, Hanley, Longton and Penkhull in 1851 endorse this picture of a restricted migrational range, with between 60 and 78 per cent of populations being born within five miles of the respective towns.[4] The parochial nature of such in-migration, combined with the importance of natural increase, did much to create an inward-looking and essentially local population in the course of the nineteenth century.

After 1851, net in-migration played a diminishing role in population change, and natural increase returned as the major component of growth, although with reduced dynamism (Table 8.1). Thus, while crude birth rates fell from 40 per 1000 in Stoke registration district in 1858–62 to 37 per 1000 in the 1890s, crude death rates declined marginally faster from 25 per 1000 to 23 per 1000.[5] This trend partly accounted for the slackening in the overall rate of population expansion in the area in the second half of the nineteenth century. At the same time, from 1871 with a slowing down in economic activity in the Potteries, particularly in the coal and iron industries, both Stoke and Wolstanton registration districts were characterized by net migration losses: in the decade 1871–81, net out-migration depleted the population increment from natural increase in these two districts by 31 per cent. This process continued for the rest of the century, contributing also to the lessening rate of population growth.

Table 8.1

Components of population change, 1841–1901 ('000s)

Registration district	1841–51			1851–61			1861–71			1871–81			1881–91			1891–1901		
	A	N	M	A	N	M	A	N	M	A	N	M	A	N	M	A	N	M
Stoke-upon-Trent	10.0	6.2	3.8	13.4	9.7	3.6	18.0	13.0	5.0	15.5	16.9	-1.4	17.2	17.4	-0.2	19.2	20.0	-0.8
Wolstanton	9.3	4.3	5.0	12.4	8.3	4.1	14.6	12.1	2.4	6.5	15.2	-8.7	8.2	14.1	-5.9	14.8	15.2	-0.4
Newcastle-under-Lyme	1.3	1.8	-0.5	3.8	3.6	0.2	5.7	4.7	1.0	4.0	6.1	-2.1	2.9	6.3	-3.4	2.4	6.4	-4.0

A: absolute change; N: natural increase; M: net migration

Source: R Lawton, 'Population migration to and from Warwickshire and Staffordshire, 1841–1901', unpublished MA thesis, Liverpool University, 1950, table 12.

While the area defined by Hargreaves contained one of the major foci of population in nineteenth-century England and Wales, its impact was dissipated by its distribution among a number of centres. The expansion of these individual settlements may be traced in some detail in the decades 1811–71 and 1891–1901, when the censuses provide population data by township and at the end of the century by borough and district. The dispersion at the beginning of the period may be demonstrated most clearly by examining population density in 1811 (Fig 8.3). A major distinction can be identified between the townships of Tunstall, Burslem, Hanley and Shelton, Penkhull with Boothen, the two Fentons, Longton and Lane End, and Newcastle, covering together 9055 acres and with densities in excess of 1 per acre, and surrounding townships below that level, with dominantly agricultural interests. However, the seven township groupings with the highest densities displayed different patterns of growth. Applying Law's criteria of urban status of a population over 2500, of a density of more than 1 per acre, and of evidence of nucleation of settlement, Tunstall and the two Fenton townships in 1811 would appear marginal as towns, still emerging from their village background. The remaining five fulfilled Law's requirements of town standing, with Hanley-Shelton possessing the largest population and Newcastle the greatest density. By 1821, all seven township groupings could be said to have acquired that status.[6]

Population growth in these towns varied over the century, with the longest established, Newcastle and Burslem, displaying the slowest rate of increase, and the newest, Fenton and

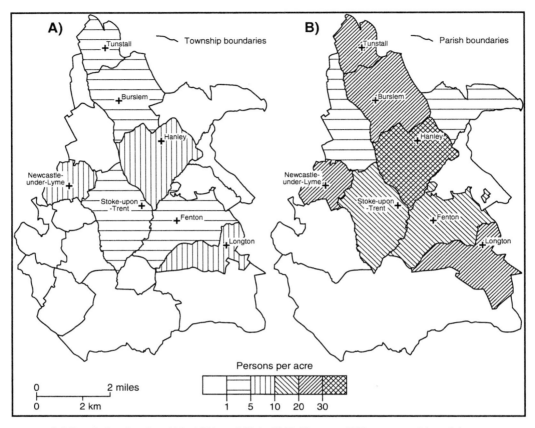

FIGURE 8.3 Population density: A) in 1811; and B) in 1901 (*Sources*: T Hargreaves, *Map of the Staffordshire Potteries, and Newcastle*, Burslem, 1832; Censuses, 1811 and 1901).

Tunstall, the most rapid (Table 8.2). The timing of expansion also differed between the individual centres. For the two northern towns, Tunstall and Burslem, major growth was concentrated in one period, 1811–51 and 1831–51 respectively. Hanley and Shelton, Penkhull with Boothen, and Longton and Lane End were each marked by two main phases of above average population increase: in the first case 1811–31 and 1851–71, in the second 1811–31 and 1871–1901, and in the third 1811–41 and 1871–1901, the last achieved largely through the addition of the built-up areas of Florence and Dresden from Blurton township, Trentham. Fenton was characterized by three main periods of population expansion, 1821–41, 1851–81 and 1891–1901, as was Newcastle in 1831–41, 1851–71 and 1881–91, but these increases tended to be less vigorous and more intermittent. Outside these years growth in each centre was below its decadal average for the period 1811–1901.

The varying pattern of population development resulted in changes in the ranking of the constituent towns (Fig 8.2). In 1811 Hanley and Shelton possessed the largest population, 9968 people, some 20 per cent more than the nearest sized town, Burslem. By 1901 Hanley still contained most people, 61,599 in all, but had extended its dominance in the area, being 50 per cent larger than the next centre, still Burslem. While the relative ranking of the six pottery towns remained virtually stable over the century, Fenton and Tunstall the two most recent

Table 8.2
Population density, 1811–1901

Townships (administrative title, 1901)	People per acre			Percentage population growth 1811–1901
	1811	1851	1901	
Newcastle (Newcastle MB)	9.6	16.1	29.7	322
Tunstall (Tunstall UD)	2.0	11.5	23.4	1162
Burslem with Sneyd and Rushton Grange (Burslem MB)	4.5	10.3	20.8	466
Hanley and Shelton (Hanley CB)	6.5	16.6	34.9	618
Penkhull with Boothen (Stoke MB)	2.4	5.8	16.4	791
Fenton Culvert and Vivian (Fenton UD)	1.4	3.2	13.0	908
Longton and Lane End (Longton MB)	6.2	19.1	20.2	726

Source: Censuses, 1811–1901

additions to the group maintaining the bottom places, the position of Newcastle underwent much change. Of the seven centres in 1811, it possessed the third largest population, but by 1901 it had declined to sixth, with just 500 people more than Tunstall. Throughout the century it grew at a rate about half that of the six pottery towns combined. Lacking the economic resources of those centres, population expansion was achieved mainly through natural increase, with crude birth and death rates lower – although comparable in direction – than those in Stoke and Wolstanton registration districts, but was depleted by large-scale net out-migration, which from 1841 to 1901 in Newcastle registration district reduced the numbers arising from natural increase by 30 per cent (Table 8.1). The population trends of Newcastle in the nineteenth century set it firmly apart from those of the pottery towns.

Despite the differing pace of change, by 1901 population was still predominantly confined to the same areas identified in 1811 (Fig 8.3). Although there had been some increase in surrounding districts through limited suburban development and small-scale industrial activity, densities remained low, far from the levels to be found in highly populated Hanley and

Newcastle. In their new administrative formats extending over 10,716 acres, the density, size and rate of growth of population of these seven township groupings establish the bases for understanding the pattern and extent of settlement change in the area.

HOUSING PROVISION

While industrial enterprises grew in number and range, and individual towns sought to provide public and institutional evidence of their status over the nineteenth century, the creation of the built landscape of the Potteries was chiefly the product of translating population expansion into housing. As with population, levels of housing provision related directly to the course of economic prosperity, and the demand for and supply of housing were subject to great periodicity. Some indication of the temporal pattern of housing provision may be derived from the census figures on inhabited houses. These data, however, are not without their problems, particularly in great cities: a consistent definition of house would not seem to have been employed prior to 1851, while the nature of the housing itself could compromise the accuracy of the returns, buildings of multiple family occupancy, cellar dwellings and court housing making it difficult to determine both the number and status of houses. While recognizing these obstacles, the inhabited house data may be less contaminated in the area under review than for other major industrial-urban centres. Although a significant concentration of people, as seven separate units, individually possessing populations throughout the period that placed them in the lower urban ranks, the towns would not have presented the problems of size to be found in enumerating housing in say Liverpool or Manchester. In addition, representatives of Burslem, Hanley, Longton and Newcastle in response to questions arising from the 1845 Royal Commission on the state of large towns and populous districts reported an absence of cellar dwellings, few buildings of multiple occupancy, the common practice being one family to a house, and although courts existed in most of them they would seem limited in extent. [7] If assumed to be reasonably reliable, the data should not be regarded as a record of housebuilding but rather of total housing stock at a given date, the figures representing the net accumulation of houses after demolition in a decade. In the absence of detailed series of housebuilding in the area, even at the end of the period, the inhabited house data from the census offer the best guide to the relative development of housing among the seven centres over the nineteenth century.

As might be expected, the growth in housing stock broadly mirrors that of population, but is subject to greater decadal variability. Overall the number of inhabited houses in the seven centres expanded more than sixfold between 1811 and 1901, with above average increase marking the years 1811–41 and thereafter only the two decades 1851–61 and 1891–1901 (Table 8.3). That general trend was not replicated by any of the towns and hides the diverse pattern of housing provision between them. Longton and Tunstall possessed two periods of above average growth in housing stock, 1811–41 and 1871–91 for the former, resulting not from new building but from the absorption of the suburbs of Dresden and Florence, and 1891–1901 for the latter. The pattern of housing expansion in Hanley was more volatile, with alternate decades displaying above and below average rates of increase. Similar fluctuations were found in Fenton and Stoke in the first half of the century, but thereafter growth was more concentrated, in the former in 1851–81 and 1891–1901, and in the latter from 1871–1901. The provision of housing in Burslem and Newcastle, the two oldest centres, was more disjointed, expansion in stock not being marked by either regularity or concentration. Despite, with the exception of Newcastle, the similarity of their economic base, the temporal supply of housing in this group of towns was remarkably individual and distinct, traits most evident in the last decade of the century, a peak

Table 8.3

Growth in the number of inhabited houses, 1811–1901

Townships	Number of inhabited houses in		Average percentage decadal growth	Actual percentage growth by decade								
	1811	1901	1811–1901	1811–21	1821–31	1831–41	1841–51	1851–61	1861–71	1871–81	1881–91	1891–1901
Newcastle	1319	4235	14	13	7	27	7	26	18	9	7	11
Tunstall	343	4058	32	55	40	90	19	31	10	–	–	29
Burslem	1657	8020	19	18	53	5	11	27	10	–	–	27
Hanley and Shelton	2054	12,882	23	32	21	31	14	38	21	–	–	25
Penkhull with Boothen	802	6343	26	28	10	43	11	28	14	–	–	41
Fenton Culvert and Vivian	517	4625	28	34	15	28	10	45	32	31	18	40
Longton and Lane End	1080	7249	24	35	43	26	10	16	16	–	–	13
Total	7772	47,412	22	27	28	28	12	30	17	–	–	35

Source: as for Table 8.2.

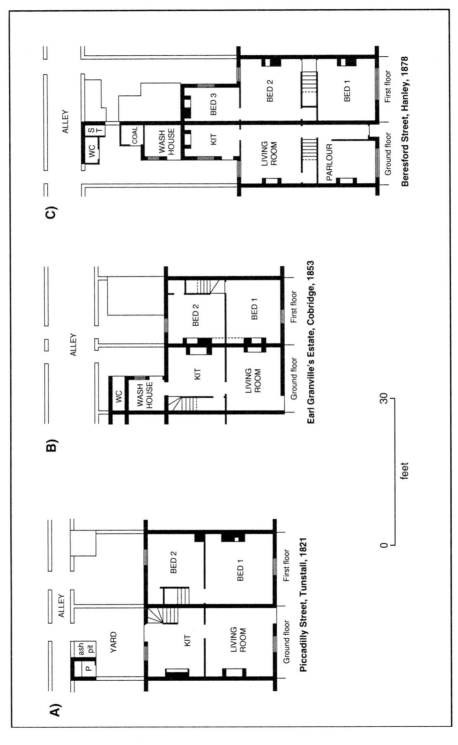

FIGURE 8.4 Plans of workers' terraced housing in the nineteenth century (*Source*: M W Greenslade, 'Burslem', in *Victoria County History of Staffordshire*, 1963, viii, 115).

in housebuilding activity generally, when Tunstall and particularly Longton recorded below average rates of increase in housing stock, Hanley about an average rate, and Burlsem and especially Fenton and Stoke well above average expansion.

Whenever built, the overwhelming majority of the housing stock was intended for working-class inhabitants. In 1845, R A Slaney in his report to the Royal Commission on the state of large towns and populous districts, while drawing attention to the neglected and cramped condition of the residences of the poorer classes in courts, alleys and narrow streets, judged the standard of housing in the towns of the area to be better than in other industrial centres he examined. Although generalizations about housing types in seven towns with different phases of growth present difficulties and ignore variations arising from individual developers and builders, and from the need to supply accommodation for a range of social standings, three major house styles have been recognized in the area in the course of the nineteenth century (Fig 8.4). At the time of Slaney's report the dominant form of housing was described as terraced, brick-built with quarry-tiled ground floors and tiled roofs, two rooms deep, each 10 to 12 ft square and two storeyed, giving a living space of four rooms. This 'cottage' plan of housing emerged as early as 1807 in Burslem, and was maintained in all the towns well after mid-century. From the 1850s the cottage plan began to be modified by the addition of a projecting wash-house and wc, as exemplified by the smaller properties built for Lord Granville's workers at Cobridge from 1853. With improvements in water supply and sanitation during the second half of the nineteenth century, many cottage plan terraces came to make similar additions. Under the influence of local government by-laws, there was a move from the 1870s to introduce the larger through terrace house (the 'tunnel-back' plan), with a rear annex allowing greater functional specialization of rooms and the provision of a third bedroom. However, in the light of building patterns in the area, the widespread adoption of this housing type had to wait until the 1890s.[8]

A broad assessment of the extent to which housing standards had developed from the four-room cottage plan of the 1840s may be made by calculating the average number of rooms per house in each town at the end of the century. By 1901, greatest change had occurred in Tunstall, Burslem, Hanley and Stoke, where between 68 and 71 per cent of the housing stock possessed five or more rooms. The rate of improvement was lower in Fenton, with 60 per cent of houses with five or more rooms. Longton and Newcastle displayed the lowest standards of housing, with only 45 and 47 per cent respectively of houses containing five or more rooms.[9] In great part, these variations reflected the impact of the differing building cycles among the towns. Thus, the last two decades of the century, when the larger tunnel-back plan began to spread, were for Longton and Newcastle unlike the other centres periods of little growth in the housing stock.

The level of middle-class housing provision was small, and by 1901 the area was noticeable for its relative lack of such properties. At the beginning of the century little distinctive middle-class accommodation can be detected. Far more discernible was the diverse pattern of development of the properties of the growing numbers of the wealthy. Thus, of pottery owners, most resided in houses attached to their works in town centres, a practice that only began to decline from mid-century. Some had erected houses detached from their potteries on the then edge of the built-up area, such as Portland House in west Burslem, belonging to the Riley family in the early nineteenth century. Others moved into the extensive surrounding rural districts. Of this group, a few rented existing properties that peppered these parts, a trend that became more popular towards the end of the century. More purchased small estates and built houses beyond the then boundaries of the towns, adding to the surprisingly high stock of

PLATE 8.1 The village of Greenfield, 1827 (P W L Adams, *A history of the Adams family of north Staffordshire*, 1914).

PLATE 8.2 A view of Hartshill, Lucy Lynam, late nineteenth century (City Museum and Art Gallery, Stoke-on-Trent).

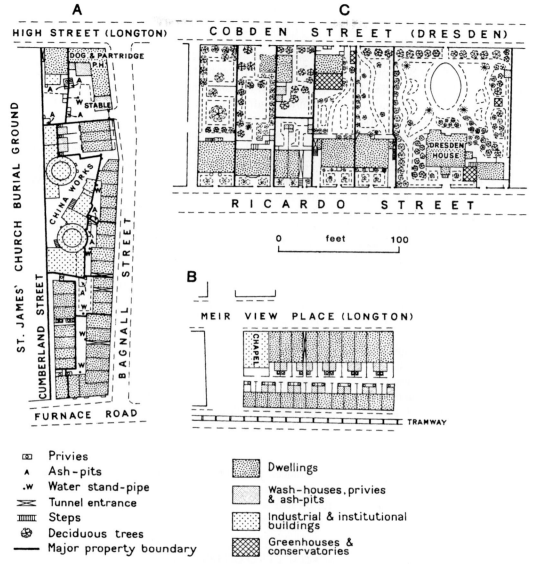

FIGURE 8.5 Housing layouts in Longton, 1879 (*Source*: Ordnance Survey, *Plan of the town of Longton, the Potteries, scale 1:500*, Southampton, 1879).

parkland and landscaped gardens (Fig 8.8). Of these some were established exclusively for personal enjoyment, such as the Mount built by Josiah Spode in 1803 to the west of Stoke centre or Bank House well to the east of Burslem erected in 1828 for Richard Riley, while others incorporated potteries and/or workers' housing to create industrial villages along the lines of Etruria. Thus, Theophilius Smith developed what came to be known as Greenfield to the north-east of Tunstall in the 1790s, comprising Greenfield Hall, a pottery works and 40 cottages, and between 1841 and 1857 Herbert Minton established a small planned community close to his house, Longfield Cottage in Hartshill, west of Stoke, with church, school and housing built in a Gothic style, both surviving as separate and distinct settlements at the end of the nineteenth century[10] (Pls 8.1 and 2).

Purpose-built housing for middle-class inhabitants, in the form of detached and semi-detached villas, can be identified in a few locations from the 1820s, as along the Waterloo Road at Bleak Hill and Cobridge. Here, however, the scheme was slow to mature, involving few houses by 1832, and from the 1850s became engulfed by terraced properties. Attempts to create exclusive middle-class enclaves were made after mid-century at, for example, Stokeville (later known as the Villas) south of Stoke centre between 1851 and 1855, and the Brampton to the north of Newcastle. Again, such developments were few and small-scale: Stokeville amounted to 24 houses and the Brampton by 1877 contained only 31 properties. More frequently in the second half of the nineteenth century, middle-class housing tended to occupy small sections of larger building schemes, quickly merging into terraced accommodation, a pattern perhaps best typified in the suburbs of Dresden and Florence established to the south of Longton in the 1860s. While the limited size and relative absence of spatial concentration of middle-class housing stock may be a reflection of the structure of the dominant industry of the area, they should also be seen as a function of population. It has been suggested that in the nineteenth century the physical entity of the town began to disaggregate into distinctive zones, of which middle-class suburbs were but one, when populations reached 50,000. While the figure was exceeded in the area as a whole by 1821, the seven towns operated as discrete centres, and at the end of the century only Hanley contained a greater population, achieved as late as 1891 and not by much.[11]

Although lacking great diversity, the housing types that developed resulted in a range of distinctive built landscapes throughout the towns of the area, which may be illustrated by examples from Longton (Fig 8.5). The housing off Longton High Street is representative of the cottage plans of around 1840. Development of the plot with an inn at its head was just starting in 1832, and by 1858 it was covered disjointedly with four courts and two terraces of cottages, all with a street frontage, and a small pottery works, a pattern that persisted to the end of the century. The improvements in terraced housing from mid-century are reflected in the properties at Meir View Place. Laid out on a gridiron plan, they demonstrate a more ordered and regular pattern, with separate street and back entrances, projecting wash-houses and wcs, and individual yards. While small in number, middle-class housing revealed greater variation in style and size, low densities and large gardens with profuse vegetation, as may be seen from the properties developed in the 1860s on a section of Ricardo Street in Dresden.[12]

SPATIAL DEVELOPMENT

The spatial pattern of housing provision is first most clearly and precisely caught in the nineteenth century on Hargreaves' survey (Fig 8.6). There the reality and relative importance of the seven major centres can be discerned: Hanley, Burslem, Longton and Newcastle emerge as well-defined urban concentrations, while Stoke, Tunstall and Fenton are less distinct, still bearing much similarity to the many smaller settlements scattered throughout the area. Superimposition of the solid geology provides an opportunity of perceiving the broad locational context of the development of these centres. Placed within the bounds of the outcrops of the resource rich Etruria Formation and Upper Coal Measures, the linearity that characterized the arrangement of the pottery towns – Tunstall through Burslem to Hanley, and Stoke through Fenton to Longton – reflected initial siting on ridges away from valley bottoms, the Fowlea

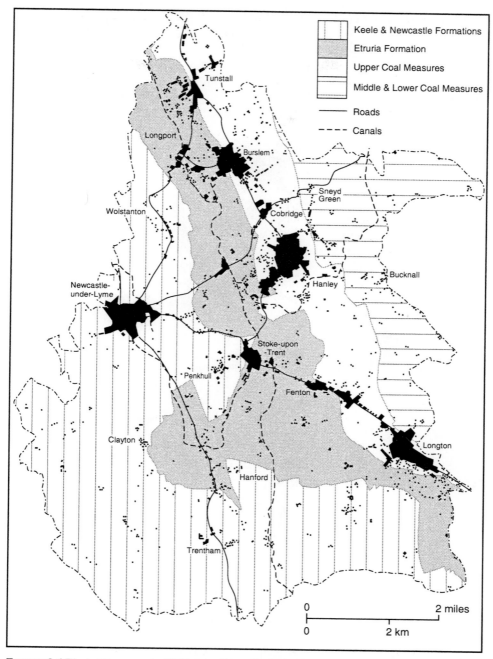

FIGURE 8.6 The built-up area in 1832 and solid geology (*Sources*: Hargreaves, *Map*; British Geological Survey, *Environmental geology of the Stoke-on-Trent area: solid geology, 1:25,000*, 1991).

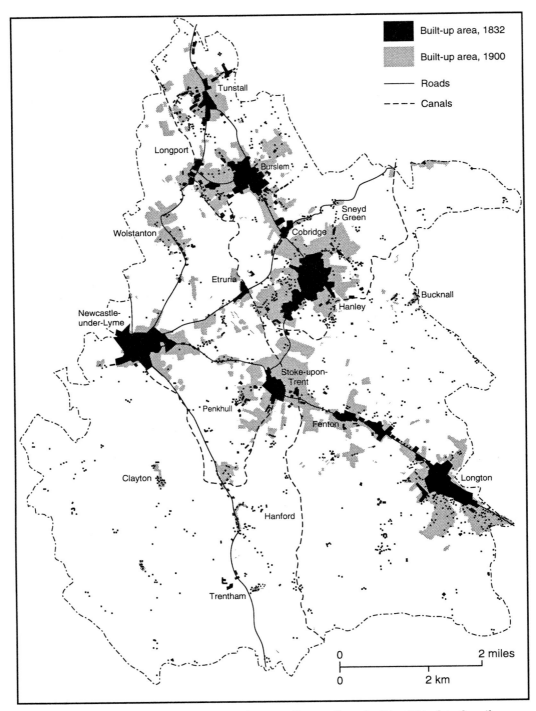

FIGURE 8.7 The built-up area in 1900 (*Source*: Ordnance Survey, *Second edition 25 inch to the mile sheets*, nos XI, XII, XVII and XVIII, Southampton, 1899–1900).

valley in the case of the former group, the Trent valley in the case of the latter, emphasized and compounded by the growth of the eighteenth-century turnpike road network. The distinctiveness of the linearity of development of the pottery settlements was early recognized, and by mid-nineteenth century it was considered that 'the best conception of the whole [district] is of one vast manufacturing street, running . . . from south-east to north-west, and swelling out to the bulk of large towns at particular spots'.[13] In contrast, Newcastle lying on the industrially limited Keele and Newcastle Formations was located in the bottom of the Lyme valley, its spread from an eleventh/twelfth-century castle site being confined by surrounding ridges, which contributed to the maintenance of a compact form.

Both Moisley and Beaver suggested that the pattern of urban development remained stable throughout the nineteenth century. Examination of the second edition Ordnance Survey 25 inch to the mile sheets, revised in 1898 and published in 1899/1900, from which the extent of growth from 1832 can be determined, would point to the need of some revision of that assessment (Fig 8.7). Although still predominantly contained within the borders of the Etruria Formation and Upper Coal Measures, the built-up area of all the pottery towns by the end of the century had been subject to intensification, through infilling, development of vacant land and redevelopment of existing plots, and to extension, even the smallest centres – Tunstall and Fenton – more than doubling their bounds from 1832. The impact of these processes may be illustrated from central Burslem. Thus, in the core of the town, the block of land between the Market Place and Queen Street, about 3½ acres, underwent constant infilling throughout the period 1832–98. To the north

PLATE 8.3 View from Etruria Hall, H Warren, mid-nineteenth century (City Museum and Art Gallery, Stoke-on-Trent).

of the Market Place, an area of open land, which in 1878 covering some 5 acres was designated a public recreation ground, was developed to contain a theatre and five rows of terraced housing by 1898. West of the Market Place, the Fountain Place Works, built in 1789 by Enoch Wood, occupied in 1832 a plot just over 8 acres, with an impressive pottery at its eastern end (Pl 7.4), and a mansion and extensive landscaped gardens on the rest. By 1878, the pottery and the mansion remained largely unchanged, but the gardens had almost disappeared, with some terraced housing replacing them at the western end of the plot. The pottery still dominated the eastern end of the plot by 1898, but terraced housing laid out in the plan of a cross had now completely displaced mansion and gardens. The expansion of Burslem westwards to Longport may be taken as an example of the extension of the built-up area. In 1832 the two settlements were separate; in the third quarter of the nineteenth-century, there began from Burslem the laying-out of streets and housing on open land to the north and south of Newcastle Street, the main route between the two; and during the 1880s and 1890s the final connection was achieved with the demolition of Longport Hall and the construction on its land, around $2^{1}/_{2}$ acres, of some 130 terraced properties. These processes, replicated in the other pottery centres, served to translate the mid-nineteenth-century image of linear and globular urban development in the area into reality. Newcastle, still physically detached from the pottery towns, conformed more to the assertion of Moisley and Beaver. Here, spatial expansion was limited, tending to be confined to the eastern side of the borough, and largely undertaken between 1832 and 1877.[14] The more than doubling of inhabited houses from 1831 to 1901 in Newcastle was mainly accommodated within the 1832 boundary of the built-up area, adding high densities to the overall low housing standards at the end of the century.

While the general pattern of urban growth in the area can be depicted, explanation of that pattern in detail has yet to be fully determined. Landownership represents a starting point, the willingness of landlords to release land for building, the rate, location and size of such land releases setting to a great extent the pace, direction and intensity of development. Certainly, within the area landowners displayed a range of attitudes to urban expansion. Thus, throughout the greater part of the nineteenth century the burgesses of Newcastle were reluctant to make available for building purposes land, lying mainly on the western side of the borough, allocated to them at the enclosure of the town's four open fields in 1816. Their resistance to selling building plots acted as an effective break to the westward expansion of the town in the period, channelled growth to the east, and forced much housing to be infill and dense in character. In contrast, the dukes of Sutherland, whose north Staffordshire estate, extending over 10,533 acres in 1859, occupied the bottom third of the area under consideration, including a significant portion of Longton, were less opposed to industrial and urban development, pleased with the greater revenues it yielded over agricultural land, especially where it could be concentrated at an effective distance from Trentham Hall. In consequence, they encouraged the growth of Longton, most actively in the provision of estate land for and in the promotion of the building of the Dresden and Florence suburbs to the south of the town in the 1850s and 1860s, completing the scheme with the donation of 45 acres for the creation in 1887 of Queen's Park.[15] At present, the pattern of landownership of the towns throughout the period is but imperfectly known: its plotting would do much to establish a spatial and temporal framework for understanding urban growth in the area in the nineteenth century.

The initial expansion of the pottery towns in the nineteenth century, in common with other rapidly industrializing centres, was accompanied by relatively little spatial order or planning. Industrial enterprises and housing advanced into the surrounding rural districts with seeming indifference to existing park- and agricultural land, producing the stark and incompatible

PLATE 8.4 Intermixing of housing and pot-banks at Longton, *c* 1900 (Warrillow Collection, Keele University Library).

PLATE 8.5 Marl hole, pot-banks and housing at Edensor, Longton, *c* 1900 (Warrillow Collection, Keele University Library).

contrasts in land use that were evident from mid-century around Etruria Hall (Pl 8.3). Within the built-up area the relative absence of spatial social segregation of housing has already been noted. More noticeable was the lack of separation of residential and industrial development. As Hargreaves' survey demonstrates (Fig 8.8), pot-banks were predominantly sited in town centres and accommodation for the workforces was built in close proximity, creating a haphazard jumble of bottle ovens and housing. As an indication of the level of that intermixing, the 534 bottle ovens plotted on that map represented a ratio of one to every 21 houses then in the six pottery towns (Pl 8.4). Such a chaotic pattern was not lost on contemporaries: J G Kohl, a German visitor to the region in the early 1840s could record that 'between the great factories, or banks, lie scattered the small houses of the shopkeepers, the workmen, the painters, the engravers, the colourmen, and others; while here and there the intervals are filled up by churches and chapels, or by the stately houses of those who have grown rich by pottery'.[16]

With the increasing number of pot-banks, this confusion in land use persisted throughout the nineteenth century, compounded by the expanding area of housing coming into direct contact with a profusion of brickfields, marl holes and collieries that originally had been located beyond the margins of the towns (Pl 8.5). However, the rate of housing provision, growing from

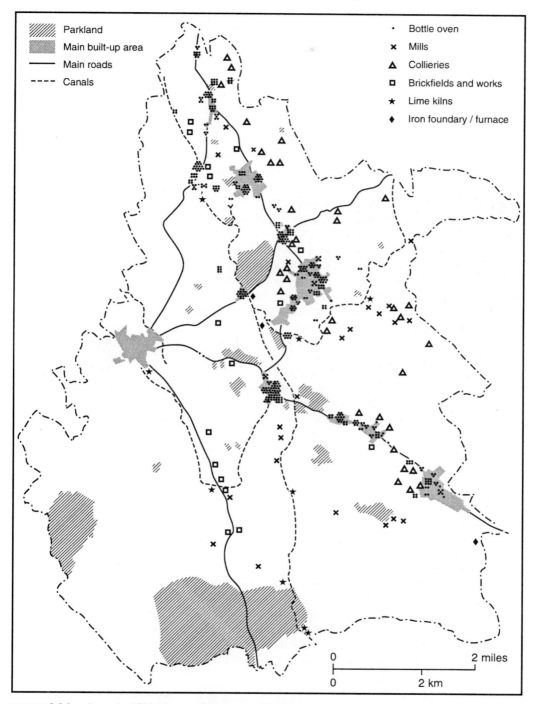

FIGURE 8.8 Land uses in 1832 (*Source*: Hargreaves, *Map*).

mid-century more quickly than the establishment of new heavy and extractive industries in the district, contributed in itself to a lessening in the intensity of intermixing. Thus, in 1900 there were 71 houses in the pottery towns to each one of the 612 bottle ovens depicted on the Ordnance Survey second edition 25 inch to the mile sheets. And from mid-century attempts were made to divorce residential from industrial uses, from the small-scale Stokeville scheme and the more ambitious Dresden and Florence suburbs of the 1850s and 1860s to the extensive development south of Hanley Park around St Jude's Church in the last years of the 1890s, containing some 450 pairs of terraced houses.

Beyond the limits of the Etruria Formation and the Upper Coal Measures, such blatant conflicts in urban land use were generally absent. Newcastle's economy over the century was based on the trades, crafts and services of a country town. Lacking extractive, manufacturing and heavy industry on any significant scale, it avoided rapid urbanization, escaping many of the social and developmental problems encountered in the pottery towns. The differences between the two may be effectively demonstrated at mid-century in terms of levels of personal wealth, a reflection of a range of aspects of urban life – housing conditions, the amount of poverty, the nature of employment and variations in income. In 1845–7, per capita payment of assessed taxes, a personal levy on the type of house occupied and establishment maintained, in Newcastle of £0.12 was double that in the parliamentary borough of Stoke-upon-Trent, comprising all the pottery towns.[17] The quality of the urban environment in Newcastle, despite failings, would seem to have been significantly better than the generality of the Potteries.

This survey has but etched an outline of the growth of the conurbation in the nineteenth century. Nevertheless, it demonstrates that the changing settlement pattern in the region should be seen at two levels. More generally, the concentration of population, the spread, type and density of housing, and the disorder of development, evident in the Potteries over the period, are traits that characterized all great centres of nineteenth-century industrialization. However, the detailed form of growth can only be understood in terms of seven main settlements, each at the lower end of the urban scale in 1801 and despite marked expansion still occupying that position in 1901, and each as the cartographic and census data reveal with individual and often differing patterns of development. It was, in the eyes of contemporaries, this mixture that made the settlement pattern in the Potteries so distinct among British conurbations.

REFERENCES

1. A D M Phillips, 'Settlement patterns in Staffordshire in the late eighteenth and nineteenth centuries', *Manchester Geographer*, new series, 6, 1985, 42–57.
2. T Hargreaves, *Map of the Staffordshire Potteries, and Newcastle*, Burslem, 1832; British Parliamentary Papers (BPP), 1845, XVIII, 'Second report of the Commissioners for inquiring into the state of large towns and populous districts, 1845', appendix, part 1, 171.
3. L Weatherill, *The pottery trade and north Staffordshire 1660–1760*, Manchester, 1971, 120–3; Census, 1831; R Lawton, 'Population migration to and from Warwickshire and Staffordshire, 1841–1901', unpublished MA thesis, Liverpool University, 1950, 169–84.
4. Censuses, 1841 and 1851; R Lawton, 'Population movements in the west midlands, 1841–61', *Geography*, 43, 1958, 164–77; D Stuart, ed, *The population of central Burslem, 1851 and 1861*, Keele University, 1973; M Breeze, ed, *Central Longton in 1851*, WEA Hanley, 1976; D A Gatley, ed, *Hanley in 1851: a survey based on the census returns*, Staffordshire Polytechnic, 1989.
5. BPP, 1860, XXIX; 1861, XVIII; 1862, XVII; 1863, XIV; 1864, XVII; 1905, XVIII, 'Annual reports

of the registrars general', 1858–62, 1881–1890, 1891–1900.

6. C M Law, 'The growth of urban population in England and Wales, 1801–1911', *Trans Inst Brit Geogr*, 41, 1967, 125–43.

7. E Higgs, *Making sense of the census*, 1989, 48–56; BPP, 1845, XVIII, 'Second report . . . into the state of large towns and populous districts', appendix, part 1, 169–76; E J D Warrillow, *A sociological history of the city of Stoke-on-Trent*, Hanley, 1960, 318–23.

8. BPP, 1845, XVIII, 'Second report . . . into the state of large towns and populous districts: report by R A Slaney', 135–6, 169–76; M W Greenslade, 'Burslem', in *Victoria County History of Staffordshire (VCH Staffs)*, 1963, viii, 114–16; C Hawke-Smith, *The making of the six towns*, Hanley, 45–9; D Baker, *Potworks: the industrial architecture of the Staffordshire Potteries*, 1991, 42–5, 79–83, 96–7; R Rodger, *Housing in urban Britain 1780–1914*, 1989, 28–37.

9. Census, 1901.

10. M W Greenslade, 'Tunstall', 'Burslem', and 'Stoke-on-Trent', in *VCH Staffs*, 1963, viii, 83, 91, 105, 112, 117, 183; Baker, *Potworks*, 39–42, 81–3, 96; J Ward, *The borough of Stoke-upon-Trent*, 1843, 102, 210, 511–13.

11. D M Palliser, *The Staffordshire landscape*, 1976, 222–8; J H Y Briggs, *The history of Longton: 1, the birth of a community*, Keele, 1982, 57–9; Greenslade, 'Burslem', 112; Baker, *Potworks*, 77–9; Rodger, *Housing*, 38–43; Hargreaves, *Map*; Ordnance Survey, *First edition 25 inch to the mile sheets*, nos XI (16), XVII (4), XVIII (10 and 11), Southampton, 1879–80.

12. Hargreaves, *Map*; Ordnance Survey, *Plan of the town of Longton, scale of 10.56 ft to the mile; Plan of the town of Longton, the Potteries, scale 1:500; Second edition 25 inch to the mile sheets*, no XVIII (10 and 11), Southampton, 1858, 1879, 1900; T R Slater, 'Urban growth and structure', in A D M Phillips, ed, *Victorian Staffordshire*, forthcoming.

13. Anon, *The land we live in*, 1848, iv, 28.

14. H A Moisley, 'The industrial and urban development of the north Staffordshire conurbation', *Trans Inst Brit Geogr*, 17, 1951, 154–7; S H Beaver, 'The Potteries: a study in the evolution of a cultural landscape', *Trans Inst Brit Geogr*, 34, 1964, 14–16; Greenslade, 'Burslem', 105–7, 135–6; Ward, *Stoke*, 260, 266–7; Hargreaves, *Map*; Ordnance Survey, *First and second editions 25 inch to the mile sheets*, nos XI (12), XII (9), XVII (4), Southampton, 1879, 1899–1900.

15. J G Jenkins, 'The borough of Newcastle-under-Lyme', in *VCH Staffs*, 1963, viii, 4, 49–50; A D M Phillips, 'A note on farm size and efficiency on the north Staffordshire estate of the Leveson-Gowers, 1714–1809', *N Staffs Jnl Fld Stud*, 19, 1979, 31–2, and 'Settlement patterns in Staffordshire', 44–5; Staffordshire Record Office, D593/H/14/3/10 a-e and 18 a-g, Surveys of the north Staffordshire estate, 1820 and 1859; Briggs, *Longton*, 48–57; Palliser, *Staffordshire landscape*, 228–9.

16. Quoted in Anon, *The land we live in*, iv, 29.

17. A D M Phillips and J R Walton, 'The distribution of personal wealth in English towns in the mid-nineteenth century', *Trans Inst Brit Geogr*, 64, 1975, 35–48.

9. Urban Institutions and Administration

J H Y BRIGGS

The early history of administration in north Staffordshire has been described as 'a palimpsest whose original parochial pattern has been overlaid by a new complexus of civil government'.[1] Add to that basic statement the interplay of formal and informal agencies and the complexity of growth becomes a fascinating riddle begging resolution. In early times the word 'Stoke' seems to have designated no more than the location of a church; and certainly until recent times most of the area was contained within the two sprawling upland parishes of Stoke and, to its north-west, of Wolstanton, with later growth into the parish of Trentham to the south (Fig 9.1). Although the parochial structure became increasingly out of touch with the pastoral needs of a rapidly increasing urban population as the pottery towns expanded in the eighteenth century, it was not until 1807 that the first legal steps were taken to create more manageable ecclesiastical districts.

Overlaid on the parish map of north Staffordshire was the manorial jurisdiction of two ancient manors, those of Newcastle and Tunstall, slightly complicated by the existence of a third manor of Fenton Culvert in the southern part of the region from the thirteenth to the sixteenth century, whose history is less well documented than that of its neighbours. Although such manorial justice was designed for the governance of agrarian societies, many aspects of local life remained under the jurisdiction and control of the lords of Newcastle and Tunstall well into the nineteenth century.

A third pattern of legal administration emerged at the end of the sixteenth century with the development of statutory obligations for the relief of the poor, which witnessed yet a further set of authorities and boundaries established. These in part served to recognize that a number of areas within the ancient parishes, such as Newcastle and Burslem, had already become civil parishes. When, in the nineteenth century, the new poor law was adopted in north Staffordshire, Stoke formed one poor law union in 1836 covering the southern part of the old parish, whilst two years later Burslem and Tunstall became part of the new Burslem and Wolstanton union. At the same time Newcastle from 1838 became the centre of a further union in conjunction with eight rural parishes to the west.

In all this there is also from the mid-eighteenth century onwards a contrast to be made between Newcastle-under-Lyme, very conscious of its heritage, memorialized in its motto, 'Ancient and Loyal', and with its twelfth-century charter and gradual development of urban institutions, however faulty they might prove in day-to-day operation, and the emerging industrial towns of the Potteries, which lacked all advantage of local government save the manorial jurisdiction that covered them as landed estates. Moreover, this was magnified by the relationship that developed between the ancient borough and its new neighbours, all too often characterized by conflict, seen particularly in Newcastle's obstruction of direct turnpike links with the pottery towns.

FIGURE 9.1 Parish boundaries in north Staffordshire, *c* 1850 (*Source*: Index to Tithe Survey, sheets 72 NW and 73 NE).

But times were changing. By 1760, Burslem had established its own market. In the previous year the Uttoxeter to Stoke road had been turnpiked and in 1763 the Burslem to Lawton turnpike linked the northern pottery towns into the national road network. Interestingly, Ward notes that 'the people of Newcastle were extremely hostile to the intended Act of Parliament for improving the thoroughfare through the Potteries, on account of the injurious effects they anticipated by the diversion of carriages and travellers from their town, and had raised every possible objection to the measure in Parliament'.[2] The completion of the Trent and Mersey Canal in 1777 put the Potteries firmly on one of the main arteries of national communications, whilst Newcastle had to make do with a branch of this.

By the reform crisis of the 1830s, economic competition had spawned political uncertainty.

As early as 1783 an attempt had been made to secure the incorporation of the whole pottery district but the only practical outcome seems to have been the impanelling of the ancient corporation of Hanley as a parody upon the real thing, a mocking way of calling attention to the desperately unsatisfactory situation produced by the absence of any instruments of local government within the pottery towns. In 1817 there were further meetings in the Potteries under the chairmanship of Sir John Heathcote to the same end, and the idea emerged again in the reform crisis of the 1830s. Twenty years later, in 1850, Robert Rawlinson, one of the most distinguished of the new public health inspectors, who came to investigate both Stoke and Hanley, was convinced that it was absolutely necessary for the north Staffordshire towns to amalgamate for the proper local government of the area to be secured.

In the first schedule of new boroughs to be enfranchised by the reform legislation of 1832, Stoke does not appear. A first amendment suggested that Stoke might receive a single member but this did not assuage local sentiment, when it compared a Potteries population of around 52,000, with Newcastle's 8000. Only after mass meetings and intense lobbying was a second member secured, in which process, not surprisingly, even the anti-reform member for Newcastle, Edmund Peel, brother to the prime minister and third son of the first baronet, was energetic in promoting the Potteries case, for a failure to establish a separate constituency would have simply perpetuated pottery influence within the borough, and indeed would have totally swamped the Newcastle agricultural and hatting interests.[3]

The common notion that the Municipal Corporations Act of 1835 provided the means whereby local government was reformed, so as to bring it into line with what the Whigs had achieved nationally in 1832, simply does not work in north Staffordshire as Table 9.1 indicates (Pls 9.1–4). Certainly, the original bill of 1833 had contained a proposal that all the new parliamentary boroughs should be incorporated, but unfortunately, for an area such as the Potteries, fraught with complex inter-community feuding, such a simple proposal did not survive in the Act as passed two years later.

Table 9.1

Urban development of the towns of north Staffordshire

Town	Borough	Town hall	Improvement commission	Board of health	Parish
Newcastle	c 1173	early 1600s/1713	1819	1850	1807
Tunstall	1894 UDC	1816/1833–5	1847	1855	1831–7
Burslem	1878	c 1761/1854/1911	1825	1850	[1807]
Hanley	1857	1791/1845/mid-1880s	1825	1859	1831–43
Stoke	1874	1794/1834 ff	1839	–	by 1086
Fenton	1894 UDC	1888	1839	1873	1838–41
Longton	1865	1814/1844/1863	1839	1862	1833–9

Until, therefore, the second half of the nineteenth century, and in some cases well into the second half, such local administration as was achieved was carried out by commissioners, trustees, boards and other locally convoked authorities. For example, the all-important market trustees in Hanley were first established in 1791, though they did not achieve statutory authority until 1813 when a private Act gave them power to purchase and hold land and buildings, to borrow for such purposes, to charge toll, and to apply any profits, once loans had been discharged, to such public works as would be of benefit to the town. Strangely, these included from the very beginning no greater

PLATE 9.1 The old Guild Hall, Newcastle-under-Lyme (Warrillow Collection, Keele University Library).

municipal concern than the payment of the organist at St John's Chapel. Significantly, the 1813 'Market House or Town Hall' was not limited to commercial functions but embraced a lock-up for the detention of offenders.[4] The market trustees, all men of substance, by their single-mindedness of commercial aim, and virtual rejection of the welfare function allowed them in the 1813 Act, made Hanley the shopkeeper to the whole conurbation and a rival to Burslem, 'the mother town of the Potteries', and Stoke, its administrative centre and municipal appellation.

In 1806 an attempt to secure a comprehensive local improvement Act could not command sufficient support, and local proprietors, for the defence of their homes, their wives and their pot-banks, had to make do with the self-help endeavours of the Potteries Central Association for the Protection of Felons, until in 1823 a further attempt was made to secure a local Act which still encountered difficulties over whether outlying potters, especially Josiah Wedgwood at Etruria, should pay the same level of rate as those whose businesses were in central Hanley and Shelton. In 1825, an Act for Watching and Lighting Hanley and Shelton was finally secured by dint of allowing the potters of Etruria to opt in at their own volition. This led to the appointment of commissioners with powers to collect an annual rate for the purposes of lighting the town, to elect a chief bailiff, and to appoint constables and watchmen.

By an amending Act of 1828 the franchise was limited to certain officers, the clergy, both established and dissenting, of the townships, and to owners of properties valued at £100 per annum and occupiers of property of half such annual value – much higher than the £28 per annum level that the Webbs believed confined the Manchester franchise to substantial traders and owners of mansions.[5] The exclusive Hanley commissioners worked through a series of committees – for rate collection, lighting, the town hall, nuisance removal, lodging house management and, at the end of the commissioners' period, a committee to consider proposals for the reform of the structure of local government. They also bore responsibility for maintaining the town's part-time fire brigade, whose efforts were often nullifield by the lack of a reliable water supply. But in 1852 a commissioners' meeting confessed that their powers under existing local Acts were 'inadequate for the purposes of the government and sanitary improvement of the townships'.[6]

A lack of resident gentry within the 'Borough of Stoke-upon-Trent', a designation used only to refer to the parliamentary borough and therefore of those eligible to act as magistrates, led in 1839, having regard 'to the very great and increasing extent of the population and manufactories', to legislation to secure the appointment of a stipendiary magistrate to administer justice within the pottery communities with lock-ups to be provided within each of the six towns in the area, six not Arnold Bennett's five, the omission of Fenton being a sin for which north Staffordshire's most famous author has yet to be forgiven by the inhabitants of that location. It was not until 1855 with the appointment of John Ridgway, manufacturer, to the bench that Hanley first secured an unsalaried resident magistrate.[7]

Significantly for future class relationships, in 1849, the 'operatives class committee', with particularly heavy polling in Hanley and Shelton, won control of the Stoke Board of Guardians over the local 'capitalists'. Initially they did well, securing the liquidation of an inherited debt of almost £7000, partly through the deployment of workhouse inmates on allotment cultivation to defray expenses, an extension of outdoor relief beyond that allowed by 'their cruel predecessors', and also effecting a check upon the insolence of local officials. Helped by better trading conditions, they successfully won an admission of rate liability out of the North Staffordshire Railway, but courted more difficulty than advantage in taking on the Hanley market trustees for similar ends, even though Stoke and Longton markets were already making contributions to their accounts. This unfortunately was construed as an outright working-class challenge to oligarchic power, and only after the informal intervention of the stipendiary magistrate did the trustees agree to pay; but the victory had only been secured at a cost of deep division within society.[8]

To start with, the agents of these various boards and commissions operated as modernizing forces, functionally addressing the most pressing needs of the community, unfettered by history and precedent. By the mid-century, however, a jungle of competing authorities led to considerable internecine strife: guardians vesus market trustees, who in their turn argued with the highway boards of the twin townships of Shelton and Hanley, whose jurisdiction overlapped with that of the improvement commissioners.

The highway boards were the authorities elected on the most democratic of local franchises, but unfortunately, especially on the Shelton board, democracy was accompanied by financial incompetence and probably petty pilfering on the part of its artisan officers, whose greatest crime was 'the damage they did to the reputation of the only democratically elected local authority in the township and to that of the working-class activists who controlled it'. With overall responsibility but too little power to act were the improvement commissioners. All this muddle and competition consumed much energy, generated a lot of heat, but did little for the good government of the area. Into such a situation came the cholera which began to appear in

PLATE 9.2 Tunstall Town Hall, *c* 1900 (Warrillow Collection, Keele University Library).

the Potteries in the autumn of 1848:[9] each of the southern towns, Hanley, Fenton, Stoke and Longton, immediately set up local committees to take appropriate action. The threat to life was so perceived as to incline local interest in the first three to seek the aid of central bureaucracy by petitioning for an inspector of the General Board of Health to make a local inspection, but Longton argued against the visit because its mortality rate was quickly brought under control, and indeed because of Sutherland patronage it had a better water supply than the other towns. Other vested interests, both populist and oligarchic, headed by Alderman Copeland, Tory MP for Stoke, also opposed the inquiry, but by then Robert Rawlinson, pre-eminent amongst the new engineers, had already been charged with the task.

By 17 June 1849 his report, together with its recommendation that a board of health be established for the whole of Stoke parish, was complete, though publication was delayed for a year. Such a general solution was too radical for local interests which opposed the Rawlinson proposals with their old separatist prejudices. Confusion reigned as proposals were made for separate boards of health, the incorporation of the parliamentary borough, and the incorporation of the separate towns. Such multiplicity of proposal proved then as subsequently a sure recipe for not changing the status quo.

A committee of operative-potters – in which the presence of Hanley chartists can be clearly detected – had indicated that desirable as reform might be they believed it an expensive luxury that they could ill afford, whereas anything short of incorporation would focus power without proper representation. 'Taxation without representation' was a principle often to be invoked in the local government controversy of these years. By contrast the Pottery Central Reform Association, embracing both electors and non-electors of a liberal mind, was totally convinced of the need for immediate action and made local government reform their platform in fighting the parliamentary seat in the Liberal interest in 1852.

PLATE 9.3 Hanley Old Council, c 1905 (Warrillow Collection, Keele University Library).

When it was decided that the best way forward was to seek incorporation for Hanley on its own, new disputes arose around the issue of whether to propose either a high or a low local rateable qualification. Moreover, the case for simply adopting the Public Health Act was run alongside this. No less a figure than Edwin Chadwick informed the Hanley commissioners that it was the unanimous view of the General Board of Health in London that conditions in Hanley were such as to require the urgent application of the Public Health Act.[10] But events were to demonstrate that central government was as yet not powerful enough to overcome local divisions, for Hanley had to be deleted from the provisional order laid before the House of Commons because of the extent of local opposition. All this demonstrates that in history delays and postponements are as important as simple patterns of cause and effect, since they embody forces of dissonance and uncertainty always present in seeking change.

The cholera came to Hanley in 1848, and there is no doubt that it sharpened minds about the need for efficient local government, but that was only secured after nine years of conflict and compromise with incorporation in 1857 and adoption of the Public Health Act two years later in 1859. Even then the process was not complete, for it was not until 1862 that the market trustees could be persuaded to transfer their prestigious assets to the new borough and not until 1870 that it became a separate policing authority.

The early years of the new authorities were mainly concerned with the issues of waste, industrial and human, smoke and sewage, both of which came under the scrutiny of government through the terms of the 1866 Sanitary Act. Chimneys designed to consume their own smoke had been commended by parliamentary hearings in 1843 and legislation for London dated to 1853. But until 1866, it has been argued, the only notice taken of black smoke in the Potteries was to use it as an argument for a wakes week excursion to sunnier climes.

But the 1860s were a critical period for the Potteries, most particularly with the extension of the Factory Acts to cover potworks in 1864; provincial life as lived in the north Staffordshire Potteries was becoming much more amenable to discipline from the agencies of central government. The smoke clauses in the new legislation prompted the local newspaper, the

Staffordshire Sentinel, to chide the youthful council with tardiness of response; 'In no other part of the United Kingdom', it asserted, 'is it more necessary to bring the Act into operation than in these towns, in which the worst evils of the clay and iron manufactures are combined.'[11]

The council took defensive action by sending a circular drawing attention to the legislation to local manufacturers and its own nuisance committee, as also by placing a notice in the *Staffordshire Sentinel*. A district conference on the nuisance of smoke was held, but this did not prevent black smoke continuing to belch forth from Stoke's many kilns and chimneys. Unconvinced by such action, a group of Stoke residents became the first to petition the Home Secretary under the Act to remove smoke control from the hands of the local council and to appoint a central government smoke inspector for the area, the threat of which produced an immediate capital expenditure by a large number of manufacturers to get their chimneys in order. The ironmaster mayor of Hanley, W S Roden, a future MP of Stoke, darkly threatened, 'The question was whether those who were so delicate should leave the district or whether the manufacturers should put an end to their manufactures.'[12]

When the petitioners applied a second time, the *Staffordshire Sentinel* hectored the council on the defaulting practice of particular councillors, whilst its columns became a kind of clearing house for practical solutions to the problem. The petitioners secured a government enquiry and Rawlinson once more came to Hanley to assess the situation. He congratulated the petitioners and in no uncertain terms told the council to comply with legislation, which it did to such an

PLATE 9.4 Fenton Town Hall, *c* 1900 (Warrillow Collection, Keele University Library).

extent that it became a model for the other towns to follow, by implementing an inspection programme and enforcing limited periods for the emission of black smoke, and by extending its concern to those who calcined iron, other ironworks, lime kilns, and brick and tile manufacture. The real solution to the problem, though, lay not with legislation or its implementation, but rather with technology, with the use of gas as a fuel, first in existing intermittent kilns in the 1880s and from the beginning of the new century in new continuous-firing tunnel kilns.

As with so many issues, as far as sewage disposal was concerned it was easier to diagnose the problem than find a solution. The woeful inadequacy of waste-disposal facilities in Hanley were made abundantly clear in Rawlinson's 1850 report: his graphic language all but sensitizes the nose to the manifest distress present throughout the townships – only half the children born could expect to survive their fifth birthday. Whilst the sanitary state of the town was perhaps the major incentive to incorporation, the new council showed itself far from capable of dealing with the situation. The cost of initiating a town-wide scheme was believed to be prohibitive, at least so long as the pottery trade suffered from the depression occasioned by the American Civil War. The council was slow to act out its role as 'guardian of the public health' of the community; after nine years of inaction the *Staffordshire Sentinel*, bemoaning the lack of an efficient sewerage system, complained: 'There is a municipal corporation, with all its stipendiaries and titular dignitaries and there are two registrars of deaths, and a beautiful cemetery, but no officer of health collects, classifies and publishes the death returns or gives analysis of the diseases which week after week result in death.'[13] Once again the search for a district solution to an interacting problem allowed the forces of torpor to triumph, and not even the threat of legal action by the duke of Sutherland whose residence at Trentham was threatened by a polluted river Trent could secure effective action. At last in the mid-1870s Hanley returned to a town scheme, just a decade before the town began to see the widespread introduction of the water closet, which could not have been introduced at any earlier juncture.

The pattern of municipal change in the other pottery towns was of a similar or even more delayed nature: a combination of intense parochialism, simple reluctance to part with funds, together with all the elitism of property-owning meant that the local community was slow to produce the institutions of local government that a growing trade, an expanding population, and the increasingly-complex realities of urban life required. Although the provisions of the Public Heath Act were widely employed to avoid incorporation, the pressures for more comprehensive instruments of local government greatly increased from the mid-century.

At the south end of the region, Longton secured a body of self-perpetuating improvement commissioners in 1839 to address the confusion of totally-unplanned urban growth.[14] Municipal development was, however, not such a hopeless endeavour but that commercial interests saw it as an area for profitable exploitation. Accordingly the Stoke, Fenton and Longton Gas Company treated with the commissioners to light the streets of the town and a market company was founded to improve trading facilities – activities in due course to be bought out by the town as its instruments of government grew in confidence.

The other face of private provision in the early Victorian town is to be seen in the strength of its voluntary societies and agencies: schools, chapels, friendly and building societies, burial and saving clubs, mechanics' institutes, co-operatives and the like. All helped both to develop the local community and in some measure to discipline it. Though these were not their only or even their principal functions, in the absence of more direct and formal means of controlling the energies of emergent industrialism they acted not only to ameliorate the distress of the victims of such social change but also to pioneer services later to be taken over by the municipality.

Friendly societies both cultivated modest savings and sought to keep their members out of the

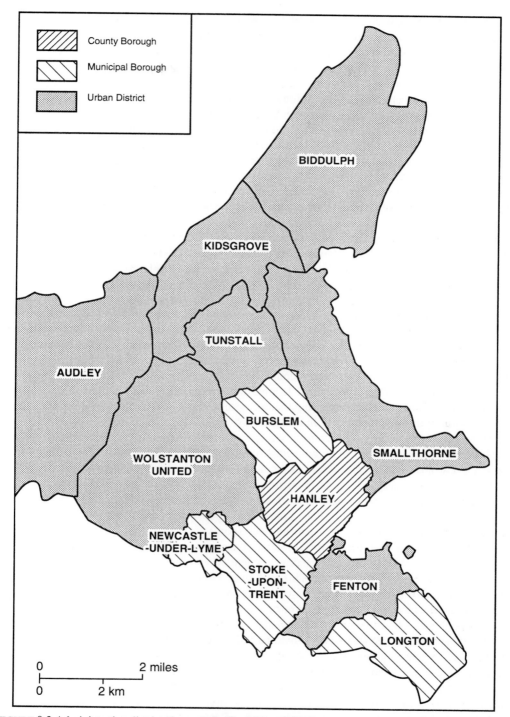

FIGURE 9.2 Administrative districts in north Staffordshire, 1908 (*Source*: T W Freeman, *The conurbations of Great Britain*, Manchester, 1959, 251).

clutches of the poor law so that the parish was spared the cost of supporting these self-helping individuals. Several of the Longton societies went beyond that and debarred benefit to those guilty of acts of 'debauchery or misconduct': the Lane End Female Friendly Society required that all its members be women of sober life and conversation 'well-affected to the present Establishment', a sure marker as to the usefulness of such bodies in an uncertain social environment. Whilst children's savings funds planted 'the germ of provident habits' in the very young, it was said of the building societies in Longton that they were 'a giant power for good [which] had born a very important share in improving, reorganizing and remodelling the town and in elevating its social status'. More particularly the Freehold Land Society sought to purchase land as a means to political enfranchisement. One witness to the factory commissioners testified: 'Industrious, thoughtful men began to see how much by care and economy they could accomplish, and to apply themselves in real earnest, and as a result of their intelligent enterprise, we have as it were, three separate new towns created, and a fourth now in course of erection.'[15]

The same commentator deplored the opposite class: 'Their life-long creed is "Sufficient to the day is the evil thereof" . . . They neither understand the theory nor the practice of economy . . . They have no value of money, except so far as it may secure their present gratifications, and never dream of providing for future contingencies.'[16] Unfortunately this pillar of the Longton Building Society movement, Enoch Palmer, than whom 'no-one was more generally respected', was found in the early 1870s to have been manipulating the books, including the invention of ficticious mortgages, in his own favour. It was possibly this incident that caused Arnold Bennett to mirror Longton's experience by commenting in *Clayhanger*, 'No stories of the defalcation of other secretaries of societies, no rumours as to the evils of the system of the more famous Starr-Bowkett Building Societies ever bred a doubt in Bursley or Turnhill [Burslem and Tunstall] of the eternal soundness of the Bursley and Turnhill Permanent £50 Benefit Building Society.' The Victorian mind hardly needed reminding that no system or organization could be immune to the moral quality or the absence thereof in the men who worked it.

More obviously working class in organization was the co-operative movement. As early as 1828, *The Co-operator* noted the 'great mass of suffering in the Staffordshire Potteries arising out of the low state of wages, the want of employment, and the high prices of the necessaries of life'.[17] Attempts at early co-operative manufacture, as also for the establishing of a potters' labour bank, seem to have foundered, not least because of the methodistical potters' suspicion of Robert Owen's atheism. In the 1880s Longton co-operators returned first to warehousing and then the manufacture of pottery with considerable success.

In the second half of the century a new start was made in retailing, which included the running of a public bakehouse, and the development of a mutual-improvement programme with the opening of a co-op reading room. This took over a tradition that dated back to the founding of a workingmen's club in 1838 which collected together a 'few of the sober and thoughtful men' at the end of a day's work to 'read or talk over subjects that interested them', which led on to the Mechanics' Institute of 1840, and the Athenaeum of the next decade. Its Longton promoters were intent that their town should be complete not only in terms of the instruments of government, not only in terms of profitable industry and environmental improvement, but also in the promotion of culture and intelligence.[18]

The political programme of the working classes was also changing. In 1842 some of the more violent aspects of the Plug Plot riots occurred in the streets of Longton, but by 1854 the leaders of Longton artisans, walking now the path of respectability, were applying to the commissioners for the use of a room in the town hall to hold meetings for responsible

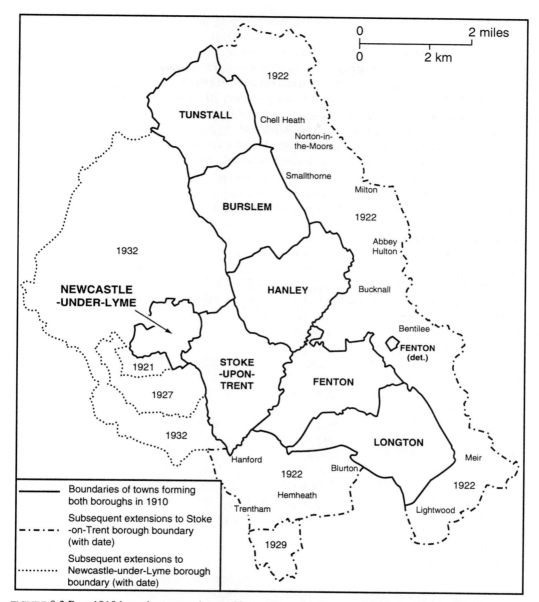

FIGURE 9.3 Post-1910 boundary extensions to Newcastle-under-Lyme and Stoke-on-Trent (*Source*: J G Jenkins, 'The borough of Newcastle-under-Lyme' and 'The federation of the six towns', in *Victoria County History of Staffordshire*, 1963, viii, 1 and 260).

discussion of local concerns. They added their voice to those who opposed the un-elected commissioners increasing their powers in 1863 and 1864 without yielding the principle of representation, which brought to a head the contention that had existed for the past six years as to how Longton was to be governed. As local government became more complex and wide-ranging, so it needed greater powers to enforce its will, but such powers could not be assigned to a body not representative of the whole community: the growth of power was accompanied by the demand that such power be democratically accountable.

Meanwhile Longton's own satellite communities of East Vale and Dresden, fearful of the higher rates that they anticipated would result from the borough's incorporation, opted out of the new borough by creating separate boards of health, leading to the accusation that their inhabitants, benefiting from the services of the borough, made no contribution to them. In 1883–4 these cheap rate areas together with Florence and Normacot were annexed by the borough. Differential levels of rates were also one of the major issues to be overcome in the moves towards federating, or more correctly amalgamating, all the pottery towns in one unitary authority some twenty years later.[19]

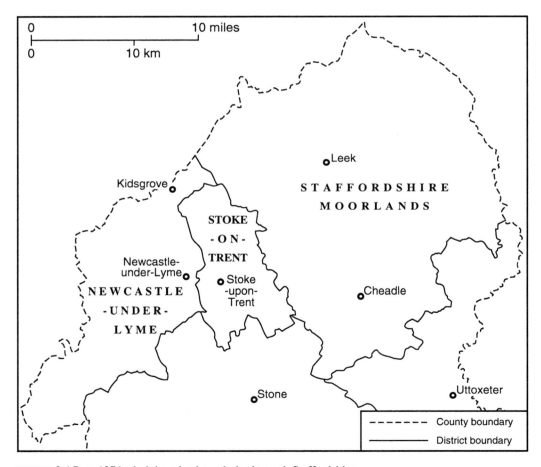

FIGURE 9.4 Post-1974 administrative boundaries in north Staffordshire.

A proposal of 1888 that the ancient county of Staffordshire should be split with the creation of a new 'County of the Potteries' foundered when the new county council legislation was amended by reducing the minimum size for an independent county borough from 100,000 to 50,000, for this enabled Hanley to secure enhanced status on its own, at the same time making the separate county proposal unsupportable. For its part, Hanley blamed the failure on Stoke's insistence on being the chief town of the new county (Fig 9.2). The new century opened with a different proposal, involving not only the Potteries but also Newcastle-under-Lyme and Wolstanton UDC. Although there were fine resolutions, legal difficulties were suggested as a reason for diverting to the less ambitious scheme of redrawing Hanley's boundaries to include the other five towns with covetous eyes being cast upon the intermediate status of much of Wolstanton. But the scheme failed anyhow because of its financial implications.

In 1905 Longton and Stoke proposed a federation of the southern three towns. However, in the course of the investigation of this proposal, John Burns, then president of the Local Government Board, became persuaded that a larger federation would have many advantages and decided to urge this solution upon the pottery towns against the vested interests of local office-holders, differential local services differentially charged, and above all a continuing parochialism. Eventually these forces were overcome even though popular votes in Fenton, Tunstall and Burslem went against the proposals, notwithstanding the duke of Sutherland's offer to endow the new county borough with his Trentham estate. After a number of petitions to the House of Lords against the proposals, the legislation securing federation was finally passed in December 1908 for implementation in March 1910, a fatal time-lag allowing for an Indian summer of anti-federationism, which gave the new county borough a difficult birth and Burslem two town halls by way of spending capital balances locally rather than see them diffused across the district. Such was the lack of trust that the first meeting of the new authority had to be held in the North Staffordshire Hotel, after which successive monthly meetings rotated around the different town halls until in October 1910 the council decided to make its permanent home in the council chamber at Stoke.

The inter-relationship of the north Staffordshire towns was not yet finished. In 1922 the borough extended its boundaries to the east and to the south. In 1925 it was granted the title of a city, and in 1928 its mayor became a lord mayor. Attempts to take over Newcastle, as well as other adjoining areas, in both 1930 and 1946, however, proved abortive. The 1930 take-over, for as such it was seen, was bitterly fought by Newcastle: their MP, Colonel J Wedgwood, led the fight and for his efforts was elected mayor of Newcastle for the following two years and became almost irremovable as the borough's MP, though now sitting in the Labour interest. The 1930 proposals, however, softened the residents of Wolstanton to their absorption into Newcastle in 1932 by the casting vote of their chairman, though 96 per cent of the electorate voted in favour, a union resolutely rejected seven years earlier (Fig 9.3).

In 1974 further changes to the structure of local government came with the implementation of the 1972 Local Government Act belatedly following on the Redcliffe-Maude Report of 1969 which had highlighted the ongoing problems of relating efficiency in regional administration to the participatory goals of local democracy. By this Act both Newcastle and Stoke became district councils of a strengthened Staffordshire County Council, which for Stoke particularly meant a considerable loss of status and political autonomy (Fig 9.4). The 1974 revisions, now almost twenty years' old, are ripe once more for modification, though it can be argued that the most critical changes have taken place in terms of the restrictions now imposed by central government on the amount of discretion allowed to governors at the more local level. Such serious national debate, as focused in the work of the present Commission on Local Government, once more provides the arena in which the ancient debates between Newcastle and Stoke are resurrected, though the spoils of the battle, in terms of real and effective powers, promise to be less than in any former period of history.

REFERENCES

1. M W Greenslade, 'The city of Stoke-on-Trent', in *Victoria County History of Staffordshire (VCH Staffs)* 1963, viii, 80.
2. J Ward, *The borough of Stoke-upon-Trent*, 1843, 29–30.
3. *Staffordshire Advertiser*, 12 March, 16 July and 30 August 1831; Herefordshire Record Office, Foxley Mss, B47/BVD/65.
4. Ward, *Stoke*, 361–4.
5. Ibid, 369–71; W E Townley, 'Urban administration and health: a case study of Hanley in the mid-nineteenth century', unpublished MA thesis, Keele University, 1969; S and B Webb, *The development of English local government, 1689–1815*, 1963, 173.
6. Townley, 'Urban administration', 128, fn 101.
7. Ward, *Stoke*, 576; Townley, 'Urban administration', 113.
8. Townley, 'Urban administration', 137–43.
9. Ibid, 160–4.
10. Ibid, 200.
11. *Staffordshire Sentinel*, 22 September 1866.
12. Ibid, 9 May 1868.
13. Ibid, 31 March 1866.
14. J H Y Briggs, *The history of Longton: 1, the birth of a community*, Keele, 1982.
15. British Parliamentary Papers, 1865, XX, 'Reports of inspectors of factories, 31 January 1865', 92 (evidence of Enoch Palmer).
16. Ibid, 94.
17. Briggs, *Longton*, 89.
18. Ibid, 96.
19. J G Jenkins, 'The federation of the six towns', in *VCH Staffs*, viii, 252.

10. The Potteries in the Interwar Period

B J TURTON

At the end of the First World War the Potteries could still be clearly identified as a cluster of largely Victorian industrial communities with an employment structure little changed from that of the mid-nineteenth century. Coal and ironstone mining, iron and steel production and above all the many branches of the ceramic industry dominated the local economy. Although the constituent towns of the Potteries had amalgamated in 1910 to form the county borough of Stoke-on-Trent each centre still retained its separate entity with its own local services and strong social affiliations and loyalties. Newcastle-under-Lyme maintained its historic and exclusive status as a municipal borough and the growing townships of Chesterton, Knutton and Silverdale were contained within Wolstanton United Urban District, whose population in 1921 exceeded that of Newcastle. To the north the mining communities of Kidsgrove and Biddulph had also kept their identity as urban districts.

Between the wars the geography of much of urban Britain underwent a revolution founded upon the decentralization of population into a suburban periphery. This process was aided by an awareness of the urgent need to improve housing and living standards and by the availability of cheap public transport, mortgages for the private housing sector and the encouragement by government through building subsidies of an ambitious programme of local authority house construction. For most towns and cities in Britain this suburban growth was focused upon a single commercial core but in north Staffordshire it had the effect of finally creating a conurbation from a loose grouping of urban centres which had possessed a coherence based upon industrialization but had, until the early 1930s, lacked a corresponding physical unity.

This expansion of residential areas was accompanied in many towns and cities by the establishment of new 'light' consumer-orientated industries, often associated with the demand for electrical appliances and, at a later stage, motor vehicles. The growing availability of reliable road freight transport in the 1920s enabled many of these new industries to occupy sites on the urban fringe alongside main roads but in north Staffordshire this type of development was restricted to Newcastle, on the main London to Scotland trunk road and the Potteries did not share in this growth.

THE POTTERIES AT THE END OF THE FIRST WORLD WAR

In 1921 the north Staffordshire urban region had a population of 334,700 distributed between the principal pottery towns, Newcastle and the surrounding and still physically separate smaller mining communities such as Silverdale and Chesterton (Table 10.1). Although these independent communities were interlinked by railways and tramways the limits of each town could still be clearly traced at the end of the war. Newcastle, for example, had a tenuous link eastwards with Stoke through Hartshill, where a ribbon growth of housing had taken place in the late nineteenth century, but elsewhere the urban fringe was marked by agricultural land, institutions such as the City General Hospital or by the low density spread of villas that formed the Brampton estate to the north of the town centre. Similarly, Burslem was separated from the built-up areas of Cobridge to the south by the Brownhills estate, with its eastern limits marked by the North Staffordshire Railway's loop-line and its western boundary by the Trent and Mersey Canal in the Fowlea valley.

Table 10.1

Population changes, 1921–45

Administrative area	1921	1931	1939	1945
Stoke-on-Trent County Borough	267,647	276,639	272,000*	264,820*
Newcastle-under-Lyme Municipal Borough	20,549	23,246	64,500*	68,300+
Wolstanton United Urban District	29,232	30,525	–	–
Chesterton	7439	6861		
Silverdale	8235	8662		
Wolstanton	13,558	15,002		
Biddulph Urban District	7931	8346		10,560+
Kidsgrove Urban District	9346	9938		14,890+

* estimated totals; + estimated totals for 1947
Sources: Census, 1921–31, and Registrar General's estimates

Employment in 1921 in the urban region amounted to 148,193, with 46 per cent in the various categories of the pottery industry. Within Stoke Borough women accounted for 56 per cent of the potteries' workforce, whereas in Newcastle and Wolstanton, where coal and ironstone mining was a significant employer of labour, the proportion of females in the labour force was much less. The collieries in the region employed about 37,000 and the iron and steel industry 3600, with a similar number in the engineering sector.

Although much of the labour force still lived within short walking distances of places of employment, especially the pot-banks of the inner urban areas, the movement of workers between the component towns of the Potteries, making use of tram and local rail services, was well established by the early 1920s. Over 17,000 of the 118,000 workers employed within the borough of Stoke travelled in daily from Newcastle, Kidsgrove, Biddulph and Wolstanton, and over one-half of the labour force resident in the last district found employment elsewhere (Tables 10.2 and 3).

Table 10.2

Employment in principal industries, 1921–45

Industry	1921	1931	1939	1945
Coal-mining	36,600	30,651	23,450	21,000
Iron and steel manufacturing	3643	2140	3867	3200
Pottery and allied trades	54,200	62,648	61,250	41,689

Sources: Census industry tables; Chamber of Trade estimates

Table 10.3

Labour mobility in 1921

Administrative area	Total occupied and resident in area	Total working in area	Total working elsewhere
Stoke-on-Trent County Borough	118,601	102,157	12,811
Newcastle-under-Lyme Municipal Borough	9,461	3,434	5,630
Wolstanton United Urban District	12,960	5,747	6,775
Kidsgrove Urban District	3,906	2,484	1,341
Biddulph Urban District	3,265	2,637	531

Source: Census industry tables, 1921

RESIDENTIAL GROWTH

Between the wars north Staffordshire shared in the national housebuilding boom and by 1930 the new private and municipal estates had been extended far enough finally to bring about the coalescence of the seven towns of the region, producing a sprawling conurbation from Newcastle in the west to Meir in the east and from Tunstall in the north to Trentham in the south.

The physical setting of the Potteries within the headstreams of the Trent had confined most urban growth before 1914 to the interfluves founded upon Coal Measure sandstones and development in the valleys had been mainly associated with mining, ironworking and clay and marl extraction. Any plans for an extension of residential areas had to contend with difficulties posed by steeply sloping land, abandoned tracts of small-scale mining where subsidence and uncharted mineshafts were serious problems, and districts where future coal extraction would be likely to create subsidence.[1] Elsewhere, and especially to the south of Newcastle and the Potteries, land that was suited to large-scale residential development was in agricultural use or contained within large estates such as Trentham. The possibilities for interwar expansion were therefore limited to only a few areas but despite the various drawbacks both Newcastle and Stoke experienced substantial growth up to 1939.

Stoke-on-Trent, in common with many other cities which saw rapid industrial growth in the nineteenth century, was by the early twentieth century aware of the deficiencies in much of its housing stock, particularly in the inner urban areas of Hanley, Burslem, Stoke and Tunstall. However serious efforts to replace substandard dwellings only began after the First World War when it was estimated that there was a national shortage of about half a million houses. The 1919 Housing and Town Planning Act required local authorities to take stock of housing needs and plan the necessary new schemes, and later in the year subsequent legislation provided building subsidies of between £130 and £160 per unit. The Housing Act of 1924 permitted higher subsidies and enabled local authorities to undertake the extensive programmes of construction which contributed so much to the overall suburban growth of the interwar period. Municipal initiatives accounted for 31 per cent of all houses built in Britain between 1919 and 1934 and both Newcastle and Stoke councils took full advantage of the 1923 legislation which required all authorities with populations of more than 20,000 to prepare housing schemes by 1926.[2]

The housebuilding programme in Stoke-on-Trent was begun in 1921 and construction continued until 1940 at an average rate of 550 units each year. Annual totals did not exceed 670 until 1936 but thereafter, with the commencement of a widespread slum-clearance programme, building rates increased although in 1938 the Public Health Department was still able to identify 150 locations where urgent action was still required, principally in Cobridge, Etruria Vale, Longport and Pittshill (Table 10.4).

Table 10.4

Housebuilding in Stoke-on-Trent County Borough, 1921–39

Year	Municipal housing	Privately-built housing	Total
1921	54	–	54
1922	102	273	375
1923	224	–	224
1924	170	47	217
1925	42	304	346
1926	404	302	706
1927	550	379	929
1928	288	301	589
1929	232	645	877
1930	327	402	729
1931	495	465	960
1932	604	484	1088
1933	676	745	1421
1934	601	1064	1665
1935	465	1059	1524
1936	1117	1045	2162
1937	922	1626	2548
1938	310	1258	1568
1939	515	747	1262

Source: City of Stoke-on-Trent, *Housing, 1919–57*, 1958.

Council housebuilding began on a modest scale in Trent Vale, Abbey Hulton, Meir and Basford on sites which could be easily acquired and developed. A total of 30 sites, each with over 50 dwellings, and many smaller housing clusters were completed by the beginning of the Second World War.[3] Large-scale estates were, however, mainly confined to areas to the east and south-east of the Tunstall-Longton urban axis on land within the existing county borough boundaries and within the parishes of Chell, Smallthorne, Milton, Caverswall and Norton which were transferred wholly or in part to Stoke Borough in 1922. By 1939 the new peripheral estates at Abbey Hulton, Carmountside, Meir and Bucknall, together with the Stanfield estate at Burslem, each contained over 450 units, the majority being semi-detached houses with three bedrooms, kitchen and living-room (Pl 10.1). This concentration on sites to the east of the conurbation, and within easy reach of many of the larger collieries, was to be continued after the war with the further development of Meir and the building of the Ubberlee-Bentilee complex adjacent to Abbey Hulton.

The history of municipal housing in Newcastle predates the 1919 legislation, with the construction in 1915 of Corporation Cottages (29 units) on a site at Castle Green to replace earlier buildings. This action was taken under the 1870 Housing of the Working Classes Act and was the first initiative in local authority housing in north Staffordshire. As in Stoke it was necessary for Newcastle Borough to acquire sites for larger housing schemes from neighbouring districts and parts of Clayton parish were acquired in 1921 and 1927. This was followed by the transfer to Newcastle in 1932 of the entire Wolstanton United Urban District, with its population of 30,000, and parts of Audley Urban and Stone Rural Districts. With the exception of the Poolfields estate built just to the west of the old town centre all the larger council housing areas were located on the borough peripheries at Clayton, Chesterton and Knutton, with the latter two schemes having been begun by the Wolstanton council prior to its acquisition by Newcastle. A total of 2703 units were provided between 1919 and 1939[4] (Fig 10.1).

The interwar construction of housing in the private sector was encouraged by the series of Property Acts passed between 1915 and 1925 to ease the transfer of small plots of freehold land to the new generation of houseowners. Land in agricultural use attracted low rents after the First World War and many landowners were persuaded to dispose of their property to speculators anxious to acquire building sites to meet the growing demand for houses from those in

PLATE 10.1 City of Stoke-on-Trent housing estates at Meir, 1945 (Air Photo Archives, Keele University). In the south-east corner is the Meir air-landing strip and the government agency factories occupied by Rootes for aircraft repair in the Second World War; in the far west lie the extremities of the pre-1914 urban area.

professional and administrative occupations. This demand was financed by building societies attracting money from investors who were reluctant in the early 1920s to support manufacturing industry, and interest rates below 4 per cent and 95 per cent advances proved an attraction to many workers.[5]

Within the city the number of units provided by the private sector exceeded the municipal totals in most years between 1928 and 1939, with building reaching a peak in the 1934–8 period, when annual totals of completions exceeded 1000 houses (Table 10.4). Available land in small plots on the margins of Tunstall, Burslem, Hanley, Stoke and Longton all attracted private builders, the predominant type of dwelling being the ubiquitous three-bedroomed semi-detached, and 'ribbon development' took place along the principal roads leading north from Tunstall to Goldenhill, north-east from Hanley to Endon and south-east from Longton towards Blythe Bridge. In particular the housing built west of Stoke centre itself towards Hartshill met that of adjacent Newcastle, establishing for the first time a physical link between market town and new industrial centres.

Private sector housebuilding within Newcastle was concentrated into several distinct areas. The larger types of semi- and detached houses on more spacious plots were located in the Westlands, founded upon the level and well-drained Keele sandstones to the south-west of the old town centre (Pl 10.2). Building took place on both sides of the Market Drayton road, with some ribbon development along the Clayton road. Other estates were mainly located to the east of the A34 trunk road in Wolstanton, Basford and Porthill, between the Lyme and Fowlea valleys. Smaller areas of private housing were also constructed in Silverdale, Knutton and Chesterton[6] (Fig 10.1).

This interwar housing expansion had a significant effect upon urban population distribution in both Stoke and Newcastle, although only about 20,000 persons were added to the total population of the conurbation between 1921 and the early 1940s. Wards in Stoke containing large tracts of poor quality nineteenth-century terraced housing lost much of their population between 1921 and the late 1930s, whereas the peripheral wards in which new estates had been built recorded very high increases. Ward 4 in Burslem, for example, lost 30 per cent and Ward 2 (Tunstall) 27 per cent but Ward 26, with the Meir municipal estate, increased in population by 68 per cent and Ward 28 (Abbey Hulton) by 167 per cent. Similar patterns of population redistribution may be seen in Newcastle Borough (Fig 10.2).

URBAN TRANSPORT

Mobility for the majority of town dwellers between the wars was largely provided by trams, motor buses and, to a much more limited extent, by suburban railway services. All three forms of urban transport existed in the Potteries and, in common with other large cities, the period 1920–30 was marked by the establishment and expansion of many small and highly competitive bus companies. The Potteries Electric Traction Company (PET) had completed a 30-mile tramway network serving Newcastle and the pottery towns by the early twentieth century and the flexibility of their services soon challenged the monopoly of the North Staffordshire Railway's system. The PET also introduced experimental motor bus services between 1901 and 1914 to act as feeders to the trams and ten private bus companies had also been established but these innovations were interrupted by the war.[7] Competition for traffic returned in 1920, however, with operations shared between twelve PET vehicles and nineteen other companies. By 1924, when PET had 27 buses in the area, it faced competition from over 80 privately-owned vehicles on 22 routes. The battle for a growing traffic was fiercest on the Tunstall-Burslem-Hanley-Stoke-Longton axis, which had attracted 29 small operators with a total of 75

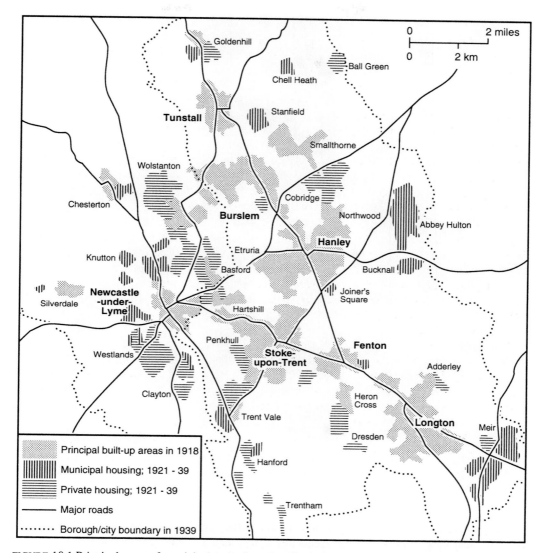

FIGURE 10.1 Principal areas of municipal and private housing built between 1919 and 1939 (*Source*: City of Stoke-on-Trent, *Housing 1919–1957*, 1958).

buses. The PET realized that the expansion of its bus fleet could best be achieved by abandoning its tramway services, which had seen a decline in their traffic from 31.58 million passengers in 1919 to 25.48 in 1924. However, the Stoke Council was opposed to this action, declining an offer to purchase the system in 1925, and PET had to secure an agreement with the Ministry of Transport to replace its trams with motor vehicles. All trams were withdrawn by mid-1928 and the PET's augmented fleet of 171 buses faced competition from 55 smaller operators by 1930.[8] At this time Stoke was one of the few large cities where the local authorities did not operate their own passenger services and the vigour of the battle between the various independent companies for traffic on the main Tunstall-Stoke-Longton route was highlighted by

PLATE 10.2 The Westlands post-1920 private housing area, 1945 (Air Photo Archives, Keele University). To the north is the Orme Road muncipal housing estate, separated from the Westlands by the main Newcastle–Nantwich road.

the traffic commissioners: 'No timetable existed and the vehicles shuttled down in a continuous game of "leap frog" with an average frequency of less than a minute at peak periods.'[9]

However, this chaotic situation was gradually resolved with a progressive series of mergers and takeovers begun by the PET in 1927. By 1939 the company, reorganized as the Potteries Motor Traction (PMT) in 1933, had acquired 25 of its smaller competitors and in 1944 it bought out Associated Bus Companies Ltd, the largest of the surviving independent operators which itself had been formed from 25 smaller firms.[10]

These interwar bus companies provided three main types of service to passengers in the north Staffordshire conurbation. Most routes, and those with the most frequent timetables, were concentrated within the built-up area, linking the various town centres and the newly-established suburbs and municipal housing estates of Stoke and Newcastle. A second category provided transport between the principal Potteries centres and neighbouring market towns such as Stone, Leek, Cheadle, Uttoxeter and Market Drayton. Finally, there was a modest development of pioneer long-distance routes between Hanley and Manchester, Chester, Derby and Birmingham.

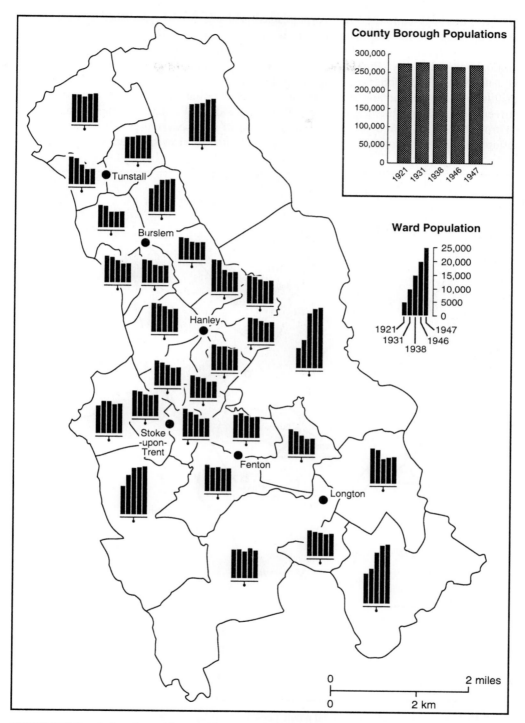

FIGURE 10.2 Population changes by ward in the city of Stoke-on-Trent, 1919–47 (*Sources*: Censuses, 1921 and 1931; Stoke-on-Trent City Council).

In 1939 the PMT carried 57 million passengers and was firmly established as the principal bus undertaking in the Potteries and the surrounding rural areas. Eighty services were in regular operation, including fifteen long distance routes to destinations such as Manchester, Birmingham and Derby (Fig 10.3). All the peripheral housing estates were provided with frequent services, Longton, for example, being linked with the Meir estates and Burslem with Smallthorne by buses running at five-minute intervals. Similar service intervals were provided between Newcastle, the municipal estate at Poolfields and the Westlands housing area.

Throughout this period of vigorous expansion of road passenger transport the North Staffordshire Railway continued to maintain its suburban services between Stoke, Newcastle,

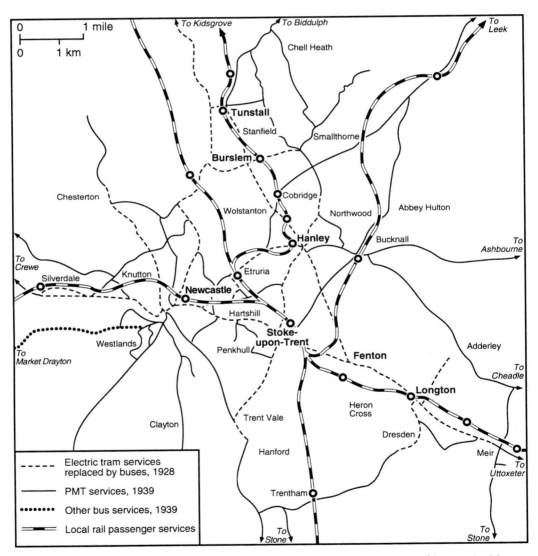

FIGURE 10.3 Development of road and rail public passenger services, 1919–39 (*Sources*: Potteries Motor Traction timetables; G K Smith, *Potteries Motor Traction*, 1977).

Leek and Kidsgrove, by way of the circuitous 'loop-line' through Hanley, Burslem and Tunstall, although traffic was much reduced from pre-war levels. In the east, however, the decline of mining in the Audley area and the fall in passenger traffic resulted in the closure in 1931 of the branch between Keele, Audley and Alsager. The Biddulph valley line also lost its passenger services in 1931.[11]

As road traffic in the Potteries expanded steadily during the interwar period the first evidence of congestion within built-up areas was seen. Stoke prepared plans for eastern and western bypasses to the main Tunstall-Stoke axis but no action was taken and it was not until construction of the A500 route in 1977 along the line of the proposed western bypass that a through road avoiding these towns was available.

MINING AND QUARRYING

In 1920 coal was being mined from over 70 pits, although 32 of these employed less than 150 workers and only nine collieries had workforces of over 1000. Production was still concentrated on the exposed field at large mines such as Victoria, Whitfield, Norton, Sneyd and Shelton Deep, but Stafford colliery and several smaller pits in the west were beginning to exploit the much greater depths of the concealed measures. These larger mines were owned by over 24 private companies, such as Shelton Iron and Steel, Florence Coal and Iron and Chatterley-Whitfield, but many lesser enterprises existed operating the smaller pits and drift mines scattered over the exposed section of the coalfield.[12]

In the mid-1920s production was disrupted by the General Strike but the north Staffordshire mines were not affected by the loss of export markets to the same extent as other British fields since much of their market was within Staffordshire and adjacent areas. There was a general trend for mining to move westwards and southwards in search of workable seams in the concealed field, with the extension of the coalfaces of Stafford and Florence collieries at depths of up to 3600 feet towards Barlaston and Meaford. New pits were also developed in the early 1920s at Chesterton, Wolstanton and Hem Heath. Extraction in the faulted anticlinal areas to the west and north of Newcastle was gradually abandoned, with the closure of pits in Kidsgrove, Talke and Apedale valley, although several drift or footrail mines survived with workforces of less than twelve.[13]

Several amalgamations of mining companies took place, with the disappearance of firms such as Robert Heath and Low Moor, which had extensive coal and ironstone interests, and eighteen of the companies recorded in 1926 had ceased to exist by 1938 (Pl 10.3). By the latter date large-scale mining was in the hands of eleven companies and several of the collieries still working the exposed field had expanded to employ over 2000 (Sneyd and Deep pits at Hanley, and Whitfield north of Tunstall). The newly opened collieries on the concealed field at Hem Heath and Wolstanton had also grown to employ over 1000 miners, and of the total labour force of 24,255 about 80 per cent were in pits with over 1000 men. Many much smaller pits had survived, however, working seams in areas abandoned by the major companies, but the number involved in the 25 mines with fewer than 100 men was only 10 per cent of the total workforce (Fig 10.4).[14]

During the interwar period quarrying of the Etruria marls and the blackband group continued as the basis of the brick and tile industry. Demand for these products rose with the expansion of housebuilding programmes and this section of the ceramics industry experienced fewer problems stemming from market fluctuations than the pottery and allied trades.

IRON AND STEEL

Ironstone extraction and the production of pig-iron was closely associated with coal-mining, several companies, such as Shelton Iron and Steel, being involved in both activities. Substantial quantities of Coal Measure ironstone continued to be mined in north Staffordshire during the interwar period with annual totals of up to 130,000 tons, but by 1940 production had ceased and ore had to imported from the east midlands and overseas sources.[15]

Five works producing pig-iron from sixteen blast furnaces were still operating in 1921 but steel manufacturing was confined to the Shelton works at Etruria (Pl 10.4). Only three firms survived the economic problems of the 1930s, however, and by 1940 the only significant smelting centres for pig-iron were Goldendale and Shelton (combined with steel). Within Stoke employment in iron and steel manufacture declined from 3761 in 1921 to 3000 in 1939.

POTTERY AND ALLIED INDUSTRIES

The locational stability of the china and earthenware pottery firms in north Staffordshire between the wars contrasts with the changes seen in the distribution of many consumer industries in other parts of Britain. The advantages of road freight transport, labour mobility conferred by the motor bus and the migration of much of the industrial workforce to new peripheral housing estates could have stimulated a similar outward movement of pottery works.

PLATE 10.3 Adderley Green colliery, 1925 (Warrillow Collection, Keele University Library). North of Longton on the exposed coalfield, this colliery produced 150,000 tons annually with a labour force of 520. Owned by Stirrup and Pye, it was closed in the post-1945 period of rationalization.

In fact, throughout the interwar period the majority of pottery concerns continued to occupy restricted sites in central urban areas which were often subject to mining subsidence and had poor access for motor lorries.

One important technological advance which required more space than the conventional premises centred around the bottle kiln were usually able to offer was the introduction of the gas-fired tunnel oven. By 1921, when the advantages of the tunnel oven were generally recognized, it was estimated that 80 per cent of existing pot-banks were too small to install this

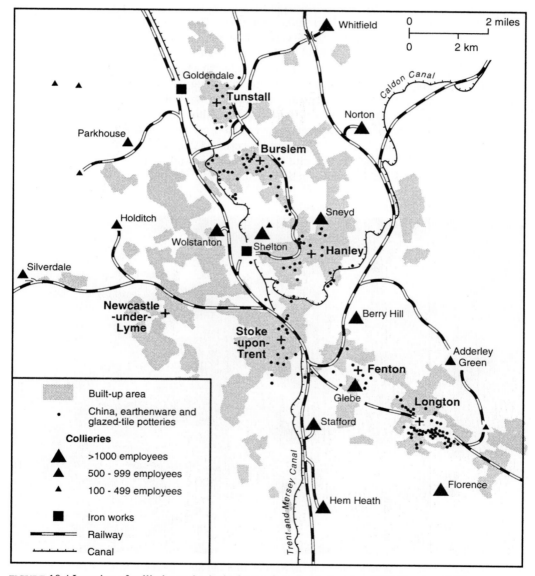

FIGURE 10.4 Location of collieries and principal manufacturing industries, 1939 (*Source: Colliery yearbook and coal trades directory*, 1938).

new equipment despite the 60 per cent saving in fuel costs that using gas rather than coal could achieve. Experiments with electric tunnel ovens had also been conducted in the pre-war period but by 1927 only two furnaces were in regular use. One tunnel oven 300 ft long had the firing capacity of six of the traditional kilns but few of the existing sites could be adapted to accommodate this length. In addition, many of the smaller family firms with fewer than 50 workers had the bulk of their capital tied up in their premises and could afford neither to finance a move out to larger sites nor to purchase the modern plant necessary to exploit the savings in production costs offered by the tunnel kiln.[16]

The British market for north Staffordshire chinaware was strongly challenged in the 1920s by imports of cheaper porcelain goods from Germany and Czechoslovakia. The situation was exacerbated by the effects of the 1926 General Strike and in 1927 the British Pottery Manufacturers' Federation was successful in obtaining a safeguarding import duty of £1.40 per cwt on all imported china for a five-year period. Electrical porcelain manufacture did not experience these problems, and benefited from the increasing market for insulators from both housing and the electric distribution industry between the wars. Production in existing works grew and three new works were opened at Hanley and at Milton, to the east of the conurbation.

A local trade directory for 1919–20 contains over 250 firms associated with the production of tiles, earthenware and china and the 1921 census records 54,200 workers in these industries in Stoke.[17] Estimates for the late 1920s cite 60,000 workers and in 1939 there were 70,000 employees, although this included those in brick manufacture. The only interwar example of the

PLATE 10.4 The Trent and Mersey Canal and the Shelton Iron and Steel Works, Eturia (Stoke-on-Trent City Council). The bridge carries the Potteries 'loop' railway across the canal; in the extreme right is Etruria Hall.

planned relocation of a major pottery is provided by Wedgwoods, whose Etruria site alongside the Trent and Mersey Canal had by the 1930s become inadequate to meet production requirements. A decision to introduce electric tunnel ovens was followed by the acquisition of land in Barlaston for the construction of new premises and employees' housing alongside the Stoke to Stafford railway. Although the chosen site was on the concealed coalfield any future mining operations would be at depths unlikely to create any subsidence problems. The transfer of production was planned to begin in the late 1930s but was interrupted by the outbreak of war and not finally completed until the 1950s.

OTHER MANUFACTURING INDUSTRIES

Unlike south Staffordshire the iron and steel industry of Stoke had never been the basis of a flourishing engineering industry. Several firms specialized in mechanical equipment for the coal-mining and pottery industries but the only large-scale works in the engineering category were the two railway locomotive works at Stoke, one owned by the North Staffordshire Railway and one by Kerr, Stuart and Company. With the incorporation of the North Staffordshire Railway in 1923 into the newly created London, Midland and Scottish Railway locomotive building at the Stoke plant was discontinued and transferred to Crewe, leaving the Stoke works to concentrate on repairs and maintenance. The Kerr, Stuart factory continued to build steam locomotives for the home and export market although its future became increasingly uncertain in the 1930s as demand declined.

Manufacturing in Newcastle was confined to papermaking and a small-scale textile industry with a specialization in fustian cutting. Six mills continued to produce fustian in the town until the late 1920s when competition from Lancashire mills with automatic equipment became too strong.[18] A uniform clothing factory was opened at Enderley Mills but the combined workforce in all these activities was insignificant and large numbers of Newcastle workers continued to find employment in the pottery and mining industries.

Industrial diversification in north Staffordshire only occurred on a very limited scale between the wars. The expansion of motor vehicle production in Britain after 1918 created a demand for components and in the 1920s the Michelin tyre company decided to move from their cramped site in Kensington, central London, to larger premises. Stoke-on-Trent City Council offered the company concessions in the supply of electricity, water and housing and in 1927 Michelin occupied a new factory in Trent Vale adjacent to the A34 and with rail access. The workforce had expanded to 1550 by 1939 and the Michelin factory was the only new enterprise of any significance to be established in the Potteries area in the interwar period.[19]

Employment in the service sector experienced little change in this period, with each of the six pottery towns and Newcastle maintaining a limited range of retailing, professional and administrative functions and no single centre growing to dominate the conurbation, although Hanley did display the greatest variety of retail facilities. At the end of the 1930s Stoke-on-Trent was still identified as one of the largest urban centres in Britain where manufacturing industry dominated the employment structure and where the 27 per cent employed in services was well below the national average.

The coal-mining, ironworking and pottery industries were severely affected by the recession of the early 1920s and the more prolonged economic depression of 1929–32 and unemployment in some districts such as Kidsgrove exceeded 22 per cent during these periods. However, these three basic activities continued to dominate the industrial structure throughout the interwar period and the introduction of alternative sources of employment had little impact upon the overall situation. Workforce numbers declined in several of the leading industries and technical changes were introduced into many of the larger pottery works, but the geographical location of almost all works remained basically unchanged until 1939. The coal-mining industry, however, experienced significant changes, with the near-extinction of deep mining in the older districts of the exposed coalfield and a concentration of new investment in the south, tapping the deeper seams of the Middle Coal Measures.

THE SECOND WORLD WAR

In 1939 the north Staffordshire conurbation had a total labour force of 162,000, with 40 per cent in the ceramic industry and 16 per cent in coal-mining. The declining iron and steel industry had about 3000 workers and engineering had a similar number (Table 10.2). This well-established structure was to be substantially altered during the early years of the Second World War as sites in north Staffordshire were adopted as strategic locations for the production of munitions and other military equipment, being just beyond the effective range of enemy bomber aircraft.[20] A government-owned Royal Ordnance factory for production of ammunition cases was built at Radway Green, to the north of the conurbation, with a second plant for shell filling at Swynnerton, between Newcastle and Stone; at peak production in the early 1940s over 35,000 were employed.

A second government initiative was the building of four 'agency factories', with almost 100,000 m² of production space for occupation by new munitions firms or by existing companies whose premises in more vulnerable districts of Britain had been damaged or destroyed by enemy action. These were situated in the Milehouse area of Newcastle, close to one of the larger municipal housing estates, and on the extreme south-east margins of the conurbation at Blythe Bridge. The two Milehouse works were allocated to British Thomson Houston for shell production and to the BSA company for manufacturing aircraft guns. At Blythe Bridge the factories were occupied by Rootes, the Coventry-based vehicle group, for aircraft repairs, being adjacent to Meir airfield. These three companies employed 8750 when working at full capacity in the early 1940s.[21]

Production of essential war equipment was also introduced into existing works requisitioned by the government. Several electrical porcelain factories, a number of small foundries and engineering works, the Michelin tyre plant, and Shelton iron and steel works came into this category. The Dunlop tyre company also took over a part of Wedgwood's Etruria factory for tyre remoulding. A total of 575,000 m² of industrial floorspace in north Staffordshire was requisitioned for wartime production, with 304,000 from the pottery industry alone.

The operation of these three categories of works on a continuous basis created a demand for a labour force which rose to a maximum of 48,000, or just under one-third of the pre-war total. Many of the key skilled personnel were drafted in from other parts of Britain and accommodated in hostels provided close to the two Royal Ordnance plants which were the largest employers. Much of the demand, however, was met by a planned redeployment of the existing workforce, particularly that in the pottery industry. An estimated 272 pottery factories existed in 1939, although about 20,000 workers were employed or on short-time.[22] Production of domestic pottery was permitted to continue during the war at only 88 of these works, with many small firms sharing their capacity. A further 32 firms ceased production entirely and over 100 premises were used solely for storage or remained empty. Large numbers of the employees displaced by this rationalization were drafted into the production of wartime equipment.

These changes in industrial structure resulting from the urgent requirements of the war effort were more significant than any of those experienced in the Potteries during the previous century. Employment in all branches of ceramics was more than halved whereas engineering, which in 1939 accounted for only 3330, expanded to occupy almost 29,000, largely due to the opening of the Royal Ordnance and agency factories. Similarly, the workforce in the 'vehicles and aircraft' category increased from 1042 in 1939 to over 5000 at peak wartime production. The distribution of employment at this time was also in marked contrast to the traditional concentration of both male and female labour in industries based upon the Potteries. The urban areas of Newcastle, Kidsgrove and Biddulph, and the rural area of Swynnerton, which together in the late 1930s had employed only 25,800, accounted for 65,700 in 1943, with women accounting for 47 per cent of this total (Table 10.5).

Table 10.5

Wartime changes in employment

Industry	1939 insured employment	Wartime peak/trough	1951 insured employment
Bricks, pottery, glass, cement	69,685	29,026	63,556
Service industries	38,456	35,971	63,002
Coal, etc, mining	27,260	24,251	20,883
Textiles, clothing	4005	3007	4163
Metal manufacture	3867	5599	6039
Engineering	3321	24,866	11,124
Wood, paper, printing	2522	1477	3428
Food, drink, tobacco	2093	1645	3315
'Other metal industries'	1971	819	1668
'Other manufacturing'	1669	3228	5073
Vehicles, aircraft	1042	5171	1194
Chemicals	894	21,076	4167

Source: A Moyes, 'The industrial economy of north Staffordshire in the Second World War', *N Staffs Jnl Fld Stud*, 16, 1976, 79.

THE POTTERIES IN 1945

At the conclusion of the war north Staffordshire faced the inevitable rundown and eventual closure of the munitions and aircraft plants established in the early 1940s. The introduction of these works had created a level of industrial diversification in the region which represented a far more balanced structure than that which had persisted between the wars. Decisions made in 1945 as to the disposal of this now surplus wartime production capacity were to have a significant influence upon the pattern of subsequent economic growth in the region and upon physical planning policies.

The two agency factories in Newcastle were to remain as engineering works after 1945. British Thomson Houston retained their premises for the manufacture of electric motors for domestic appliances and the BSA plant, which had been leased by Rolls Royce in 1944, was taken over in 1946 by Rists Wires and Cables, producing electrical components for vehicles. The Rootes company had no wish to retain their Blythe Bridge agency works after the war and in 1946 the larger of the two premises was occupied by the Simplex domestic appliance firm. Numbers employed fell rapidly at the two Royal Ordnance factories but both were retained for the continuing manufacture of munitions in the postwar period, thus maintaining employment levels in these peripheral rural areas.

The pottery industry was in urgent need of rebuilding and re-equipment in the immediate postwar years. Much of the female labour force which had been occupied in light engineering during the war was reluctant to return to the china and earthenware industries, and manufacturers realized that the all-important export trade could only be re-established with improved and more efficient methods of production. A contemporary review of the industry recommended improvements in factory layout in order to increase output per man-hour and the replacement wherever possible of bottle kilns by tunnel ovens, whose advantages in terms of fuel efficiency had been demonstrated in the interwar period.[23] However, the adoption of electric and gas ovens was a slow process and in 1945 the landscape of industrial north Staffordshire was still dominated by the distinctive outline of the bottle kiln, some 900 being recorded as standing in that year.[24]

CONCLUSIONS

North Staffordshire shared in the nationwide process of suburban growth between the wars and acquired many of the features of the mid-twentieth century conurbation. The ambitious housing programmes promoted by municipal and private enterprise after 1921 had been necessarily halted during the war but many of the peripheral areas of expansion such as the Westlands in Newcastle and the Meir and Abbey Hulton estates in Stoke still had ample land for further growth, although developments had to wait until building restrictions were relaxed in the 1950s. However, its industrial structure retained its dominant nineteenth-century character. Despite a reduction in the size of their workforces the mining, iron and steel and ceramic industries still accounted for the major part of the employment structure at the end of the interwar period and the geography of their location was still largely determined by the geology of the Coal Measures. A temporary change in this well-entrenched situation was brought about by the introduction of the armaments plants between 1939 and 1945 but with the conclusion of the war the region looked once more to its traditional industries for its economic future.

REFERENCES

1. H A Moisley, 'The Potteries coalfield: a regional analysis', unpublished MSc thesis, Leeds University, 1950.
2. G E Cherry, *Cities and plans*, 1988.
3. City of Stoke-on-Trent, *Housing 1919–1957*, 3rd ed, 1958.
4. Information supplied by Housing Department, Newcastle Borough Council, 1992.
5. Cherry, *Cities*, 93–4.
6. W M Williams and D T Herbert, 'The social geography of Newcastle-under-Lyme', *N Staffs Jnl Fld Stud*, 2, 1962, 108–26.
7. J W Day, *Wheels of service 1898–1958*, Stoke-on-Trent, 1958.
8. G K Smith, *Potteries Motor Traction*, 1977.
9. C I Savage, *An economic history of transport*, 1959.
10. Smith, *Potteries*, 88–9.
11. B J Turton 'The changing railway network of Staffordshire', *N Staffs Jnl Fld Stud*, 4, 1964, 76–88.
12. Town and Country Directories Ltd, *Potteries and district trades directory 1917–8*, Manchester, 1918.
13. *Colliery yearbook and coal trades directory*, 1916 and 1938 eds.
14. Ibid.

15. Moisley, 'Potteries coalfield', 139.
16. *Staffordshire Sentinel, Sentinel yearbook of the Potteries and north Staffordshire*, Hanley, 1928.
17. A P Llewellyn, *North Staffordshire: its trade and commerce*, Derby, 1921.
18. P J Bemrose, 'Mines and mills' in J Briggs, ed, *Newcastle-under-Lyme 1173–1973*, Stoke-on-Trent, 1973, 98–108.
19. Moisley, 'Potteries coalfield', 140.
20. A Moyes, 'Second World War manufacturing and its significance for north Staffordshire' in A D M Phillips and B J Turton, eds, *Environment, man and economic change*, 1975, 315–35.
21. A Moyes, 'The industrial economy of north Staffordshire in the Second World War', *N Staffs Jnl Fld Stud*, 16, 1976, 73–84.
22. Ibid; *Pottery gazette and glass trades review directory*, 1940.
23. Board of Trade, *Working party report on pottery*, 1946.
24. S H Beaver, 'The Potteries: a study in the evolution of a cultural landscape', *Trans Inst Brit Geogr*, 34, 1964, 20–1.

11. The Potteries: A Question of Regional Identity

M W GREENSLADE

The Potteries region can claim to be unique, in this country at least, in being named after its staple product. The nearest rivals are the Stannaries of Devon and Cornwall and the Dukeries of Nottinghamshire, but neither is completely analogous. One is an area of jurisdiction over tin mines, the other a district of ducal estates. It has been suggested that the Sheffield region would be similar if it were called the Cutleries, or south-east Lancashire if it were known as the Spinneries; all that we have is Manchester as Cottonopolis.[1] It has been further suggested that the nearest analogy is to be found elsewhere in Staffordshire, where much of the south is known as the Black Country. That name, however, is thought to derive from the atmosphere created by the coal and iron trades rather than from their products.

There is the extra complication that there may still be some south of Watford who imagine that the Potteries is anyway part of the Black Country. Such a view could perhaps have been forgiven in the days before gas and electric firing and clean air, when the universal bottle oven produced a black pall mixed with the fumes of iron and steel furnaces. Arnold Bennett described it as the 'necessary grime' of the Potteries, observing tersely of this local characteristic that he did not think the region would ever be described – 'Dante lived too soon'.[2]

The use of a collective name for the settlements that were to become the six towns of Tunstall, Burslem, Hanley, Stoke-upon-Trent, Fenton and Longton dates from the eighteenth century when the pottery industry was becoming well established. Robert Plot, writing on Staffordshire about 1680, noted only Burslem, describing it as carrying on 'the greatest pottery they have in this county'.[3] In the early eighteenth century it was still the main centre: a list for that period compiled by Josiah Wedgwood, admittedly some 60 years later, detailed 43 potworks in Burslem and its immediate neighbourhood, with only seven in Hanley, two in Stoke, and no mention of anywhere else.[4] It was a different matter by July 1750 when Dr Richard Pococke came to north Staffordshire on his travels through England.[5] He found a whole area engaged in potmaking, and he noted 'kilns built in shape of a cone, which make a very pretty appearance, there being great numbers of them in all the country beyond Newcastle'. That town was 'the market town and capital of the Pottery villages', and Pococke found 'some few potters' working there. Having inspected their products, he set off into the hinterland:

On the 6th I went to see the Pottery villages, and first rid two miles to the east to Stoke, where they make mostly the white stone. I then went a mile north to Shefly [Shelton], where they are famous for the red china; thence to Audley [Hanley] Green a mile further north, where they make all sorts, and then a mile west to Bozlam, where they make the best white and many other sorts, and lastly a mile further west to Tonstall, where they make all sorts too, and are famous for the best bricks and tiles; all this is an uneven, most beautiful, well improved country, and this manufacture brings in great wealth to it; and there is such a face

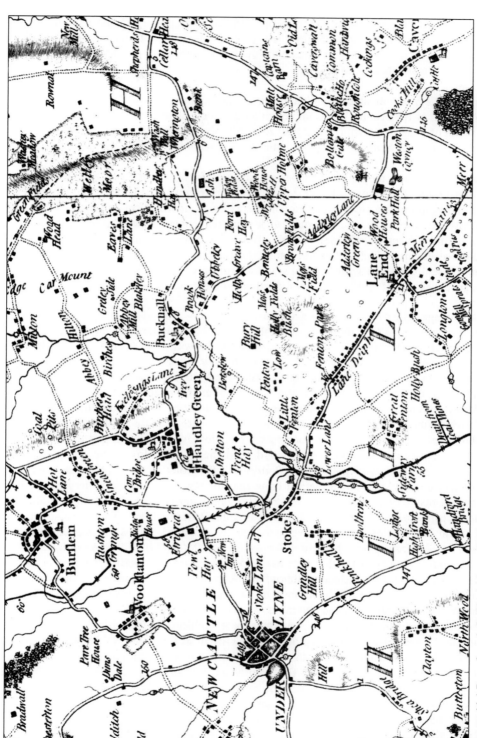

PLATE 11.1 Part of north Staffordshire, c 1775, from a map by William Yates at the scale of 1 inch to 1 mile.

of industry in all ages and degrees of people, and so much civility and obliging behaviour, as they look on all that come among them as customers, that it makes it one of the most agreeable scenes I ever saw, and made me think that probably it resembles that part of China where they make their famous ware.

Clearly a pottery region, already with a distinctive appearance, was well established.

By the end of the century it was taking on an urban character, even if it was that of a sprawl rather than of a distinct town (Pl 11.1). In John Aikin's *A description of the country from thirty to forty miles round Manchester* of 1795, the relevant section is headed 'The Potteries':

About a mile from the borders of Cheshire, the Staffordshire potteries commence at a village called Goldenhill, from whence to the other extremity of the pottery at Lane End is something more than seven miles; a considerable part of which, by joining together, strikes the traveller as but one town, although under different names . . . in all probability the various towns and villages of Goldenhill, Newfield, Smithfield, Tunstall, Longport, Burslem, Cobridge, Etruria, Hanley, Shelton, Stoke, Lower Lane, Lane Delf, and Lane End, will ere long be so intermixed with buildings as to form only one town and one name. At a little distance they are all of them already ranked under the general name of *The Pottery*.

The passage reflects the confusion which many writers showed when trying to find a name for the new region. Was it the Potteries or the Pottery? The writers may not always have been clear themselves whether they meant the region or its potworks. For Pococke in 1750 it was 'the Pottery villages'. Arthur Young in *A six months tour of the north of England* of 1770 recorded that 'I had the pleasure of viewing the Staffordshire Potteries'. *Bailey's western and midland directory* of 1783 has an entry for the whole under the heading 'Newcastle-under-Line, Staffordshire, and neighbouring Potteries'. That is modified in *Bailey's British directory* of 1784, which under the heading 'Newcastle, Staffordshire' has the subheading 'Potteries, in Staffordshire' and then deals with each place, beginning with Burslem and ending with Lane End. On the other hand Josiah Wedgwood used the singular form when he published *An address to the young inhabitants of the Pottery* in 1783. John Byng in 1792 described visiting 'the pottery country' and noted that 'at Lane End the population of the pottery commences'.[6] The agronomist William Pitt, in his *General view of the agriculture of the county of Stafford* of 1794, managed to refer to both the Potteries and the Pottery within a single paragraph on the area. Aikin in 1795, as quoted above, was equally confused, but as his account progressed through the different places he settled firmly for the Pottery. In 1798 *The universal British directory* made a clear distinction between region and works. Covering the area in its fourth volume under Newcastle, it had a subheading 'Account of the Potteries, or Manufactories of Staffordshire Ware in the neighbourhood of Newcastle' and started with Goldenhill: 'At this place the Pottery commences and continues to Lane End'.

The plural form of the region's name became established in the early nineteenth century, presumably a reflection of the region's rapid growth at that time. In 1808 the register of St Luke's, Onecote, a chapelry in the Moorlands, recorded the burial of Samuel Alcock, 'a young man out of the Pottery'.[7] In the same year William Pitt, in a second edition of his *General view*, settled for the Potteries, and in 1817, in his *Topographical history of Staffordshire*, 'this opulent and interesting district of the county' was the Staffordshire Potteries. A public meeting at Hanley in 1817 passed a resolution regarding arrangements for future meetings which designated Hanley 'the most central place of meeting for the Potteries at

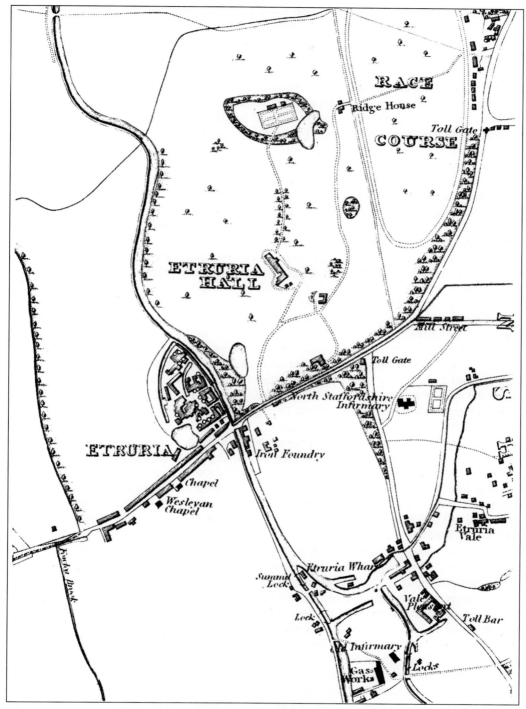

PLATE 11.2 Etruria in 1832 from a map by Thomas Hargreaves at the scale of around 6 inches to 1 mile.

large'.[8] When the first history of the region was published by Simeon Shaw in 1829, he called it *History of the Staffordshire Potteries*, it being a study of 'that interesting and opulent district, named – THE POTTERIES, – because almost exclusively appropriated to manufactories of Porcelain and Pottery'.

In 1834 William White's *History, gazetteer, and directory of Staffordshire* went so far as to reverse the position of the Potteries as an adjunct to the borough of Newcastle-under-Lyme. There is a long section on the Staffordshire Potteries, 'this grand seat of the porcelain and earthenware manufactures', to which a Newcastle directory is tacked on. Later there is a separate account of Newcastle, including the eyebrow-raising statement that the directory of the town is inserted 'immediately after the *Directory of the Potteries*, of which populous district this town may be considered as a western suburb'. At least that insult to Newcastle's dignity was removed from White's next edition in 1851, although the relationship between ancient borough and parvenu towns remained delicate.

The name had become established, but what of the soul behind it? There Josiah Wedgwood had stepped in to show that there was more than just clay and money involved.[9] Certainly he was a practical working potter who dominated the revolution in the pottery industry in the later eighteenth century and was a leader of the ancillary movement for turnpiking and canal building. He was also an astute business man who cultivated the leaders of society. At the same time Wedgwood's interests extended to scientific learning and artistic discovery, though still largely for their application to the making of pottery.

He became interested in contemporary archaeological excavations in Italy, where Greek vases were being discovered in Etruscan tombs and were mistakenly thought to be of Etruscan origin. Thus when he built a factory, house and village on an open site west of Hanley, he called it Etruria, apparently at the suggestion of his friend Erasmus Darwin of Lichfield (Pl 11.2).[10] He inaugurated the factory in June 1769 by personally throwing six vases in black basalt, which were later sent to London to be painted with red classical figures copied from a plate in Sir William Hamilton's *Etruscan antiquities*. They were inscribed with details of their production and the proud boast 'Artes Etruriae Renascuntur'. Wedgwood had in fact begun producing what he called Etruscan bronze vases at his Burslem works in 1768. In 1769 he took out a patent for an encaustic enamel to be used for imitation of painting found on antique vases. In 1770 he moved on from Etruscan ornamental ware to the production of Etruscan teapots. Something of the same inspiration is found a century later when two suburbs of Longton were laid out in the 1850s and 1860s as Florence and Dresden. Florence was developed on land belonging to the third duke of Sutherland, and the name was that of his eldest daughter. Dresden was the work of the Longton Building Society (Pl 11.3).[11]

Wedgwood was also capable of more down to earth propaganda. In 1783 he produced a pamphlet to justify the suppression of a food riot at Etruria, *An address to the young inhabitants of the Pottery*, urging his young readers not to be led astray by the violent example of their elders. Typically he sent an inscribed copy to Queen Charlotte.[12] In his peroration he invited his readers to ask their parents what the area was like when they themselves were young. Their answer would, he claimed, reveal a state of poverty far greater than was now known:

Their houses were miserable huts; the lands poorly cultivated, and yielded little of value for the food of man or beast, and these disadvantages, with roads almost impassable, might be said to have cut off our part of the country from the rest of the world, besides rendering it not very comfortable to ourselves. Compare this picture, which I know to be a true one, with the present state of the same country. The workmen earning near double their former wages –

their houses mostly new and comfortable, and the lands, roads, and every other circumstance bearing evident marks of the most pleasing and rapid improvements . . . Industry has been the parent of this happy change . . . and how far these improvements may still be carried by the same laudable means which have brought us thus far, has been one of the most pleasing contemplations of my life.

It was a view which had already been expressed by John Wesley on a visit to Burslem in March 1781:[13]

How is the whole face of this country changed in about twenty years. Since the potteries were introduced, inhabitants have continually flowed in from every side. Hence the wilderness is literally become a fruitful field: houses, villages, towns, have sprung up; and the country is not more improved than the people.

By the early nineteenth century six towns were rapidly crystallizing out of the numerous small settlements and had become known as the Potteries. The name, however, was a geographical expression imposed from above and outside rather than a sign of a corporate identity. Even in the 1860s, according to Arnold Bennett writing forty years later, one went from Burslem to Longton 'as one now goes to Pekin'.[14] Throughout the whole of the nineteenth century, these pottery communities displayed a marked reluctance to abandon their separate and independent existence, most clearly demonstrated in the individual development of local government in the region. Indeed, the persistence of these traits, as shown in chapter 9, did much to retard, complicate and flaw the process of urban federation at the beginning of the twentieth century.

PLATE 11.3 Inspiration and reality: Dresden, Longton, *c* 1900 (Warrillow Collection, Keele University Library).

At the same time there were numerous institutions which transcended particularism. Names like the Pottery Subscription Library (1790), the Pottery Philosophical Society (1820), the Pottery Mechanics' Institution (1826), and the Potteries Schools of Design (1847) suggest an appeal throughout the area, even though the institutions tended to be based in Hanley, already the leading town. The North Staffordshire Infirmary, which in 1819 replaced a 'house of recovery' for the poor opened in Etruria in 1804, aimed to serve an even larger area than the Potteries.[15] A succession of newspapers served the Potteries from 1809, culminating in the *Staffordshire Sentinel* in 1854. In 1873 the paper became the *Staffordshire Daily Sentinel*, the first daily to be published in the county. As the *Evening Sentinel* it remains a north Staffordshire institution.[16] In 1843 there appeared what its author fairly described as 'a copious general history of the district known as the Staffordshire Potteries' – *The borough of Stoke-upon-Trent* by John Ward, a Burslem lawyer. Though inevitably the core of the book is the history of each town, the work is also a general survey of the area.

The expansion of local communications also brought some unity.[17] The turnpikes and the canals of the eighteenth century and the railways of 1848–9 were concerned primarily with long-distance transport. The railway from Stoke to Manchester, however, had a station at Longport (for Burslem and Tunstall) and from 1864 one at Chatterley (for Tunstall), and there was a station at Longton on the line from Stoke to Uttoxeter, with another at Normacot from 1882. The era of local transport started in 1862 when a horse-drawn tram service was introduced between Hanley and Burslem, the Staffordshire Potteries Street Railway built by George Train of Boston (Mass). A steam tramway was started between Stoke and Longton in 1881 and was extended to Hanley and Burslem in 1882. Electricity replaced steam in 1899, and the line was further extended to Tunstall and Goldenhill in 1900. After some false starts a regular motor-bus service began in 1913. Meanwhile the Potteries Loop Line brought a local railway service to the northern part of the area. The first part, running from the main line at Etruria as far as Hanley, was opened in 1864. It was at last extended to Cobridge, Burslem and Tunstall in 1873, to Goldenhill in 1874, and back to the main line at Kidsgrove in 1875.

In the early twentieth century the Potteries acquired a new sort of identity in the works of Enoch Arnold Bennett (1867–1931).[18] The son of the upwardly mobile Enoch Bennett, potter, schoolmaster, pawnbroker and solicitor, Arnold was born in Hanley and grew up in Burslem. At the age of 21 he left for London to work in a solicitor's office, but he was soon embarked on a literary career.

On 29 September 1896 he recorded in his journal that he was to begin a new novel that night. What he later described as 'my Staffordshire novel' gave him some initial trouble, and in September 1897 he was in Burslem seeking inspiration: 'the grim and original beauty of certain aspects of the Potteries has fully revealed itself for the first time . . . This romance, this feeling which permeates the district, is quite as wonderfully inspiring as any historic memory could be.' The book was finished at 2.45 am on 17 May 1901 and was published in 1902 as *Anna of the five towns*. It was the first of a series of novels and short stories recreating the Potteries of his Victorian youth and the contemporary Edwardian scene. Although he made his home in France for ten years from 1902 and wrote much else, he continued to tap the local vein. Planning what was to be *Clayhanger* in October 1909 he noted:

I find that if I am to begin my new novel on 1st Jan. 1910, I must make a series of small preliminary inquiries. I do this at perhaps the rate of half an hour or an hour a day. I have read *When I was a Child*, and all I need of Shaw's *North Staffordshire Potteries*, and tonight I re-read the 'Social and Industrial' Section of the Victoria History, which contains a few juicy items that I can use.

PLATE 11.4 Industrial landscape, L G Brammer, *c* 1935 (City Museum and Art Gallery, Stoke-on-Trent). An image of the Potteries by a local artist produced at the time of Priestley's visit and confirming his view of the region.

Towards the end of his life he singled out *The old wives' tale* (1908), *Clayhanger* (1910) and *The card* (1911) as three of his four best works – the fourth was *Riceyman Steps* (1923), where he gave Clerkenwell in London something of the Potteries treatment.

Bennett turned the six towns of Tunstall, Burslem, Hanley, Stoke, Fenton and Longton into five – Turnhill, Bursley, Hanbridge, Knype and Longshaw, with Bursley naturally having a central role. He explained his reason for omitting Fenton when declining an invitation from the Fenton Traders to speak at their annual dinner:[19]

> The sound of the phrase 'Six Towns' is not so good as the sound of the phrase 'Five Towns'. 'I' in 'Five' is an open vowel. 'I' in 'Six' is a closed vowel, and is not nearly so striking. To my mind a broad sounding phrase for the district was very important. It is also to be remembered that Fenton had not then the same status as it has now.

Events, people and places appeared in the novels and stories thinly disguised, so that it is possible to produce an identification down to smallest details.[20] The result is a landscape of a vividness unsurpassed in English literature, bathed in a light both tender and sardonic and touched by both humour and pathos.

A kindred if less romantic light has been shed on the region in recent years by the work of the Victoria Theatre. In 1962 the Studio Theatre, a touring company pioneering theatre in the round, made Stoke-on-Trent its permanent home, converting the disused Victoria cinema in Hartshill into a theatre in the round. In 1986 it was replaced by the specially built New Victoria

Theatre on a site at Basford provided by the borough of Newcastle-under-Lyme. As part of its work as a community theatre rooted in the life of north Staffordshire and supported by the local authorities, the 'Vic' under the direction of Peter Cheeseman has presented not only plays with a local setting – including adaptations of Bennett's work – but a notable series of documentaries on the life of the district. Based on local events and derived from primary source material, including personal reminiscence and folk-songs, the documentaries began with 'The Jolly Potters', describing the life of potworkers in the mid-nineteenth century. Later topics included the Civil War in Staffordshire, the federation of the six towns, the fight to preserve Shelton Bar steel works, Hugh Bourne, the local pioneer of Primitive Methodism, and Josiah Wedgwood. The most successful was *The Knotty*, the brilliantly told story of the North Staffordshire Railway. First produced in 1966, it had 84 performances locally. It was also performed in Cardiff at the invitation of the Welsh Arts Council, and in 1969 it was taken to Florence as the British contribution to the Rassegna Internazionale dei Teatri Stabili.[21]

J B Priestley, touring England in 1933 to write his *English journey* of 1934, found the Potteries unique in their product, their bottle ovens like 'some monstrous Oriental intrusion', their pall of smoke, and 'their remote self-contained provincialism'. There was a 'mythical city of Stoke-on-Trent', with a population of nearly 300,000 but no real existence: 'There is no city . . . when you go there, you still see the six towns, looking like six separate towns' (Pl 11.4). Other writers, before and since, have been equally forthright.[22] One of the more recent, Sir Nikolaus Pevsner, found Stoke-on-Trent in the early 1970s 'an urban tragedy. . . There is no centre to the whole, not even an attempt at one, and there are not even in all six towns real local centres.'[23] Clearance and conservation have been a feature of the late twentieth century, with ambitious new building – notably in Hanley, which even has a Unity House. The Garden Festival on the derelict Shelton Bar site at Etruria in 1986 stimulated new developments, even making a future for the Potteries as a tourist attraction. Yet it can still be claimed that for many local people the city remains mythical and that they identify rather with their own local town.

In 1974 there came a new complication. In the local government reorganization of that year the city had hoped that it would become the core of a Greater Stoke-on-Trent embracing Newcastle, Crewe and Congleton. Instead it became part of the county once more. It was allowed to keep its city status and its lord mayor, and some powers were delegated by the county. Even so Staffordshire County Council has more power over the area than it had before federation. In the 1990s reorganization is once again on the local government agenda. Within a few years the Potteries could have yet another new identity.

REFERENCES

1. H Owen, *The Staffordshire potter*, 1901, 1–2.
2. A Bennett, 'The death of Simon Fuge', in *The grim smile of the five towns*, Penguin ed, 140.
3. R Plot, *The natural history of Staffordshire*, Oxford, 1686, 122.
4. E Meteyard, *The life of Josiah Wedgwood*, 1865, i, 191–2.
5. J J Cartwright, ed, 'The travels through England of Dr Richard Pococke' *Camden Soc*, new series, 42, 1888, 6–8.
6. C Bruyn Andrews, ed, *The Torrington diaries*, New York, 1970, iii, 126.
7. Staffordshire Record Office, D3816/1/1, 6 June 1808.
8. J G Jenkins, 'The federation of the six towns', in *Victoria County History of Staffordshire (VCH Staffs)*, 1963, viii, 253.
9. A Finer and G Savage, eds, *The selected letters of Josiah Wedgwood*, 1965.
10. D King-Hele, *Doctor of revolution*, 1977, 74.

11. B Young and J G Jenkins, 'Longton', in *VCH Staffs*, viii, 227.
12. In the William Salt Library, Stafford.
13. *The journal of the Rev John Wesley A M*, Everyman ed, iv, 202.
14. A Bennett, *The old wives' tale*, Everyman ed, 11.
15. M W Greenslade, 'Hanley' in *VCH Staffs*, viii, 160, 170–1.
16. *The Sentinel story, 1873–1973*, Hanley, 1973.
17. E J D Warrillow, *A sociological history of the city of Stoke-on-Trent*, Hanley, 1960, 56–77; M W Greenslade, 'Tunstall' and 'Burslem', in *VCH Staffs*, viii, 85, 110; Young and Jenkins, 'Longton', 228.
18. L G Wickham Legg, ed, *Dictionary of national biography, 1931–40*, 1949, 66–70; F Swinnerton, ed, *Arnold Bennett: the journals*, Penguin ed, 1971, 22, 33–4, 67, 268.
19. E J D Warrillow, *Arnold Bennett and Stoke-on-Trent*, Hanley, 1966, 51–2.
20. As is done ibid.
21. Peter Cheeseman's introduction to *The Knotty*, Methuen playscript, 1970.
22. C Hawke-Smith, *The making of the six towns*, Hanley, 1985, 76–80.
23. N Pevsner, *The buildings of England: Staffordshire*, Harmondsworth, 1974, 252.

PART THREE

The Contemporary Conurbation

12. Economic Structure: Employment Patterns and Prospects

L ROSENTHAL AND P LAWRENCE

In 1939, the city of Stoke-on-Trent contained 296 smithies and stabling establishments.[1] In 1992, no smithies remained. Change such as this in the structure of an economy – local, regional or national – is inevitable, and is often taken to reflect the necessary dynamism and mobility of factors of production required for the efficient allocation of resources. Where horse-drawn transport declines, motorized transport grows. In 1939, the city of Stoke-on-Trent also contained thirteen coal-mines, two blast furnaces, and over 350 pottery (and related) factories and pot-banks. By 1992, no blast furnaces remained, the last two coal-mines were, at the time of writing, under notice of closure, and the number of pot-banks had decreased by three-quarters.

Traditionally, the Potteries has seemed, and has often been presented in economic terms as, a specialized and isolated locality, with a distinct and long-established industrial character based upon pottery, coal and steel. This economic specialization has left its mark upon the region in many ways, not least in moulding the characteristics of the local labour market, in perceptions of the character of available labour on the demand side, and in the skills required by local vacancies on the supply side of the market.

The concern here is to map the changing structure and pattern of the employment and industry of the Potteries over the period since the Second World War. As it will be shown, there have been dramatic changes in the relative importance of the staple industries that have characterized the region since the industrial revolution. That the characteristics of local economies change over time is certainly no surprise. However, when reviewing the research undertaken on the Potteries economy,[2] it is, perhaps, more surprising how constant have been the fears of those researchers, concerning the need to diversify the industrial base of the area and encourage the services sectors. The follower of current local trends will no doubt concur.

Living and working in an area makes one well aware of its quirks and special nature, lovable or otherwise. There are many unique facets of the Potteries economy, as it will become more obvious. Nevertheless, in concentrating on the Potteries, the reader should bear in mind that it may be that there exist here no more unique features than may be boasted of by other comparable, well-established industrial cities.

STRUCTURAL CHANGES IN EMPLOYMENT, 1945–71

The local joke has it that Stoke-on-Trent escaped bombing during the Second World War because the *Luftwaffe* concluded from reconnaissance that they had done it already. During the war, Stoke's situation in an area designated 'safe' had led to major ordnance-related investment (nearby at Radway Green and Swynnerton), and much inward, if temporary, relocation of industry, which laid the ground or provided the factory space for the relative expansion of general engineering in the area during the 1950s and 1960s.[3] There had also been some expansion in coal production, and although the tableware and sanitary ware sections of the pottery industry had been largely closed down for the duration of the war, the pottery industry's infrastructure, equipment and buildings remained intact. Although some diversification was evident, the domination of the area by pottery, steel and coal was largely the same in 1951 as it had been in 1939.

The structure of the industrial base, 1951–71

In 1951, the census recorded the sectional industrial classification of the employed population of the Stoke-Newcastle conurbation as shown in Figure 12.1. For comparison, the same breakdown is presented for England and Wales for 1951 as part of Figure 12.2. The nature of the Stoke-on-Trent conurbation as an industrial city is shown clearly here. Some 66 per cent of the employed population were recorded in either mining (8 per cent) or manufactures (58 per cent); and for England and Wales the comparable total figure was 40 per cent. The rather limited extent of employment within the service sectors in the city is also evident in these figures. Furthermore, of the employment in mining and manufactures, pottery and coal-mining have together formed the bulk. Figure 12.3 shows a breakdown of the share of employment in the city taken by pottery, coal-mining, and all other manufacturing over the years from 1951. In 1951, of the total in mining and manufactures, pottery and ceramics took 49 per cent and mining over 12 per cent. The share of other manufactures was only some 37 per cent.

The importance of the pottery and ceramics industry to the area, obvious though it seems, can be further underlined. The figures used in these calculations refer to direct pottery and ceramics manufacture. The area also contains a great variety of other firms, even within manufacturing, which though not counting as part of the ceramics industry, nevertheless service and cohabit with ceramics, such as kiln suppliers, other pottery process machine manufacturers, design and lithography firms, suppliers of colours and other raw materials, as well as the firms supplying necessary transport, construction and finance. Up to the present, over 75 per cent of the UK national pottery employment is concentrated in the city. Figures 12.1 and 2 also trace the changes in the reported shares of the major industrial classifications in employment over the

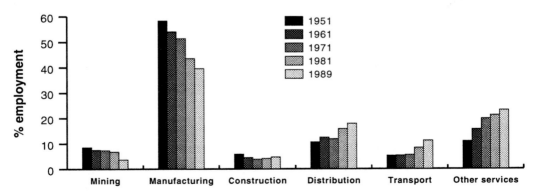

FIGURE 12.1 Employment in Stoke-on-Trent by industrial classification, 1951–89 (*Sources*: Censuses, 1951 and 1961, for Newcastle-under-Lyme and Stoke-on-Trent; censuses of employment for Stoke-on-Trent Travel-to-Work Area, 1971, 1981, 1989).

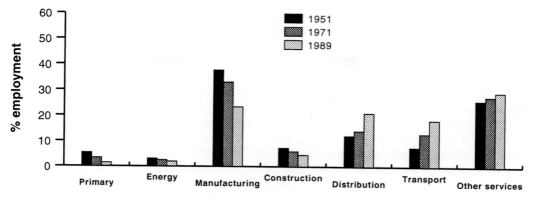

FIGURE 12.2 Employment in England and Wales by industrial classification, 1951–89 (*Sources*: Census, 1961, for 1951 data; censuses of employment, 1971, 1989).

period 1951–71. The total shares of mining and manufactures in employment fell from the 66 per cent of 1951, to 61 per cent in 1961, and to just over 58 per cent in 1971. These falls were rather sharper than those for England and Wales as a whole. At the same time, the service sector shares were rising, from just over 27 per cent in 1951 to over 36 per cent in 1971. All of this rise can be traced to the public and professional sectors, and reflect the rising numbers employed within the education and health sectors of the area (including Keele and Staffordshire Universities and their precursors); again, these are rather sharper than the national rises. However, not only had there been a shift from manufacturing to services, but substantial shifts were occurring within the manufacturing sectors.

Within the mining and manufacturing sectors, total employment was falling in the city over the period, but this was unevenly spread around the sectors making up this broad grouping. Over the twenty-year period, pottery and ceramics employment fell by around 15,000 jobs, mining by 5000 and metal-manufacturing by 1300, evidence of the long-running decline of the importance of these industries in the area, and in the economy at large. Within the pottery and ceramics industry, the period up to 1971 saw an immense amount of change, with the introduction of new technology, organization and methods, causing productivity to rise much more quickly than the market was expanding. One consequent effect was that from 1958 to

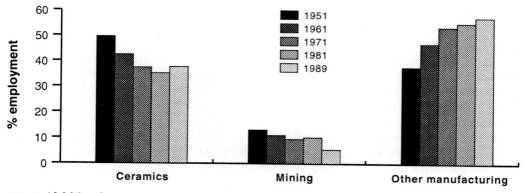

FIGURE 12.3 Manufacturing employment in Stoke-on-Trent, 1951–89 (*Source*: as for Fig 12.1).

1968, the proportion of the region's school-leavers entering ceramics halved.[4] The most (literally) obvious changes concerned the final replacement of the traditional coal-fired bottle kilns with electric and gas-fired kilns. This new technology, well established in the larger facilities long before 1939, in combination with the implementation of the Clean Air Acts after 1956, left fewer than 30 of the estimated 2000 bottle kilns of 1938 remaining in operation by 1964.[5] By the end of the 1960s, Burchill and Ross reported that the 'pall of smoke hanging over the area [had] now completely disappeared'.[6]

Gay and Smyth present a careful picture of the ceramics industry up to the early 1970s. Tunnel kilns and other continuous-firing processes, replacing earlier batch-firing methods, encouraged the pursuit of economies of scale in production and the 'substitution of scientific attitudes for craft attitudes'.[7] The period also witnessed a bewildering number of mergers, acquisitions and takeovers, with associated relocations and restructurings of production, disguising in many cases what would otherwise have been simple closures. By 1971, when Allied English Pottery acquired Doulton and Co, the three giant firms of Doulton, Wedgwood and Worcester Royal Porcelain were supplying two-thirds of the domestic tableware market. Single firms dominated both tile manufacture (H and R Johnson) and electrical insulators (Allied Insulators). Gay and Smyth noted that the number of domestic tableware firms fell from 230 in 1935 to 75 in 1970; the number of tile manufacturers down from 50 to 14; and the number of sanitary ware manufacturers from 30 to 12. Even though employment totals fell substantially, the total output of the industry rose by around 25 per cent between 1951 and 1969, indicating a much more rapid rise in the productivity of labour in the industry. Gay and Smyth argued that given the low value-added per worker and the limited amount of mechanization, such productivity improvements were easy to achieve.

Within mining, the contraction of the industry in the area was associated with a gradual reduction of the number of working pits, and the abandonment or consolidation of their workings. Postwar employment in the north Staffordshire coalfield peaked in 1958 at 21,200 men in 21 collieries.[8] By 1960–1, there were seventeen pits, and thereafter the rate and scale of colliery closures and consolidation in the area accelerated. During the 1960s, pits closed at Mossfield and Park Hall in 1963, at Glebe in 1964, at Foxfield in 1965, and at Parkhouse in 1968, and the Sneyd and Deep pits were consolidated into Wolstanton in 1967. Employment had fallen to 11,000 by 1968, and production and employment in mining in the area continued to concentrate at fewer pits at Chatterley Whitfield, Florence, Hem Heath, Holditch, Silverdale, and Wolstanton. By 1967, Hem Heath and Florence were employing one-third of the men, and contributing nearly 40 per cent of the output of the coalfield.[9]

However, during the same period 1951–71, there had been a substantial rise in the employment within, and relative importance of, manufacturing outside these traditional areas of coal and ceramics. The most dramatic changes were evident in general engineering, and especially the electrical engineering and rubber manufacturing areas. Rubber manufactures in the area are entirely within the Michelin company. The Michelin tyre company had arrived in Stoke in 1927, but production facilities had greatly expanded over this period. Within the general engineering sectors, Rist's had arrived during the wartime relocations and permanently settled immediately after the war, supplying electrical wiring to the midlands car industry. Tube Investments (Creda) had set up at Blythe Bridge in the early 1950s, and the English Electric-ICL and GEC-Elliot Automation facilities at Kidsgrove can be dated from 1954. These large, new industries have had important effects of the degree of diversification within the local economy. From 1951 to 1971, manufacturing in industries outside the pottery, coal and metal-forging sectors increased its employment by some 18,000. Importantly, this meant that the share of manufacturing employment in non-traditional areas of manufacturing rose from 37 per cent to nearly 53 per cent.

Clearly, in the period from 1945 to 1971, the local economy had witnessed a substantial increase in the diversification of its industry. Within manufacturing, some of this diversification was due to the declines in employment in ceramics and mining, but more was due to the appearance or expansion of new firms and manufacturing sectors, especially those in engineering and rubber. Similarly, there had been growth in employment within the public, education and health sectors of the services.

Unemployment levels, 1951–71

The image of Stoke, with declining staple industries, would perhaps suggest that unemployment problems would set the city apart, but the recorded unemployment figures tell a rather different story. For the period of the 1950s and 1960s, as shown in Figure 12.4, the official, registered unemployment rate for the city never rose above 3 per cent, and was below 2 per cent for most of the period. The absolute numbers recorded as unemployed in the city remain below 5000 for the entire period up to 1970, and below 2500 for more than half the period. Indeed, there was a labour shortage in the city for much of the period, with, for example, miners relocated to the Potteries coalfield during the 1960s to offset local recruitment difficulties.

For comparative purposes, Figure 12.4 also includes the national unemployment rates for the same period, and it can be seen that the two series mirror each other, for the most part rising and falling together over the cycles of the times. However, the unemployment figures for Stoke show unemployment rates which for the majority of the postwar period lie below those for Great Britain as a whole. Not only were the unemployment rates very low absolutely, they may be argued to have been low relative to the rest of the economy also. Compared to both the pre-war period and to the period after 1970, for the Stoke-on-Trent area, the 'long boom' can be viewed without misplaced nostalgia.

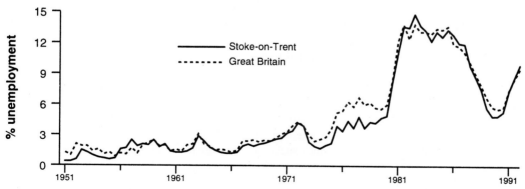

FIGURE 12.4 Unemployment rates in Stoke-on-Trent and Great Britain, 1951–92 (*Sources*: Area statistics tables of the *Ministry of Labour Gazette, Department of Employment Gazette, and Employment Gazette.* All figures are for March and September of each year, March 1951 to March 1992, unadjusted for seasonal variation. Unemployment percentages for Stoke-on-Trent and adjacent exchanges before 1960 use the 1960 working population as a denominator).

A TURN FOR THE WORSE: 1971–81

If the local economy in its new industrial areas and services had boomed during the 1950s and 1960s sufficiently strongly to offset the decline of employment in the more traditional sections, the period after 1971 saw further declines in all manufacturing areas, but this time with rather fewer offsetting factors.

The industrial base, 1971–81

The sectoral distributions of employment over the 1970s is again illustrated, for the Stoke-on-Trent Travel-to-Work-Area (TTWA), in Figure 12.1. The general trend away from manufacturing and towards the service sectors is again clearly evident. Similarly shown is the acceleration in the decline of manufacturing employment after 1979, where the national rise in unemployment following the early policies of the Conservative administration had disproportionate effects in the manufacturing sectors. Given that Stoke-on-Trent had a disproportionate employment share in manufacturing this led to a relatively sharper rise in local unemployment than for the UK as a whole.

Nevertheless, the figure may give, perhaps, a misleading impression that services were in some ways expanding quickly. In fact, services rose only by about 4000 jobs (around 2 per cent of the labour force) over the decade 1971–81 within the Stoke TTWA. On the other hand, employment totals within the manufacturing sector fell by around 28,000 jobs over the decade, and most of this was concentrated in the five-year period after 1975. Unlike the previous decade, all the components of the manufacturing sectors contracted, such that relative shares within manufacturing did not alter much, as shown by Figure 12.3.

The major job losses in manufacturing were concentrated in pottery and ceramics, with a 12,000 decline in employment in the area. Again, most of the falls occurred during the final years of the 1970s, a period when the gradual loss of once-traditional markets of the pottery industry was worsened by the overvaluation of sterling. There was a number of factory closures within the ceramics sector between 1978 and 1981, including Wedgwood's closure of its Tunstall plant in 1981 and the closure of the Royal Doulton Regent Works in 1980, each with over 700 job losses. The pottery industry's production figures fell from an index of 100 in 1975, as recorded in the Business Monitor, to 75 in the second quarter of 1982. The ever-continuing round of acquisitions and mergers was maintained, with Royal Worcester merging with the US-owned Carborundum Tableware (including Spode in Stoke) to form Royal Worcester Spode in 1976.

For the pits, Chatterley Whitfield, which had been the first British pit to produce a million tons per annum, closed in 1977 with the gradual exhaustion of the western edge of the north Staffordshire coalfield, but as part of the heritage industry has been transformed into an underground museum. The most celebrated local closure concerned the loss of steel-making at Shelton Bar in Etruria, finally closed in 1980. Around 3500 metal-manufacturing jobs were lost in the area over this period when the steel-production facilities were removed. Nevertheless, metal-working and rolling still continues successfully at the remaining part of the British Steel site.[10]

The evidence presented here would suggest that the traditional three-way dominance of ceramics-mining-steel within the economy of the area had by 1981 been replaced by a looser four-way dominance of ceramics-mining-rubber-electrical engineering. This concentration of employment in the city into just a few sectors (an oft-repeated statistic) seems to reinforce the view that Stoke is somehow special or isolated. However, all industries tend to be unevenly spatially distributed around economies, and a similar argument about unusual concentration of particular industries could probably be made for many other cities of equivalent size.

The isolation of the north Staffordshire economy was examined in a 1980 study by Pullen and Proops.[11] This was based upon an input-output model of the area's economy for 1977, which traced the relative importance of links that local industry had with other local industry (mostly sales and purchases), compared to the links it had with industry elsewhere. Clearly, the more and stronger the links that local firms have with other local firms as suppliers or customers, and the less they have with non-local firms, the more 'isolated' in economic terms will be the local economy; and the more separated will be the local economy from wider national events. The results of the exercise demonstrated a high degree of integration of the local economy with the rest of the national economy and, therefore, a low degree of isolation of the local economy in 1977. That the local economy shared the national experience of the dramatic downturns in the state of the economy towards the end of the 1970s is further reinforcement of this argument.

Unemployment, 1971–81

As it would be expected from the depressing account above, the unemployment rate in the region saw a sharp rise at the end of the 1970s, although the worst of this recession was to be felt into the 1980s. The progress of the unemployment rate for Stoke-on-Trent for this period, and for the British economy as a whole, can be seen in Figure 12.4. For the Stoke area itself, the unemployment rise was spectacular at the end of the 1970s. The Stoke TTWA saw unemployment in absolute numbers rise above 10,000 for the first time during the winter of 1979–80, above 20,000 for the first time during the winter of 1980–81, and climbed over 30,000 for the winter of 1981–82. At its peak, the unemployment rates in the city hovered close to 15 per cent.

Although there is evidence of a rising level of underlying unemployment, along with the rest of the UK, dating from the early 1970s, the severe downturn following the Conservative election victory of 1979 is a conspicuous feature, and the resultant high levels of the unemployment rate, both locally and nationally, continued well into the mid-1980s. Comparing local and national situations, it may be seen that, again, during the decade of the 1970s, the Stoke unemployment rate stayed well below the national level, by a matter of one to two percentage points. Only at the very end of the decade did the local rate equal or overtake the national rate, indicating that this recession hit the local area, with its manufacturing bias, relatively more severely.

INTERESTING TIMES, 1981–PRESENT

The recession that began at the start of the 1980s continued at a high level in terms of unemployment until around 1986, both nationally and locally, and again the local manufacturing and mining sectors bore the brunt of these events. The census of employment records a fall in manufacturing employment in the Stoke TTWA of a further 12,000 over the 1981–9 period, although total employment in the area rose by some 3000, illustrating a remarkable rise in employment in the service sectors.

The industrial base, 1981–present

The changing distribution of employment over the major sectors in the 1981–9 period for the Stoke TTWA can be seen from Figure 12.1. Comparison with Figure 12.2, which shows the national England and Wales proportions at the end of the period, makes it clear that the local economy again shared what was an important national switch in the proportions employed in these sectors. Not only Stoke, but the economy as a whole, saw substantial shifts from manufacturing and energy (including coal extraction) towards the service sectors, especially distribution, transport and communications, and financial services.

Within the manufacturing sectors locally, the changing proportions of employment between ceramics, mining and other manufacturing is shown in Figure 12.3 By 1989, the proportion of the working population employed in manufacturing in Stoke TTWA had fallen below 40 per cent for the first time, down by 20 percentage points since 1951, and the proportion employed in mining had fallen below 5 per cent of total employment in manufacturing and mining, down from close to 10 per cent in 1951. Some of the slack has been taken up by the rises in the distribution, transport and other (professional, public, financial) service sectors, but unemployment has taken the remainder. It is reported that 10 per cent of the working population is now engaged in retailing in the area.[12] The ceramics sector can be seen to have begun to reverse its relative decline among the other manufacturing sectors of the area. However, Figure 12.3 should be viewed in the context of falling totals employed in the manufacturing sectors in all areas, where the most obvious trend concerns the likely end of mining locally. Looking back on this period does not make comfortable reading.

For the pottery industry, the 1980s saw substantial new investment in many areas of ceramics manufacturing, with the increased introduction of fast-firing furnaces and other production-time reduction methods, and the increased use of mechanization and flow-line production methods, and the way seems open to further application of modern production engineering and computing skills. There has been a reduction by most enterprises of the number of lines carried, so that processes economical only with long production runs have become more and more applicable. It is likely that the more traditional craft-based skills will continue to decline in importance.

The ever-continuing reorganization of the industry continued at the same high pace apparent since 1950. In the decade to 1985, Benington reported 35 major plant closures in the city, and the elimination of one-third of the ceramics industry's capacity (and employment).[13] Ownership of firms continued to change hands. Of the more important, in 1986 Wedgwoods were taken over by Waterford, who had some other local pottery interests, to become Waterford Wedgwood; Royal Worcester Spode have been acquired by Derby International; Coloroll acquired both Staffordshire Potteries and Biltons in 1986, and then collapsed spectacularly in 1990, leaving its pottery subsidiaries (including Royal Winton) to management and other buy-outs; and Aynsley China was also subject to a management buy-out from Waterford Wedgwood in 1987. The five years, 1985–90, were reported to have seen one-half of the industry changing hands. By 1990, acquisitions, mergers and the relocation and rationalization of the constituent firms have resulted in an estimated one-half of the total employment in the industry locally being held by just four ceramics firms (Waterford Wedgwood, Doulton, Churchill, H and R Johnson), and an estimated 80–85 per cent of local pottery employment concentrated in the top ten firms.[14] Casual observation, and the lessons of history, indicate the whirling dances of ceramics industry organization and reorganization will not end quite yet.

Nevertheless, the Stoke pottery industry remains an important and impressive economic machine. Although employment has been reduced by some 50 per cent since the 1950s, the industry provides some 30,000 jobs in Stoke, and the area produces 75–80 per cent of UK pottery output. Ceramics continues to export about one-half of its entire output, which still covers the range of ceramic products from figurines through tiles, hotel and tableware, electrical insulators and switches to nuclear reactor components. Development and research continue into new applications and uses, with the fastest growing use of engineering ceramics in vehicle manufacture. Wedgwood and Royal Doulton remain among the largest and most prestigious ceramics firms in the world.

In mining, the industry is likely to have ceased entirely in the area well before the end of the 1990s. From some 10,000 employed in the industry in 1971, 5800 remained at five pits by the start of the 1984–5 miners' strike. Of these five pits, just two, Silverdale and Trentham, survived into the 1990s, employing a total of just 4000. Holditch in Newcastle-Chesterton was employing 700, and Wolstanton some 900 before they closed in 1989; and Hem Heath and Florence have been amalgamated into the super-pit at Trentham.[15]

In common with manufacturing and general engineering elsewhere in the economy, the local representatives of manufacturing outside mining and ceramics have also been reorganizing and restructuring over the 1980s. The Michelin plant saw a large redundancy in 1985–6, when the manufacture of several product lines was transferred from Stoke, and the employment levels (at a peak at nearly 8000 in the 1970s) had fallen to around 3500 at the end of the 1980s. Although Michelin now has claims to be the world leader in tyre production, its local levels of output are highly dependent upon vehicle manufacture. New technology and more reliable and hard-wearing products have been a feature here.

Within the electronics-electrical engineering sectors, the very promising concentration of plants along the A34 has not turned into the major core of a North Staffordshire Silicon Pot-bank as sometimes foreseen. As the Training and Enterprise Council report states, the local electronics-electrics firms form 'rather a selection of large firms in a variety of markets than an electronics "sector"'.[16] ICL's plant, which now concentrates on printed circuit production, has brought some small satellite firms, but fierce competition in electronics has seen ICL close its two smaller local plants at Hanley and Newcastle in the early 1980s, and transfer other departments away from its major local Kidsgrove plant in 1982. Rists (Lucas) and Michelin are very dependent on their customers in the vehicle manufacturing industries, whilst the white goods products of Creda are linked to the movements of the housing market. Neither housing nor vehicles has seen current booms. Century Oils in Hanley have a new industrial lubricants plant since 1988, and are important suppliers to US industry.

Some of the more obvious expansions within the service sectors can be seen at the Festival Park. There was much temporary employment at the Stoke Garden Festival in 1986, built on the site of the closed Shelton Bar steel works in Etruria. Site development following the festival has been very successful in attracting retailing, leisure activities (cinemas and watersport), a hotel, and business servicing facilities. As services are provided, for the most part, by small firms in dispersed units, it is less easy to trace the course of service sector employment by looking at individual firms. By the early 1990s, the six largest employers in Stoke-on-Trent were Waterford Wedgwood, Royal Doulton, and Michelin in the private sector, and Staffordshire County Council, Stoke Council, and the local health authority in the public sector. In 1990, Benington reported that ten organizations provided over 50 per cent of jobs in the city.[17]

It is not a difficult task to paint a bleak picture of the north Staffordshire economy at the moment, and the planning authorities of the area have publicly expressed their concerns about the local economy, and called for Assisted Area status.[18] The major cited argument is that the area has effectively lost mining and steel-metal manufacturing of its traditional sectors, so that instead of being a three-sector dominated economy, it is now one-sector dominated.

Unemployment, 1981–present

It has been noted how the major recession that accelerated at the end of the 1970s continued at a high level in the area up to the mid-1980s. This is plotted on Figure 12.4, and the course of unemployment in the area is clearly demonstrated. Unemployment began to fall very rapidly after 1986, to below 10 per cent by 1987, and to marginally below 5 per cent in 1989. In 1988 unemployment numbers were below 20,000 and below 10,000 by 1989. Unhappily, this recovery has, in the late 1980s and early 1990s, gone into reverse, and unemployment is again rising steeply. In all of this, the local economy has shared the experience of the economy as a whole. Although the early 1980s saw the Stoke unemployment rate rise marginally above that for Great Britain, the Stoke rate has hovered at or around the national rate, and mirrored national trends and cycles over most of this period.

Stoke-on-Trent City Council points out that the Stoke TTWA is extensive, and the officially reported unemployment rate for the area as a whole fails to illustrate the problems of the city itself.[19] Their own estimates for the city, rather than the wider travel-to-work area, lie 1½ percentage points above those illustrated on Figure 12.4, and mostly well above the UK rates. They also present ward-based estimates of unemployment, showing wide variation within the city, with unemployment blackspots apparent in some areas, especially Shelton and Brookhouse. Newcastle-under-Lyme's Economic Monitor argues that the unemployment rate in the local economy, although clearly tied to the national rates, tends to be rather more volatile, falling more sharply during depressions and recovering more quickly during upturns than the national figures.[20]

EARNINGS: A LOW WAGE REGION?

The Potteries is commonly regarded as a low-wage and low-earnings area. This view is perhaps reinforced by its poor environment and ageing housing stock, and by its image as a region dominated by declining manufacturing industries. The area is also relatively deficient in occupations at the higher-paid end of the scale. Figure 12.5 shows the share of occupational classifications in the Stoke TTWA compared with the West Midlands and with Great Britain for 1981. As it may be seen, Stoke's occupational distribution has proportions below those for the

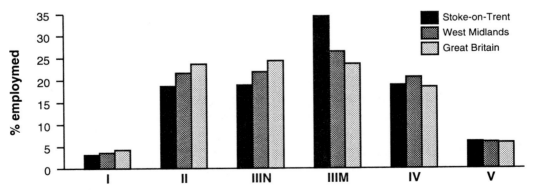

FIGURE 12.5 Occupational classifications in Stoke-on-Trent Travel-to-Work Area, the West Midlands and Great Britain, 1981. Occupational classifications are: I, professional, etc; II, intermediate, supervisory; IIIN, skilled non-manual; IIIM, skilled manual; IV partly skilled, semi-skilled; and V, unskilled (*Source*: Census, 1981, small area statistics).

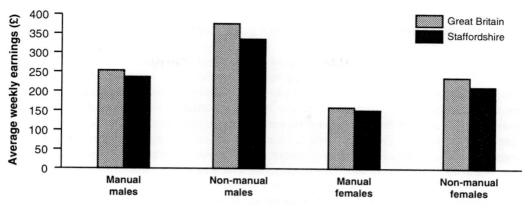

FIGURE 12.6 Average weekly earnings in Staffordshire and Great Britain, 1991 (*Source*: Department of Employment, New Earnings Survey, 1991).

West Midlands and for the nation as a whole for the professional, intermediate and skilled non-manual sectors, all of which tend to be high-paid occupations. Stoke further possesses a substantial proportion, above the regional and national share, of skilled manual workers, mostly in factory-based skills. In addition, female participation in the pottery industry is, and historically always has been, very high. The rather lower average earnings obtained by females compared to males can be expected to influence the level of earnings of the Potteries labour force as a whole.

All these factors tend to indicate that the Potteries earnings levels may be relatively low. Hard earnings data support this perception, although in this case data are only available for the whole of Staffordshire. The reader should be aware that the rest of Staffordshire tends to higher earnings, lower unemployment, and higher proportions in higher skilled occupations than Stoke-on-Trent.[21] The New Earnings Survey notes that in Staffordshire average earnings are below the national average for manual and non-manual males, just below the national average for manual females, and well below for non-manual females. A similar pattern can be observed when comparing Staffordshire earnings to those of the West Midlands region, with the exception of manual females, who do a little better in Staffordshire. Figure 12.6 compares

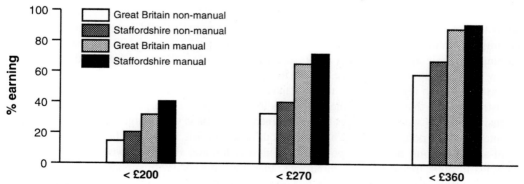

FIGURE 12.7 Distribution of weekly earnings in Staffordshire and Great Britain, 1991 (*Source*: as for Fig 12.6).

average earnings for Staffordshire in 1991 with those for Great Britain as a whole. While in 1978 Staffordshire average earnings were at 98.8 per cent of the national average, by 1991 they had fallen to 93.6 per cent.

This view is underlined by consideration of the lower-earnings end of the distribution (Fig 12.7). For 1991 the New Earnings Survey records that while nationally 31.6 per cent of male manual earnings are below £200 per week, for the West Midlands this proportion is 32.4 per cent, and for Staffordshire 40.3 per cent. A similar pattern can be observed for the higher income ranges, and for the other groups of workers, although manual females do slightly better than the other groups. Tables 12.1 and 2 set out the cut-off earnings levels for the lower and upper deciles for selected categories of labour, with regional and national comparisons, for the two years, 1978 and 1991. The data show some widening of earnings dispersion within the county, and between the county and the country as a whole, with a higher proportion of people at the lower end of the earnings profile than before, suggesting some special adverse effects for the county from the restructurings of the 1980s. At the upper end, a wider Staffordshire-Great Britain dispersion is most obvious among non-manual male earnings. Similar shifts can be observed in the Staffordshire-West Midlands relationship, though from very different base positions in 1978.

Table 12.1

Weekly earnings of top and bottom deciles in Staffordshire, the West Midlands and Great Britain, 1978

Occupational classification	Bottom 10 per cent with earnings under (£)			Top 10 per cent with earnings over (£)		
	Staffs	W Midlands	GB	Staffs	W Midlands	GB
Manual males	53.4	55.2	53.4	114.0	108.4	112.2
Non-manual males	56.7	57.2	57.7	139.0	136.8	150.4
Manual females	37.6	34.4	37.0	65.9	68.6	67.1
Non-manual females	35.9	35.9	37.1	86.8	85.9	88.8

Source: Department of Employment, New Earnings Survey, 1978.

The causes of these earnings relativities are usually laid at the door of the pottery industry. Various writers on the industry have noted that pottery workers' earnings are well below averages for manufacturing industry as a whole.[22] Indeed, Haggar *et al* present evidence to show that in the nineteenth century, north Staffordshire potteries paid lower wages than other ceramics manufacturers in the UK.[23] The New Earnings Survey of 1991 reveals ceramics earnings for male manual workers at 89 per cent of the manufacturing average and even a little below the non-manufacturing male manual average.

Gay and Smyth reject not only the explanation for the relatively low earnings in the pottery industry, but also that these earnings are really low. They prefer to argue that pottery is a labour intensive industry with high prices being obtained for products with a high labour content. They maintain that the pottery industry has low labour costs because it employs largely unskilled and semi-skilled labour, a high proportion of which is female. However, when compared with earnings in other industries for similar jobs, then they suggest, with supporting evidence, that pottery workers, especially women, in fact do relatively well.[24]

Nevertheless, that there is a good explanation for the level of earnings does not negate the

Table 12.2

Weekly earnings of top and bottom deciles in Staffordshire, the West Midlands and Great Britain, 1991

Occupational classification	Bottom 10 per cent with earnings under (£)			Top 10 per cent with earnings over (£)		
	Staffs	W Midlands	GB	Staffs	W Midlands	GB
Manual males	142.1	149.5	149.3	350.4	348.5	375.5
Non-manual males	163.0	170.5	178.7	516.0	531.1	602.0
Manual females	99.0	97.5	100.5	218.5	214.8	233.6
Non-manual females	119.6	124.9	131.0	349.8	348.6	324.9

Source: Department of Employment, New Earnings Survey, 1991.

view that the Potteries is a relatively low-wage area, nor remove the suspicion, however circumstantial, that low pottery wages have driven down general wage levels in the area. Although Gay and Smyth claim that had wages really been low, the industry would have lost its labour force, it could equally be argued that lack of alternatives precluded such a movement.

CONCLUSIONS

It is clear that the Potteries region, though its industry is special, specialized and concentrated in particular industrial sectors, is in no way peculiar. The Potteries economy has had a post-war history that to a substantial extent mirrors that of the economy of the UK as a whole. During the 1950s and 1960s, the long boom brought high employment levels, low unemployment levels, new investment and reorganization in traditional sectors, and new industries to increase the diversity and variety of the economy. The 1970s brought a severe economic environment, which accelerated the problems and decline of manufacturing, and multiplied unemployment levels, with what employment expansion there was being concentrated into service sectors. There were major shifts in employment patterns and structure over the period, and in the distribution of employment between manufacturing and services. Such a story can be told equally for the nation and for the local region.

Within the service sectors, although the share of the local region in professional service occupations and in non-manual occupations in general has increased substantially since 1951, it is still a long way from national averages. It may be that future prospects for the local economy are effected by an 'unattractive' local labour pool, with a high concentration of industry-specific skilled and semi-skilled workers, and few professional/white collar skills. There still remains a relatively low take-up of further education and skills training; and Stoke-on-Trent may well have been hurt by its failure to acquire Assisted Area status. Although unemployment rates have remained at or below the national and regional levels for much of the postwar period, the area remains a low-earnings and low-pay economy, and the local economy has failed to experience a rise in other industrial sectors to match the declining influence of its traditional industrial employers. Like it or not, the future prospects of the economy of the Potteries region are still ultimately and intimately bound up with the fortunes of the ceramics industry.

REFERENCES

1. A J Reeves, *Post-war employment in Stoke-on-Trent*, Hanley, 1945.

2. Ibid; R L Smyth, 'Economic growth in north Staffordshire', *N Staffs Jnl Fld Stud*, 3, 1963, 88–93; A Moyes, 'Employment change in the north Staffordshire conurbation, 1951–1966', *N Staffs Jnl Fld Stud*, 12, 1972, 83–100; R Imrie, *Industrial restructuring in a dominated labour market: the case of Stoke-on-Trent*, Department of Town Planning, University of Wales Institute of Science and Technology, Planning Research Paper No 106, 1988; J Bennington, *Stoke-on-Trent: a local economic strategy for a period of transition*, Economic Development and Tourism Committee, Stoke-on-Trent, 1990.

3. A Moyes, 'Second World War manufacturing industry and its significance for north Staffordshire', in A D M Phillips and B J Turton, eds, *Environment, man and economic change*, 1975, 315–35.

4. D L Gregory and R L Smyth, *The worker and the pottery industry*, Studies in the British Pottery Industry No 4, Keele University, 1971.

5. R G Haggar, A R Mountford and J Thomas, 'Pottery', in *Victoria County History of Staffordshire (VCH Staffs)*, 1967, ii, 1–67. The exact date and place of the last bottle-kiln firing in Stoke as part of normal operations has proved an elusive datum, but could not have occurred much beyond the mid-1960s. D J Machin and R L Smyth, *The changing structure of the British pottery industry, 1935–1968*, Studies in the British Pottery Industry No 2, Keele University, 1969, record eleven remaining 'in operation' in 1965, and Moyes, 'Employment change', notes the last went out of use in 1967. Certainly, the passing of the old coal-fired bottle kilns was substantially unnoticed and unmourned at the time. There was a last firing of a bottle kiln at the Gladstone Museum, Longton, during 1978 to mark the end of this era.

6. F Burchill and R Ross, *A history of the Potters' Union*, Hanley, 1977, 218.

7. P W Gay and R L Smyth, *The British pottery industry*, 1974, 14.

8. A J Taylor, 'Coal', *VCH Staffs*, ii, 1967, 81–5.

9. A Moyes, 'Post-war changes in the distribution of employment and population in north Staffordshire', unpublished MA thesis, Keele University, 1971.

10. British Steel were employing 440 workers at the rolling mill and finishing shed at the site in 1992.

11. M J Pullen and J L R Proops, 'Input-output analysis and the north Staffordshire autarky myth', *N Staffs Jnl Fld Stud*, 20, 1980, 41–61.

12. Staffordshire Training and Enterprise Council, *North Staffordshire labour market assessment: summary report*, Prepared by Pieda plc, 1992.

13. Bennington, *Stoke-on-Trent: a local economic strategy*.

14. Staffordshire Training and Enterprise Council, *North Staffordshire labour market assessment*.

15. Both Silverdale and Trentham remain under threat of imminent closure at the time of writing.

16. Staffordshire Training and Enterprise Council, *North Staffordshire labour market assessment*.

17. Bennington, *Stoke-on-Trent: a local economic strategy*.

18. Partners Group, *Review of the Assisted Areas of Great Britain*, Representations by the Partners Group for the Stoke-on-Trent-to-Work Area, 1992.

19. Stoke-on-Trent City Council, *Stoke-on-Trent City Plan, 1989–2001: draft technical report*, 1989.

20. Newcastle-under-Lyme Economic Monitor, *The 1989 census of employment: a summary of findings*, Newcastle-under-Lyme Borough Council, 1992.

21. Staffordshire Training and Enterprise Council, *Staffordshire skills audit: summary report*, Prepared by Pieda plc, 1991.

22. Gay and Smyth, *The British pottery industry*, 209; Burchill and Ross, *Potters' Union,* 258–9; R Imrie, *Industrial restructuring in the British pottery industry: a crisis for labour and locality*, Department of Town Planning, University of Wales Institute of Science and Technology, Planning Research Paper No 107, 1987, 50.

23. Haggar *et al*, 'Pottery', 48–9.

24. Gay and Smyth, *The British pottery industry*, 209–10.

13. Economic and Industrial Diversification: Changing Policies, Technologies and Locations

R M BALL

This chapter focuses on the pattern and process of change in the area economy of the Potteries in the postwar period. Of course, despite the myriad of changes, there are continuities, remnants of the past that retain, in a variety of ways, their hold on the complexion of the area economy, and this is an integrating theme of the chapter. The discussion traces the geographical implications of the movement towards a diversification of the area economy that has occurred since 1945 – both in terms of broad economic structure and the precise nature of the industrial base – but also considers the extent to which the legacy of the past economy manifests itself in the present. From a geographical perspective it discusses the character of the contemporary economy, the range of new manufacturing activities and the gradual emergence of a more substantive service sector and explores a range of related locational issues. The conurbation is portrayed as an 'intervention backwater', problematical in its own way but neglected by most regional and urban policies, that is gradually, through a combination of private sector and local authority initiatives, fighting off its image as an old, overdependent and rundown industrial area that has little potential for future development.[1]

Incompleteness, lack of continuity of definition and availability, inaccessibility, and modest quality in the local data base are familiar frustrations for economic geographers studying local economies. As such, and not surprisingly, information on the changing structure of economic activity in the Potteries region is similarly 'thin on the ground'. Official sources are either small samples (census of population, economic activity data) produced relatively infrequently or lack continuity of definition, coverage and comparability over time (census of employment). Moreover, much spatial analysis is based on employment and/or unemployment data so that it is, in effect, spatial labour market analysis.

This chapter tries to avoid that focus, but unfortunately, such a stance means that, by necessity, we must work with little or no comprehensive data. It is necessary to assemble evidence from a wide variety of research and data sources if anything more than an ephemeral assessment is to be made. Building on past research findings or academic commentary, it uses a variety of sources, including official data, sector sources, evidence from research on specific dimensions of the area economy, local economic survey work, private sector sources, and local authority research and intelligence material.

The theme of continuity and change is a valuable framework for the assessment of any area economy. In the Potteries conurbation, whilst the traditional ceramics sector continues to provide a vital cornerstone for the area's jobs and prosperity, it has changed significantly since 1945 in its size-structure, in its ownership, its technological profile, and in its employment base. As already demonstrated in chapter 12 it is still there and still dominant, but unsurprisingly, the nature of the product, the way it is produced and the kinds of jobs provided have changed dramatically. The deep-mined coal industry retains a production presence in late 1992 but it is fragile, uncertain and a shadow of its postwar base level, and even what capacity remains is under pressure from cheaper methods such as open-cast. By the mid-1990s its continuity of presence may well only survive as remnants in the landscape – in the villages and derelict sites of former pit complexes – or as industrial heritage sites for tourism and leisure development.

GEOGRAPHICAL PERSPECTIVES ON THE DEVELOPING ECONOMIC BASE OF THE REGION

The previous chapter has provided a broad background picture of the developing postwar conurbation economy and highlighted key features of its dynamism. This chapter, taking a selection of these and other issues, emphasizes the geographical dimension of development. This involves the investigation and analysis of trends at two broad, and not necessarily discrete, spatial scales: the first, focusing on the relative position of the locality – the conurbation economy – in its global context; the second, assessing the nature and implications of the changing distribution of economic activity within the area. This is a useful structure for reviewing geographical change in the conurbation economy.

In these terms it is necessary to consider a number of interconnected locational and development factors that pertain to and influence the area's economic progression. This requires an assessment of the geographical dimension of factors such as the industrial decisions made by key players (both private and public sector) in the area, the attractiveness of areas outside the region as a focus for development that might conceivably have located in the Potteries, technological and organizational changes, transport and accessibility issues, the role of local authority economic planning and the contribution, albeit minimal, of central government spatial policies to the development of the area. All impinge on the character of the conurbation economy.

The relative geographical position of the conurbation economy: global considerations and external connections

In a variety of ways the position of the Potteries conurbation in the wider global economy is vital for an understanding of its development, not least of all because global influences directly condition the character of the local economy. Moreover, in a related sense, it is important to judge how the area has developed relative to other areas, and to consider the influence of external factors and issues. Sometimes, external forces have worked in the area's favour. For example, as Fogarty shows in his study of postwar 'reconstruction' problems,[2] during the Second World War a number of general (precision) engineering firms were shifted to the area on strategic criteria, something of an irony in that, as a consequence of its distance from the country's major conurbations – its marginality – north Staffordshire was positively rewarded. Some of the 'newer' manufacturing industries of the area owe their initial facilities to this legacy. Elsewhere, the impact of external relationships has been less positive; for example, the dependence of its key industries on external, often export markets. In all these respects, geography really does matter.

The 'booming towns' research of Champion and Green provides an indication of the contemporary geographical position of the area, although only in terms of employment structures (Table 13.1). Relative to the national average representation of 'traditional' industries, the Potteries is one of the more specialized localities in Great Britain. There are few areas with a greater representation. In terms of contemporary growth activities such as business services, whilst the conurbation has secured a modest share and with almost average growth in that sector in the 1980s, it is underrepresented compared to the average locality. The traditional base continues to dominate.

Table 13.1

The relative position of the Potteries conurbation in traditional industries and business services in the late 1980s, by local labour market areas (LLMA)

Percentage employment (September 1987) in	Stoke-on-Trent LLMA	Great Britain		
		Median LLMA	Best LLMA	Worst LLMA
Traditional (primary, utilities, manufacturing) industries	46.1	31.7	12.6	58.1
Business services (including banking, finance, insurance)	6.0	6.7	20.6	1.7
Percentage change in employment in business services, 1984–7	11.2	13.9	83.2	−38.0

The Stoke-on-Trent LLMA is based on the CURDS, Newcastle-upon-Tyne, functional regions framework and includes the conurbation plus peripheral commuting areas.
Source: A G Champion and A E Green, *In search of Britain's booming towns*, Centre for Urban and Regional Development Studies, University of Newcastle-upon-Tyne, 1985.

The degree of geographical specialization of the contemporary economy is indicated by calculating a simple measure of spatial concentration – the location quotient. As Table 13.2 shows, location quotients in excess of 1.0 (indicating an average representation) occur only in a narrow band of activities, mainly mirroring the traditional base of the area economy. Unsurprisingly, of particular note is the 'manufacture of non-metallic products', a sector that includes much of the ceramics industry, whereas particularly underrepresented activities tend to be in the service sector.[3] Clearly, an examination is needed of the global setting of major economic activities in the conurbation, as well as an investigation of external pressures and sources of assistance, if the area's postwar geographical development is to be effectively charted.

Some global factors and the local development of the ceramics industry
Despite optimism in the immediate aftermath of war, the ceramics industry proved to be a slow growth area. Although varying in its performance by product type, it suffered from a relative lack of domestic product demand in the late 1940s and 1950s, and lost some export markets (for example in Australasia) through tariff changes. Largely linked to global markets and foreign competition, each of the five major segments of activity – tableware; gift ware; tiles; sanitary ware; and industrial ceramics – has had a different but in most cases chequered developed since the 1950s. For example, the vitally important tableware market in North America was choked in the 1970s by high prices, at least partly engendered by the overvalue of sterling against the US dollar. At the same time, the period saw strong competition from both traditional and emergent

Table 13.2

Industry classes with high location quotients in the Stoke-on-Trent area, 1989*

Industrial class	Location quotient	Employment ('000)	Percentage of total employment
Manufacture of non-metallic products	19.1	32.3	17.6
Coal extraction/manufacture of solid fuels	5.3	4.1	2.3
Rubber and plastics processing	4.2	7.6	4.1
Manufacture of office and data processing equipment	3.0	2.0	1.1
Owning and dealing in real estate	1.4	1.6	0.9
Education	1.0	14.2	7.7

* Data in this table are not comparable with Table 13.1, as they are based on an area that covers Stoke-on-Trent, Newcastle-under-Lyme and Staffordshire Moorlands (Fig 9.4).
Source: Census of employment, 1989.

producers – Japan, West Germany and Taiwan. Tiles have been particularly affected and afflicted by high quality imports from Iberia and Italy, whilst sanitary ware additionally suffers from any recession in the construction industry. Competition led to the demise of many of the least competitive firms and to the emergence – largely through acquisitions – of a small number of dominant, multi-plant firms such as Wedgwood and Royal Doulton. Both these firms have since been acquired by non-local interests and this reflects the increasingly 'remote-controlled' character of the Potteries economy.

It is interesting to note that the vast majority of UK ceramics production – around 75–80 per cent – remains firmly entrenched in the Potteries conurbation. Geographically, there has been no domestic decentralization tendency: for example, the formation of branch plants in Assisted Areas has not been a feature of ceramics, although, in a process of 'internationalization' as a response to the erosion of overseas markets, some of the larger firms have invested in and/or acquired mass production facilities outside the UK, leaving the specialist niche markets to Potteries production. The forces of inertia have been particularly dominant in the industry – probably the prime example of an industrial concentration in the UK spatial economic system. The importance of labour skills and technical 'know-how', established patterns of operation through supplying industries, and perhaps the continuing influence of traditional family control, if only through representation on the boards of multi-plant businesses, are some of the factors involved.

Technological changes have also been important in conditioning the character of the industry. The sector was described by Rodgers as 'archaic' in the early postwar period but, since the early 1950s, many processes have been automated (for example, sorting, glazing and printing), precipitating the shedding of labour (as reflected by membership of the Ceramics and Allied Trades Union which fell from over 41,500 in 1980 to 31,300 in late 1988). There has been a major shift towards continuous firing using gas- or electricity-powered kilns. Pressures to increase productivity in the face of competition and lost markets led to various technical changes: in the 1960s and 1970s, in order to reap economies of scale, product ranges were narrowed, with the tendency already noted for a switch towards customized items. Inevitably, this led to the abandonment of many of the older, less suitable factory premises in areas such as Burslem. Close relationships between retail chains and pottery producers have stimulated the use of 'just-in-time' production methods[4] and in this regard, the central geographical position of the area has proved important.

In some respects, the local development of the conurbation has been left behind by the global development of new product areas. According to a report produced for Stoke-on-Trent City Council in 1989,[5] one sector of great untapped potential is that of advanced ceramics (electroceramics; engineering ceramics). The Potteries was the birthplace of advanced ceramics in the 1950s yet, due to a lack of national investment and state support, this potential source of diversification was barely exploited, and other national economies, such as Japan, have benefited. However, there is now a recognition of the potential. Major private sector and educational research organizations engaged in advanced ceramics are located in the conurbation together with the combined expertise of the traditional pottery manufacturing and supply industry. Unfortunately, the overbearing tradition of the area, until recently the lack of business parks and some key skills, and the absence of national long-term investment have continued to act as a brake on diversification via the so-called 'new ceramics'.

By the late 1980s it was apparent that the character of the ceramics industry had changed quite substantially since the 1950s: fewer producers using less of the factory stock, with a very different organizational structure from that of the early postwar period, significantly controlled from outside the local area and using much less labour, but still exerting a dominant influence over the area economy. The implications of these changes for the internal economic geography of the conurbation will be discussed later.

The global and the local: steel, coal and the rest

Outside ceramics, one of the most controversial local events in the postwar development of the Potteries conurbation economy and one that remains firmly in the consciousness of local people was the closure in 1980 of the British Steel Corporation works at Shelton Bar. Shelton Bar was a small steel-making plant that produced high-quality, light steel beams for the expensive end of the steel market. Reflecting in part the raw material base of the north Staffordshire coalfield, steel-making had been carried on continuously since 1841 at Shelton, and at its peak the plant employed nearly 5000 workers. Although the rolling mill and complex was retained (and survives in an efficient state today), the closure was controversial for a number of reasons. Shelton Bar was a large employer in a community within the conurbation that depended – economically and socially – on the works. More than that however, it had relatively modern steel-making equipment and with some modest investment the workforce claimed (through its Shelton Action Committee) that it could produce steel as cheaply as the large new integrated plants at coastal locations proposed under the BSC plan. The highly cost-effective rolling mill at Shelton was to be retained in any case but the SAC argued that it would be cheaper to produce steel using scrap-fed electric arc furnaces at Shelton than to ship it in from Scunthorpe. BSC claimed that there was not sufficient scrap steel for the development of electric arc furnaces and were sceptical of the cost estimates. Not least, any decision to retain small plants could threaten the viability of their concentration-integration strategy. Steel-making ceased at the site, the electric arc scrap proposal never saw the light of day, and the conurbation economy lost over a 1000 jobs and a major source of demand. The works had 7000 suppliers of equipment and materials within a 40 km radius, many of whom were local, and monthly purchases were over £2 million.[6] As with the ceramics industry, the changing face (in this case, the demise) of a traditional industry can only be understood in the context of its global position within a production system and strategy for development clearly influenced by external (non-local) forces and decisions.

The influence of global decisions and factors is nowhere more evident than in the coal-mining industry. Clearly an important part of the industrial heritage of the Potteries conurbation,

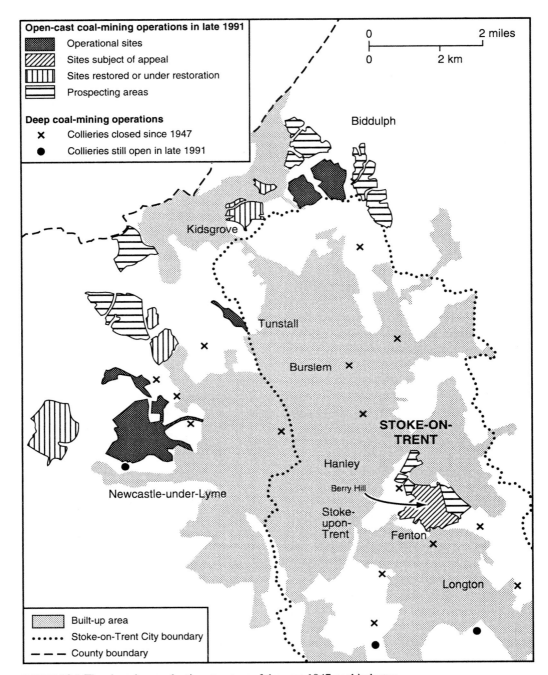

FIGURE 13.1 The changing production structure of the post-1947 coal industry.

in the 1990s it is a shadow of its early postwar incidence. The demise of the local steel works, the switch to electric- and gas-fired kilns in pottery production, together with the general decline of markets for coal, the relatively low cost of imported coal, and the concentration of domestic demand around the power generation core have precipitated its decline. In mid-1992 there were just two pit complexes remaining – Trentham and Silverdale. Unfortunately, in an industry dominated by pressures for cheaper imported sources for the power industry and by privatization and the so-called 'dash for gas', the future was less than assured and both were nominated for closure in the October 1992 British Coal cutbacks. The ensuing public and political outcry resulted in a reprieve for Silverdale and a small question mark beside the Trentham closure decision, but their survival over anything more than the short term seems unlikely.

Other important events for coal-mining involve both positive and negative developments in the locality. In the latter case, the relocation of British Coal's regional headquarters to Cheshire further eroded the level of mining-related activity; on a more positive note, the former mining complex at Chatterley Whitfield has become the location for British Coal's archival collection and thus has considerable potential as a heritage site for tourism and leisure. In addition, and as part of a drive to develop this site as a tourist attraction, coal-mining on a modest scale may recommence in 1993.[7]

Although the deep-mined sector has continued to decline, there are important additional continuities in the economic presence of the industry in north Staffordshire. Shallow deposits of coal in many parts of north Staffordshire mean that British Coal has been able to exploit (and propose exploitation of) reserves by open-cast methods, so that the economic activity of coal-mining remains in the area, albeit at only a fraction of the production levels attained throughout the postwar period (Fig 13.1). Open-cast coal is cheaper (on a par with imported coal), but generates its own tensions within the locality. Relatively few jobs are created, and many of them are non-local as British Coal tends to contract out exploitation. Moreover, the landscape and the quality of life of those in the vicinity is severely disrupted over the exploitation period, and the image of the region may not be enhanced by the physical presence of such activity. Between 1974 and 1992, eight sites, covering an area of over 700 ha and containing some 10 million tonnes, have been granted permission for open-cast coal-working in north Staffordshire and there are several additional prospecting sites. Particularly controversial amongst recent proposals has been Berry Hill, a visually prominent site in the heart of the conurbation. This proposal to mine 0.9 million tonnes over almost five years (the level of output that the Trentham complex could in the early 1990s produce in six months), it is argued, runs counter to the agreed strategy for environmental and economic regeneration in the conurbation and is in conflict with the commitment towards tourist development.[8]

Whilst traditional specializations, if not volumes, remain at least partially intact, there has been a gradual development in the conurbation of a modest array and scale of other manufacturing activities. These have been either activities linked to the traditional ceramics base – machinery, materials – or developments associated with the post-1970s expansion of small manufacturing businesses. Although the Potteries has a relatively poor record in this domain,[9] it has spawned a variety of activities, from those again linked to the ceramics or engineering base to new activities in areas such as plastics and food processing. Some firms have 'overspilled' into the Potteries from the West Midlands or Manchester conurbations; others have set up manufacturing–distribution activities to take advantage of the good accessibility of the area; some have been attracted by the relatively low-cost operating environment and the availability of cheap premises. In general though, there have been no substantive in-moves.

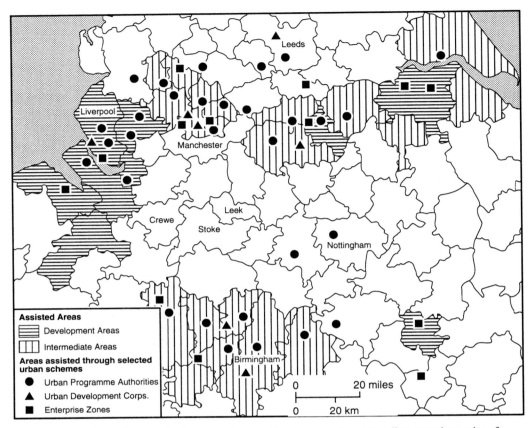

FIGURE 13.2 The Potteries conurbation as an 'intervention backwater': surrounding areas in receipt of assistance through regional and urban policy.

The lack of global recognition: the Potteries conurbation as a non-Assisted Area

Despite innumerable proposals and protestations from the local authorities,[10] the Potteries has rarely received central government support through either regional or urban status. Representations for Enterprise Zone allocation, applications for both Assisted Area and Inner Area status (all following from the post-1970s rationalizations), and proposals for RECHAR support in the early 1990s have fallen by the wayside, up against a central government that has resolutely refused to respond to the needs of the area. With the exception of the Derelict Land Grant, the term 'intervention backwater' accurately reflects this situation (Fig 13.2; Pl 13.1). Such neglect is interesting because the strength of the case has often seemed strong. The conurbation is very characteristic of an old industrial centre with problems of a poor-quality built environment comparable to those of areas that have long been provided with government assistance through regional and/or urban aid. Ironically, its generally low unemployment rate – at least partly a result of undercounting given the traditional involvement of women in the ceramic workforce – coupled with other less tangible political factors has served to deny it regional and urban support. In these terms, and given coal closures, perhaps only for the time-being, the policy emphasis in the conurbation is firmly set at the local scale.

PLATE 13.1 Local sensitivities and emotive responses: the Potteries region as an 'intervention backwater'. A cartoon by Dave Follows published in the *Evening Sentinel* newspaper in 1984 at the time of the mid-1980s review of regional policy and of the decision not to grant Assisted Area status to the Stoke-on-Trent Travel-to-Work Area (Reproduced by permission of the artist and Staffordshire *Sentinel* newspaper).

THE LOCAL DIMENSION: GEOGRAPHICAL CHANGE WITHIN THE CONURBATION ECONOMY

At the local scale, a wide range of factors has influenced the changing geography of economic activity in the conurbation. These include technological changes affecting the viability of particular plants or operating areas; the varying potential that areas within the conurbation have shown for exploiting contemporary economic opportunities, including variations in accessibility and proximity to the M6, differing suitability for retail development, and differences in industrial heritage potential; and local authority economic policies in as much as they have influenced the local direction and degree of economic change.

For example, as a consequence of product development, and organizational and technological changes in the ceramics industry discussed earlier, many of the smaller, family pottery firms ceased to operate. Between 1951 and 1966 Moyes estimated that 166 establishments closed,[1] whilst during the 1979–83 'shake out', when 25,000 jobs were lost from ceramics nationally, around 50 firms went out of business. Most were relatively small (50 employees or less) and virtually all were located in the core pottery manufacturing areas within the conurbation – Burslem, Stoke, Longton and Hanley in particular. Some were taken over by larger firms, but many disappeared from the scene altogether. Trends like this gave rise to a problem of unutilized (vacant) industrial premises (vips). For example, survey work completed in the mid-to-late 1980s estimated that in 1985 there was over 3 million sq ft of available floorspace in 264 separate premises in Stoke-on-Trent alone, and much of this 'problem' was focused on Burslem and Hanley (Fig 13.3), where many of the less easily re-usable premises were located.[12] The issue of underutilized industrial floorspace is one example of the differing potential evident within the conurbation. Some areas have benefited from the modest diversification that has in consequence occurred. For example, industrial premises located adjacent to new or improved access routes have tended to be refurbished and/or re-let as going-concerns more readily (Pl 13.2).

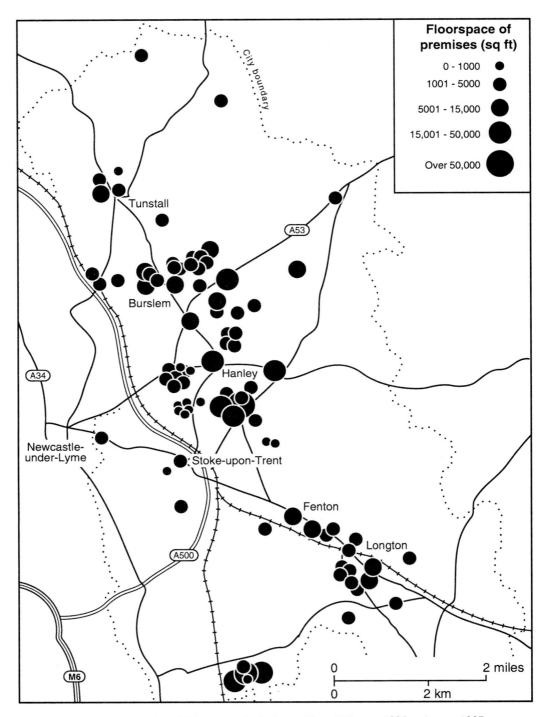

FIGURE 13.3 Industrial premises falling vacant in Stoke-on-Trent, February 1985 to August 1987.

More generally, the quality of the infrastructural base has been an important factor in the changing locational structure of the conurbation. For example, in the core industrial areas, many internal roads were originally constructed for modest traffic flows and for purposes that differ from those of a modern integrated industrial complex. Indeed, in the early days of industrial development in the core area it was the canal system which carried most of the raw materials and outputs of the key pottery-based industries. Aside from the construction of the M6 motorway in the early 1960s and the major impact that it must have had on the regional accessibility of the conurbation, over the course of the postwar period substantive improvements have been made to the area's internal infrastructure. In the 1970s, the so-called D road (A500) – a route first mooted in the 1930s – was completed. This provides both Stoke and Newcastle with greater access to the M6 through a D-shaped loop (Fig 13.4; Pl 13.2) that, cutting across the conurbation, links up with junctions 15 and 16 of the motorway. This road has enhanced the development potential of sites adjacent to the loop.[13] More recently there have been several congestion-easing schemes, including a new road around Hanley – the emergent retail centre of the conurbation – and plans for major improvements in Longton and Tunstall (Fig 13.4). These initiatives will all serve to enhance the attractiveness of heartland locations for development purposes, something that is vitally important for their future economic progress.

PLATE 13.2 The A500 (D road) Loop (Jeffersons Air Photography, Liverpool). Completed in 1981, the D road provided an important new source of access to the A34 trunk road and the M6 motorway, helping to open up the core of the conurbation economy and to regenerate areas adjacent to the route.

The growth and development of local authority involvement

In the face of central government reluctance to resource and support the Potteries region, local authority involvement in the economy was active and expansive from the late 1970s. Prior to local government reorganization in 1974, urban localities were primarily engaged in providing for whatever development happened to occur rather than actively intervening in its promotion.

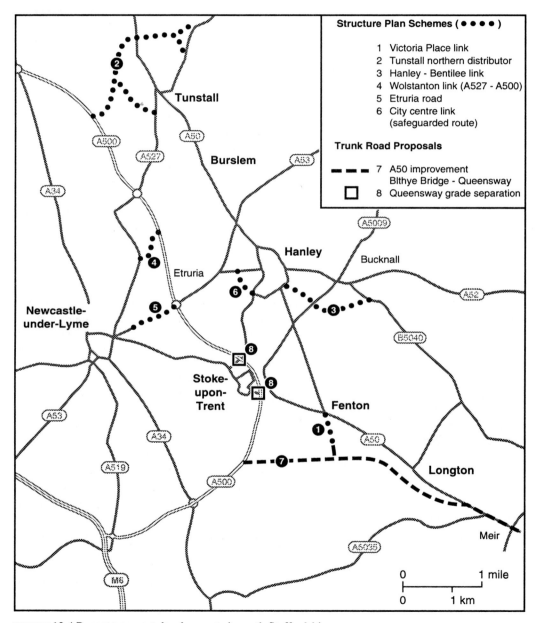

FIGURE 13.4 Recent transport developments in north Staffordshire.

Against this background there has been a variable approach and degree of involvement among the three authorities concerned, Stoke-on-Trent City Council, Newcastle-under-Lyme Borough Council, and Staffordshire County Council, all pursuing their individual economic strategies, not always obviously in tandem with each other. In general, the 'local' approach to regeneration has involved a number of key strands, focusing on indigenous industry, inward investment, small business formation and advice policy, infrastructural development, marketing and tourism, policies for training, for developing the public sector, and for increasing involvement at a European Community scale, and with a commitment to public-private partnership.

Of the two district authorities, Newcastle was the first to develop industrial development planning, and this has occurred in three phases. From 1974–9 the emphasis was on employment generation, setting the basic foundations of a local economic policy by developing industrial estates and the town centre. From 1979–87 a more reactive/first-aid approach was adopted in the face of increasing unemployment. This nurtured a wide range of policy initiatives from business growth through small factory construction and advice to inward investment strategy. Finally, since 1987 there has been a more proactive approach in which quality of development – particularly in the areas of office and retail provision – has been sought.[14] In general, however, there is recognition that in all areas traditional manufacturing must also play a central part in any regeneration. For example, the emphasis in Stoke's local economic policy, as gradually developed since the early 1980s, has been more orientated towards that sector, although the growth of services is also seen as a major need. As the city of Stoke-on-Trent Economic Development Strategy argues, there is a primary need to defend, develop and modernize the indigenous manufacturing industries, technologies and skills as well as to diversify on the basis of pre-existing strengths.[15]

Locational change in the conurbation manufacturing-mining economy
The theme of continuity and change is particularly appropriate in assessing the post-1945 locational distribution of economic activity in the conurbation. For example, it is apparent that there is a clear retention of activity in the historical urban-industrial heartland of the conurbation. This is the belt running from Tunstall and Burslem through Hanley to Longton, essentially located and evolving on physical and raw-material access grounds.[16] Particularly since the late 1970s, there has been notable selected brownfield development within the heartland, in particular utilizing former colliery, pottery or other derelict sites. Aside from the usual range of selected conversions and infills that might be expected in any old industrial area, industrial estate development using one or more of a number of sources of finance (for example, British Coal financial support, Derelict Land Grant aid, and local authority finance) has been a prime vehicle for regeneration. In this sense, the pattern of industrial land-use has barely changed but the activities involved and the kinds of local operating environment have greatly altered. Such developments have also fostered service activity and, for example, new educational developments in the 1970s (the former Polytechnic and the Sixth Form College) were both located on reclaimed sites in the heartland.

The conversion of industrial space in the conurbation has taken two forms. First, there has been a variety of pockets of relatively small-scale conversion – ranging from use (of site or buildings) change to the subdivision of premises for small businesses – which mostly involve private firms, either disposing of premises acquired through takeover, or developing unused capacity.[17] Second, there has been the marginally more grandiose, and certainly more identifiable, larger-scale industrial estate and business park developments, often originating in the public domain (Fig 13.5). These are mainly either British Coal developments on former

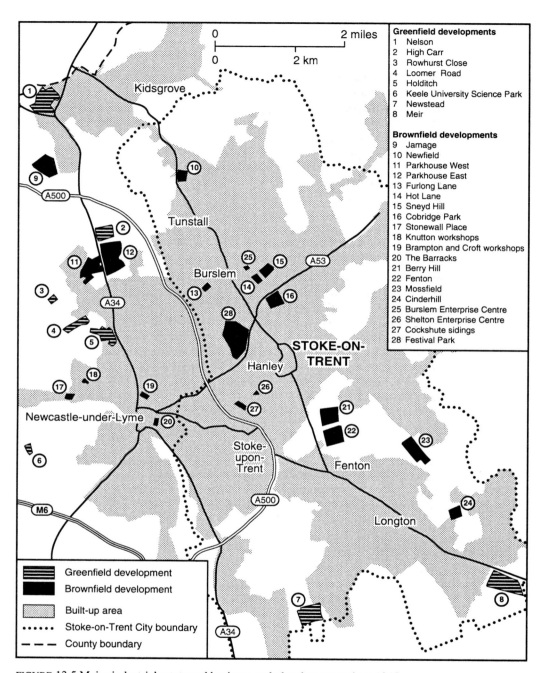

Greenfield developments
1 Nelson
2 High Carr
3 Rowhurst Close
4 Loomer Road
5 Holditch
6 Keele University Science Park
7 Newstead
8 Meir

Brownfield developments
9 Jamage
10 Newfield
11 Parkhouse West
12 Parkhouse East
13 Furlong Lane
14 Hot Lane
15 Sneyd Hill
16 Cobridge Park
17 Stonewall Place
18 Knutton workshops
19 Brampton and Croft workshops
20 The Barracks
21 Berry Hill
22 Fenton
23 Mossfield
24 Cinderhill
25 Burslem Enterprise Centre
26 Shelton Enterprise Centre
27 Cockshute sidings
28 Festival Park

Greenfield development
Brownfield development
Built-up area
Stoke-on-Trent City boundary
County boundary

FIGURE 13.5 Major industrial estate and business park developments since 1945.

colliery sites (Sneyd Hill or Mossfield in Stoke) or local authority inspired conversion and organized development, sometimes initially in partnership with private developers (as at Parkhouse in Newcastle). Individual firms or groups of firms have occasionally been major catalysts in the redevelopment of sites, for example, the former local authority airfield at Meir, part of which is now an industrial estate. Most schemes have been brownfield development, the exceptions being Nelson, Holditch and High Carr in Newcastle, and Meir and Newstead on the periphery of Stoke. The last two estates were originally planned in the late 1950s, but most brownfield developments are more recent, largely deriving from the opportunities brought about by the chance to obtain Derelict Land Grants following the contraction of established, traditional industries, and hence their premises, in the early-to-late 1970s.

The most recent initiatives have been business park or enterprise centre developments designed to encourage and nurture new small concerns, and not exclusively in manufacturing. For example, in Stoke-on-Trent there are two Enterprise Centres in refurbished and converted buildings, all substantially funded by local authority resources, and one development inspired by a British Rail supported scheme at Cockshute, linked to Community Partnership – a local liaison between industry, local authority and British Rail (Fig 13.5). The Science Park at Keele University, part funded by Newcastle-under-Lyme Borough Council, is designed to nurture high technology developments. In all parts of the conurbation, but especially Newcastle, the focus has been gradually shifting in the last few years, with a number of private sector business park developments designed to attract commercial activities.

Vips provide both a potential problem and a source of available activity space. In this respect, research on the reoccupation of formerly vacant industrial premises in Stoke between 1987 and 1989 yields interesting data not only on the areas that have suffered from plant abandonment but also on the character of the 149 new occupants.[18] Around 46 per cent of new occupants in 1989 were engaged in manufacturing but relatively few were entirely new businesses. Most were local relocations, expansions, or reopenings of buildings that had been previously 'mothballed'. In the traditional pottery-manufacturing centres, there were numerous examples of pottery manufacturers or materials suppliers occupying former vips, particularly in Longton and Burslem. Outside the Potteries' traditional manufacturing sectors, a substantial number of occupations involved locally-orientated service businesses, mainly retail and wholesale distribution, or specialist services such as cleaning, car servicing and computer software installation. Amongst the remainder was the expansion of Cauldon College into premises formerly occupied by a textile firm and certainly vacant in both 1985 and 1987. All this evidence evokes a rather parochial image of the Potteries' recent economic development.

However, and despite the modest record of new firm growth in the region, there were numerous examples amongst the new occupants of the kinds of small businesses that were prominent in new enterprise growth throughout the economy in the 1970s and 1980s. Double-glazing manufacturing (Longton, Burslem and Hanley), specialist plastics moulding (Burslem), security services (Fenton) are good examples of small businesses – new or relocating to larger premises – that are typical of the 1980s, and that tend to occur in industrial sectors where there are limited economies of scale and relative ease of entry into business, and which have often inhabited part or all of the premises left vacant by the rationalization of traditional industries (Fig 13.3; Pl 13.2).

Since 1945 there has been some economic development outside the heartland. Contemporary industrial development has adopted peripheral locations away from what Rodgers calls the 'urban tangle of the six towns'. In part this has been necessitated by the limited availability of land ready and suitable for development – itself partly associated with the tightly-defined green belt on the perimeter of the conurbation – and the high costs of regeneration in the heartland. This has involved both new industrial groups locating in greenfield sites or, in the earlier part of the postwar period, in former wartime shadow factory space (ICL in Kidsgrove), and new developments by existing businesses (the Royal Doulton factory at Baddely Green), or the dispersal of investment in existing activities (such as pottery production and materials supply at Meir). Locations have been along main routes, for example, around the A34 trunk road to the south and north of the conurbation. The decentralization of the Wedgwood factory complex to Barlaston – completed by the mid-1950s – is a classic example, as is the development of the Nelson Industrial Estate to the north of the conurbation in the late 1950s.

Locational change in the conurbation service economy

The modest scale and development of its service-industry base has long been a limiting factor in the development of the Potteries conurbation. Indeed, Fogarty in 1945 called for a new focus for services – a compact, conveniently-situated and attractive shopping, business and recreational centre, perhaps with a concentration of services natural to a regional capital.[19] Although great strides have been made in the 1980s and 1990s, particularly in developing Hanley as a major shopping centre and in the development of Newcastle town centre, there is still only limited representation of some services, particularly footloose producer services (Table 13.1).

In the area of retailing it might be argued that the Potteries has experienced a transition, from being 'undershopped' (that is, with less than its expected level of retail facilities) to being 'overshopped' in the 1990s. The spatial structure of the conurbation as it existed in the early 1950s produced a retail facility spread across the area's various urban centres. Lacking an identifiable regional centre, most of the constituent towns were underprovided in terms of retail outlets. The retail boom of the early 1980s resulted in a real augmentation of the range of activity throughout the area.

In the wake of the 1986 National Garden Festival on a large derelict area in Shelton, the Festival Park site was developed as a mixed industrial-commercial-leisure and retail park (Pls 16.2 and 3). The initial intention had been for a more dominant manufacturing use of the reclaimed site but developers willing to put in substantial factory space in advance of occupation could not be found. Retail development thus filled an important need, not just in terms of shopping capacity but also in terms of development. The Potteries Shopping Centre in Hanley, with 0.5 million sq ft of space attracted a variety of multiple stores that were new to the conurbation (Pl 14.1). In Newcastle, a deliberate policy aimed at activating underused or unused town centre sites was operated by the local authority from the 1970s. Between 1980 and 1986 retail floorspace in the town increased by 19 per cent.[20] The conurbation has been transformed from underrepresentation of retail facilities in the past to a point where commentators are suggesting, in the light of economic recession, that there is now overcapacity. This is particularly important for the emergent retail centre of Hanley.

In this way, the changing geography of the conurbation service economy has been partly connected to the differential potential of areas within it to adopt and exploit new economic opportunities in the post-1945 period. Two further examples can be cited. First, the drive for diversification in the 1990s has precipitated a recognition of the potential role in future economic development of tourism, mainly by definition in the older industrial areas of the conurbation. Economic diversification is seen by development professionals as a vital need for the conurbation economy and, in the wake of successful promotion elsewhere, tourism has gradually gained credence as a potentially fruitful future growth area. All local authorities have

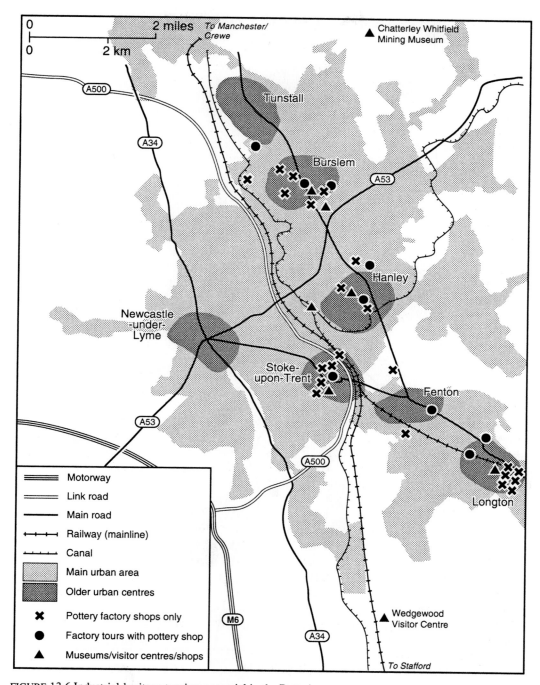

FIGURE 13.6 Industrial-heritage tourism potential in the Potteries.

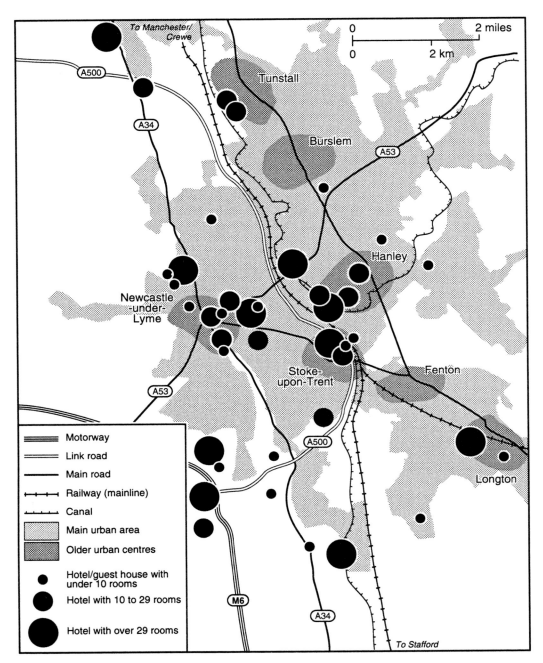

FIGURE 13.7 The accommodation base in north Staffordshire.

jumped on the 'tourism bandwagon' and, in particular following the recommendations of the Heart of England Tourist Board in its *Tourism action programme for north Staffordshire*, there is a real commitment to tourism in the area. At first sight this may seem a longshot. However, the region has a unique industrial heritage in the pottery industry with valuable potential in the 'pits' dimension. It is well placed for business tourism and, although held back by a negative physical image, is assisted by the catalyst of quality household names, such as Wedgwood and Royal Doulton. With major industrial heritage attractions – the Wedgwood Visitor Centre; the Gladstone Pottery Museum; Chatterley Whitfield Colliery and Mining Museum and dozens of factory shops and tours – mainly located in the older urban centres that need new economic initiatives, together with a solid accommodation base (Figs 13.6 and 7), there is great potential in this area of activity.[21]

A second pertinent example concerns warehousing-distribution potential. As might be expected given the geographical position of the conurbation and its good access to the north-west and west midlands, warehousing and distribution developments have been increasingly evident since the 1960s.[22] These have been particularly prominent in areas close to motorway access points. Thus, the Parkhouse Industrial Estate in Newcastle, developed on a former colliery site, attracted a number of distribution sections of either established manufacturing firms or of specialized distribution companies to a location close to the M6 motorway (Fig 13.5).

THE CONURBATION ECONOMY IN THE 1990S AND BEYOND: CHALLENGES FOR LOCAL ECONOMIC POLICY

Against the background of the various trends discussed in this and other chapters, there are clearly many challenges facing local economic planning in the 1990s – some general, others local in origin, all topical – and it is perhaps appropriate to end on such a note.

Mobilizing resources for local initiatives

There is a need to raise the modest resources available for local economic planning and to convince central government of the benefits that a fuller degree of support for the local economy might bring. Access to European Community sources has also been limited in the past, and there is clearly scope for levering monies in the future. A recent decision to put EC funds into a scheme to regenerate the Gladstone-St James area of Longton is a start.

Although it may well be changing in the 1990s – indeed, the local enterprise agency, Business Initiative, has assisted over 2000 new business start-ups since 1981 – there has in the past been a certain complacency on the part of local industry, and it is a challenge for local economic planning to mobilize the private sector and to spell out again the benefits that greater local economic strength may produce for local business. A recent initiative by Stoke-on-Trent City Council evaluating the needs for regeneration through a 'corridor' strategy was designed with this purpose, and indeed spelt out the private-sector resource needs.[23]

Locational demands and the challenge for local policy

An underlying feature of the geography of the region's economic development in the 1980s and 1990s concerns a partly implicit debate that has been taking place over the needs of urban regeneration and the, albeit costly, development of unattractive brownfield sites as set against the demands of business for a high-quality operating environment to match that on offer elsewhere in the midlands and south Cheshire – essentially less costly and less constrained greenfield locations. Indeed, the task is to more than match competing areas given the non-availability of most regional and urban assistance in the Potteries. There is pressure on the

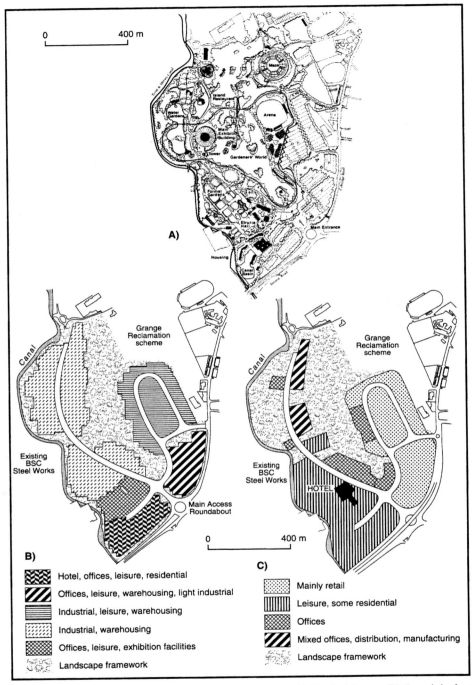

FIGURE 13.8 The Stoke-on-Trent National Garden Festival site: A) Festival layout; B) the original post-Festival development intentions; and C) the nature of the final development.

lower-cost and more attractive sites on the periphery of the conurbation. Of course, greenfield developments may be detrimental to any policy of urban-physical regeneration if they divert attention and resources away from the needs of the conurbation centre, but they may be necessary if a broadening of the economic base – urban economic regeneration – is to be nurtured.[24] The need, if feasible, is for internal regeneration. As demonstrated at arguably the conurbation's most famous brownfield location, the Garden Festival site (Fig 13.5), with the right local attitude and crucially with adequate resources, regeneration is achievable, even if it may not provide precisely the type of development sought (Fig 13.8; Pl 16.3).

Parallel paths or a shift towards integrated initiatives: the challenge for local policy
Certainly until the mid-1980s, district authorities in the Potteries operated separate policies, despite the endeavours of the structure plan. More recently, a certain congruence seems to have emerged, a shift towards a more integrated approach to local economic planning. This has been stimulated by at least three factors: the production of the north Staffordshire tourism action plan[25] and the nature of the tourist product, with accommodation strengths in Newcastle and attractions in Stoke, demanding a sub-regional approach; joint liaisons in business advice precipitated by a realization of the value of such partnerships during a period of economic stringency; and a recognition of the need to bid jointly for central government's attention in the quest to gain urban and regional assistance.[26] In effect, there is a requirement for an integrated economic development strategy for the whole of the conurbation and this, long recognized by many in local government, has gradually filtered through at a political level.

These are, of course, only some of the challenges facing local economic planning in the conurbation in the mid-1990s. Internally, the integration of land-use and economic policy itself presents a challenge for local policy. Rather more disquieting for all authorities there is the debate about unitary authority status. The county council already accepts that Stoke-on-Trent should seek such status, but one wonders about Newcastle on the western flank of the conurbation. It is connected at the eastern side and already contained within the travel-to-work area, and decisions about unitary status are awaited with great interest.

CONCLUSIONS

Like any other conurbation, the Potteries economy has changed its geographical complexion in many ways since 1945. The global economic setting of the area has substantially affected its character and there has, in addition, been a variety of locally-induced changes. However, there are continuities, remnants of the past that in some senses impose constraints on development: the problem of derelict and vacant buildings in Stoke is just one of those; yet others – for example, the 'quality' name of parts of the ceramics sector – represent positive features. Despite gradual diversification, the area remains dominated by its key industry and that base may be vulnerable in the increasingly global economy of the mid-1990s and beyond. As local economic and land-use planners have long realized, the area needs to diversify but not to deny its manufacturing specialism. Just as Rodgers argued back in the late 1970s, the area needs something to spearhead its growth.[27] Not a new town as it was suggested at the time, but an industrial and infrastructure-led solution and one that must involve the private sector as well as the public. In these terms, the area is perhaps a strong candidate for an injection of public infrastructural support over a finite period, something that might act as a catalyst for private industrial investment and, in such terms, stimulate rather than tinker with the process of regeneration.

REFERENCES

1. H B Rodgers, 'The west midlands and central Wales', in G Manners *et al*, *Regional development in Britain*, 1972, 204–12.
2. M Fogarty, *Prospects of the industrial areas of Great Britain*, 1945, 324–32.
3. The dependence of north Staffordshire on employment in this sector tightened in the late 1980s from a location quotient of 17.5 in 1982 to 19.1 in 1989; Staffordshire Training and Enterprise Council, *North Staffordshire labour market assessment: summary report*, Prepared by Pieda plc, 1992.
4. R Imrie, 'Industrial restructuring, labour and locality: the case of the British pottery industry', *Environment and Planning*, A, 21, 1989, 10–16.
5. M Prees and P Field, *Stoke-on-Trent and the new ceramics*, Industrial Development Unit, Stoke-on-Trent City Council, 1989; Staffordshire Development Association, *Staffordshire: a leading world centre for advanced ceramics*, 1992.
6. P Mounfield and S Jones, 'Shelton in decline', *Geog Mag*, 51, 1979, 509–10.
7. R M Ball and M Metcalfe, 'Tourism at the margins: pits, pots and potential in the Potteries locality', *Proceedings of the tourism in Europe conference*, Durham, 1992.
8. The results of a public local inquiry held in early 1992 on this proposal are awaited. It is particularly sensitive when nearby British Coal expect to close the Trentham colliery complex in 1993.
9. Staffordshire Training and Enterprise Council, *North Staffordshire labour market assessment*.
10. Newcastle-under-Lyme Borough Council, *Response to the white paper: regional industrial development*, 1984; Stoke-on-Trent Council *et al*, *The case for north Staffordshire and the case for inner area funding*, 1985 and 1991.
11. Imrie, 'Industrial restructuring', 10–16.
12. R M Ball, 'Vacant industrial premises and local development: a survey, analysis and policy assessment of the problem in Stoke-on-Trent', *Land Development Stud*, 6, 1989, 105–28.
13. Especially sites such as those at Sideway and Ravensdale: see chapter 16.
14. Newcastle-under-Lyme Borough Council, *Policies for the council's promotion of the local economy*, 1990.
15. Stoke-on-Trent City Council, *Economic development strategy, 1991–2001*, 1991.
16. Rodgers, 'The west midlands', 206.
17. R M Ball, *Vacant industrial premises in Stoke-on-Trent: a survey and analysis with some policy suggestions for the 1990s*, Report to Industrial Development Unit, Stoke-on-Trent City Council, 1989.
18. Ibid.
19. Fogarty, *Prospects of the industrial areas*, 324–32.
20. Newcastle-under-Lyme Borough Council, *A guide to the borough*, 1987, 13.
21. Ball and Metcalfe, 'Tourism at the margins'.
22. With a location quotient of 0.9 in 1989 for retail distribution and 0.8 for wholesale distribution, the area cannot claim any great concentration.
23. Stoke-on-Trent City Council, *Facing the challenge*, Stoke Corridor Regeneration Discussion Document, 1992.
24. The fact that some of the likely greenfield locations are beyond the planning jurisdiction of the conurbation authorities (the cluster of services at Stone) adds fuel to the controversy and points to the need for a regional view of the distribution of economic activity.
25. Heart of England Tourist Board, *Tourism action programme for north Staffordshire*, Worcester, 1987.
26. Parnters Group, *Review of the Assisted Areas of Great Britain*, Representations by the Partners Group for the Stoke-on-Trent Travel-to-Work Area, 1992.
27. Rodgers, 'The west midlands', 210–12.

14. Planning the Conurbation

A L MURRAY

The post-war planning of north Staffordshire has had to wrestle with the land-use inheritance of two centuries of industrial and mining activity. The introduction of statutory plans, both strategic and local, after the last war together with detailed systems of development control had, therefore, to address a region where urban development and mining was already scattered over a substantial area along the old A50 and west of what became the A500 road in Newcastle-Stoke. Mining activity for surface, shallow and deep coal, for clays and other minerals, as well as scarring the landscape, had already produced an open-structured urban development pattern with housing and industry characteristically intermixed but often spread around sites still in use for active mining, for the storage of mine waste or reserved for long-term clay extraction.

With the progressive introduction of better firing techniques after the Second World War in the ceramic industry and the switch to other fuels, the city, which slowly emerged from under its blanket of smoke, was visually and functionally deficient. Built structures (housing and industry) were often old and obsolescent, roads and infrastructure were not related to modern needs and frequently also affected by age and mining subsidence. Mining activity worked to a traditional, piecemeal pattern which frequently left sizeable areas derelict or occupied by mining waste, some of it burnt and thus capable of re-extraction for other purposes. A stable, if narrowly-based, industrial structure, traditionally working on a low margins, helped to sustain a general tolerance of low urban environmental standards.

This broad pattern is illustrated in Figure 14.1, which shows the extent of the built-up area at 1945, with subsequent stages of development at 1963, 1975 and 1990. These intervals, although not even, are the only ones comprehensively available from Ordnance Survey maps and the extant records of planning departments. The figure reveals the area's continued open-structured nature, the extensive infill development, and the progressive urbanization of the southern and eastern rims. In 1945, continuous urban development was most notable in the north of the city running along the two main northbound ridges from Hanley to north of Tunstall and some distance to the east (through Northwood). Further continuously-developed areas ran north-westwards from the Stoke centre to Newcastle and beyond in the west, and from Fenton to beyond Longton in the south. Apart from the east central side of the conurbation (the Berry Hill area), itself an abandoned shallow mining district, much that remained within these largely-developed tracts was also urban in the broader sense, often partially or wholly derelict, or used for land-extensive waste storage or tipping purposes.

It was this situation which the first post-war planning proposals sought to address. This began with the advisory plan prepared by Abercrombie and Jackson in the immediate post-war years, just as the first steps to introduce statutory town planning procedures were being taken (Table 14.1). Development plans were then prepared for areas of the city and the surrounding county during the 1950s. The county plan included attempts to prepare detailed proposals for towns such as Newcastle, Stone and Leek. The proposals for a statutory north Staffordshire green belt were drafted by the county council in 1957 but not subjected to the normal procedure for seeking approval from the relevant Minister of State. Formal proposals were, however, adopted in 1967 and after the consideration of objections were approved by the minister in 1971. Matching proposals for green belt within the city area were included with the Stoke-on-Trent City Council's first review plan prepared in the early 1960s, again not to receive full statutory endorsement for several decades.

Table 14.1

North Staffordshire: post-war development planning

Plan	Agency	Date of preparation
North Staffordshire Plan	Abercrombie and Jackson (advisory document)	1949
County Development Plan	Staffordshire County Council	1951
City Development Plan	Stoke-on-Trent City Council	1956
Green Belt Plan: North Staffordshire	Staffordshire County Council	1956 Draft / 1967 Adoption
North Staffordshire Strategy	Staffordshire County Council / Stoke-on-Trent City Council	1969
City Plan Review	Stoke-on-Trent City Council	Late 1960s
Town Maps: Newcastle-Kidsgrove	Staffordshire County Council	During 1960s
Structure Plans: Stoke	Stoke-on-Trent City Council	1974
Staffordshire	Staffordshire County Council	1974
Structure Plan Review	Staffordshire County Council	1982
Structure Plan Review	Staffordshire County Council	1989

In the late 1960s also, a planning strategy document, prepared jointly by the Staffordshire and Stoke authorities, discussed the scope for 'overspill' assimilation into the north Staffordshire-south Cheshire region – a prospect stimulated by the preparation of regional development strategies for both the North-West and West Midlands Regions. In both cases, the congestion problems of the larger conurbations figured greatly as did alternative strategies for accommodating burgeoning housing needs. Reference was made to the difficulty for the city of Stoke-on-Trent in simultaneously carrying through its urgent programme of urban renewal and revitalization, and accommodating growth from Birmingham or the north-west conurbations. It was also recognized that any 'overspill' of population to the area would need to be matched by a substantial injection of new employment since the main local economic sectors of pottery and mining were not growing. Green belt policy, it was being suggested, was important not only to contain the growth of the conurbation but also to channel growth and redevelopment back into the city and to facilitate a strategy of redistributing growth to planned locations well removed from the inner conurbation edge within and beyond the green belt.

The early 1970s saw the progressive introduction of the new style (conceptual) structure plans for the city and the county which moved from static zoning concepts to an attempt to focus concern upon new and redevelopment areas, together with related economic, environmental and infrastructure strategies. Since then, these original strategic plans have been reviewed twice, the first to incorporate experience after local government reorganization in 1974 and to re-emphasize the commitment to strategic and local planning to the new county and district planning authorities. The second review of the county structure plan submitted to

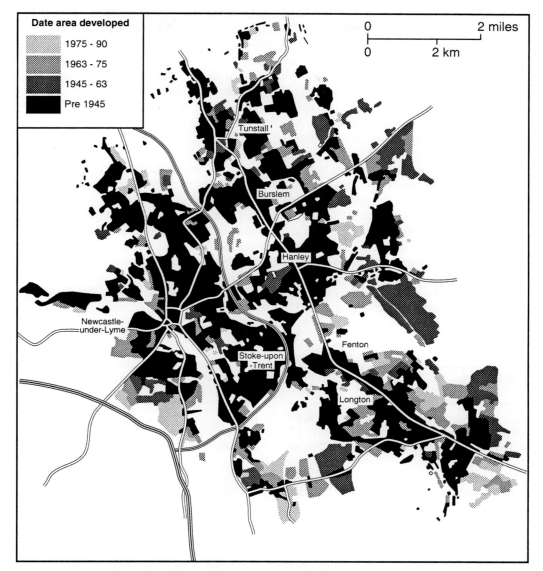

FIGURE 14.1 The north Staffordshire conurbation: post-war development.

government in 1989 provided an opportunity to roll forward plans for a further decade to 2001 and to re-assess their policy content.

Local plans prepared since the mid-1970s are now also into their second cycle, the first round following on the approval of the original structure plan in 1978 and the second round for a further decade of development needs consequent on the approval of the county structure plan in 1991. The first round of plans focused only on parts of the conurbation, and was affected by differences of approach by individual districts. Newcastle-under-Lyme Borough Council sought to provide a full areal coverage, whilst local plans in Stoke-on-Trent concentrated on particular localities recognized as needing special attention, such as the Hanley centre (Hanley Axis Plan). Elsewhere, local planning briefs were used extensively to control the process of land-use change. In some notable cases, these were the subject of some public involvement but not to the degree required for statutory plans. Under the most recent Planning Act, there is a requirement for all local plans to provide a total areal coverage and this is reflected in the approach now taken in the city, Newcastle and the adjoining Staffordshire Moorlands.

The development of this planning system must be seen in the context of the region's economic and demographic structure. As chapters 12 and 13 have indicated, the north Staffordshire economy has exhibited significant shortcomings over the last forty years, with its near-static overall employment levels and its inability to match centres of more rapid growth elsewhere in the country. Population trends in the region in the period 1951–91 have similarly displayed a lack of dynamism. Absolute numbers in the three north Staffordshire district areas (Stoke-on-Trent, Newcastle-under-Lyme, and Staffordshire Moorlands) making up the region grew slightly in the 1950s and 1960s, but in the last two decades have undergone an overall decline, with a 1991 population estimated at below that of 1951. The region's share of national population has consistently fallen for the last four decades, the largest shortfalls occurring in the 1960s and 1980s (Table 14.2). Within the region, there have been distinct contrasts between the three district areas. Stoke-on-Trent has experienced consistent population loss, particularly from 1961 to 1981; Newcastle-under-Lyme expanded until 1971 and has subsequently declined; and Staffordshire Moorlands, growing up to 1981, is now witnessing falling numbers.

Table 14.2

Population changes, 1951–91

District	Population				
	1951	1961	1971	1981	1991
Newcastle-under-Lyme	104,600	114,600	120,000	118,200	117,800
Staffordshire Moorlands	75,300	78,000	90,200	96,100	94,300
Stoke-on-Trent	279,900	277,300	265,200	252,500	244,300
Total	459,800	469,900	475,400	466,800	456,400
North Staffordshire's population as a percentage of national total	0.94	0.92	0.88	0.86	0.82

Sources: 1951–81: county census vols; 1991: census, county leaflet.

Besides natural increase, two factors are known to be affecting the population level in north Staffordshire; the first concerns local migration from the city to adjoining towns and settlements, the second longer distance migration. Since the areas covered by the modern districts east and west of Stoke (Staffordshire Moorlands and Newcastle) embrace both town and country they, to a degree, provide pointers to patterns of local migration. The aggregate migration figures for all three districts give a measure, undoubtedly incomplete, of the longer distance movements (Table 14.3). Stoke has consistently been an area of out-migration from 1951 to 1991, although the reduction in scale since 1971 partly reflects successful urban regeneration strategies. Newcastle and Staffordshire Moorlands up to 1961 and 1981 respectively benefited from local in-migration, but since those dates they have joined Stoke as areas of migrational loss. In the region as a whole longer distance out-migration has been both high and continuous over the last forty years. In combination with falling rates of natural increase, this feature accounts for the lack of absolute population growth and in itself is a clear indicator of the poor performance of the north Staffordshire economy.

Table 14.3

Causes of population change in north Staffordshire, 1951–91

District	1951–61		1961–71		1971–81		1981–91	
	Natural* increase	Migration+	Natural increase	Migration	Natural increase	Migration	Natural increase	Migration
Newcastle-under-Lyme	9530	530	6330	−980	1260	−3050	700	−1160
Staffordshire Moorlands	2,190	510	5290	6850	1480	4450	190	−2030
Stoke-on-Trent	13,990	−16,610	11,920	−23,910	160	−12,910	2750	−10,940
Total	25,710	−15,570	23,540	−18,040	2900	−11,510	3640	−14,130

* Natural increase: births minus deaths recorded.
+ Net residential migration: difference between natural increase and total population change.
Sources: as for Table 14.2

These interconnected demographic and economic themes have remained of basic concern in the strategic planning of the conurbation. They have underlain the efforts made both to improve the physical environment of the city and its infrastructure and to attract new employment, and also the successive attempts to change perceptions of the area held by government and in Whitehall, views which consistently prevented designation of north Staffordshire from any form of industrial policy support.

DEVELOPMENT IN THE POST-WAR PERIOD, 1945–60

The first fifteen years after the end of the war saw the completion of north Staffordshire's first advisory land-use plan and, drawing heavily upon it, the statutory development plans for the administrative areas of Stoke-on-Trent and the surrounding county, together with a first attempt to define a green belt.

Features of north Staffordshire particularly highlighted in the Abercrombie and Jackson analysis included: 'lack of industrial diversification' and a 'monotonous class structure'; a poor urban environment, the city being seen as 'a good place to get out of', obsolete living standards and thus a need for new development; much surface subsidence and dereliction; and a lack of industrial sites and poor quality public services. Aims identified for the plan to relate to these deficiencies were to define new areas for urban development, especially for housing, retail and industry and measures for urban transport; to identify and, where necessary, safeguard important open areas to meet the needs for agriculture, recreation and land extensive areas (especially mining); and to identify strategic improvements to communications.

Particular features of the very detailed plan for urban development stressed the need to avoid peripheral 'one-class housing ghettos' with long work-journey distances – a strangely prophetic concern in relation to post-war development in many British cities; the low degree of scope to attract new inward investment from abroad in the light of the poor urban environment; the need to raise the quality and facilities of the Hanley centre to enable it to perform its real function as a regional centre; the difficulty of improving environmental standards given the low general expectations and high tolerance especially of smoke, dirt and industrial blemishes (firm public intervention being seen as essential to redress this imbalance); and the scope for new urban development within and adjacent to the 'conurbation' as well as elsewhere in the region, in towns and settlements from Leek in the east to Ashley-Loggerheads in the west.

Within the city of Stoke, the first city development plan contained proposals for major new areas for housing development at Bentilee east of Hanley, a peripheral location but central to the north-south spread of the Victorian pottery towns. Smaller developments were proposed to the south-west of Longton and in other locations within the A50 corridor running through the city. No large-scale areas for clearance and redevelopment were defined in the plan, individual proposals having to rely upon individually-justified housing clearance procedures. Some rationalization of industrial uses were proposed but no major changes of use. The city's first major new industrial estate at Newstead was planned in the late 1950s. Major improvements to highways were limited to the A500, the eastern link road providing a link northwards from Bentilee – a concept only finally abandoned twenty years later owing to the practical difficulties of securing the land-use changes necessary to bring it about.

In the surrounding county, the 1951 county development plan gave admirably explicit regard to many of the new ideas which had emerged over the preceding decade concerning planning. Industry 'should have room to expand and progress . . . and have good access to its raw materials and markets rather than . . . hampered and restricted by incompatible developments'. For housing and community needs 'people should live in comfortable and convenient houses and neighbourhoods with shops, playgrounds, schools and employment near at hand rather than in slums and obsolescent housing away from what they need and mixed up with all kinds of incongruous buildings and activities'. Planning strategy was, therefore, to seek urban redevelopment for housing and other uses where it met these objectives but to channel the 'overspill' growth to locations where development could heal past mining scars and help to bring needed amenities to existing settlements.

Although generous space provisions to allow for relatively low-density housing were made (4–15 dwellings per acre, compared with the 40–50 per acre densities inherited from the late Victorian period), land-use proposals for industry were modest. This was less a conscious decision than reflection of two primary features of the area: first, the low scope for attracting newer types of industry, especially that unrelated to ceramics; and second, the relatively intensive nature of existing industrial development, with high employment densities and multi-storey patterns of development. The county development plan, for instance, made the assumption that existing firms' needs could be met within their present sites, whilst for new industry a net increase in area of one-third over twenty years was envisaged – by itself a vision of heroic proportions.

DEVELOPMENT, 1960–75

The relatively slow progress made in overcoming the formidable array of environmental problems in Stoke-on-Trent in the decades after the war stemmed in part from the intrinsic pattern of obsolescence of sites and buildings, both houses and factories. Progressive redevelopment, only ever pursued in north Staffordshire on a small-scale basis and very rarely involving business uses, could only achieve localized effects, often submerged by newly-arising dereliction resulting from mine or factory closures. New developments following the proposals of the city and county plans were, apart from major new housing areas as at Bentilee and Blurton, frequently smaller scale and scattered across the whole conurbation. These schemes were also able to take advantage of the land reclamation work which particularly in the 1960s and early 1970s began to bring about major changes in the visual environment of the city.

During this period, large areas of derelict collieries, marl workings and other tipped areas were reshaped and relandscaped, ceasing to be the eyesores they had once been. Associated dust and sedimentary run-off from such sites were also reduced. Only rarely did such projects produce land which was reusable because of the substantial costs involved in physical investigation and rendering sites safe for building purposes. Such difficulties related in part even to sites previously built upon, since it was not uncommon for old mine shafts to be discovered beneath housing erected in the Victorian era, and active deep mining under much of the city might be expected to expose sooner or later any risks which were taken with buildings.

A feature of the Newcastle area was the scope offered by the absence of environmental problems for relatively attractive housing to be progressively developed to the south-west of the town. The Newcastle town map envisaged these newer housing areas, together with a 'fairly large' allocation of 73 acres for industry in the borough, to supply needs in the period 1951–71. Industrial allocations proposed for the borough for the subsequent twenty years in the 1974 structure plan amounted to 300 acres, a four-fold increase. As a result of major public objections, this provision was subsequently reduced to 200 acres.

DEVELOPMENT, 1975–90

With the arrival of a new Planning Act in the early 1970s, steps were taken by both the county and city authorities to prepare strategic plans to take development policy forward for a further twenty years. A high degree of collaborative work between authorities enabled the new structure plans which emerged in draft form in 1973 to be related. A general strategy of encouraging continued rehabilitation of the urban core of north Staffordshire was endorsed in both plans. The Stoke plan strove to reduce the rate of population loss, in part by finding new attractive private housing sites as well as by securing industrial expansion.

Quality employment sites were, however, still hard to define and much reliance was placed upon the reuse of former industrial, clay-industry or colliery land. The largest area of flat land in the city, at the former Meir airport, was earmarked for housing to accommodate an acknowledged shortage of suitable sites capable of being developed for higher-quality private housing. After the consolidating practices of the 1960s and 1970s, much of it 'fitted in' to the existing urban area in both north and south of the city especially near Longton and west of Newcastle centres, the late 1970s saw a return to larger development sites for housing such as those south of Newcastle centre (Clayton) and in the southern part of the city at Trentham, Longton and Meir. Only one major site in the north, at Birches Head, was identified for residential purposes. Industrial sites were recognized north of Newcastle, but almost entirely on reclaimed land. Other areas, even further out, were marked for industry, but only slow progress was made in the face of stability and infrastructure problems.

Retail development in this period included major out-of-centre developments for superstores and other 'drive-in' needs, especially at the former steel works site on the edge of Hanley centre. In addition, some successful urban redevelopment schemes were carried out in the larger cores, particularly the Potteries Shopping Centre in Hanley (Pl 14.1), and in Newcastle. Difficulties persisted for many of the smaller traditional centres, which still lack more modern facilities for the pedestrian and car-borne shopper.

Since the early 1970s, statutory planning has continued to focus on the objectives of regenerating the urban core of the Potteries whilst avoiding further urban sprawl around the

PLATE 14.1 Central Hanley, 1992 (Jeffersons Air Photography, Liverpool). The dominance of the Potteries Shopping Centre in the urban core is plainly visible.

edges. Housing schemes in the 1980s were characterized by a wide mix of scattered developments, both on greenfield sites and urban infill. Industrial and office activity was almost all concentrated on previously developed areas, notably at the former Shelton steel works, the site of the 1986 National Garden Festival and also the location of the largest retail-leisure scheme in north Staffordshire. This concentration on reused land has become a matter of growing concern to the local authorities, as the failure of north Staffordshire to provide attractive greenfield-site options was increasingly seen as a major factor explaining the low success in encouraging inward investment projects and fostering high quality 'flagship' developments by established local companies. The response has been to seek peripheral green belt sites, where land is otherwise not available, a strategy which has yet to overcome the rigorous policy constraints now in place to prevent development in such areas.

CONCLUSION

In relation to the original strategic diagnosis put forward in the first north Staffordshire plan, the region's problems have remained remarkably intractable. The area still lacks industrial diversification, even if the dominance of mining and pottery has greatly reduced. A particular deficiency is the absence of more rapidly growing 'sunrise' industries, such as those which have led to the especially rapid post-war growth of the South-East Region of the UK. Environmental deficiencies remain not only in an absolute sense, especially in the older urban A50 corridor, but also in a relative sense compared with suburban areas on the periphery and green belt settlements further out. Living standards have improved for the majority. Poor-quality housing is limited to the older cores of the pottery towns. Thanks to the lack of truly large-scale redevelopment or peripheral council housing developments, north Staffordshire has been spared the severe cases of 'social obsolescence' and alienation, which have afflicted some metropolitan post-war housing estates. Surface subsidence and dereliction are still a feature of life in north Staffordshire, as any visit to the city by rail will testify, despite the decades of intensive action to reclaim and restore derelict sites. Social tolerance of such conditions is, however, decreasing rapidly as revealed in the much stronger resistance to new mineral working, waste disposal or open-casting proposals. A lack of suitable industrial sites in the region remains a problem. There is, however, no absolute shortage of land, but more a lack of quality sites capable of attracting large-scale new investment. While the region's communication patterns are progressively being improved, relating to motorway and trunk routes from, within and across the developed area, these schemes have been slow to be completed and have only rarely been associated directly with large-scale development or redevelopment. So far, at least, no major reversal has been secured in the progressive decline in bus and rail patronage.

In terms of the key objectives identified in this original post-war plan there remains a need to define further land for urban development. Housing sites can still be found throughout the conurbation in part on areas released from industrial or other uses. Industrial secondary sites are also plentiful. There is, however, a shortage of premium industrial locations, well-related to motorway or dual carriageway connections. Urban transport has continued to suffer from a progressive switch to the use of the car. The lack of focused patterns of development in the area has compounded this problem. As congestion has begun to build, concern with new public transport solutions is growing. Safeguarding of open space within and around the urban area has been achieved, particularly through land reclamation. Much more may, however, be needed if further colliery closures occur. More intensive use of some of the reclaimed sites could still call for further substantial investment. Further major improvements to the highway system of the city are offered by currently-planned trunk and county road schemes. The A50 scheme in particular, to the south-east, and the Tunstall northern distributor roads, to the north-east, promise substantial improvements. Complete grade-separation of all remaining junctions on the core road corridor of north Staffordshire is also in prospect. There remain problems of traffic management around all the conurbation's centres, a need for better east-west connections, especially between Newcastle and Stoke-on-Trent, and a necessity to explore other improvements associated with the longer-term search for the expansion of the urban area.

The picture is, therefore, one of a mixture of successes and failures. Strategic planning has been remarkably successful in resisting the centrifugal tendencies of new housing development, by sustaining strong green belt protection and settlement concentration policies. Environmental policies have played a part in helping to encourage continuing property investment in the urban core but only in rare cases has new housing development land been created. Industrial policy only had modest objectives in terms of meeting locally-generated needs. Whilst these may have been met, the strategic necessities of diversification are now leading to a trenchant re-assessment of means to change the 'profile' of the whole area with a view to inward investment promotion, a triggering of higher levels of confidence in reinvestment in the urban core, and the identification of high-quality employment sites on the urban periphery.

15. The Social Structure of Stoke-on-Trent: A Spatial Perspective

D J EVANS

The nature of industrialization and the individual character of urban development have had major impacts of the social structure of the Potteries. While bearing a similarity to other conurbations that underwent rapid, nineteenth-century industrialization, the social structure of the region has been subsequently modified by the relative absence of dynamism and structural change in its economy and by the relative stagnation of its population to produce a distinctive pattern. The purpose of this chapter is to present a contemporary assessment of the overall social structure of Stoke-on-Trent, and to demonstrate, in cartographic form, the varying socio-spatial character of the city. Pressures of space have precluded a similar analysis for Newcastle-under-Lyme, but that omission is fortunately countered by the borough being the focus of a series of innovative studies of spatial-social structure from the 1960s onwards.[1]

The determination of social structure and its spatial expression is made difficult through the lack of appropriate data arranged in a suitable areal framework. The most valuable source for such studies is the population census. Since 1961, census data have been made available for small areas or enumeration districts. Up to the 1981 census, these are the smallest spatial units for which information can be obtained. The average population size of such areas in urban locations is 500.[2] The data provided by the census are wide-ranging, including detail on housing, demographic and socio-economic aspects of the population. It does, however, exclude any attitudinal material on opinions and perceptions, and some key social indicators such as religious affiliation and income. Nevertheless, since the data contained in the census is so comprehensive and given the fact that, unlike other surveys, the population has a legally-binding duty to complete census forms, it represents an effective source for examining socio-spatial structures. The census for 1991 has been slow to emerge, and at present the most up-to-date census data are those for 1981. Although a decade old, this material provides the most intimate and precise picture of the spatial pattern of social structure in Stoke-on-Trent.

To illustrate the socio-spatial pattern of the city, use has been made initially of ten individual variables in the census, and subsequently of an amalgamating classification of the enumeration districts based on forty census variables. Of the selected ten individual variables, which have been plotted for each enumeration district in Stoke-on-Trent, variable 1 is a measure of social class, variables 2–5 represent different housing tenure categories, variable 6 distinguishes housing quality, variable 7 indicates employment levels, variables 8–9 portray age structure, and variable 10 displays ethnic structure. The classification combining forty census variables is known as the Acorn classification. This groups enumeration districts that possess a similar profile of characteristics across the forty variables. The practice of grouping enumeration

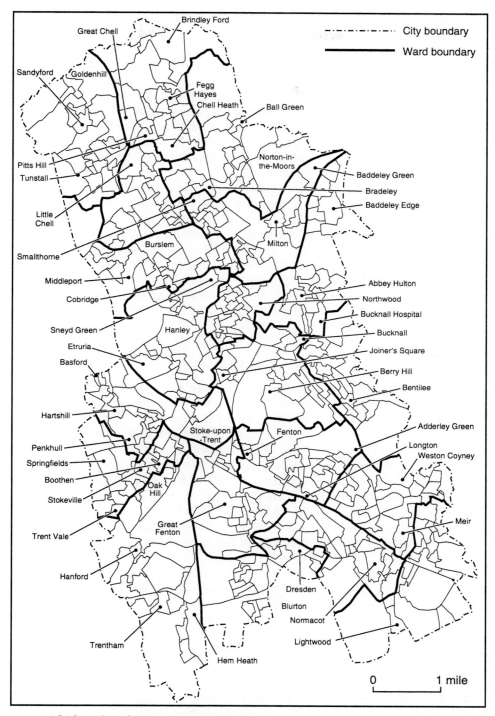

FIGURE 15.1 Location of named enumeration districts.

districts with similar characteristics across a range of census data follows in the tradition of social area analysis and factorial ecology.[3]

Along such lines, several social area studies of Stoke-on-Trent have been undertaken, most notably that by Jackson and Oulds.[4] However, the analysis provided by the Acorn classification is to be preferred in that it incorporates a greater number of census variables than such studies (Jackson and Oulds making use of thirty variables), which results in a more comprehensive and precise assessment of social structure. More importantly, the existing social area analyses have been devised to relate directly to Stoke-on-Trent: their potential for comparison with other parts of the country is limited. In contrast, the Acorn classification was designed to be applied nationally, and its use allows the scores obtained in Stoke to be placed firmly in a country-wide context.[5]

Before examining the spatial pattern of these various social indicators, it is important to remember that the city in 1981 had a socio-economic composition orientated to the lower groupings. Only 14 per cent of employed men and 11 per cent of employed women in that year were in social classes 1 and 2, compared to 29 and 22 per cent respectively in Great Britain as a whole. At the same time, the city had been experiencing population loss, through out-migration and falling rates of natural increase (Table 14.3), with numbers declining by 9.8 per cent between 1951 and 1981. And finally, the distributions of these variables have to be seen in the context of a number of urban centres that go to make up the city. To aid the following analysis, a location map of the enumeration districts mentioned in the text has been prepared (Fig 15.1).

INDIVIDUAL VARIABLES

The distributions of the individual variables have been plotted by enumeration district in Figures 15.2–6, and the salient features of the pattern of each are here summarized.

Persons in social classes 1 and 2 (Fig 15.2A). The areas with a high percentage in these social classes include peripheral locations in the south, most notably Trentham, Lightwood, and parts of Weston Coyney; the Hartshill and Penkhull areas on the western side of the city; the districts near Bucknall Hospital and Baddeley Green on the eastern fringe; and Brindley Ford in the north. In addition, enumeration districts with relatively high percentages in this category can be found in Smallthorne and Pitts Hill in the north of the city.

Council-rented accommodation (Fig 15.2B). Districts with high percentages of this type of accommodation include Blurton and Meir in the south; Bentilee and Abbey Hulton in the east; and Smallthorne, Norton-in-the-Moors, Chell Heath and Middleport in the northern part of the city.

Owner-occupied accommodation (Fig 15.3A). Trentham, Weston Coyney, Adderley Green, Berry Hill, Baddeley Green, Sneyd Green, and parts of Burslem and Bradeley emerge as areas with high proportions of owner-occupancy.

Rented furnished accommodation (Fig 15.3B). This form of accommodation is highly localized in Dresden, Stokeville, Basford, Hanley and Cobridge.

Rented unfurnished accommodation (Fig 15.4A). Enumeration districts with high concentrations of this accommodation are found in Weston Coyney, Meir, and parts of Longton, Fenton, Hanley, Cobridge and Burslem.

Accommodation lacking bath or inside wc (Fig 15.4B). Normacot, Fenton, Stoke, Abbey Hulton, Hanley, and parts of Middleport and Tunstall are marked by high readings of this variable.

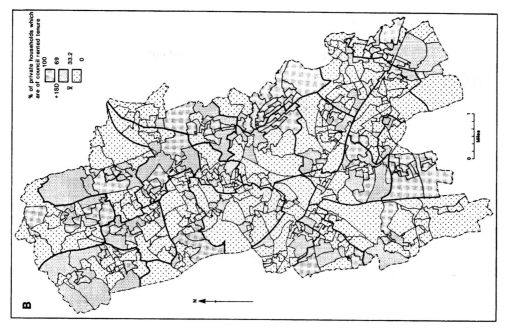

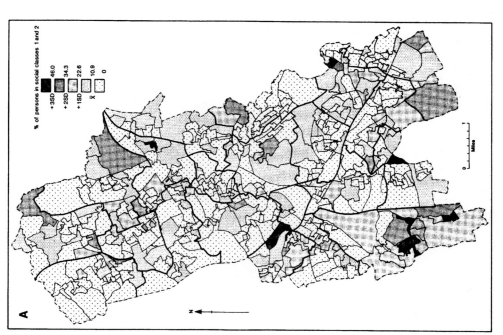

FIGURE 15.2 The distribution of A) persons in social classes 1 and 2, and B) council-rented accommodation (*Source*: 1981 census, small area statistics).

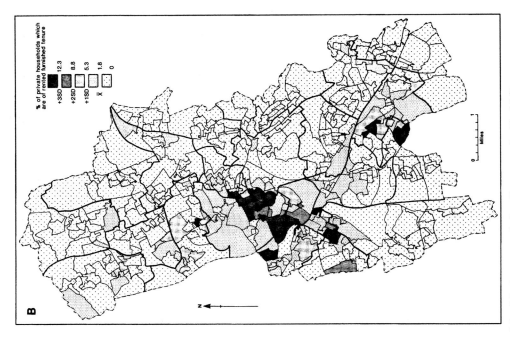

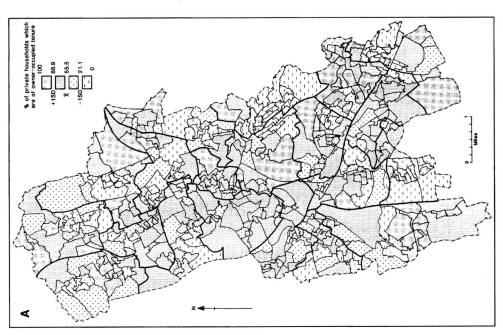

FIGURE 15.3 The distribution of A) owner-occupied accommodation, and B) rented furnished accommodation (*Source:* as for Fig 15.2).

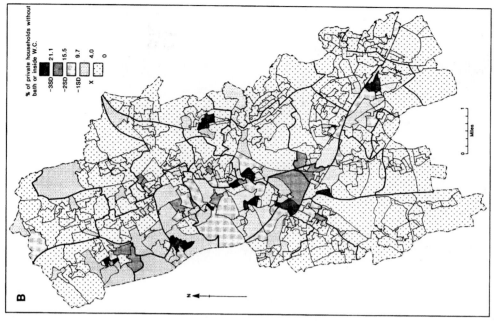

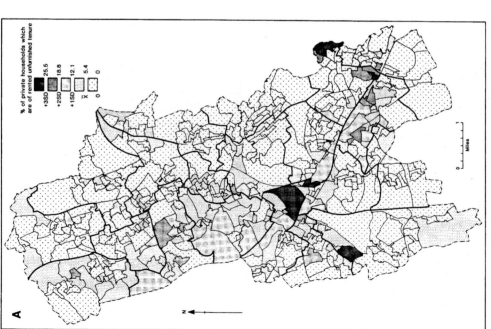

FIGURE 15.4 The distribution of A) rented unfurnished accommodation, and B) accommodation lacking bath or inside wc (*Source*: as for Fig 15.2).

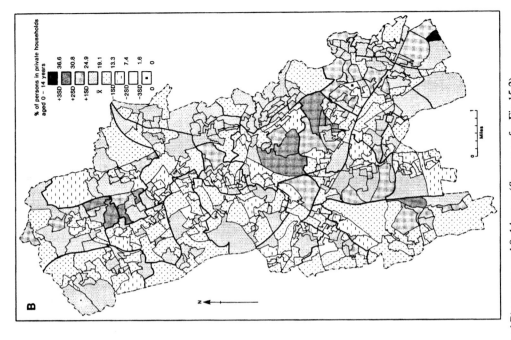

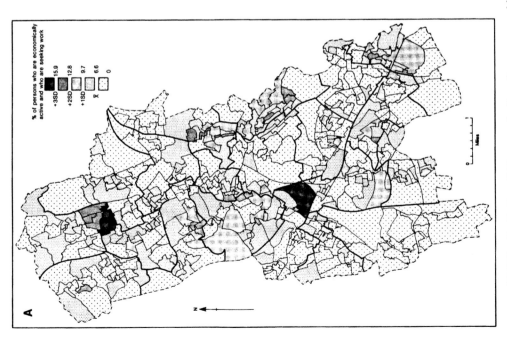

FIGURE 15.5 The distribution of A) economically active persons seeking work, and B) persons aged 0–14 years (*Source*: as for Fig 15.2).

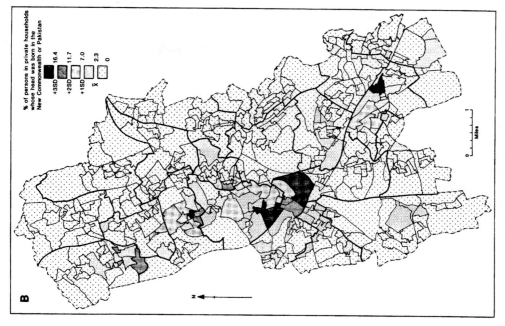

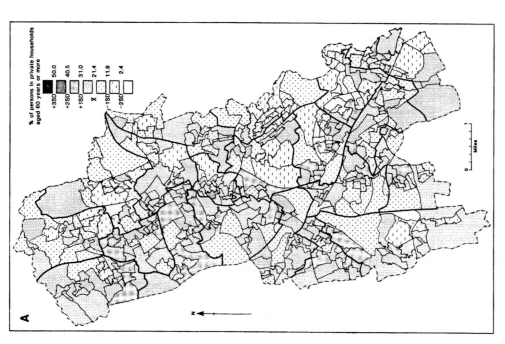

FIGURE 15.6 The distribution of A) persons aged 60 years and over, and B) New Commonwealth and Pakistani population (*Source*: as for Fig 15.2).

Economically active persons seeking work (Fig 15.5A). This category is relatively highly represented in Blurton, Meir, Stoke, Bentilee, Abbey Hulton, Cobridge and Chell.

Persons aged 0–14 years (Fig 15.5B). Children in this age group are relatively well represented in Hem Heath, Meir, Weston Coyney, Berry Hill, Adderley Green, Stoke, Northwood and Chell Heath.

Persons aged 60 years or more (Fig 15.6A). Oak Hill, Fenton, Joiner's Square, Hanley, Sneyd Green, Burslem, Tunstall and Little Chell possess high proportions of the elderly.

New Commonwealth and Pakistani population (Fig 15.6B). This population group has greatest concentrations in Normacot, Longton, Stoke, Northwood, Cobridge and parts of Tunstall.

Besides the intrinsic interest in and planning implications of the precise location of these key social variables, the distributions together point to distinct patterns emerging in the social structure of the city. The extent and nature of this spatial variability in social composition may be determined more fully by examining the Acorn classification.

SOCIAL GROUPING OF ENUMERATION DISTRICTS

Of the overall Acorn classification, ten groups have distinct presences in Stoke-on-Trent, ranging from Group B to Group K. These are characterized as follows:

Group B: modern family housing, higher incomes, young families;

Group C: older housing of intermediate status, pre-1914 housing which is not necessarily in poor condition, elderly population;

Group D: older, terraced housing, pre-1914 housing which may be lacking in amenities, young families;

Group E: council estates, category 1 – skilled workers, young families;

Group F: council estates, category 2 – elderly population;

Group G: council estates, category 3 – the most serious social problems, such as unemployment and single parent families;

Group H: mixed inner metropolitan areas, pre-1914 housing, rented as flats or as terraced houses which may be poor in amenities, cosmopolitan population;

Group I: high status non-family areas, older houses in which families have been replaced by single people or childless couples, above average incomes;

Group J: affluent suburban housing, older residents, older children;

Group K: better-off retirement areas.

The proportion of enumeration districts in Stoke-on-Trent falling into each of the Acorn groupings is recorded in Table 15.1, as are the appropriate proportions for the population of the whole of Great Britain. In Stoke a high proportion (72.2 per cent) of enumeration districts belong to three groups, C, D and F. This concentration emphasizes the dominance of older housing, council estates and elderly population in the city. Indeed, in comparison with the country as a whole, Stoke is marked by an over-representation of these three groups, Group D being more prominent than the other two. Under-representation in Stoke occurs most notably in Groups K, G, I, J and H, revealing a relative lack of affluent areas with different kinds of demographic and family structure, of inner city areas with cosmopolitan populations, and of council estates with most serious social problems.

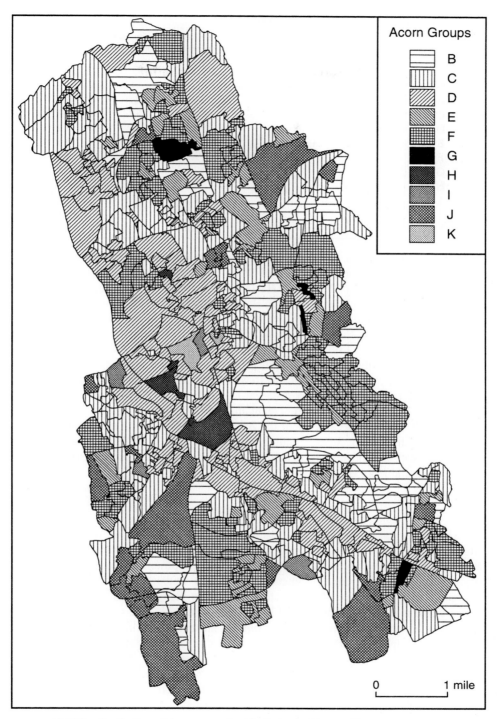

FIGURE 15.7 The distribution of Acorn groupings in Stoke-on-Trent, 1981.

Table 15.1

Social structure in Stoke-on-Trent and Great Britain, 1981

Acorn group	Percentage of enumeration districts in Stoke	Percentage of GB population	Ratio of Stoke figures to GB
B	11.7	16.8	0.7
C	28.7	17.7	1.6
D	22.6	4.3	5.3
E	7.8	13.0	0.6
F	20.9	9.1	2.3
G	1.0	7.3	0.1
H	1.1	3.9	0.3
I	0.8	4.2	0.2
J	4.2	15.9	0.3
K	0.4	3.8	0.1

The distribution of Acorn groupings by enumeration district presents an overview of the spatial complexity of the social structure of Stoke-on-Trent (Fig 15.7). Group C is found in Sandyford, Baddeley Green, Burslem, Hartshill, Bucknall, Stokeville, Dresden, Fenton, Longton and Meir, and Group D in Tunstall, Hanley, Boothen, Fenton, Longton and Meir. Both groupings characterize the nineteenth-century urban centres of the Potteries. Enumeration districts falling into Group F – in Trent Vale, Blurton, Meir, Bentilee, Abbey Hulton, Norton-in-the-Moors, Chell Heath, Little Chell and Middleport – represent the main post-1919 local authority housing areas of the city. Relatively affluent social areas are marked by Groups B and J. The former, possessing slightly lower incomes but more children than Group J, are located in the Baddeley Edge/Milton, Northwood, Great Chell, Berry Hill, Weston Coyney and Hem Heath areas, the latter found mainly in Trentham, Hanford and a few enumeration districts in Sneyd Green. The only other category of the Acorn classification with a representation well in excess of 1 per cent among Stoke's enumeration districts is Group E, indicative of areas of council estates with a child-rearing structure, with occurrences in parts of Blurton, Bentilee, Trent Vale, Meir and Fegg Hayes.

APPLICATIONS

The Acorn classification permits the construction of a cross-section of the socio-spatial structure of Stoke-on-Trent. Such patterns that can be discerned are both a reflection of the past growth of the city and an indication of future developmental needs. In addition, the classification provides a sampling framework for further studies of the social make-up of the city, and an analysis of the fear of crime can be cited as an example of its use in this fashion.

Fear of crime is defined in the second British crime survey as 'a shorthand to refer to any anxiety about becoming a crime victim',[6] rather than actual victimization. Surveys of this phenomenon were first conducted in the USA but now several studies have been undertaken to examine the problem in this country. These have been carried out at both national – the three British crime surveys, two of which include analyses of fear of crime – and local scales. Fear of crime is seen as a bigger problem than crime victimization itself, since fear affects more people and may have debilitating effects on lives through restriction of movement.[7] The third British crime survey indicated that the most common crime was vandalism, affecting 15 per cent of

Table 15.2

Characteristics of survey respondents

Characteristic		Percentage of respondents	Characteristic		Percentage of respondents
Sex:	male	46.8	*Age:*	16–19	7.2
	female	53.2		20–25	18.2
				26–30	8.8
Marital status:	single	36.0		31–40	11.7
	married	41.7		41–50	10.2
	separated	1.4		51–60	10.3
	divorced	4.3		61–70	11.7
	widowed	16.6		71+	21.9
Tenure:	owner-occupied	64.7	*Years resident in area*:	0–2	20.1
	local authority	7.9		3–5	14.4
	housing association	4.3		6–10	10.8
	privately rented	20.2		11–15	5.8
	tied to job	2.9		16–20	5.7
				21+	43.2
Employment status:	full-time	15.8			
	part-time over 10 hours	7.2	*Age at end of education*:	under 15	33.1
	part-time under 10 hours	0.0		15	16.5
	unemployed	12.9		16	15.8
	sick/disabled	2.9		17	4.8
	retired	33.1		18	5.7
	housewife	12.3		19	1.2
	student	15.8		20+	7.1
				still in education	15.8
Children under 16:	households with	29.0			
	households without	71.0			

households[8]: fear levels are much higher than this. At the same time, fear of crime may also be subject to amelioration to a greater extent than crime itself. Whilst real crime appears to rise inexorably, fear of crime being an attitude of mind may be capable of greater management and reduction.

Three enumeration districts in Stoke-on-Trent were chosen within which to conduct interviews relating to fear of crime in March/April 1992. The questions employed were those devised by the 1984 British crime survey,[9] so as to allow a measure of comparison. Local surveys of fear of crime in Hammersmith and Fulham, Islington, West Kensington, and Hilldrop have also used similar questions, again facilitating comparison with the figures from Stoke.[10] The enumeration districts were adjacent but belonged to different Acorn types, namely Groups H, D and C. These groups, according to the second British crime survey, possess respectively high, medium and low risk of crime.[11] Respondents at 38.9, 31.7 and 39.7 per cent of the houses in each district were interviewed, and the characteristics of the sample are noted

Table 15.3

Overall fear levels

Nature of question	Fear levels	Percentage response in				
		Stoke*	Hammersmith	Islington	W Kensington	Hilldrop
Safety in walking alone in area after dark	very safe	8.6				
	fairly safe	31.6				
	bit unsafe	40.4				
	very unsafe	19.4				
Home burgled and goods stolen	very worried	56.1 ⎫				
	fairly worried	27.3 ⎬	60	56	63	52
	not very worried	10.8				
	not worried	4.3				
Being mugged and robbed	very worried	50.4 ⎫				
	fairly worried	17.3 ⎬	47	46	55	52
	not very worried	24.5				
	not worried	7.9				
Being raped	very worried	41.2				
	fairly worried	8.8				
	not very worried	16.2				
	not worried	15.4				
Being sexually molested or pestered	very worried	44.9				
	fairly worried	11.6				
	not very worried	25.4				
	not worried	15.2				
Home or property damaged by vandals	very worried	56.5 ⎫				
	fairly worried	28.3 ⎬	50	46	57	46
	not very worried	10.9				
	not worried	3.6				
Being attacked by strangers	very worried	50.4 ⎫				
	fairly worried	25.2 ⎬	44	38	51	49
	not very worried	19.4				
	not worried	4.3				
Being bothered or insulted by strangers	very worried	23.0 ⎫				
	fairly worried	26.6 ⎬	30	26	28	31
	not very worried	34.5				
	not worried	14.4				

* The percentage 'don't know' response has not been listed

in Table 15.2. In terms of Stoke as a whole, the sample is over-representative of the elderly, owner-occupiers, privately rented households, under-representative of local authority residents and households with children under sixteen, but mirrors the gender division.

The levels of fear exhibited by all interviewed, without any disaggregation, may be seen in the responses to questions about the individual's general feeling of safety in an area and about specific crimes (Table 15.3). The data reveal that within Stoke the most feared crimes are burglary and vandalism to home or property, the least feared insults or bother from strangers. More importantly, however, the data demonstrate the existence of relatively high levels of fear of all aspects of crime in the city, much greater than levels recorded in both national and other local surveys. Thus, 59.7 per cent of respondents admitted to feeling a bit or very unsafe in their home area, compared to 31 per cent reported in the 1984 British crime survey. In Stoke 56.1 per cent were very worried about having their homes broken into and goods stolen, and 50.4 per cent about being mugged and robbed: the comparable figures in the 1984 British crime survey were 23 and 20 per cent respectively.[12]

Again, comparison of the two most worried categories in Stoke and in other localities, largely London based, of a range of crimes from burglary, mugging and robbery, vandalism to home or property, attacks by strangers to insults or bother from strangers indicates that levels in Stoke are never less than 13 percentage points greater than the highest rating elsewhere (Table 15.3). The fear of crime questions were subsequently analysed by the individual area of survey and by a range of demographic and socio-economic attributes. This procedure showed the following variables to possess the most numerous, statistically-significant relationships with the fear of crime: age, sex, residential stability, and age when completed education. These data point to a fearful group in Stoke who are elderly, female, with low levels of education, and a lengthy period of residence in their respective areas.

Police-recorded crime in the city does not at first sight indicate a high incidence of crime: in 1991 the rates were 1.0 per 100 adults for violence, 4.1 per 100 households for burglary, and 3.8 per 100 households for theft of a motor vehicle. The 1992 British crime survey suggests that police figures need to be inflated by 75 per cent for vandalism, 55 per cent for burglary, and 7 per cent for vehicle theft to compensate for under-reporting and under-recording of crime. If this is done, the rates for Stoke rise to 1.6, 6.4, and 4.0 for these three categories of crime. These figures are comparable to the averages disclosed in the British crime survey for these crimes of 1.5, 6.8, and 3.5 respectively: only in the case of vehicle theft is the figure for Stoke distinctly higher.[13] The overall crime figures for Stoke-on-Trent are likely to be skewed geographically to certain areas, given that the 1992 British crime survey indicated that districts marked by Acorn Groups G, H and I were at highest risk, and those by Groups B, C, J and K at lowest risk. Even so, the high levels of fear of crime both overall and amongst the particular social groups identified in this survey appear to be irrational, in the light of the victimization rates in the city. Given its prevalance, however, fear of crime in Stoke warrants further investigation, especially the role of victimization in causing fear and its relationship to the physical and social decline of neighourhoods, approaches which reinforce the need for an understanding of the city's socio-spatial structure.

REFERENCES

1. For example, W M Williams and D T Herbert, 'The social geography of Newcastle-under-Lyme', *N Staffs Jnl Fld Stud*, 2, 1962, 108–26; D T Herbert, 'Social area analysis: a British study', *Urban Stud*, 4, 1967, 41–60; R Barr, 'Newcastle-under-Lyme: a computer based social area classification', *N Staffs Jnl Fld Stud*, 15, 1975, 41–5.

2. D Rhind, *A census user's handbook*, 1983, 44.

3. D T Herbert and C J Thomas, *Urban geography: a first approach*, 1982, 277.

4. G Jackson and G Oulds, *A social area analysis of Stoke-on-Trent*, Occasional Paper in Geography No 4, North Staffordshire Polytechnic, 1984.

5. M Hough and P Mayhew, *Taking account of crime: key findings from the second British crime survey*, Home Office Research Study No 85, 1985, 95.

6. Ibid, 33.

7. Ibid, 39.

8. P Mayhew and N A Maung, *Surveying crime: findings from the 1992 British crime survey*, Home Office Research and Statistics Department, Research Findings No 2, 1992, 69.

9. Hough and Mayhew, *Taking account of crime.*

10. K Painter *et al, Hammersmith and Fulham crime and policing survey,* Centre for Criminology, Middlesex Polytechnic, 1989, and *The West Kensington survey final report*, Centre for Criminology, Middlesex Polytechnic, 1989; B D Maclean *et al, Preliminary report of the Islington crime survey*, Centre for Criminology, Middlesex Polytechnic, 1986; J Lea *et al, The Hilldrop environmental improvement survey*, Cente for Criminology, Middlesex Polytechnic, 1988.

11. Hough and Mayhew, *Taking account of crime*, 74.

12. Ibid, 37, 73–4.

13. Mayhew and Maung, *Surveying crime.*

16. Dereliction and Environmental Regeneration

P T KIVELL

Any overview of land dereliction in north Staffordshire would be bound to confront two very general observations. On the one hand there is the depressing realization that the landscape, together with its associated water courses and atmospheric conditions, could suffer such gross degradation and dereliction. On the other hand, this is partly balanced by the tremendous progress made in land restoration, especially over the past generation.

There is no hiding the fact that half a century ago much of the landscape of north Staffordshire presented a picture of singular decay. Even by comparison with the degraded conditions of other heavy industrial regions at the time, the Potteries suffered a uniquely heavy burden of environmental squalor. What had brought the region to this situation is, of course, clearly understood and straightforward to grasp. Above all it was the combination of economic geology, industrial structure and the historic lack of effective mechanisms of planning and control.

The dominant economic activities of the area had, for over two hundred years, been dependent on extractive industries which had scarred the landscape in a variety of ways and in a multiplicity of locations. Above all the extraction of coal, ironstone, and a number of different clays, marls and sands had left the area pockmarked with artificially created hills and hollows, many of which were very large. Most of the manufacturing industries which locally made use of these mineral resources were themselves relatively dirty or polluting in their nature. The iron and steel works, the brick and tile manufactories and even the pot-banks themselves, from which emerged the finely crafted pottery ware, all created waste materials, smoke and other by-products which degraded the land and surroundings. The absence of legislation and the relative poverty of the agricultural land in the local area meant that there was neither legal control nor economic competition to restrict the prevailing degradation of the land. Not until the end of the Second World War, and in particular the passing of the Town and Country Planning Act of 1947, was there an effective institutional framework to prevent the worst abuses.

Formally the situation was surveyed by Beaver in what was to become nationally a pioneering investigation of land dereliction and reclamation.[1] In 1943 Beaver documented 53 coal-mines, 32 brickworks and 19 tileworks in north Staffordshire. Using maps prepared from air photographs, he assessed the extent of derelict land (Table 16.1), although with changing definitions and survey methods this should be taken only as a crude approximation.[2]

DERELICTION IN THE MODERN PERIOD

The mid-1960s represent an important period in reviewing dereliction and reclamation in north Staffordshire. In particular, it was the time at which central government attention began to focus on the problem, and grants were made available to local authorities to undertake major

Table 16.1

Derelict land in north Staffordshire, 1945

Administrative area	Area (ha)
Stoke-on-Trent County Borough	932
Newcastle Municipal Borough	444
Newcastle Rural District	155
Kidsgrove	223
Biddulph	24
Total	1778

Source: S H Beaver to city of Stoke-on-Trent Planning Department, 28 November 1946.

programmes of reclamation. Before looking at the reclamation, however, it is necessary to understand how the nature and scale of dereliction was evolving. Many commentators agree that this period marks a watershed in the development of British industry. Certainly, after the mid-1960s it is clear that a number of hitherto important industries entered a phase of profound restructuring as they began to be affected by new working practices, notably mechanization, by a new world economic order, with greater competition from newly industrializing overseas countries, and by changing patterns of demand for traditional products. As a result, many important industries, and individual plants, entered a period of decline.

A rash of colliery closures reduced the total number of deep-shaft mines operating to fifteen by 1964, plus a number of small, privately licensed pits. The number of iron and steel works had been contracting for many years, but the closure of Shelton Bar in 1980 removed the last remnant of iron and steel making from the region. The all important pottery industry, including brick and tile making as well as the tableware division, continues to be a mainstay of the local economy, but here too processes of rationalization and mergers have reduced the number of individual establishments and caused the abandonment of many marl pits. Alongside the closures and contractions in all of these sectors there has been a declining need for various parts of the infrastructure, so the abandonment of railway lines, public utilities and other installations has also contributed to the creation of derelict and vacant land.

The nature of the problem represented by derelict land is relatively easy to envisage. It is a waste of a valuable economic resource; a disincentive to development which deters new investment and handicaps the modernization of the region, not just where it occurs but also by blighting much wider areas beyond its immediate boundaries; and an environmental and aesthetic eyesore which casts a pall over whole communities, encourages outward migration and, in some cases, is plain dangerous.

It is an often repeated fact that Stoke-on-Trent had more derelict land, and a higher percentage of its area derelict in 1968, than any other local authority. In assessing the extent of dereliction, clearly the definitions used and the methods of collecting the information are important. Both of these have changed over time, making exact comparisons difficult, but in recent years a number of central government studies have made it possible at least to attempt the task. Since 1964, the then Ministry of Housing and Local Government, and subsequently its successor the Department of the Environment, has regularly requested information from local authorities concerning the amount and nature of derelict land in their administrative areas. Information was collected in terms of the official definition of 'land so damaged by industrial or other development that it is incapable of beneficial use without treatment'. A government survey was undertaken in 1974, but the published figures were not broken down into local authority districts. Changes in the requirements of the official returns affect the validity and comparibility of the figures, but the situation for north Staffordshire up to 1980 has been fully documented by Kivell et al elsewhere.[3] In the 1980s growing government attention was focused on the problems of derelict land, especially in the context of its role in the problems of the inner city and the processes of urban regeneration. This was accompanied by major Department of the Environment surveys, based on local authority records in 1982 and 1988.[4]

Table 16.2 summarizes the situation as far as it is realistically possible. It must be stressed that these figures are only approximations. Apart from the changing political and administrative conditions under which they were collected, it should also be remembered that the figures represent only snapshots in a continuously evolving situation. The total stock of derelict land at any one time is the result of flows into and out of the system; new dereliction is constantly being created, and some sites are taken out of stock as they are reclaimed for development. Large areas can be added overnight, as with the closure of the Shelton steel works which added 66 ha to the total. In addition, the surveys exclude significant areas, such as damaged land which is subject to enforceable planning conditions or which is in a redevelopment scheme, 'naturally derelict land', and land which although damaged has blended into the landscape over time. By 1974, Stoke-on-Trent had lost its unenviable position at the top of the national league table of dereliction (to Wansbeck in Northumberland), but its total of 517 ha still represented 5.6 per cent of the city's administrative area.[5] Even more alarming were local authority figures for Stoke-on-Trent which indicated that in 1984 nearly one-eighth of the city's land was derelict, potentially derelict, or neglected. Table 16.2 confirms that it is the area's mining history which has been responsible for the bulk of dereliction, but the composition of the figures for 1988 illustrate how the impact of general industrial closure, especially in the manufacturing sector, made a substantial contribution during the recessionary years of the 1980s.

Table 16.2

Derelict land in Stoke-on-Trent and Newcastle-under-Lyme, 1974–88

Type of dereliction	Area (ha)					
	1974		1982		1988	
	Stoke	Newcastle	Stoke	Newcastle	Stoke	Newcastle
Spoil heaps	119	157	78	166	138	61
Excavations and pits	99	10	67	25	10	7
Railways	24	3	10	36	18	26
Mining subsidence	–	–	–	–	18	0
General industrial	–	–	–	–	68	9
Other forms	275	103	157	79	9	8
Total	517	273	312	306	261	111

Sources: 1974, local authority records; 1982 and 1988, Department of Environment surveys.

Some of the characteristics of dereliction are revealed by Table 16.2. Thus, it is clear that the mining and quarrying industries have been prime causes, with excavations and pits and spoil heaps of various kinds dominating the picture. Dereliction has been created partly by the closure of establishments in particular locations, perhaps because of resource depletion or

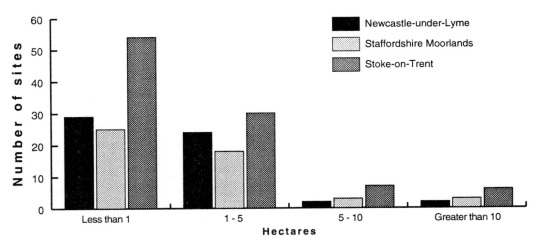

FIGURE 16.1 Derelict sites remaining in north Staffordshire, April 1990, by size.

industrial change, partly by associated tipping and subsidence, and partly by low standards of planning control and environmental care in the past. Various forms of damage can thus be inflicted, from closure of plant on otherwise flat, relatively undamaged, land through to very substantial alteration of the land's surface and sub-surface structures, including in some cases severe contamination. Because of the nature of the local geology and the industries affected, the incidence of derelict land in north Staffordshire has always been widespread throughout the region rather than being concentrated in isolated pockets.

Ownership of the land is an important consideration in this context for two reasons. Firstly, there is the question of whether the land is owned by private or public sector interests, for this will affect its eligibility for reclamation grants. Secondly, the number of separate owners involved in any one site is important, for this will affect both the process and the speed with which parcels of land can be assembled for treatment. In north Staffordshire, ownership through the 1980s was split approximately evenly between public and private sectors, but the public sector's share has been falling slowly and in 1992 it represented 47 per cent of the remaining derelict sites.

Figures for 1990 showed that there were still over 500 ha of derelict land on more than 200 sites in north Staffordshire.[6] The predominant type of dereliction was in the form of spoil heaps and, as Figure 16.1 indicates, the great majority of the total occurred on small sites of less than 2 ha. Remaining dereliction is still found throughout the area but there are particular concentrations around the northern parts of Stoke-on-Trent (Fig 16.2).

LAND RECLAMATION

If the record of dereliction in north Staffordshire is a grim one, it can be largely offset by the bold and successful record of land reclamation undertaken in recent years. Most of the credit for this must go to the local authorities, working closely with the Department of the Environment and making use of central government grants. In the process, north Staffordshire has gained an international reputation for its successful treatment of dereliction. Since the end of the Second World War, a number of distinct periods can be recognized, although it is important to add that in recent years the legislative frameworks and directions have changed a number of times, and economic circumstances have altered, causing consequent changes in the pattern of land restoration.

The first major period is represented by the twenty years following 1945. Prompted by the overwhelming drabness of its local environment, the city council of Stoke-on-Trent embarked on a modest programme to reclaim derelict land, mainly of small sites, for housing, educational and industrial after-uses. Despite the absence of government grants, a total of some 485 ha were reclaimed by 1967. Initially, this effort began to reduce the overall stock of dereliction, but during the latter part of the period, despite active restoration, a fresh spate of colliery closures saw the total begin to rise again.

A second, and vitally important, phase of reclamation activity was ushered in by the announcement in 1967 (Circular 17/67) that the government would pay a 50 per cent grant towards the losses incurred in the reclamation of derelict land outside the various assisted areas. These levels were subsequently raised to 75 per cent in 1970 and to 100 per cent in 1975, and much of north Staffordshire was designated a Derelict Land Clearance Area. In stressing the importance of government grants, it should not be forgotten that significant amounts of restoration were also undertaken without them. For example, local authorities undertook some schemes which were profitable (through the sale of restored land for development), some schemes which were dual purpose (for example, the filling of old quarries through controlled refuse tipping), and some restoration occurred as a part of other development work done by either public or private sector bodies. However, it was the availability of grants, plus the increasingly urgent need to improve their environments and rectify long-standing shortages of public open space, that prompted local authorites in the area to embark upon a massive programme of land restoration.

The organizational frameworks adopted were important considerations in this process. The local authorities, notably the city council of Stoke-on-Trent and the borough council of Newcastle-under-Lyme were the key players, but Staffordshire County Council and the West Midlands Regional Office of the Department of the Environment were also important. Within Stoke-on-Trent, where the problem was greatest, the main elements were the establishment of a Derelict Land Working Party (consisting of representatives from the city council, the Department of the Environment, land-use consultants and British Coal), and of a Land Reclamation Committee on the city council, and the employment of land-use consultants for much of the design work. Individual planning officers and councillors also had great influence on the outcome. In the early 1970s the city took the relatively unusual step of preparing a subject plan to deal with the treatment of derelict land and its future use as a separate land-use issue.

The record of achievement is an impressive one, in both quantitative and qualitative terms. As with dereliction, the figures for restoration do not lend themselves to very straightforward comparisons during this period. There were, for example, changes from a calendar year to a financial year in collecting data, and some figures are incomplete, but overall it is possible to estimate that in the period 1965–74, Newcastle restored 96 ha and Stoke 588 ha, a total of 684 ha. There was a noticeable increase towards the end of this period as some of the larger schemes prompted by the availability of grants reached fruition. Disappointingly, the net reduction in the amount of dereliction was considerably less than this because new areas were continually being declared.

This was the period when Stoke, in particular, decided to launch a 'crash' programme of reclamation on a few, high-profile, large sites, designed to make an immediate impact on the environment. A brief examination of a few of these is instructive.

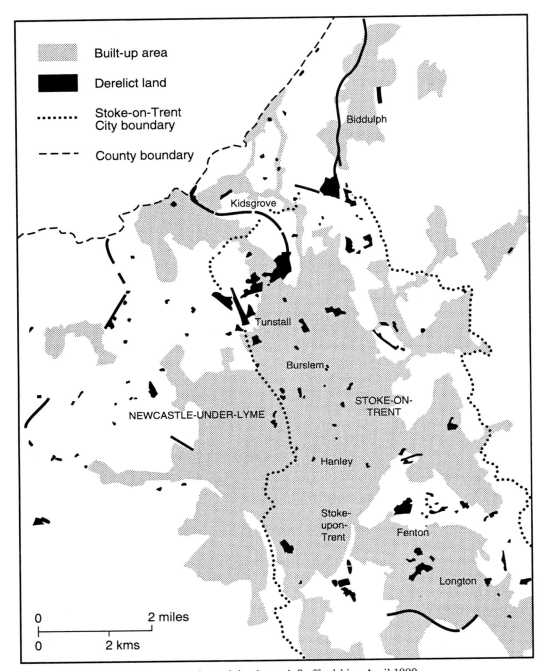

FIGURE 16.2 Location of derelict land remaining in north Staffordshire, April 1990.

Central Forest Park was declared the first priority area for reclamation in 1967. The site, covering 52 ha, had seen coal extraction from Hanley Deep Pit for almost one hundred years until its closure in 1961, and marl extraction for an adjacent brickworks. The landscape consisted of three enormous cones of colliery shale, extensive areas of gullied mining wastes, deep shafts, water-filled marl pits, disused mineral railways, and decaying buildings. Vegetation was sparse at best and the area had been subjected to fly-tipping. This oppressive site attracted early attention because of its strategic location close to Hanley, the area's main shopping and commercial centre, the impact it had on the city due to its size and the height of its spoil heaps, the potential it offered for immediately improving the city's image, and the willingness of the owners to make part of the land immediately available. Clearly there were practical, as well as financial, limits on what could be done with such a severely damaged site, so the designers conceived of a 'Forest Park'. This involved substantial, but nonetheless partial, reshaping of the spoil heaps through cut-and-fill operations, the application of topsoil, sewage sludge and fertilizer, and the establishment of a semi-natural landscape of wood, grassland and footpaths. The completed scheme was handed over to the Parks Department in 1974. With such a degraded site it would be unrealistic to expect an absence of problems, and there have been short-term difficulties with erosion, fires, the establishment of some of the vegetation, and pollution in the lakes, but the park has now taken its place both as a valuable asset close to the city centre, and as a major improvement to the city's environment.

A second major scheme, which had some objectives similar to those of the Central Forest Park, was that at Westport Lake. At this site, alongside the Trent and Mersey Canal in Longport, a lake and associated pools had appeared after subsidence in the 1890s. By 1970, when reclamation commenced, the lake was surrounded by other forms of dereliction, including shraff tips, a marl hole, marshy ground and derelict railway lines. Its position, adjacent to the main London-Manchester railway line and the newly opened D road (A500), maximized its impact on the local scene. This combination of character and location gave it tremendous potential for recreational use and environmental improvement after reclamation. Its other attraction as an early candidate for restoration was that it offered maximum improvement potential for modest capital investment. The major part of the scheme, which consisted of dredging and making a beach around the lake, topsoiling and planting the surrounds, and laying -out footpaths, was completed very quickly and opened in 1971. Subsequent phases were completed by 1979, giving a total of nearly 40 ha. Early plans to provide for swimming in the lake were thwarted by pollution, but the site quickly became popular for walking, picnicking, model boating, fishing and nature study in a city which, at that time, was markedly short of public open space.

Another recreational facility, although very different in character from Westport Lake, was created by one of the largest reclamation projects of this era at Park Hall Country Park, on the eastern fringe of Stoke. Here, an area of some 177 ha of sandy heath vegetation and birch-oak woodland, which had originally been a deer park, had been brought increasingly into agricultural use in the nineteenth century. In the period 1939–70, sand and gravel extraction on a large scale totally altered the landscape and left much damage. A master plan for its conversion to a country park was approved in 1973, and detailed ecological and design studies took place. Although there were some severe problems to be tackled, in the form of pit-shafts, settling lagoons and various types of tipping, there was also a number of advantages which the site offered for recreational use. For example, the surface geology, being Bunter sandstone, was relatively clean and attractive when compared to other derelict sites in the region, and the nature of the quarrying operations had resulted in a varied and exciting landscape which included some dramatic cliffs and canyons. As with the two previous schemes, a relatively low-cost reclamation brief was pursued and major earth moving and other expensive works were minimized. The park, which was substantially completed in the late 1970s, now offers a valuable recreational resource, complete with a warden service, and it was awarded first prize in the RICS and Times Conservation Awards scheme.

Alongside these major schemes, designed to maximize rapid environmental improvement and to provide much needed public open space, the city also undertook many smaller projects. Notable amongst these was a series of 'greenways' which provided a network of interconnected footpaths and cycleways by re-using derelict railway lines. Another interesting scheme was that at Chatterley Whitfield colliery in the north of the city, where controlled tipping of waste was used to facilitate land reclamation in the final few years of the life of the pit. Subsequently a mining museum was opened.

In Newcastle too, the need to provide public open space was also a major motivation in reclamation schemes. Although these schemes were smaller than those described above, they made a significant contribution to the improvement of the local landscape. In particular, reclamation sites in the Lyme valley close to the town centre, at the Whammey in Knutton and at Bathpool Park, and elsewhere in Kidsgrove were important. Even more significant, from some points of view, was the effort which Newcastle put into reclaiming derelict land for commercial and industrial after-use. Notable amongst these were the Jamage Estate at Talke Pits, which is now largely occupied by major retail stores and industrial warehouses, and the Parkhouse Estate astride the A34. This latter project, which replaced derelict clay workings, a

PLATE 16.1 The Parkhouse Estate, Newcastle-under-Lyme (P T Kivell). Astride the A34 road, major new industrial and commercial activities have replaced a derelict colliery and tileworks.

colliery and tileworks, was started in 1975, at which time it was the largest industrial development in north Staffordshire. It was an early example of a joint development between the local authority (Newcastle Borough Council) and a private developer (W A Blackburn Ltd), an arrangement which was to become generally more common in the 1980s. Parkhouse is considered a prestige development with easy access to the M6 motorway. By 1989, 45 ha of land had been developed, providing up to 4000 jobs in a mixture of industrial, warehousing and office activities (Pl 16.1).

In such an ambitious, rapid and varied programme as that undertaken in north Staffordshire between 1965 and 1979, it is inevitable that some elements were less successful than others. For example, some of the vegetation failed to establish itself, continued erosion scarred some of the re-contoured spoil heaps, maintenance costs proved higher than expected, some of the footpaths and fittings presented a primitive image, and occasionally pollution recurred on reclaimed sites. In a very few instances, whole projects failed to achieve their primary aim, as at Clanway Stadium. However, the overall judgment of land reclamation during this period must be that it achieved, for quite a modest investment, a major and resounding success for the region, which set it well on its way towards shaking off one of the gloomiest industrial heritages imaginable.

After 1979 a further phase of land reclamation was introduced in north Staffordshire. Partly this was a shift stemming from the fact that some of the largest and most pressing local eyesores had now been dealt with, but there was also a need to respond to major national economic and political changes. In short, the newly elected Conservative government signalled its clear intention to emphasize policies of inner city redevelopment and economic regeneration. The reclamation of derelict land was expected to play its part in this process. Derelict Land Grants were to continue (indeed they were increased nationally from £8.25 million in 1974/5 to £75 million in 1985/6), but growing emphasis was to be placed on 'hard' end-uses, such as industry and commerce which would provide jobs, and on encouraging activity and investment from the private sector, either in joint schemes with the public sector or as the sole agents of reclamation.

Perhaps as a reflection of growing government concern, the published figures relating to land reclamation became rather more detailed and reliable at this time. National surveys were undertaken in 1982 and 1988. From these it can be established that Stoke and Newcastle together reclaimed 790 ha between 1974 and 1982, and a further 435 ha from 1982 to 1988. Up until 1988, notwithstanding government emphasis upon 'hard' end-uses, it was public open space which formed the great bulk of local reclamation schemes. It can, of course, be argued that the area still needed recreational facilities, that open space was one of the cheapest and most effective uses of reclaimed land, and that it did make a major contribution to economic

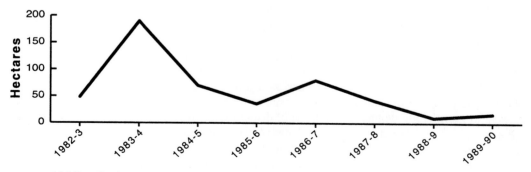

FIGURE 16.3 Derelict land reclaimed in north Staffordshire, 1982–90.

regeneration by making the area more attractive to inward investment. Any visitor to the area in the 1980s would find it hard to deny that further environmental improvement was a high priority. A particularly powerful contrast was available, here as in many other industrial cities, by crossing the area first by car and then by train.

Throughout the 1980s derelict land remained a major issue both in Staffordshire county structure plans and in local plans. One early initiative was the North Staffordshire Land Renewal Plan, covering an area of 4600 ha to the north and west of the town of Newcastle, but also embracing small parts of Stoke and Staffordshire Moorlands. It was an area in which the effects of over two hundred years of disjointed mining and quarrying were overwhelmingly obvious. A multiplicity of shafts, structures, spoil mounds, slag heaps, brickworks, tileries, and clay pits combined to produce a landscape which was not as spectacularly derelict as some other parts of the Potteries, but which was depressingly dreary. Altogether almost one-fifth of the designated area was covered by mineral workings, derelict land or tipping sites. To complicate matters much of the mineral extraction was still active, in the form of British Coal deep mines and privately licensed pits, currently operational clay pits, albeit often with intermittent operations, and the reworking of spoil heaps for red ash, coal and other minerals. Above all, open-cast mining, in which there was growing interest, was creating the most massive alterations ever seen to the local landscape. Not all of these elements were as problematic as they might seem at first sight for some of the activities had planning conditions attached, and others could be used constructively in the reclamation programme.

Reclamation in the North Staffordshire Land Renewal Area has proceeded through four distinct routes. Firstly, local authority land reclamation schemes: these schemes, which have taken place both with and without grant aid, are exemplified by Leycett colliery (reclaimed to grazing land prior to use as a country park), by later phases of the Parkhouse Estate, and by the scheme to provide public open space on 73 ha of previously colliery and gasworks land at Birchenwood, which was financed by the recovery of coal from the site and the sale of land for housing; secondly, private restoration: this takes a number of forms, some quite small, as for example where farmers might fill in a railway cutting to extend their usable land, to large schemes such as the self-financing scheme being undertaken by British Coal to reclaim part of the derelict Holditch colliery site through coal recovery; thirdly, reclamation incidental to other development: one of the commonest variants of this form is the use of tipping to reclaim quarries and other large holes, as being undertaken at Bemersley, but the reworking of old spoil heaps to extract minerals also affords valuable opportunities; and lastly, reclamation in association with open-cast coal-mining: open-cast coal-mining is a controversial activity in some respects, but it can undoubtedly play a major role in land reclamation. Within the area under review it has already contributed to major improvements at Bateswood, Leycett and High Lane, and crude calculations in 1980 showed that if all of the executive's proposed sites were authorized they could reclaim half of the derelict land in the Land Renewal Area.[7]

Within the city of Stoke-on-Trent, undoubtedly the largest and most prestigious reclamation scheme of the decade was connected with the 1986 National Garden Festival and the subsequent development of Festival Park as a joint venture between the city council and St Modwen plc (Pls 16.2 and 3). Here on a site of 67 ha, only half a mile from the city centre, was an extraordinarily degraded landscape of disused steel works, mine shafts, waste deposits, tar lagoons and abandoned industrial buildings. After unsuccessful attempts to secure Enterprise Zone status, or European Community funding, the city succeeded in attracting a major Garden Festival. Before this could be held, extensive reclamation had to be undertaken. This was done with the aid of a large Derelict Land Grant: it involved moving 1.4 million m³ of earth, the

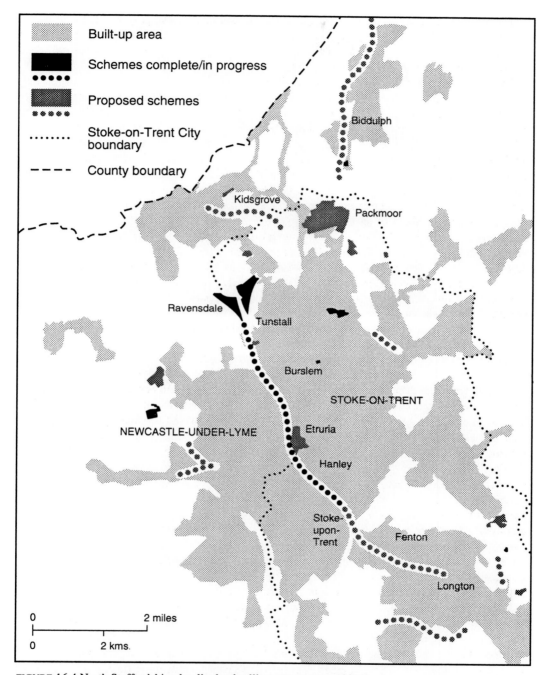

FIGURE 16.4 North Staffordshire derelict land rolling programme, 1992/3.

PLATE 16.2 The proposed site of the National Garden Festival in 1984, after the closure of the Shelton Bar Iron and Steel Works (Stoke-on-Trent City Council).

PLATE 16.3 The National Garden Festival site, 1992 (Jeffersons Air Photography, Liverpool). The area developed by St Modwen plc as a commercial, leisure, manufacturing and retail complex bears little resemblance to its earlier appearance.

laying of 24 km of pipework and 3.7 km of roads, at a total cost of £9.5 million. The Garden Festival itself was a success, although poor weather contributed to a smaller than expected attendance. Interest from developers following the Garden Festival was slow to materialize, but fortunately, as the national and local economies improved in the late 1980s, the site's advantages, including its strategic location, became more attractive and today it boasts an impressive range of uses (Fig 13.8). Two and a half thousand people work at Festival Park and it can be considered one of the most successful attempts in Britain to use Garden Festivals for the revitalization of a decaying urban area.

Despite the success of the Garden Festival site, the 1980s were difficult times in which to maintain the momentum of large programmes of restoration in north Staffordshire, and this is reflected in Figure 16.3. There were severe pressures on government expenditure, and changes in the administration of Derelict Land Grant meant that only single schemes could be put forward for approval on an *ad hoc* basis. Towards the end of the decade the share of Derelict Land Grant allocated to the West Midlands Region fell, and north Staffordshire had to compete both with areas which had Inner City status and with major priorities such as the limestone quarrying district of the Black Country.

Greater coherence, continuity, and the ability to tackle longer-term schemes, returned to the reclamation effort in 1989 with the adoption of a rolling programme involving the three district authorities and Staffordshire County Council. This programme recognized that many parts of the area still suffered from the twin handicaps of poor ground conditions and a sub-standard physical environment. The overall aims were to use land reclamation to bring forward new,

PLATE 16.4 Derelict land at Ravensdale (P T Kivell). Reclamation is already well-advanced as part of the rolling programme to create land for new jobs.

high-quality employment sites; inject confidence in the older urban areas; and upgrade the area's image by coordinated environmental improvement. In the relatively booming conditions of 1989, only 32 ha of prime quality sites were available in north Staffordshire, split between Festival Park, Parkhouse and the Keele University Science Park, so the need to provide additional space was paramount. The rolling programme, started in 1989, identified 206 ha of development schemes for industry and housing, 75 ha for environmental improvement and public open space, and a further 50 ha for longer-term treatment. Two key sites have important roles to play in the provision of land for employment; one is of 68 ha at Ravensdale (Pl 16.4) and the other is 52 ha of mostly privately owned land adjacent to the A500 at Sideway. In both cases business parks and industry are planned. But these areas are held back by poor ground conditions (including some severe contamination), lack of infrastructure and multiple ownership, all of which Derelict Land Grant is designed to tackle. It is estimated that almost half of the industrial land requirements for the foreseeable future could be met from reclaiming derelict land.[8] The broad outline of current reclamation under the rolling programme is indicated in Figure 16.4.

In addition to these major schemes, the local authorities are also undertaking and encouraging a range of other initiatives. For example the Brighter Track project, a joint venture between Stoke-on-Trent City Council and British Rail to improve the environment along main railway corridors has now been running for four years. Particular encouragement is also being given to private landowners to make use of the grants of 80 per cent of net costs which are available to them, especially given that 60 per cent of remaining dereliction in the city is in private ownership.

Finally, it is worth briefly summarizing the current grant and national policy situations. Department of the Environment policy continues to emphasize the importance of Derelict Land Grants in urban revitalization, but in a Derelict Land Grant Advice Note of 1991 the Treasury signalled a switch in emphasis back to 'soft' end-uses – for public open space and environmental improvement. Between 1990/1 and 1992/3 the total Derelict Land Grant for England was increased from £72 million to £106 million, but in the latter year, Stoke-on-Trent's share of this was a modest £695,000. At the time of writing there is a government proposal to establish an Urban Regeneration Agency charged with responsibility for revitalizing derelict and vacant land and buildings. This would take over, and coordinate existing city grants, Derelict Land Grants and the work of English Estates, but its likely effect remains to be seen.

CONCLUSION

Land reclamation has been, and remains, a crucial element in the transformation and modernization of the physical, economic and social landscapes of north Staffordshire. In a region which has received nothing from the multiplicity of Assisted Area and Inner City aid programmes over the years, the importance of Derelict Land Grants cannot be overemphasized. These grants have contributed to the success of one of the most effective and impressive records of industrial land reclamation to be seen anywhere. Since 1945 over 2400 ha of derelict land have been reclaimed in north Staffordshire, the great majority of it in the last 25 years. The visual impact which this has made upon the local environment is both obvious and dramatic, but it is also measurable in more tangible terms such as a reduction in population out-migration from the urban area, the attraction of new industrial and commercial investment, and an increase in the number of visitors.

As the task has progressed it has become in some ways more difficult. The early parts of the programme dealt with some of the larger sites in a very pragmatic way, but those which remain today tend to be the smaller and more complicated ones. It is also the case that modern reclamation mostly takes place to much higher technical standards than before. The mammoth task is not yet quite finished; there remain, at the time of writing, approximately 300 ha of dereliction, and new areas are still being created, but the rolling programme currently in motion provides an encouraging mechanism for further reductions in this total.

REFERENCES

1. S H Beaver, 'Minerals and planning', *Geog Jnl*, 104, 1944, 166–93, 'Surface mineral working in relation to planning', *Jnl Royal Institution Chartered Surveys*, 29, 1949, 325–39, 'Land reclamation after surface mineral workings', *Jnl Town Planning Institute*, 41, 1950, 146–51, and 'An appraisal of the problem', in W G Collins, ed, *Proceedings of the derelict land symposium, 1969*, Leeds, 1970, 3–9.
2. Figures calculated by S H Beaver in 1945 and supplied by letter to the city of Stoke-on-Trent Planning Department, 28 November 1946.
3. P T Kivell, P W Bush, A W Bannell and M Fenn, *An evaluation of land reclamation policies in north Staffordshire*, Department of the Environment and Keele University, 1985.
4. Department of the Environment, *Survey of derelict land in England, 1982*, 1984, and *Survey of derelict land in England, 1988*, 1991.
5. City of Stoke-on-Trent, *Report of the Director of Planning and Architecture to the Planning Committee*, 1985.
6. Figures from Stoke-on-Trent City Council and Newcastle-under-Lyme Borough Council Planning Departments, August 1992.
7. Staffordshire County Council Planning Department, *North Staffordshire land renewal plan: survey and issues*, 1980.
8. Stoke-on-Trent City Council *et al*, *A joint submission for a north Staffordshire derelict land rolling programme: land reclamation into 1992/93*, 1991.

17. Health Profiles, Provision and Planning

M E SUMMERLY

The present North Staffordshire Health Authority shares its boundaries with the three northernmost local government districts in the county of Staffordshire, from east to west the district of Staffordshire Moorlands, the city of Stoke-on-Trent and the borough of Newcastle-under-Lyme (Fig 9.4). The population numbers some 460,000 according to the 1991 mid-year estimates of the Office of Population Censuses and Surveys (OPCS). About two-thirds of that population resides within the conurbation of Stoke-on-Trent and Newcastle-under-Lyme. In comparison with many other health districts, it is relatively stable with only small inward and outward movements of people. This makes it convenient to undertake longitudinal epidemiological studies of health and disease.

HEALTH PROFILES

Demography

Demographic and certain health data have been available for over a hundred years based on local government areas and it has been possible to study the local population using data from OPCS and from accessing the annual reports of the former medical officers of health of Staffordshire County and Stoke-on-Trent County Borough. Over the century various local government boundary alterations have occurred but these have been only marginal, and the opportunity, therefore, is presented of comparing the changes in the population's health over that period in the area covered by the present North Staffordshire Health Authority.

When considering health (or rather ill-health) in a population, it is essential to know its demographic characteristics because it is obvious that such factors as the age and sex composition will profoundly affect the type of ill-health or disability found within it. Census material gives this information and, therefore, a study can be made of the populations counted at the 1891, 1921, 1951 and 1981 censuses. The 1891 census was based on registration districts while those for 1921 and 1951 used local authority areas, of which there were twelve in 1921 and eight in 1951. By 1981, data were available by health districts.

The 'population pyramids' at the various censuses are shown in Figure 17.1, revealing how their shape has altered as the older age groups have increased in number and the younger have decreased. That figure also provides an indication of the population structure as OPCS predicts it in 2010, one year before the next but one census. In 1891, 49 per cent of the population were aged under 20 years and 2 per cent over 70. By 1981 the proportion of the population under 20 years had decreased to 28 per cent and the proportion over 70 years had increased to just over 9 per cent. These changes in the period have been brought about by two factors. One is the dramatic decrease in childhood death rates, especially in the first year of life, and the other is a

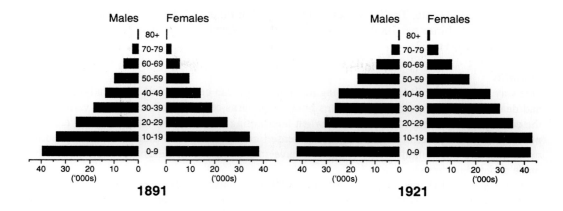

1891

1921

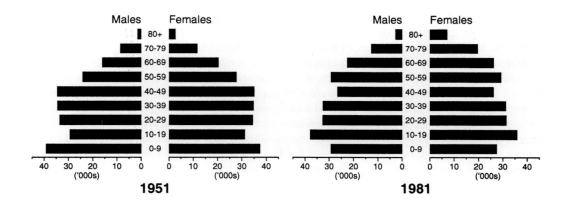

1951

1981

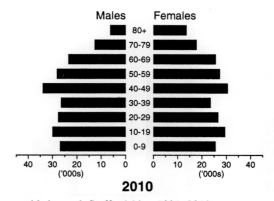

2010

FIGURE 17.1 Population pyramids in north Staffordshire, 1891–2010.

decrease in fertility rate. The latter factor is illustrated in Figure 17.2, where it can be seen that, whereas in 1891 births per 1000 women aged 15–44 years were approximately 167, by 1981 the number had fallen to 62.

Mortality

One way in which the ill-health occurring in a population can be identified is by studying deaths and death rates and Figure 17.3 indicates how the patterns of causes of death have varied over the century. Caution has to be exercised when interpreting these data because over the years the number of post-mortems performed has increased considerably and diagnoses have become more accurate as methods of investigation have improved. Nevertheless, deductions can be made about major trends.

It can be seen that infections and respiratory disease between them accounted for almost 40 per cent of deaths in 1891, and cancer and circulatory disease, the latter including both heart attacks and stroke, accounted for about 8 per cent. By 1981, however, deaths from infections have decreased to 1 per cent of the total and these and deaths from respiratory disease account for only 11 per cent of the total, whereas deaths from circulatory disease have increased to 50 per cent and those from cancer to 23 per cent. This pattern of cause of death, of course, reflects the increase in the number of older people in the population and the adverse environmental influences to which they have been exposed during their lifetimes.

In his report for 1891, the medical officer of health for Staffordshire, Dr George Reid, who had been in post for just over three years, was concerned about deaths from infectious disease. Overall in north Staffordshire there were 850 deaths from what was termed in those days zymotic disease, which included typhoid and other enteric fevers, diphtheria, scarlet fever, measles and whooping cough. Most of the deaths from these conditions were in young children. Deaths from tuberculosis were counted separately (although they have been incorporated in the figures with the infections), and in 1891 Dr Reid recorded 569 deaths from tuberculosis (called phthisis at this time). In 1981, sixteen people in the district died from infectious disease, nine of these deaths being due to tuberculosis.

Infant mortality, that is the number of deaths in the first year of life per 1000 live births, has fallen considerably over the century. In 1891 the rate was 147 and this figure excluded Biddulph because data for that town were not available. By 1981 infant mortality had fallen to 12.9. In his annual report for 1891, Dr Reid expressed dissatisfaction at the high rates of infant

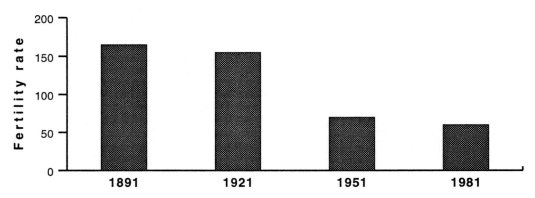

FIGURE 17.2 Fertility rate in north Staffordshire (births per 1000 women aged 15–44 years), 1891–1981.

mortality in the county, particularly in urban areas, and he noted that the three-year average for infant mortality for the years 1889–91 was highest in Longton and Tunstall at 223 and 225 respectively. Figure 17.4A shows how infant mortality has fallen over the century.

Deaths from pregnancy and childbirth have also declined. In 1891, 1 per cent of deaths was due to this cause and by 1921 the proportion had fallen to 0.1 per cent. Figure 17.4B appears to indicate that by 1951 there had been a considerable increase, again to 1 per cent of total deaths, but this was because deaths from abortion, which had not been considered in either 1891 or 1921, by that date had been added to those due to pregnancy and childbirth. In 1981 the proportion had fallen to 0.2 per cent of total deaths, the important factor in the decline being the introduction of the Abortion Act in 1967 which has virtually eliminated deaths from septic abortion.

Reasons for the changing disease patterns over time
The decline in death rates which has occurred over the last century has been due almost entirely to a decrease in mortality from infectious diseases. McKeown and Lowe have suggested a range of factors which influenced this decrease. Firstly, standards of nutrition were raised stemming

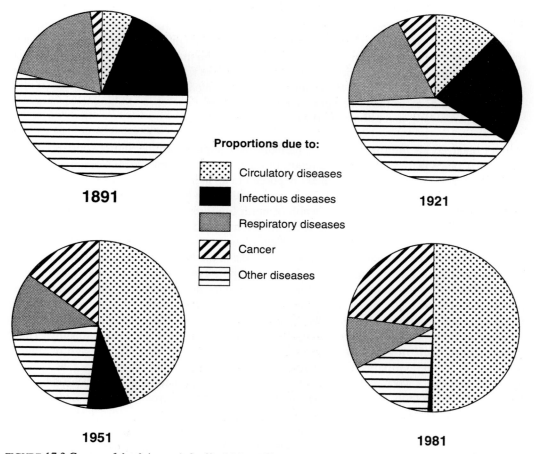

FIGURE 17.3 Causes of death in north Staffordshire, 1891–1981.

from an increase in food supply as a result of the agricultural revolution in the early eighteenth century and the development of scientific agriculture in the nineteenth century; secondly, the industrial revolution produced a growth in the nation's wealth; thirdly, the environment was improved following various Public Health Acts from 1848 onwards, ensuring the provision of a clean water supply, efficient and safe disposal of sewage, better housing and a reduction in atmospheric pollution; fourthly, change in reproductive behaviour, which led to a fall in fertility rates, resulted in a reduction in the number of children produced by each family; and finally, certain medical measures, particularly immunization and more effective treatment brought about by advances in medical science, produced their results from the second quarter of the twentieth century onwards.[1] This last factor, however, has contributed relatively little to the overall decline in deaths during the century as a whole.

At present there are epidemics of heart disease, cancer and strokes. The north Staffordshire population has higher death rates from these conditions than the average for the nation as a whole. Associated risk factors are well known and include smoking, excessive alcohol consumption, unhealthy diets and lack of exercise.

Occupation and health

According to Dr Greenhow, the average expectation of life in the pottery districts of Stoke-upon-Trent and Wolstanton is extraordinarily short. Although in the district of Stoke only 36.6 per cent and in Wolstanton only 30.4 per cent of the male population over 20 years of age are employed in the potteries, among these men in the first district more than half, and in the second about two-fifths, of the deaths are due to pulmonary diseases affecting the potters . . . of all the diseases they [the potters] are especially prone to chest disease, to pneumonia, phthisis, bronchitis, and asthma (Karl Marx, *Das Kapital*).

Marx obtained his information from a parliamentary inquiry into the Staffordshire potteries, which took place in 1860, and from a report of the Children's Employment Commissioners in 1863. Occupation is, of course, extremely important to an individual's health because industrial processes produce an environment which, if uncontrolled, can adversely affect the well-being of the workforce. No discussion on the health of north Staffordshire over the years could ignore the effect which the major occupations of the district have had on the working population.

One of the first doctors to tackle the problem of occupational health was Dr John Thomas Aldridge. In 1862, he was elected consultant physician to the North Staffordshire Infirmary, and became certifying factory surgeon to the Stoke-upon-Trent district. He was particularly interested in respiratory disease and lead poisoning, and the health problems associated with the pottery industry gave him much opportunity to study these conditions. At a lecture in 1886 at the Wedgwood Institute in Burslem he described symptoms of lead poisoning in the pottery industry as follows: 'The subjects of lead poisons are assuredly objects of sympathy. Their illness shows itself in a sallow, pale face, expressive of weakness, hunger and damaged nutrition; in abdominal pains and constipation; and troubles of the digestive organs.'[2] As a result of Aldridge's work and the concern voiced by other influential people at the time, the Factory and Workshop Act was passed in 1891 which empowered the Home Secretary to formulate special rules for those occupations which he felt were dangerous to health. As a consequence lead poisoning became a notifiable disease in 1895. In addition to these respiratory disorders in the region described by Marx, there was a further related problem arising from the use of powdered flint in the very early years of pottery-making. Powdered flint not only had to

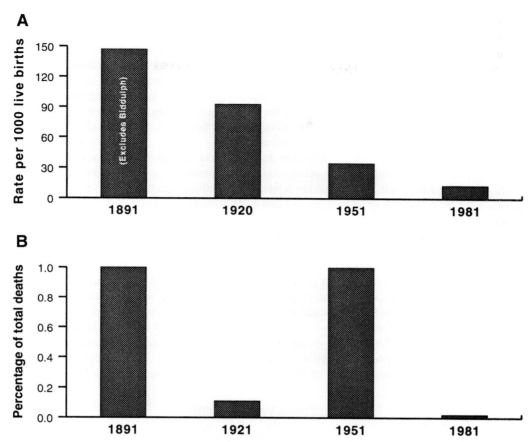

FIGURE 17.4 A) Infant mortality in north Staffordshire, 1891–1981; B) Deaths from pregnancy and childbirth in north Staffordshire, 1891–1981.

be removed from the biscuit ware after firing but was also employed as bedding for chinaware. Both processes created fine clouds of silica dust which affected the lungs and produced silicosis.

Coal-mining was a major industry in north Staffordshire during the nineteenth and twentieth centuries. Working conditions were hazardous – explosions from gas, flooding, and faulty equipment were the main factors behind most mining accidents and north Staffordshire had its fair share of these. Between 1866 and 1942 deaths in the north Staffordshire coalfield in principal disasters (those involving the deaths of at least ten men and boys) numbered 726.[3] Apart from the risk of accidents, much disability and death resulted from the dust generated from coal and rock in the mining process. The occurrence of pneumoconiosis, silicosis, and emphysema among miners has been well documented. Less well known is the miners' disease of nystagmus. The working conditions which prevailed in the mines in the earlier part of this century led to a progressive loss of control over the musculature of the eye and gradual blindness.

Iron and steel production was similarly important in the region as a major source of employment from the mid-nineteenth century. There were ten blast furnaces in the district in 1880 but the industry gradually declined and now there is none left. The main health problems associated with this work were respiratory diseases due to the dust generated in the extraction of metals from the ore and also cataracts due to exposure to the intense heat of molten metal.

The rubber industry developed in north Staffordshire in the twentieth century in response to the demands for the production of motor vehicles and insulation for electrical cabling. Probably the most important health risk associated with rubber manufacture was the development of bladder cancer in some workers exposed to beta naphthylamine. Exposure to this substance ceased after 1950 following identification of the hazard. A screening programme was set up for those people engaged in the process involving this particular chemical, enabling the early detection and prompt treatment of bladder cancer.

The textile industry in north Staffordshire has, of course, for several centuries been centred on Leek. In his book entitled *The hygiene, disease and mortality of occupations*, published in 1892, Dr Aldridge noted: 'At the period when Dr Greenhow conducted his inquiry, the silk towns were notorious for their high rate of mortality from consumption and, in a less degree, from respiratory maladies. Since then a vast improvement has taken place in this matter and in the case of Leek, one of the towns of which I have very precise particulars, the mortality from consumption has fallen to about the level of towns generally.'[4]

National concern about the working environment and its effect on the workforce began to be expressed in the late eighteenth and early nineteenth centuries, and legislation was gradually introduced covering, for example, the employment of children and women, working hours and practices. The working environment itself was also subject to government scrutiny, benefiting the health, safety and welfare of workers. Of recent laws, one of the most important is the Health and Safety at Work Act of 1974, with its regulations to control substances hazardous to health (COSHH). There is no doubt that legislation has had a most powerful and favourable influence, improving the health of the workforce of this country probably more than any other factor.

HEALTH SERVICE PROVISION

In common with the rest of the country the delivery of health services in north Staffordshire evolved gradually from early beginnings in the church and later as a result of the enactment of the Elizabethan poor law. By the turn of this century health services were provided by a variety of organizations and individuals but no one body was charged with overall responsibility.

Secondary care services (hospitals)
Hospital services were provided by either boards of guardians of poor law institutions, local government or voluntary bodies. Local government hospitals were largely concerned with infectious diseases and mental illness, although some general hospital work took place as a result of the authorization by Parliament in 1867 of the construction of hospitals to provide a more acceptable standard of care than that provided in the poor law institutions. Although initially it was not intended that poor law institutions should furnish hospital services, many who were admitted to them were sick and required such treatment. They also provided for destitute people with infections, for those who were helpless and infirm, for those termed 'lying-in women' and for certain mentally-handicapped people. The poor law institutions at the turn of the century in north Staffordshire included the Stoke-upon-Trent Union (on the present City General Hospital site), the Wolstanton and Burslem Union (now Westcliffe Hospital), the Leek Union (now Moorlands Hospital) and Cheadle Union (now Cheadle Hospital).

Infectious disease and fever hospitals included Bucknall, Newcastle (later renamed Lymewood), Bradwell, Stanfield, Cheadle and Leek Hospitals. They were administered by local government, sometimes being jointly administered where it was more economic to do so. For instance, Bradwell Hospital served the urban district councils of Audley, Kidsgrove, Smallthorne and Wolstanton, while Bucknall Hospital served the councils of Hanley, Stoke and Fenton. In general, infectious diseases hospitals (fever hospitals) admitted cases of scarlet fever, diphtheria and enteric fever (including typhoid). Smallpox, however, was still a concern, although relatively uncommon by the beginning of the century. Nevertheless, the various local government councils in north Staffordshire felt that there should be some provision if required. Accordingly, in 1902 a joint smallpox hospital district was formed consisting of the boroughs of Hanley, Burslem, Longton, Newcastle-under-Lyme and Stoke-upon-Trent, the urban districts of Audley, Fenton, Kidsgrove, Leek, Tunstall and Wolstanton, and the rural districts of Cheadle, Newcastle-under-Lyme, Stoke-upon-Trent and Leek. A hospital was built at Bagnall for people with the disease, although patients with tuberculosis were accepted for admission if the hospital had no cases of smallpox.

In the early years of this century increasing concern was voiced about death from and health problems associated with tuberculosis. Compulsory notification of tuberculosis was introduced in 1912; in the following year the Public Health Act of 1913 required all county and county borough authorities to devise schemes for its prevention. A joint venture was undertaken by Cheshire County Council (the originators of the scheme), Chester City and Birkenhead, Stockport, Stoke-upon-Trent and Wallasey Borough Councils, resulting in the building of the Cheshire Joint Sanatorium at Loggerheads which was opened in 1923. At this time it was located in Shropshire but with subsequent local government boundary changes it came within Staffordshire County Council's curtilage. The reason for this combined venture was that the councils concerned administered areas where mills, potteries, engineering and extraction industries were sited – all of which were associated with a high incidence of pulmonary disease. In addition in north Staffordshire, following the 1913 Act, tuberculosis dispensaries were established in Shelton, Newcastle, Leek, Cheadle and Biddulph.

Institutional provision for people with psychiatric illness was considered essential in the late nineteenth and early twentieth centuries. By 1892 the county asylum (now St George's Hospital) at Stafford had become overcrowded. The board of guardians of the parish of Stoke-upon-Trent, therefore, decided to provide two pavilions, one for males and one for females, on land between the workhouse school and London Road. These were completed in 1894 and could take up to 140 patients. At about the same time the county council also decided to extend the provision for psychiatric patients by building a hospital on 175 acres of land in the parish of Cheddleton. The foundation stone was laid in 1895 and the hospital was opened in 1897. It was designed to accommodate 300 male and 300 female patients with provision in the plans for an extension to house a further 200 patients. Some twenty or so years later, it was decided that an institution was required for people with mental handicap (now called learning disabilities), and Stallington Hospital was opened in 1930 by the city of Stoke-on-Trent following the purchase of Stallington Hall, formerly a private residence. Bagnall Hospital (now called the Highlands) was converted to cater for people with learning disabilities and transferred to Stallington Hospital Management Committee from Stoke-on-Trent Hospital Management Committee in 1959.

Much general hospital work at the turn of the century was carried out in voluntary hospitals, and in the region these included the North Staffordshire Infirmary, the Haywood Hospital, Longton Cottage Hospital and Leek Memorial Hospital. Whereas local-government administered hospitals had certain statutory duties with respect to their services, voluntary hospitals were able to choose their patients. These patients paid either as individuals or through insurance, although in some instances treatment was given free. The last obtained admission upon the recommendation of a subscriber to the hospital. Some idea of the restrictions placed upon admission to voluntary hospitals can be gained by the report of the Haywood Hospital in 1915. Ordinary patients (there were six beds for private patients) obtained admission on the following system of recommendation: 'persons subscribing an even number of guineas being entitled to that number of out-patient recommendations and half that number of in-patient recommendations'. Further admissions were available at the rate of 12s 6d for each additional out-patient and 2 gns for each additional in-patient recommendation. Another note stated that 'no person shall be eligible for admission as an in-patient or for treatment as an out-patient whose circumstances in the opinion of the house committee enable him to pay for such medical treatment as his condition requires'. Subscribers were asked to 'direct in-patients to be sent as clean as possible, and with a proper change of linen, a hairbrush and comb and a knife, fork and spoon'. The admission policy decreed that 'no lunatic and no person suffering from any form of contagious or infectious disease, confirmed consumption, ulcerated legs of long standing, cancer (not permitting of operation), puerperal fever or any incurable disease, no female far advanced in pregnancy may be admitted as an in-patient'.

Primary care services (general practitioner and community health services)
At the turn of the century there was only a limited form of publicly-provided general practice and this was for the destitute. It was administered under the poor law and serviced by part-time general practitioners who were poorly paid. No other forms of publicly-provided primary care were available. People not eligible to receive general practitioner services under the poor law rules had to arrange to pay personally for them. Many took out voluntary insurance or subscribed to friendly societies to cover such costs. One of the first publicly-provided primary care services to be created for the individual was the school health service. This developed partly from a general concern about the welfare of children, and partly from the inspection of recruits for the army for the Boer War revealing that 40 per cent were unfit for service. As a result the Education Act of 1907 required that school children should be medically inspected at regular intervals. These inspections identified much untreated illness and disability, and local education authorities began to provide treatment particularly for eye, orthopaedic and skin problems. In north Staffordshire the county borough of Stoke-on-Trent developed its own school health service as did the municipal borough of Newcastle-under-Lyme. The remainder of the district was covered by Staffordshire County Council school health service.

In England health visiting began in Manchester in 1862. At first it was a voluntary service, but later became salaried. By the time Stoke-on-Trent became a county borough in 1910 there were six health visitors working within it – all with certificates. There were also some voluntary health visitors to whom the official visitors referred healthy infants. Overall, however, this second publicly-provided personal health service was not universally established until after the First World War when the Maternity and Child Welfare Act of 1918 secured services for pregnant women and pre-school children.

As with the school health service in north Staffordshire, Stoke-on-Trent County Borough, Newcastle Municipal Borough and Staffordshire County Council were the responsible bodies for providing maternal and child welfare services through ante-natal and post-natal clinics, domiciliary midwifery, health visitor services and child welfare clinics. The last provided infant food, routine inspection of infants and pre-school children and limited treatment facilities.

Publicly-provided health services were further expanded by the National Health Insurance Act of 1911. This applied to a strictly-defined type of employed person and did not cover any dependants. It offered treatment by a general practitioner but not by a hospital or consultant, and was administered locally by insurance committees which were quite separate from local government.

Midwifery as a publicly-provided service in the community became properly established in 1936 with a salaried municipal midwife service administered by local government. Previously the Midwives Institute had been founded in 1881, and in 1902 the first Midwives Act marked the beginning of standardized training and regulated practice. At the beginning of the century most midwives were in private practice, while a few, employed by teaching hospitals, provided a 'district' service. As hospital midwifery practice increased and the birth rate declined, many private midwives went out of business and after 1936 domiciliary midwifery was largely a local authority monopoly.

Until the introduction of the National Health Service in 1948 district nursing was provided by a variety of organizations. Although of the opinion that it was best to nurse sick people in infirmaries, the Local Government Board considered in 1892 that, where the sick person had to be nursed at home, he or she could be provided with a nurse by the board of guardians. Many unions, particularly in London, employed their own district nurses, but others preferred to use nurses supplied by the various nursing associations and the Queen's Institute. These Queen's Nurses, as they were generally known, received six months' training and those who were destined to work in rural areas completed a further three-months' training in maternity work. The following is an extract from the 1938 report of the medical officer of health of the city of Stoke-on-Trent:

Nursing Arrangements in the City.
The following Voluntary Associations provide and pay the nurses as set out:
The Tunstall Nursing Institution, 1 Nurse.
The Burslem District Nursing Association, 2 Nurses.
The Hanley Nursing Association, 2 Nurses.
The Stoke Nursing Association, 1 Nurse.
The Fenton Nursing Association, 2 Nurses.
Longton District Nursing Association, 2 Nurses.
Norton District Nursing Association, 1 Nurse.

Background to the development of the National Health Service
As can be seen, by the second quarter of the twentieth century there was a multiplicity of provision of health services. Destitute and impoverished persons had access to general practitioner and hospital services through public assistance; general hospital provision was divided between local government and the voluntary organizations; therapeutic primary care was available from general practitioners for payment; and preventive care, together with a small amount of therapeutic care, was provided by local government.

The financial problems which were to escalate over the next few years, especially for voluntary hospitals, were presaged by the experience of Biddulph Grange Orthopaedic Hospital. This was originally a private house developed from an old farmhouse in the 1840s. In 1923 it was handed over by the then owner to trustees who formed the governing body of the Staffordshire Orthopaedic Hospital at Biddulph. It was opened as a children's orthopaedic hospital in 1924 for the treatment of diseases and disorders of bones and joints such as rickets, tuberculosis, congenital malformations, osteomyelitis and the long-term effects of accidents. Unfortunately, it was not financially viable, was placed on the market and sold to Lancashire County Council for £10,000 in 1926. They used it for the provision of treatment for physically-handicapped children from east Lancashire, although children from other counties could be admitted on payment of a fee by the local authority concerned.

By the late 1930s the costs of medical care were beginning to cause problems. Over half the population had to meet their own costs or seek assistance from the poor law. Voluntary hospitals were in great financial difficulties: many were small and inadequate, but because of limited funds could do nothing to remedy this. In north Staffordshire in 1938 the North Staffordshire Royal Infirmary, Longton Hospital, the Cripples Aid Society (now Hartshill Orthopaedic Hospital) and the Haywood Hospital formed the North Staffordshire Voluntary Hospitals Contributory Association. Workpeople in the district agreed that between 1*d* and 3*d* per week could be deducted from their wages for the benefit of the association. In addition, certain establishments agreed to subscribe to it and the association itself organized fund-raising activities such as flag days, summer carnivals, whist drives and various other entertainments. Funds so raised were to be distributed in the following proportion: North Staffordshire Royal Infirmary 78.5 per cent, Longton Hospital 6.5 per cent, Cripples Aid Society 3.5 per cent and the Haywood Hospital 11.5 per cent.

The public hospitals run by local government were also in serious financial difficulties and standards within them varied according to the wealth and initiative of individual authorities. The development of the North Staffordshire Royal Infirmary and the City General Hospital, within half a mile of each other, had been quite separate, as indeed had the development of the other voluntary hospitals in the district. There was no collaboration between the various institutions to try to utilize their resources efficiently and to provide a comprehensive service. Thus in north Staffordshire, immediately before 1948, general medical services were provided at all the voluntary hospitals and by the local authority at the City General Hospital. Surgery was undertaken at all these hospitals and also at Biddulph Grange Hospital, which continued to be administered by Lancashire County Council education committee. Maternity services were provided by local government at Leek Moorlands, the City General, the Limes and the Fanny Deakin Hospitals and by the voluntary hospitals at the North Staffordshire Royal Infirmary and the Haywood Hospital.

As a result of all the problems facing the delivery of health care, the NHS was introduced in 1948. This brought a comprehensive health service for all, free at the point of delivery, financed mainly from general taxation and marginally from national insurance contributions. The result of the NHS Act was that all hospital services were brought under public control. England and Wales were divided into fourteen regions in each of which a regional hospital board was made responsible for planning and administering hospital and specialist services. Exceptions to this were undergraduate teaching hospitals, which were administered separately by boards of governors and were directly responsible to the Minister of Health. In north Staffordshire the hospitals became responsible to the Birmingham Regional Hospital Board and on a wall in the boardroom at the North Staffordshire Royal Infirmary there is a notice which succinctly describes the location and organization of the hospital services in the district following the introduction of the NHS. It reads as follows:

The following hospitals in North Staffordshire were transferred to and vested in the Ministry of Health on the 5th July 1948:

1. NORTH STAFFORDSHIRE ROYAL INFIRMARY
2. CITY GENERAL HOSPITAL
3. HAYWOOD HOSPITAL, BURSLEM
4. LONGTON HOSPITAL
5. HARTSHILL ORTHOPAEDIC HOSPITAL
6. BIDDULPH GRANGE ORTHOPAEDIC HOSPITAL

7. CHESHIRE JOINT SANATORIUM
8. STANFIELD SANATORIUM, BURSLEM
9. THE LIMES, MATERNITY HOSPITAL, HARTSHILL
10. FANNY DEAKIN MATERNITY HOSPITAL
11. LEEK MEMORIAL HOSPITAL
12. LEEK ISOLATION HOSPITAL
13. LEEK MOORLANDS HOSPITAL
14. CHEADLE HOSPITAL
15. CHEADLE ISOLATION HOSPITAL
16. BUCKNALL ISOLATION HOSPITAL
17. BRADWELL ISOLATION HOSPITAL
18. NEWCASTLE ISOLATION HOSPITAL
19. BAGNALL ISOLATION HOSPITAL
20. BETLEY COURT REHABILITATION CENTRE
(WESTCLIFFE HOSPITAL – Joint User)
CHEST CLINICS AT SHELTON, LEEK, CHEADLE AND BIDDULPH.
LEEK ORTHOPAEDIC CLINIC.
SPECIAL TREATMENT CENTRE, SHELTON.

The Control and Management of this group of hospitals was granted to the STOKE-ON-TRENT HOSPITAL MANAGEMENT COMMITTEE on behalf of The Birmingham Regional Hospital Board.

The Management Committee was renamed the NORTH STAFFORDSHIRE HOSPITAL MANAGEMENT COMMITTEE on April 1st 1965 and on the 1st April 1969 amalgamated with ST EDWARD'S HOSPITAL MANAGEMENT COMMITTEE AND STALLINGTON HOSPITAL MANAGEMENT COMMITTEE.
The following hospitals were added to the group:
ST EDWARD'S HOSPITAL, STALLINGTON HOSPITAL, BAGNALL HOSPITAL.

Local government had thus lost its hospitals but it retained responsibility for personal health services, such as the school health service, maternal and child welfare and other preventive services, including vaccination and immunization. It also took on responsibilities for ambulance services and the care and aftercare of certain sick and handicapped persons.

The administration of general medical and dental services, pharmaceutical and supplementary ophthalmic services was combined under local executive councils, the boundaries of which coincided with those of local government. Thus, in north Staffordshire there was a Stoke-on-Trent Executive Council for the city and a Staffordshire Executive Council for the remainder of the area. Local government health services and local executive councils continued in this way until both the NHS and local government were reorganized in 1974. As far as health was concerned this resulted in the formation of Staffordshire Area Health Authority which took over all the personal health and ambulance services formerly in the hands of local government. The executive councils disappeared and were replaced by Staffordshire Family Practitioner Committee serving the whole county. Staffordshire Area Health Authority lasted for eight years until there was a further restructuring in 1982 which resulted in the creation of the present three district health authorities within the county boundary.

The NHS after 1948

The new NHS found itself with considerable challenges. A major one was the imbalance between hospital provision and the health service needs of local populations. North Staffordshire Hospital Management Committee had inherited eight infectious diseases hospitals (including the Cheshire Joint Sanatorium) at a time when such maladies were in rapid decline and when there were growing pressures from the increasing burden of degenerative disorders as a result of the ageing population. Over the course of the next few years Stanfield Sanatorium and Bucknall, Bradwell, Newcastle and Bagnall Isolation Hospitals were all converted for the care of aged people. Bucknall Hospital, however, retained two wards for infectious disease. Leek Isolation Hospital was demolished and Cheadle Isolation Hospital eventually became a private nursing home for the elderly.

As tuberculosis declined, Cheshire Joint Sanatorium began to operate on patients with cancer, bronchiectasis and minor conditions such as hernias. In 1962 open-heart surgery began there. The isolated position of the hospital created difficulties for this type of work, and it eventually closed in 1969, with facilities being transferred to the City General Hospital and the North Staffordshire Royal Infirmary. Bagnall Isolation Hospital closed in 1958 and reopened the next year to accommodate people with learning disabilities to relieve overcrowding at Stallington Hospital.

Very little new hospital building took place in north Staffordshire for almost forty years following the introduction of the NHS. That which did occur was at the Hospital Centre where a new Central Outpatients Department was opened in 1964, a new Maternity Hospital in 1968 and a Central Pathology Laboratory in 1975. Three new wards, a day hospital and rehabilitation centre for the care of elderly persons opened at the City General Hospital in 1972. With the opening of the Maternity Hospital, the Fanny Deakin Hospital was closed, being then reopened in 1971 to provide care for younger disabled people. In the community, the city of Stoke-on-Trent was particularly active in the building of health centres and in 1974 at the time of the reorganization, Staffordshire Area Health Authority inherited eleven health centres in north Staffordshire, nine of them within the city.

Recent developments

It became obvious in the late 1970s that if the residents of north Staffordshire were to receive a high standard of modern hospital care then something would have to be done about the fragmentation of surgical services, the inadequate provision for elderly people, and the poor state of much of the building stock. In 1984 a consultative document, *The pattern of hospital services in north Staffordshire* was produced to address these problems. It noted that 'The three new schemes, to be built at a cost of £32,750,000, involve the replacement of existing hospitals for the elderly at Bradwell/Lymewood and Cheadle and also the building of a 349-bedded Surgical and Paediatric Unit on the City General Hospital site. The scheme which will probably have the most far reaching effect on the district and its service is the Surgical and Paediatric Unit on the City General Hospital site. This scheme, as well as replacing existing hospital beds on the City General Hospital site, will result in an extra 87 beds for surgical patients at the City General, an extra 5 Operating Theatres and a new Children's Unit with its own Day Hospital. This will provide the Operating Theatres and beds to cut surgical waiting lists and enable the Authority to cease surgical operations at a number of smaller Hospitals.'[5]

The last four years have seen these schemes come into being. The opening of the new Bradwell and Cheadle Hospitals for the care of elderly people, and the refurbishment and extension of the Moorlands Hospital, again mainly for the same category of patient, occurred in

1988. The new Paediatric and Surgical Unit was inaugurated in 1990. Longton Hospital was closed that year but reopened in 1992 having been renovated and refurbished to cater for elderly people with both physical and mental illness. All in-patient surgery in north Staffordshire is now undertaken at the Hospital Centre, emergency work being carried out on the Infirmary site and elective (planned) surgery on the City General Hospital site. Leek Memorial and Biddulph Grange Hospitals have been closed, while the old Cheetham's (children's) Hospital was pulled down when the children's beds were transferred to the new building. Dilapidated and inconvenient gynaecological wards were also demolished. The centralization of surgical work at the Hospital Centre created space at the Haywood Hospital so that the residents of the Fanny Deakin Hospital were able to be moved there, where they now benefit from the excellent rehabilitation facilities. The Fanny Deakin Hospital has subsequently been shut.

Currently, new medical beds are being built on the City General Hospital site, so enabling all such beds to be under one roof at the Hospital Centre. The present medical wards at the City General Hospital will then be refurbished to make them suitable for the care of elderly people, facilitating the closure of Westcliffe Hospital. The building of new orthopaedic wards will begin at the City General Hospital in 1994 and they are due to open in 1996 to replace the Hartshill Orthopaedic Hospital. A new psychiatric unit at the City General Hospital site, on which building will start in 1996, will replace the acute admission wards at the City General and St Edward's Hospitals.

The present organization of health services in north Staffordshire

The implementation of the NHS and Community Care Act 1990 has produced a period of accelerating change in the organization of health services which is likely to continue for some time. The alterations began in September 1990 when district health authorities were restructured and their membership reduced. At the same time family practitioner committees were replaced by family health services authorities, and general management was introduced into that organization. The purchasing and provision of health services became separated. District health authorities have been given the responsibility for determining the health service requirements of their resident populations and have to place contracts for these services with provider units, which need not necessarily be restricted to those within their district boundaries. As a result, in the first financial year of activity – April 1991 to March 1992 – the North Staffordshire Health Authority placed contracts with hospital and community units within its own district, with hospitals and units in the two other Staffordshire health authorities and with various units in Cheshire, Derbyshire, Shropshire and Birmingham.

The Act also made provision for general practitioners with lists above a certain size, if they so wished, to be funded to purchase certain services for patients on their registers. Two group practices in north Staffordshire became fundholders in the first year and a further five practices have expressed a wish to join this scheme in 1993. There was also provision in the Act for hospitals and community units to apply for trust status and become self-governing, thus relinquishing their management accountability to district health authorities. In 1993, the Hospital Centre Acute Unit in north Staffordshire is to become an independent trust and it is likely that the Combined Health Care Unit, which provides elderly care, mental health, learning disabilities and community services, will eventually seek this status.

As a consequence of the community care aspects of the 1990 Act, Staffordshire County Council's social services department will from 1993 take the lead-role in determining individual care packages for the elderly, for people with mental health needs, learning, physical and sensory disabilities, and for others within a number of groups who may well need long-term social care. Wherever possible people will be supported so that they may remain in their own homes. This change in organization and practice requires radical rethinking of current attitudes to ensure that the needs of users and their carers become paramount and the claims of professionals and their services take second place.

THE FUTURE

There has been a growing realization in recent years that increasing investment in expensive, high-technology investigation and treatment brings diminishing returns and that the most effective and economic way to improve the health of the population is by focusing on primary prevention – dealing with the causes of disease and disability rather than treating them once they have arisen. The first important document produced by the Department of Health dealing with this aspect of care was the White Paper *Prompting better health* published in 1987.[6] It recognized the importance of primary care in the prevention of disease and disability and the promotion of health. It was translated into action in a new contract for general practitioners introduced in 1990. This laid down targets for certain preventive procedures including immunization coverage and cervical cytology uptake. It has considerably affected the pattern of general practice already so that instead of responding to requests from patients, practitioners are actively initiating preventive procedures and carrying out health promotion programmes with their practice populations.

A most important publication in 1991 was the consultation paper on the *Health of the nation*. This was followed in 1992 by the publication of the White Paper[7] with the same title. It was the first time that government had produced a strategy for health. In practical terms it has set targets for a reduction first in death rates from coronary heart disease, certain cancers, suicides and accidents, and second in incidence rates in certain cancers, gonorrhoea and adolescent pregnancy. Priorities are likely to change as disease patterns alter, and targets for other conditions will be set in future years. One result of this rebalancing of the emphasis between prevention and treatment will be an increasing need for multi-disciplinary and multi-agency working.

While it is right and proper to emphasize the importance of health promotion and the prevention of disease, there is still a considerable amount of ill-health to be dealt with as a result of genetic and past environmental influences. Here also, some radical rethinking has been taking place, particularly the questioning of long-held, unsubstantiated beliefs about the necessity for long in-patient stays. This move began in the late 1960s with the rapid discharge from maternity units of women following a normal delivery when previously they had been kept in hospital for ten days after the event. In the early 1970s the adverse effects on children of admission to hospital became widely recognized and wherever possible they are now treated at home or as day patients. If they do need admission to hospital, however, parents are actively encouraged to remain with them.

More recently it has become apparent that certain conditions and procedures for which people used to be admitted to hospital for several days can be treated in a day. Moreover, developments in anaesthesia and in minimally-invasive surgical techniques through endoscopes (so-called keyhole surgery) and the use of lasers mean that many patients can be treated for a wide variety of conditions on a day basis. Day surgery is welcomed by most patients and the Royal College of Surgeons has estimated that approximately half of non-emergency surgery could be performed in this way. The development of 'hospital at home' schemes may well further decrease the need for lengthy post-operative stays or, indeed, any in-patient stay for many people.

Perhaps one of the most exciting developments for many years has been in the field of genetics. There is possibility that very soon certain serious genetic diseases may be treated by genetic modifications of human body cells. At present much genetically-determined disease is impossible to cure. Some is capable of identification in the ante-natal period when parents can be offered a termination of pregnancy if they so wish. It may be that gene therapy will eliminate the necessity for termination in these cases and also enable treatment of those genetically-determined conditions which become apparent after birth or develop at a later stage of life. Obviously, this therapy offers significant benefit to certain individuals but there are also concerns about the ethics and the possible adverse consequences of such procedures.

REFERENCES

1. T McKeown and C R Lowe, *An introduction to social medicine*, Oxford, 1974.
2. E Isaacson, *The forgotten physician*, nd (copy in North Staffordshire Medical Institute Library).
3. A J Taylor, 'Coal', in *Victoria County History of Staffordshire*, 1967, ii, 92–4.
4. J T Aldridge, *The hygiene, diseases and mortality of occupations*, 1892.
5. North Staffordshire Health Authority, *The pattern of hospital provision in north Staffordshire: a consultative document*, 1984.
6. Department of Health and Social Security, *Promoting better health (Cmd 249)*, 1987.
7. Department of Health, *Health of the nation (Cmd 1986)*, 1992.

18. Education in Stoke-on-Trent: The Two Towns Project

T BRIGHOUSE

Let Stoke-on-Trent stand as proxy for the development, the strengths and the weaknesses of the English and Welsh education system. It has all the symptoms of the educational problems which have hobbled the development of the UK, whether one considers its economic or its spiritual well-being. It is a strange, complicated and in the end depressing tale of national misunderstanding and mismanagement, coupled with local pride, good intentions and bad luck. The outcome is the high price that is paid in the vicious circle of low investment, low skills and low expectations (Fig 18.1). There is no escaping the feeling among the majority of the nation's population that education is something to be got over as soon as is decently possible. In consequence we are in danger of becoming a society beached on the worst of all possible off-shore European islands, as a post-industrial society with ever higher crime rates, high unemployment and accumulating evidence of decline. What will be suggested is that what 'we' (and by that is meant a partnership involving the Staffordshire Local Education Authority, the local universities – Keele and Staffordshire – and other interested partners) are adopting in a small part of Stoke-on-Trent represents the kernel of an idea which could change all that and transform educational aspirations and real achievements in the inner city.

Stoke schools were planned, opened, maintained, reorganized and ultimately sometimes closed to respond to the role the community was destined to play, either in Britain's industrial revolution or in the changes in educational theories and fashions during the same period. For example, one of the primary schools in Stoke was actually paid for by the Michelin Company, the 'Mich' as it has been affectionately known by the young people in the local schools. An example of being affected by educational fashion is the Sixth Form College which was one of the earliest pioneers of that type of institution in the country. It was opened as the first purpose-built college in the country by Harold Wilson in its new buildings on a memorable day in April 1970.

Elsewhere in this volume others have remarked on the importance of the coal industry and the pot-banks to the local economy. As those industries demanded more cheap, unskilled or semi-skilled labour, so the housing and schools expanded: as they contracted, so painfully have the schools. Of course, the trends have not quite matched because the contraction of the 1930s was concealed by a rise in the school-leaving age, which brought a greater demand for school places. Later, however, in the 1970s and 1980s the demographic decline caused by a fall in the birth rate was reinforced by a contracting demand too for unskilled and semi-skilled labour.

Stoke was at first proud of the creation and achievements of its grammar schools, but by the 1960s it was persuaded along with most of the rest of the country that the price of success for the few – about 20 per cent who passed the 11+ exam – was at the expense of reinforcing the expectation of failure for the many (about 80 per cent) in the secondary modern schools.

VICIOUS CIRCLES

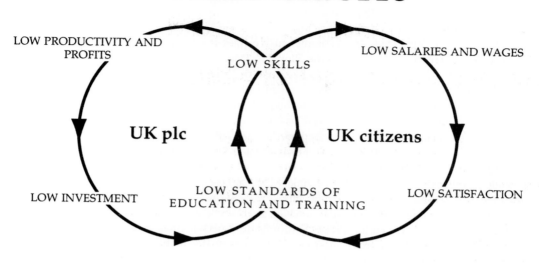

VIRTUOUS CIRCLES

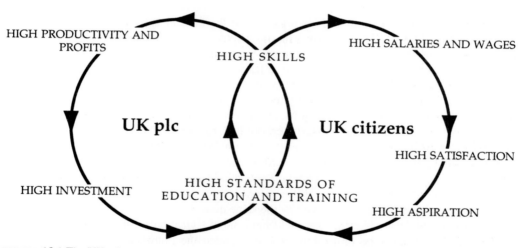

FIGURE 18.1 The UK education dilemma (*Source*: Royal Society of Arts, *The role of post-compulsory eduation and training*, 1990).

Comprehensive ideals were, therefore, embraced as they were in the whole country, not because somebody had worked out how to run the schools which would provide success for the whole ability range but because the evident injustices of any selection process at the age of eleven could scarcely be justified. Harold Wilson, in launching Circular 10/65, did so on a promise of 'grammar school education for everyone'. In the years that were to follow, the teachers in Stoke tried to make sense of it on the ground. Mostly and not unnaturally they organized their comprehensive schools into A, B, C, D, E, F, G and H general ability 'streams', so that pupils could move up and down without the difficulty which would have obtained when they were separate schools. Subliminally, of course, the feeling of failure for those in the bottom of eight streams was difficult to overcome.

When Stoke reorganized along comprehensive lines it embraced a transfer age of twelve, following the recommendations of the Plowden Report, thus establishing first, middle and combined schools for pupils aged 5–8, 8–12 and 5–12 respectively. Indeed, Stoke researched far and wide before embarking on the changed system: it even published for its teachers *The American journey*, a description of the outcome of a visit to the USA to establish the lessons to be learned from that country's long-established comprehensive schooling system. Its secondary schools in the main – there were exceptions for the Catholics – took youngsters to the age of sixteen when they could transfer to the newly-created Sixth Form College at Fenton. For those unable to obtain a place there or with a more practical bent, there were places available in Cauldon College or Stoke-on-Trent Technical College. By the late 1970s, however, Stoke had a bad bout of 'falling rolls' – the jargon phrase educationalists used to describe the problems caused by a declining school population which itself was the outcome of ever lower birth rates following the baby boom in the 1960s. Staffordshire, which had taken over local government's responsibility as the LEA from Stoke-on-Trent County Borough on reorganization in 1974, finally grappled with the problem in the early 1980s. The age range was changed back from twelve to eleven and middle schools, so recently established, were abolished and first and middle schools were combined as primary schools. At first the extra age group thus transferred to the secondary schools was reckoned to 'do the trick' so far as the worst of falling rolls was concerned for secondary education. There were to be some closures and amalgamations, but not as many as would have had to have been the case if the transfer age had been retained at age twelve. Or so it seemed. In fact, it was a messy miscalculation: the numbers in one age group, which was the important factor rather than the total number across the age range 11–16, had been overestimated. A second wave of reorganizations followed three or four years later as the full impact of falling rolls was properly appreciated.

Some secondary schools had a half-life of a year or two. Identities were lost, created and lost again. All the teachers lost their jobs, applied for them again and lost them once more. As the new schools were so messily created at the end of the 1980s, the national government claimed that the Great Debate, which James Callaghan had launched about quality in his Ruskin speech of 1976, was to be concluded in the Education Reform Act of 1988. For Stoke teachers in Stoke schools it was heralding yet more turmoil of change after a most troubled decade.

In summary, Stoke-on-Trent had lived by the same double standards as the rest of the nation: education's success was rationed. There was one sort of education for the leaders and another for the led. In the main the future leaders had attended the grammar school, while the led attended 'all age' and, after the Second World War, new secondary modern schools. There were, of course, individual pupils who beat the 'failure' designed into the system, but the 11+ exam reduced the total pupil cohort to a grammar school select band of 20–30 per cent, which diminished once again to a tiny fraction going on with their education after the old School Certificate (later O Level), having reached the age of sixteen. It is difficult to believe that in the 'good old days' of the 1950s, 85 per cent left school with no examination qualification at all. Many of the grammar school 20 per cent left at fifteen or sixteen to take apprenticeships or to enter jobs that would enable them slowly to climb the ladder of the professions. The few who stuck to the last final lap between sixteen and eighteen were reduced to about 3 per cent who entered higher education. Those who had been sifted long ago at the 11+ exam went to work as soon as they could, in the factories, in the pot-banks or on the land. There was some economic, if not moral, justification for such a system. The heavy industries – coal, steel, ship-building, manufacture, the mills and the pot-banks – demanded millions of people prepared to take an unskilled or semi-skilled job. True, the same industries provided a number of jobs for the well-educated who trained for specialist employment and leadership, but the proportion was comparatively insignificant. Stoke-on-Trent represents not commuter land but any of the proud Victorian midland and northern cities: its story could be that of Newcastle upon Tyne, Leicester, Manchester, Sheffield or Leeds. South Wales would understand it too and so would the inhabitants of Belfast and Glasgow. Some people always railed against the unfairness of the system but most were so busy and fulfilled going about their worthwhile tasks, whether skilled or unskilled, that they did not give it too much thought.

All that has now changed. There are no longer millions of unskilled and semi-skilled jobs. Technology has transformed society. We live uneasily with three million or more unemployed. Moreover, the government has set new targets for higher education. The 3 or 4 per cent reckoned capable of taking advantage of some form of higher education in the late 1950s is now considered to be 30 or 40 per cent.

'Never mind lad, I have had a word with the foreman down at the pot-bank and there is a place for you there, when school's over' is a comment that was once frequently heard in many a Potteries' home, when difficulties were encountered at school. Meanwhile, in the schools in the face of pupils' lack of commitment and achievement, teachers shrugged in despair, wondering understandably what could be expected from children whose families lacked any educational ambition or were unsupportive, even hostile to the whole process. It was hard to escape the view that such families regarded school as little more than a child-minding service. In the main a compromise was tacitly agreed between home and school – the worst sort of collusion in the turbulence of adolescence: 'You don't bother us and we won't bother you'. Nowadays amongst the unemployed, the parents can remember the comments about the 'job on the line', but it is not one that they are likely to make to their own youngsters who are having trouble in their teenage years. They know their own jobs as adults have gone, or will shortly go, and their despair communicates itself to the next generation.

The tale of educational management in Stoke, therefore, is not all that different from the rest of the UK. In the post-war period education had been regarded in an uncomplicated way, as a 'good thing' which it could be assumed most of the community would value in some way. Little attention needed to be paid to the way it was done in a classroom.

It is important to make clear that none of this is to be laid at the door of individual teachers. It was simply the climate which affected all they did. Much of what went on in individual classrooms was outstanding with some extraordinary and inspired teachers who unlocked rich veins of talent in many youngsters and adults. Stoke, indeed, with its great artistic tradition can probably point to more of that than most. What was singularly lacking, however, both at national and local level, was any focused attention to the development of quality. Educational administrators and their politicians assumed that, as they built more science laboratories, more modern language facilities, more youth clubs and more adult education centres, quality would be their inevitable companion as they expanded the 'good thing', namely ever more 'educational opportunities'. Of course, they knew the qualities and skills of the teacher in the classroom were important but they believed – although with the benefit of hindsight it can be seen to be an inadequate belief – that the solution lay mainly in *how* teachers were *initially* trained. It is difficult to remember that, until the publication in 1979 of Michael Rutter's *Fifteen thousand hours*, most people had thought that schools could not make much of a difference to your life's chances. His research and the findings of HMI in *Ten good schools* changed all that. It ushered in a decade when researchers such as Peter Mortimore, Barbara Tizzard, John Tomlinson, Sally Tomlinson and a host of others (all of whom took account of the much more extensive research in the USA and Canada) began to reveal more and more about school success.[1] Gradually, it has become possible to identify characteristics of successful schooling. Even more promising has been the analysis of some of the processes of schooling and how they might be made more rather than less successful. Sadly, such research was not available to national and local policy makers at the one point in our history when one educational policy was poised to break the cycle of deprivation.

It was in the late 1960s. A H Halsey had written his seminal book *Origins and destinations*,[2] which exposed the failure of the grammar school system to even up life's chances for the children of the working class in places like Stoke-on-Trent. (Indeed his influence acted as a spur to the comprehensive movement.) He became adviser to the Labour government and for a brief period aided and abetted by others, such as Michael Young, Halsey persuaded the Labour ministers to launch the educational priority programme (EPA). Stoke like other heavily industralized areas benefited from its follow-up, the social priority area programme (SPA). This development the LEAs of the time saw as a means of getting both new school buildings to replace those which were worn out and more money for teachers. A few LEAs intervened in the pre-school years with expanded nursery education provision. The 'Red House' project in Denaby in the West Riding was one of a few which pioneered work with families in disadvantaged areas. For most LEAs, however, it was an opportunity to get more cash and to do more of what was 'a good thing'. There was even a legitimate concern that to label schools as SPA was to reinforce the 'leper effect', thereby reinforcing the very under-achievement which the scheme was intended to overcome.

Not only did this one attempt precede our knowledge of successful schools, it was also launched prior to the emerging evidence of the 'Headstart' programme launched in the USA in 1965, which involves the parents and starts at the birth of the first child. This scheme has subsequently justified pre-school investment by evidence of enormous saving in public expenditure in special programmes and custodial provisions in the teenage years[3] (Table 18.1). In any case the oil-crisis swept away the EPA programme. Not only was it launched ahead of its time and without the benefits of the research into effective schooling and the value of nursery provision but it also preceded the change in the industrial outlook which, with chronic high unemployment, underlines the need now for a changed educational agenda.

It is, however, possible to see from the evidence of the EPA project all those years ago, the three important factors which contribute to changed outlook. They are all to do with attitudes and expectations among first teachers, secondly pupils and thirdly the parents. If logic suggests that of these groups teachers are the first and the most important group to tackle – it would after all be fairly pointless to attempt to change the hopes and aspirations of children and parents if they continue to attend schools where the prevailing attitude remains 'Well what more can you expect of these children' – it is by no means clear that the other two will follow automatically without some form of intervention. Far more conducive to improvement in any case would be a determination to do something about all three interest groups more or less simultaneously.

Table 18.1

The effects till age nineteen of high quality nursery education in the USA

Categories	Group who attended pre-school	Group who did not attend pre-school
Percentage employed	59	32
Percentage graduating from high school or equivalent	67	49
Percentage with college or vocational training	38	21
Percentage ever detained or arrested	31	51
Percentage of school years in special education	16	28
Rate of teenage pregnancies per 100 (females only)	64	117
Functional competence score (highest possible score = 40)	24.6	21.8

Source: Quoted in K Sylva and P Moss, *Learning before school*, National Commission on Education Briefing Paper No 8, 1992.

THE TWO TOWNS PROJECT

It is a combination of the above events, projects and history which the Two Towns Project in Stoke-on-Trent has sought to address. What is the Two Towns Project? The towns concerned are Tunstall and Burslem, two of the constituents of the city of Stoke-on-Trent. The project was born in 1989 as a result originally of discussions between Keele and the county chief education officer. The purpose is to raise ambitions, expectations and achievement among the young people in the locality. Although the starting point is the three county high schools in the area – Brownhills, Haywood and James Brindley – the intention is ultimately to affect for the better the educational culture of the whole community.

Initially, a steering group agreed targets for attendance, GCSE performance, staying-on rates post-sixteen, and entrance to higher education. The steering group is led by Staffordshire's chief education officer, Dr Philip Hunter, and includes representatives of the Sixth Form College, Stoke-on-Trent College, the Newcastle Tertiary College, the three 11–16 high schools in Tunstall and Burslem, the two universities and representatives of the LEA inspectorate and careers service. The intention beyond the targets is, as implied, to transform expectations and achievements amongst students in the three high schools and ultimately in the whole community.

At first the scheme coupled self-generated interventions within the schools themselves with a promise to the youngsters and their parents at about year 9 (age 13+) that the two universities would between them guarantee entry to higher education on the single proviso that the aspiring student was of serious intent and could show that he/she was committed to the study which he/she wished to pursue. Representatives of higher education appeared at parents' evenings and awards' ceremonies and broadly speaking, the message was encapsulated as follows:

It used to be the case that when we were young in the late 1950s, 3 per cent of the age group went on to university: now 17 per cent go on and the government intends that between 25 and 30 per cent will take advantage of university by the time you leave school. In the past people in this area have been under-represented and have not had their share of that expansion. The Two Towns Project has been set up because in this proud community which has contributed so much to the industrial wealth of the nation, there are diminished employment prospects. Youngsters, who have left school in the past to take jobs in local industries and business, will find that they are disappearing. It is vital that you believe in your special talent and abilities – your teachers believe that every one of you has that special talent – and that you turn it into reality. You have probably not thought seriously of staying on post-sixteen, still less of going to university. We want all of you at least to think both these things are a possibility and we are promising to give you extra help to do it. Local businesses are behind us.

The schools will provide extra clubs and classes – there will be summer schools including some at the university – and you will be guaranteed entry either to Stoke, Newcastle or the Sixth Form College and then on to a university to anyone who wants it enough.

Most important, however, has been the way in which each school has systematically tackled the issues of school improvement. Research on school effectiveness tells everyone all the characteristics evident in successful schools. What the research does not reveal as obviously is how a school can become a place where these characteristics appear.

At Keele a centre for successful schools has been established. It is a combination of research and consultancy activity: case studies in twenty comprehensive schools in six authorities have been undertaken and workshops have been provided for others to disseminate the lessons which emerge. These studies have identified various classifications which imply processes that can be tackled with greater likelihood of success. These process classifications are as follows:

Process	*Positive characteristics*
1. Leadership (at all levels within the school).	Associated with strong, purposeful . . . more than one style effective.
2. Management and organization.	Clear, simple (not over-elaborate – the larger the school the more difficult).
3. Collective self review.	Involving all staff and leading to overall aims, principles and as part of a review of all innovation and practices over a period.
4. Staff development.	Systematic and involving both collective and individual needs.
5. Environmental building. Uplifting ethos.	Visually and aurally with positive behaviour patterns among school staff and pupils. High expectations.
6. Teaching and learning	Debate among teachers about curriculum and teaching methods – leadership evidenced by head.
7. Parental involvement.	Emphasis on parents as prior and joint educators.

It is of course only a start to seek to identify the processes and the detailed characteristics associated with them. For a school to claim success it should:

be impatient to improve the educational progress and scholastic success of all pupils. Educational progress and scholastic success will certainly cover success in our national curriculum elements of knowledge, understanding science, social, personal, and aesthetic awareness and practical competencies. The school will have measures for each of those and will be seeking principally for the individual and each successive age group to improve on previous performance: it will be mindful of but not preoccupied by the comparative success of other schools both in very different and apparently comparable circumstances. Above all it will be devoted to finding the particular talent of each and every one of its pupils as a foundation on which to build confidence in other activities.

involve parent(s) as closely as possible in the educational and scholastic progress of their children.

employ staff who are generous and intellectually curious besides being competent in a variety of techniques of classroom and whole school activity. By 'generous' we mean teachers who are prepared to treat children as they might become as opposed to as they sometimes infuriatingly are and who feel obliged to go far beyond the call of 'duty' for their pupils. Such teachers will be optimistic, self-critical and as we have implied intellectually curious in their subject and about the age range of children whom they teach.

have pupils who in their everyday behaviour in the classroom, in the corridors and above all in the playground and outside the school and the local community, show that they think of others, eschew violence orally and physically as a means of settling arguments and take seriously their obligations to others as members of the school and a wider community.

At first Brownhills High School, Haywood High School and James Brindley High School in their different ways have sought to tackle each of these issues. Their initiatives have ranged from reviewing the way in which decisions are made through the responsibilities within the school management process to comparing notes on parents' evening. Daybooks have been started, homework practices rigorously evaluated, marking schemes checked, and extra classes and clubs have been laid on and marketed. The translation of values and expectations into appropriate rewards-and-punishments systems has begun. It is not the purpose of this chapter to chronicle the detail of the various measures undertaken. It is important to stress, however, that the Two Towns exercise has shown the importance of 'melody' or 'pitch' in school improvement exercise: it is simply not enough to believe there is a detailed – as opposed to a broad-brush – recipe which can be applied to effect school improvement in every case. What works in one place may not work in another. The important ingredient is the way in which the processes are carried out. This seems to confirm that management by the objective approach (target setting) will bring only partial success unless the drive for quality within an institution encompasses a trust in individuals at all levels to make wise choices when faced with divergent possible answers. Wise choices are at the heart of the processes of school improvement. Any school taking seriously the issue of improvement recognizes the highly-skilled judgments that need continually to be made about the context in which various measures are taken.

In addition to the simple factual outcomes, attention has been given to devising a means of assessing pupils' attitudes towards their teachers and their commitment to work, and a similar approach is being pioneered to the same end for parents. This development was part of our work on school effectiveness, based on the assumptions of John Gray in Sheffield who had outlined *inter alia* three key factors or performance indicators which might be a reasonable proxy for school's success: academic progress; pupil satisfaction; and whether or not a child has a meaningful relationship with at least one member of staff.

So far most work at Keele has been on pupil satisfaction where an instrument has been devised consisting of about 40 questions which cover certain important information in respect of pupil habits, such as the number of nights out a week, their time spent on homework and watching television, and also, *more importantly*, it includes questions which enable us to ascertain three factors: *their attitude to their teachers; their commitment to their work; and their general satisfaction with schooling.* In our more general work with schools we are careful to secure that the questionnaire is administered in controlled circumstances, for example, at the same time of the school year and to a random 25 per cent sample of each age group. In this way schools are able to analyse their comparative positions against the growing average response as well as against schools chosen to represent broadly similar circumstances. Over a period they will be able to measure pupil satisfaction, attitude and commitment against their own previous scores and see whether school improvement measures have had any effect.

In the Two Towns themselves, however, more extensive surveys were carried out on the attitudes held by all students in their last year of compulsory schooling. We sought to establish their attitudes in particular towards staying on. Moreover, we compared them with those of a group of youngsters in a very similar area of Manchester, a more cosmopolitan city which acts as a greater magnet to new commerce and population. The studies carried out in both cities indicated a correlation between staying on post-sixteen and whether one or more of the parents stayed on post-sixteen; the students had enjoyed their education in secondary schools; and they thought that a particular course of action led to personal financial advantage. Our interpretation of the work has relied not merely on the questionnaire but more extensive interviews with a sample of the young people involved.

The second point has given evidence for the schools to follow up in their school improvement strategies. The first and third factors have underlined the need to find new ways of affecting the general cultural expectations of the community if yet more generations of citizens are not to be tempted towards short-term financial reward at the expense of developing their full potential both for their own good and those of others.

There is now established a growing confidence within the secondary schools of the Two Towns about raised expectations. There is, however, unambiguous agreement that such progress while encouraging – staying on rates post-sixteen have more than doubled as have GCSE success rates (Tables 18.2 and 3) – conceals the need to do far more to change the climate as far as pupils and parents are concerned. It still remains the case that it is better for a youngster within his or, less obviously, her (girls' attitudes are more positive towards schooling than boys) peer group to disguise a determination to succeed. Moreover, the prevailing culture outside the school in a period and an area of high unemployment remains one of resigned despair. Stoke has more than its fair share of crime, drugs, and families wrestling with inadequate or no housing.

So what is the next step for the Two Towns project and what are the implications for the rest of the education system? First we are aiming to reaffirm our shared intentions by drawing together various interest groups – inspectors; pre-five agencies in the statutory and voluntary sectors; primary schools; business and community interest groups; parents and the various support agencies such as educational welfare and school psychology. The outcome is intended to be an ongoing forum for representatives of such groups to come together locally to take stock of progress and setbacks encountered, so that the alliance, rather than the disaggregated sum of the individuals, seeks to tackle the issue. It is hoped that most importantly the pre-school agencies will be better coordinated, schools will steadily improve, and there should be a gradual turnaround in peer group and parental pressure in favour of the efforts being made by the staff in schools.

Table 18.2

Staying-on rates post-sixteen, 1989–92

Area	Percentage of pupils staying on				Percentage increase in staying-on rate, 1989–92
	1989	1990	1991	1992	
Two Towns average	22	26	35	46	109
Stoke-on-Trent average	29	31	42	49	68
Staffordshire average	40	46	52	59	48
National average	48	53	61	–	–

Source: UK Heads of Careers Service Group, *The 1991 school leavers' destination report*; Staffordshire Careers Service.

What, however, does this project really represent that is replicable and how might it be spread? The involvement of a university with a LEA and a Training and Enterprise Council seems to be a factor of some importance. The missing agencies are police, social services, health, housing and recreation; in this event the advent of unitary authorities following the present review of local government, which seems likely to be guided by community interest and identity, seems to offer promise of solving at least some of the difficulties of different agencies not acting in concert to solve common problems. The active involvement and commitment of *all* agencies are vital if a catalyst is to be applied to the process of changing a community's culture away from despair towards achievement.

Secondly, we return to the points already made. We know far more about school improvement than at any previous time in the development of our education system. While it would be dangerously simplistic to suggest that the application of the various strategies towards school improvement would be productive without due allowance for context, it is certainly the case that no school gets worse which adopts these stratagems and most seem to improve. What is now needed is a much more vigorous dissemination of findings and a concentration of effort on disadvantaged urban areas where the benefits of school improvement and community regeneration are most needed.

As we have found in the Two Towns, however, school improvement is not enough. So what more is to be done? As a nation we have a choice. On the one hand we can continue to apply

Table 18.3

Percentage of pupils achieving five or more GCSE grades A to C

Area	Percentage of pupils					Percentage increase in number of pupils, 1988–93
	1988	1989	1990	1991	1992	
Two Towns average	10.4	14.6	12.5	16.4	19.8	90.4
Staffordshire average	22.6	27.0	29.3	32.1	33.2	46.9
National average	25.4	28.9	31.2	34.2	38.1	50.0

Source: Staffordshire Education Department, examination statistics.

sticking plaster, increase the police, patch up the physical and human damage which increases year by year, and admire those who devote their life – a diminishing number – in uncoordinated but heroic attempts to change the climate in such communities from despair to hope and a reasonable expectation of success. On the other hand we could build on what research has shown in the last 25 years, namely that the cycle of failure can be reversed especially now that we have ceased to ration success to the highest reaches of the education system.

We now need the creation of a community development programme built on the principles and lessons of 'Headstart', the education priority area programme, and more recently city challenge. The target would quite consciously be those communities where the closure of long-standing or heavy industries has left the population in economic trauma and despair. No longer in such communities can one generation pass on to the next the security of unskilled or semi-skilled employment. In such circumstances crime, drugs, drink, debt, despair and destabilization of decent living beckon. A focused programme could reverse that. What are the educational ingredients of such a community development programme? There are probably five:

Pre-school programme. We know from the 'Headstart' programme in the USA and from work in Scandinavia (Table 18.1) there is even an economic pay-off as well as the moral justification in investment in the pre-school years. The ingredients may vary but it certainly includes an educational role for a health visitor and a coordinated local approach for the provision of care and education from birth by child-minders, volunteers and all the statutory agencies represented by social services and education which together should organize extended day-care facilities beyond school hours and terms. The key to this will be to give primary headteachers in their communities and their governing bodies (with appropriate extended representation to reflect such a new interest) the responsibility to make contact at birth with the mother of each child so that toy library facilities and pre-school packages can be made available.

The primary years. As already implied, home-school liaison – the lessons of the shared reading and the maths schemes – must be disseminated. Schools should be staffed differentially – there should be at least two adults to each class. Schools need to have access to shared group workshops on school improvement practices as outlined above. The schools will also have access to a primary room in their local partner secondary schools. Curriculum continuity by way of environmental projects need to start in primary and be completed in secondary schooling. They can make use of such a facility. In the later primary years youngsters should have access to the Youth Awards Scheme, pioneered in Bristol, which enables in-school and out-of-school achievements to be seen in a progression of personal development which can lead to university. By this time too the youngster should start to have access to 'education extra'.

Education extra. A range of programmes, clubs and opportunities would be provided after school at weekends and in holiday periods. The features which would characterize this provision would be that it would be mixed-age and interest led. In this way individuals of all ages would cheerfully be able to use the programme as 'enrichment', 'substitution' or 'compensation' for the level of education which they have already achieved. Various people will contribute to these programmes – members of the community, the best of the staff in the school and the best staff from local universities and other visitors. What is envisaged is something analogous to what in the past has been seen as adult education programmes but different from them in that a high proportion of those participating will be the young, who regard the programme as part of their educational commitment in 'an out-of-school curriculum'. It will, moreover, be necessary not to confuse it with community programmes of recreation or after school care. The education extra clubs and workshops will be umbilically linked to the schools, for it is primarily the expectation of the younger generation which must be our priority to crack the cycle of deprivation and failure.

The secondary years. From the lessons of the Two Towns and all the research on school effectiveness, there is a myriad of school improvement initiatives which can be taken. In the teenage years where there is a dip in pupil motivation and expectation – in what is now called years 8, 9 and 10 – there is a need for intervention to mitigate the turbulent effects of peer group pressures. Extra classes for volunteers after school – quite different from education extra – seemed to be a promising way of legitimizing an ethos of achievement among that age group. There are, of course, other measures which work in practice and these are well rehearsed in the literature. What is now needed is to avoid their occurring simply in isolation. Staff who succeed against all the odds need to feel the warmth of allies in similar situations. That requires a national initiative.

Opportunities post-sixteen. Messages of the lifelong nature of educational opportunity and personal development need to be overt as well as subliminal. To be controversial it is about the one area of human activity where I am comfortable with the notion of propaganda. That is why the programme of 'community development' described here needs locally the active priority involvement of tertiary colleges, colleges of higher education and universities. Again the lessons of the Two Towns and other places suggest the 'accreditation' of schools by universities through their records of achievement. Messages to parents need to appear in school prospectuses from colleges and universities, explaining that higher education is no longer rationed but available to their children. There is a range of other measures including attendance at parents' evenings from representatives of the next stage of education. One of the lessons of the Two Towns is the need for universities to have criteria for local admission different from those applied to national applicants.

These five ingredients will only succeed if they are implemented by a committed partnership of a local LEA within a unitary local government authority which will thereby necessarily incorporate recreation, housing and social services, so that a holistic view can be taken of the issues. That authority too will need to link with other social agencies separated from it, such as the police and the health service. The whole of the local community needs to be on board: that means the voluntary bodies and the media as well, of course, as the local employers.

If there could be a national commission to oversee the scheme so much the better, for it would then be possible to share the lessons of the successes and setbacks encountered on the way. The local partnerships require charismatic leadership. Such leadership needs to come from reformed LEAs in partnership with a university. The LEAs of the future will be agencies quite different from the past. Compulsory competitive tendering, the removal of responsibilities for further education and higher education, the combined effects of the rules of local management and the prospective rearrangement of management for the careers service and inspection mean that LEAs will not be providers of service themselves, save in services to individuals for grants, but rather securers of provisions. They will be less concerned with being a manager, a planner, an organizer, still less a major employer. Freed of those time-consuming activities, which involve often a conflict of loyalty, and armed with the evidence of school effectiveness and improvement, they could become the leaders of a crusade for education improvement and for the development of quality in education. There are likely to be more and smaller LEAs as a result of the forthcoming reorganization of local government, a commission for which is suggesting that a sense of identity will be a key criterion for the emerging new pattern. It should, therefore, be possible to have a clearer focus for the sort of task argued for here as a result of the experience locally in the Two Towns of Stoke-on-Trent. A LEA for Stoke-on-Trent would know both the areas and the priorities to target. Much of the time of their leading members and officers would be spent in showing interest and celebrating the progress being made.

So far no mention has been made of the cost to transform inner city areas. Of far greater importance than the extra resources necessary – and justice demands some redistribution of wealth towards such areas – is the shift of priorities of those involved. Part of the condition of a grant to a local university could be its demonstration of the spending of a small percentage of its budget in support of such work. Similarly, the local authority concerned could have targeted funds and the Charity Commission could, through a local community chest, harness the efforts of charitable trusts and industrialists to the recreation of self-confidence and competence in such neglected and abused communities. The TECs could also be required to focus a percentage of their grant. In short, partnerships could be guaranteed through funding mechanisms.

The reasons for previous lack of success are complex. Initiatives such as the education priority area programme were tried before knowledge of school improvement was developed: moreover, they were wounded by the obstacles of a previous local government reorganization in 1974, with no continuity of personnel, and they eventually ran into the buffers of an oil-crisis which put an end to the 'party' of local government public spending. But now it is known that the 'Headstart' programme in the USA did work: now we are aware of how schools can be improved even if nobody any longer has any grand ideas of extravagant public expenditure. So a scheme could initially be targeted to those metropolitan districts where there is the need and where in any case local government is not to be reorganized. And where it is to be reorganized we already know the order of that reoganization. Derby, Bristol, Stockton, Hartlepool, Middlesbrough, Hull, Scunthorpe, Grimsby and Durham are all in the first phase of local government reorganization.

There is an American saying that 'if something is not broke it don't need fixing'. That is true of much of the English and Welsh education system. Schools in Burford, in Sonning Common, in Ripon, in Thirsk, and in the rural areas 'don't need fixing'. Of course, there is under-expectation and under-achievement in all areas, but often it is within communities with high expectation where the odds are that a younster will be swept along by the pressure of a peer group to succeed. That is simply not true in the inner city areas. The challenge of the ten years which will straddle the dawn of a new millenium, from 1995 say to 2005, is whether we can ourselves organize and harness the knowledge we possess to make the next big push forward in educational progress.

REFERENCES

1. T Brighouse and J Tomlinson, *Successful schools*, 1991.
2. A H Halsey, *Origins and destinations: family, class and education in modern Britain*, Oxford, 1980.
3. K Sylva and P Moss, *Learning before school*, National Commission on Education Briefing Paper No 8, 1992.

19. Cultural Traditions in the Potteries

RAY JOHNSON

The Potteries conurbation has a traditional image of smoke and grime even today, nearly forty years after the Clean Air Act. The old skyline of bottle-shaped pottery kilns helped make it recognizably different from other industrial cities, and its quirky accent and dialect – now helping to sell nostalgic books on 'Arfer Towk Rate' (how to talk right) – set it apart from its more familiar neighbours Manchester and Birmingham.

Arnold Bennett, a native of the Potteries, claimed, 'My native heath . . . has the reputation of being quite unlike the rest of England, but when I set foot in it after absence, it seems to me the most English piece of England that I ever came across. With extraordinary clearness I see it as absurdly, ridiculously, spendidly English.'[1] Although London and Paris nurtured him, Bennett's roots lay in the smoky air and cobbled streets of the pottery towns he immortalized, and which provided the background for his formative years. It was Bennett more than anyone, who gave the 'Five Towns' a national and international profile. His books celebrating the life of the townsman, as Thomas Hardy's celebrated that of the countryman, achieved universality in a regional setting.

Neither the image of Stoke-on-Trent nor that of the individual towns is associated with culture. Even in the ceramics field, the image is that of the safe, the well-known and the traditional. By contrast, in the 1930s, innovative potters such as Clarice Cliffe and Susie Cooper were linked to Stoke-on-Trent, and this was reflected in outsiders' perceptions of the city'.[2] Any attempt to 'represent' Stoke-on-Trent in any art or media form is immediately rounded upon from within the Potteries as missing the target. Being a linear city, with nearly twelve miles between the most distant boundaries, makes for much variation in character – even in dialect and accent – and activity. Hanley (the 'town centre') is both the major town and a barrier beyond which there is little need to travel. (People from Tunstall or Burslem rarely – some never – visit Longton or Fenton, and vice-versa.) Stoke-on-Trent lacks the 'feel' of cities of comparable size; there is very much a 'small town' atmosphere here.

In terms of major professional venues for theatre, concerts and other art forms, the area is relatively poorly equipped. Despite a good, modern museum and theatre (the New Victoria), many of the larger venues are in a poor state of repair. Although the Queen's Theatre in Burslem has had its auditorium refurbished with new seating, this has been done primarily to make what was once a ballroom multi-purpose again. The Theatre Royal in Hanley – reopened just over ten years ago – has never received a full refurbishment, and still looks dowdy inside. The Victoria Hall in Hanley is the chief, and acoustically best, concert hall, with the King's Hall in Stoke occasionally used for cultural events. Other large venues (ex-cinemas, ex-chapels) are closed and empty, and have been so for some years. The Empire – a Victorian theatre in Longton, long closed and due to be restored and reopened by a repertory company – was recently burned down. There are, of course, many smaller venues, some in community or council buildings, others in educational institutions. Although the council owns or manages a range of buildings, it rarely promotes directly arts events.

Perhaps we should be looking for culture with a small 'c'. The city is made up of many small community units, and people identify with these rather than the conurbation as a whole. It is inadequate to consider it simply as one city or as six towns. A short journey of, say, half a mile from Porthill to Burslem takes one through Longport, Trubshaw Cross, Dalehall and Middleport – all recognized communities.

There has been, since Wesley, a strong methodist tradition, and this nonconformism has had its cultural offshoots – music being the strongest tradition, and strongest in choral singing, glee clubs and brass bands attached to religious groupings. Mixed- and male-voice choirs are the most numerous, with choirs such as the Ceramic City Choir and the Daleian Singers among the best respected. Music has probably always been the most practised art form in the city, with more musical events than any other advertised in the local press. Most amateur associations and societies are concerned in some way with music as audience or performers.

Bennett, in a visit to a music-hall entertainment at the Grand Theatre, Hanley, commented on the performance of a group of 'songsters':

There were twenty of them standing in a sort of flattened semi-circle – the women in white and the men in scarlet hunting coats, with the conductor in knee breeches and silk stockings. Ordinary northern men and women – you could tell that – but they had class. They could really sing. They really had voices. They brought the house down every time! It was the folk themselves giving something back to the folk in artistic form.[3]

Music-making here was regarded as equal to the best in the land during the nineteenth century, up to the early years of Beecham: Elgar's 'King Olaf' was premiered in Hanley's Victoria Hall. The Victoria Hall, the Queen's Theatre, Burslem, the Lecture Theatre in the City Museum and Art Gallery, the chapel at Keele University and the New Victoria Theatre are now the main venues for concerts of classical music. The Theatre Royal, Hanley, presents musicals by the long-established amateur operatic societies, although the North Staffordshire Operatic Society (recently celebrating its centenary) still presents its shows at the Queen's Theatre, Burslem.

As for dance, there are thirty or so privately run dance schools in the city, but few touring professional dance companies come here. The Theatre Royal has been the major venue for visiting companies, but the smaller Mitchell Memorial Theatre, mostly used for the staging of amateur drama, is favoured for more experimental dance groups. There is still no dance studio available for public access and for dancers to 'work out' in on a regular basis. In the 1950s and 1960s, however, the city was a popular venue for visiting dance companies such as Sadlers Wells and the Arts Council's 'Ballet for All' scheme, and their performances were always well supported.

Clog dancing was as popular here as in other northern conurbations. Bennett, after his visit to the Grand Theatre, Hanley, wrote:

The most touching item for me was a lady clog dancer. Hanley was the centre of a land of clogs – I've wakened in winter darkness to the sound of clogs on slushy pavements. And when I think of clogs I think of the knocker-up, and hurried fire-lighting, and tea and thick bread, and the factory gates, and the terrible time-keeper standing there with his clock! Now clogs have nearly gone out of the working life – but here they re-appear in clog dancing! Once done in public houses by people who next day would clatter to work in clogs!

As I lumbered home in the electric tramcar – besieged by printed requests from the tramway company not on any account to spit – I could not help thinking and thinking, in a very trite way, that Art is a wonderful thing![4]

With regard to popular music, the present scene is much less dominated by large venues than was the case in the 1950s and 1960s. The Embassy Ballroom, in Burslem, was the main stage for jazz bands, and big bands, jazz bands and rock groups played at such arenas as the Embassy, Trentham Gardens Ballroom and the town halls. In the early 1960s, Stoke boasted the very first disco outside London – the Place – which is still one of the most popular night clubs. Large dance and performance venues were also built: the Adulte in Burslem (now demolished), the Crystal (now Fatty Arbuckle's) in neighbouring Newcastle and Jollees in Longton (now closed). The Stoke Folk Club was started up in the early 1960s at the Red Lion public house in Stoke, and remained very popular through to the 1970s. The folk music scene is still part of the national folk club circuit, and is based at the Albion public house in Hanley, the Potteries Folk Club holding an annual festival with visiting artists. The 1980s was the era of the Bridge Street Arts Centre in Newcastle as a major venue for jazz and other music, and for major visiting performers. It is now less prominent, and the main rock venue is the Wheatsheaf public house in Stoke, although many local pubs regularly put on live bands. On surprising thing is that the Potteries has never produced a band or solo artist of national stature, unless one accepts the Climax Blues Band or Jackie Trent.

But the large music societies, and choral singing, would most identify the tradition of music in the city. 'The Potteries sings because it is racially musical', said Bennett in his journals; 'it rushes away from the factory gates to the rehearsal room because it does veritably love music. . . This is amateurism at its best. I do not know how many choral societies there may be in the Potteries; but when recently one of its favourite conductors died, five choirs and ten thousand people attended his funeral.'[5]

The other great passion Bennett observed was for football:

Grown men no longer play at marbles, as they used to when I went to school. Of the more ancient diversions, pigeon-flying alone remains a very harmless hobby. Football alone reigns supreme and has no serious rival. The Potteries was one of the first centres of football, and in the history of the Association game the name of Stoke-on-Trent is glorious. Football has the characteristics of force and violence and spectacular bigness which could not fail to attract such a race as the potters. Cricket is much practised, and golf waxes yearly, but there is nothing like football in North Staffordshire. . . There you have the Pottery character symbolised: Football and Music![6]

One surprising omission is a tradition of local folk-songs. It is odd that a large conurbation, largely devoted to one industry, that of making pottery, should not have given birth to folk-songs with local themes. Of course, the area also has a strong mining community, but the miners' folk-songs are imports from other coal-mining communities. One or two local songs were recorded as part of the research for an early Victoria Theatre documentary, but local folk-singer Jeff Parton suggests that it is more likely that in the Potteries folk-songs were not researched and noted as in other areas, and such that existed have now been lost, rather than there being no folk-songs at all. But it has also been argued that all the local creative singing energy went into choral singing, glee clubs, chapel singing and hymns. In this 'chapel' culture in the past, each small pot-bank was a patriarchal working unit, with masters and workers worshipping and singing in the same chapel. In Wakes week (August Bank Holiday) there were always chapel outings – regular visits to Derbyshire for clear air and clean thoughts. There were Sunday-school outings and, on Good Friday, children at the north end of the conurbation were walked to Knypersley Pool, some picnicking, some staying over for Easter weekend. Within the six towns, there was the annual Trentham Thursday during Wakes week, many people journeying to Trentham by canal, and masters and workpeople mixing freely and socially for the one time in the year. Perhaps the nearest semblances to folk-songs are those locally-written, anonymous poems featured in Victorian copies of the workers' publication, the *Potter's Examiner*, and set to music (sometimes to traditional tunes) by Jeff Parton and others for inclusion in the Victoria Theatre's musical documentaries.

The visual arts and drama follow a less strong tradition. Of greatest cultural importance in the visual arts has been the pottery industry itself. The local body of artistic talent has hung on the coat-tails of the pottery industry. Up to the seventeenth century, local pottery design can be regarded as a folk art, a high point being the energetic and bold slipware designs on the large 'Toft' platters, many examples of which are on show in the City Museum. Since the eighteenth century, many artists who came or who were brought here worked for the pottery industry. Pottery design has always required a plentiful supply of artistic cannon-fodder, from top designers down to the army of ceramic decorators.

There is probably more artistic talent per square mile in Stoke-on-Trent than any other city. Most of the local art activity still bears allegiance to that pottery-based tradition. The craft attitude has been paramount: whatever the piece of work, it must be well made and well done. Ideas have generally been subjugated to craft, in the broadest sense of doing a job well, but that has often become an end in itself whether or not the particular piece deserved that amount of attention.

Traits of the pottery industry have permeated to other local art activity. And, unlike other places, women have always been an important group in local artistic activity. Many women work as paintresses and decorators, and women have always been wage-earners since the growth of the pottery industry. It is productive, cultural work, and many named artists are women.

The Burslem Art School has a strong history of nurturing, with a vocational bias, artistic talent in the region. It has acted as a humane-cultural centre, much more than a mere training school. Many of its ex-students have gone on to form societies – with people pooling their creative resources and putting on exhibitions. Artists tend not to get together, but here they have founded very active societies – there has clearly been a *need* to get together. There is still also much home-based painting activity, and most of this would never feature in exhibitions.

Non-ceramic artists in the Potteries have tended to fall into two categories: those who become well known and *leave*, and those who remain and are not nationally recognized. It has always seemed a place to get away from in order to get on: there are many good artists who have come *from* Stoke-on-Trent. As for subject matter, it has been observed that many local artists have remained parochial – looking inwards at immediate and local issues, rather than having a universal outlook. C W Brown, Reginald Haggar, Jack Simcock, and now Arthur Berry clearly take their inspiration from the local scene, although, in the 1950s in particular, there was a feeling that what is regarded as great art always *is* very provincial. Indeed, in a letter to a Lucie Simpson in June 1903, Arnold Bennett wrote:

I have been well satisfied with the great reception of the book [*Anna of the Five Towns*], but I dare say that you are aware that in the Potteries itself it has been gravely misunderstood by a lot of people . . . I don't comprehend your general objection to 'provincial novels', seeing that the majority of all the greatest novels in the world are provincial.[7]

There are possibly fewer nationally-recognized creative figures in the Potteries than in most comparable conurbations, and most left the district – from Arnold Bennett, Havergal Brian, and Oliver Lodge to novelist Charles Tomlinson, playwright Peter Whelan, and poet John Wain. However, when it comes to the amateur tradition, then the area has been rich in the various artistic activities.

Like many cities, Stoke-on-Trent has always received a large proportion of its culture 'on tour'. It has had its share of all kinds of theatre. The Theatre Royal has had famous touring companies, as had previous theatres such as the Grand and Empire. The New Victoria Theatre has acquired a national reputation for its innovative musical documentaries, and is committed to staging a blend of theatre classics and contemporary plays, and to experiment. There is an ongoing debate as to whether it justifies its subsidies or whether it is just a drain on local resources which could be better deployed elsewhere. Like all provincial theatres, it has been accused of entertaining at the expense of the less well-off, drawing 78 per cent of its audience from the upper socio-economic groups in the area, representing but 28 per cent of the total population. But its artistic director, Peter Cheeseman states that subsidies make the plays accessible to the whole community by bringing down ticket-prices. There is also a commitment to developing its writers, directors, actors and other personnel who are then used in commercial theatre and other media nationally.

Since the 1970s, there has been a move to generate new local theatre writing. My Stoke Original Theatre was formed to commission plays and shows from local writers, and these have been toured and performed both in the area and at the Edinburgh Festival Fringe. At present, Big One Productions is commissioning new plays by established local writers to be presented professionally on both local and national touring circuits.

The amaetur activity is prolific, drama groups utilizing the council-owned Mitchell Memorial Theatre, the Theatre Royal, Hanley, and the Queen's Theatre, Burslem, to stage a wide selection of plays and musicals. These are localized but well-supported organizations for enthusiasts. They are able to run under their own financial steam, and do not seek subsidies. It is part of the strong tradition of self-help in the region, and of reluctance to look elsewhere for development. There is the ethic of hard work and 'looking after our own'.

There are various cultural communities within the city, but their cultures are not reflected in the city's public profile – from groups from other parts of the UK to Poles, Hungarians, Chinese, Asians and Afro-Caribbeans. There are many 'hidden' ethnic-group activities, often practised in homes or the workplace in the absence of sufficient and suitable venues. This gives them no prominence as such, but they are now a significant part of Stoke's cultural fabric.

The Potteries is made up of small, busy communities, and many cultural pursuits are 'invisible'. Indeed, it has often been referred to as a 'cultural desert'. There is much home-based arts and craft activity, linked to limited exhibition or performance space, accessible to a wide range of people. And the Potteries likes to read and hear about itself, hence the success of local radio, press, and publications of local video cassettes, stories and dialect tales. As far as other forms of writing are concerned, public readings, discussions and poetry readings are rare, and the Arnold Bennett Literary Society is the only major group based on the written word.

The conurbation's press and radio stations play an important role in entertaining and informing the population with material of regional concern. An interesting development which was broadcast for just under two years was a Potteries-based radio soap 'The Colcloughs', a twice-weekly, independent production on BBC Radio Stoke, employing professional actors and a trio of local writers. The alternative use of various mass media is now emerging as an important community activity. There has been an active amateur film society in the area for over sixty years. Now local community groups video-record or otherwise document their proceedings. The group Reels on Wheels takes and projects commercial feature films in local towns with no cinema. Accessibility to locally-made cinema, independent and other archive film material has been made possible, in the form of film shows, video compilations and documentaries, by my collection catalogued as the Staffordshire Film Archive.

It has been said that the major cultural developments in recent years have been those instigated by people and institutions coming from outside the area to paint, write, sing, perform, and document the Potteries and its traditions. And while local people may be wary of these 'furriners', they prove an eager audience. But the focus of their own activities remains their own community. This is part of the identity of Stoke-on-Trent. The adherence of loyalties to the smaller societies, the communities and particular towns within the city means that the Potteries *as a whole* may not be symbolized by its culture. 'The arts and culture are about the creation and transmission of a sense of identity. They could play a crucial and constructive role in reversing stereotyped images of what Stoke is about, as well as rediscovering and revealing its underlying vibrancy.'[8]

REFERENCES

1. J Hepburn, ed, *Arnold Bennett: sketches for autobiography*, 1979, 125; see also F Swinnerton, *Arnold Bennett: the journals*, Penguin ed, 1971.
2. C Landry, ed, *A cultural strategy for Stoke-on-Trent*, Comedia Consultancy, 1990.
3. Hepburn, *Sketches for autobiography*, 130.
4. Ibid, 133.
5. Ibid, 143.
6. Ibid, 142.
7. J Hepburn, ed, *Letters of Arnold Bennett*, 1968, ii, 177.
8. Landry, *A cultural strategy*.

Index

Figures are indicated by 'f', plates by 'p' and tables by 't', immediately before the page number.